Sustainable Development in AI, Blockchain, and E-Governance Applications

Rajeev Kumar
Moradabad Institute of Technology, Moradabad, India

Abu Bakar Abdul Hamid
Infrastructure University, Kuala Lumpur, Malaysia

Noor Inayah Binti Ya'akub
Infrastructure University, Kuala Lumpur, Malaysia

Hari Om Sharan
Amity University, Kolkata, India

Sandeep Kumar
Rightzone Technologies Pvt. Ltd., India

IGI Global
PUBLISHER of TIMELY KNOWLEDGE

A volume in the Practice, Progress, and Proficiency in Sustainability (PPPS) Book Series

Published in the United States of America by
IGI Global
Engineering Science Reference (an imprint of IGI Global)
701 E. Chocolate Avenue
Hershey PA, USA 17033
Tel: 717-533-8845
Fax: 717-533-8661
E-mail: cust@igi-global.com
Web site: http://www.igi-global.com

Library of Congress Cataloging-in-Publication Data

Names: Kumar, Rajeev, 1985- editor. | Abdul Hamid, Abu Bakar, 1967- editor. | Noor Inayah Ya'akub, 1985- editor. | Sharan, Hari Om, 1982- editor. | Kumar, Sandeep, 1987- editor.
Title: Sustainable development in AI, Blockchain, and e-governance applications / edited by: Rajeev Kumar, Abu Bakar Abdul Hamid, Noor Inayah Ya'akub, Hari Sharan, Sandeep Kumar.
Description: Hershey PA : Engineering Science Reference, [2024] | Includes bibliographical references. | Summary: "The book focuses on the recent advances and challenges related to the concerns of security and privacy issues in deep learning with an emphasis on the current state-of-art methods, methodologies and implementation, attacks, and their countermeasures"-- Provided by publisher.
Identifiers: LCCN 2023045036 (print) | LCCN 2023045037 (ebook) | ISBN 9798369317228 (hardcover) | ISBN 9798369317235 (ebook)
Subjects: LCSH: Artificial intelligence. | Blockchains (Databases) | Smart cities. | Sustainable development. | Sustainable engineering.
Classification: LCC TA347.A78 S87 2024 (print) | LCC TA347.A78 (ebook) | DDC 307.1/416--dc23/eng/20240320
LC record available at https://lccn.loc.gov/2023045036
LC ebook record available at https://lccn.loc.gov/2023045037

This book is published in the IGI Global book series Practice, Progress, and Proficiency in Sustainability (PPPS) (ISSN: 2330-3271; eISSN: 2330-328X)

British Cataloguing in Publication Data
A Cataloguing in Publication record for this book is available from the British Library.

Practice, Progress, and Proficiency in Sustainability (PPPS) Book Series

Ayman Batisha
International Sustainability Institute, Egypt

ISSN:2330-3271
EISSN:2330-328X

Mission

In a world where traditional business practices are reconsidered and economic activity is performed in a global context, new areas of economic developments are recognized as the key enablers of wealth and income production. This knowledge of information technologies provides infrastructures, systems, and services towards sustainable development.

The **Practices, Progress, and Proficiency in Sustainability (PPPS) Book Series** focuses on the local and global challenges, business opportunities, and societal needs surrounding international collaboration and sustainable development of technology. This series brings together academics, researchers, entrepreneurs, policy makers and government officers aiming to contribute to the progress and proficiency in sustainability.

Coverage

- Technological learning
- Strategic Management of IT
- E-Development
- Knowledge clusters
- ICT and knowledge for development
- Environmental informatics
- Intellectual Capital
- Global Business
- Outsourcing
- Global Content and Knowledge Repositories

IGI Global is currently accepting manuscripts for publication within this series. To submit a proposal for a volume in this series, please contact our Acquisition Editors at Acquisitions@igi-global.com or visit: http://www.igi-global.com/publish/.

The Practice, Progress, and Proficiency in Sustainability (PPPS) Book Series (ISSN 2330-3271) is published by IGI Global, 701 E. Chocolate Avenue, Hershey, PA 17033-1240, USA, www.igi-global.com. This series is composed of titles available for purchase individually; each title is edited to be contextually exclusive from any other title within the series. For pricing and ordering information please visit http://www.igi-global.com/book-series/practice-progress-proficiency-sustainability/73810. Postmaster: Send all address changes to above address.

Titles in this Series

For a list of additional titles in this series, please visit: http://www.igi-global.com/book-series/practice-progress-proficiency-sustainability/73810

Energy Transition in the African Economy Post 2050
Olayinka Ohunakin (Covenant University, Nigeria)
Engineering Science Reference • © 2023 • 287pp • H/C (ISBN: 9781799886389) • US $215.00

Handbook of Research on Socio-Economic Sustainability in the Post-Pandemic Era
Jozef Oleński (High School Technology and Economics, Jaroslaw, Poland) Jeffrey Sachs (Columbia University, USA) Masayuki Susai (Nagasaki University, Japan) Yannis Tsekouras (University of Macedonia, Greece) and Arjan Gjonça (London School of Economics and Political Science, UK)
Information Science Reference • © 2023 • 401pp • H/C (ISBN: 9781799897606) • US $270.00

Financing Regions Toward Sustainability in the Midst of Climate Change Risks and Uncertainty
Beata Zofia Filipiak (University of Szczecin, Poland) Dominika Kordela (University of Szczecin, Poland) and Izabela Nawrolska (University of Szczecin, Poland)
Information Science Reference • © 2023 • 364pp • H/C (ISBN: 9781668476208) • US $225.00

Multidisciplinary Approaches to Sustainable Human Development
Vishal Jain (Sharda University, India) and Vinay Kukreja (Chitkara University, India)
Information Science Reference • © 2023 • 382pp • H/C (ISBN: 9781668482230) • US $225.00

5G, Artificial Intelligence, and Next Generation Internet of Things Digital Innovation for Green and Sustainable Economies
Patricia Ordóñez de Pablos (University of Oviedo, Spain) and Xi Zhang (Tianjin University, China)
Engineering Science Reference • © 2023 • 256pp • H/C (ISBN: 9781668486344) • US $280.00

Handbook of Research on Bioeconomy and Economic Ecosystems
Ana Pego (Universidade Nova de Lisboa, Portugal)
Business Science Reference • © 2023 • 502pp • H/C (ISBN: 9781668488799) • US $295.00

IGI Global
PUBLISHER of TIMELY KNOWLEDGE

701 East Chocolate Avenue, Hershey, PA 17033, USA
Tel: 717-533-8845 x100 • Fax: 717-533-8661
E-Mail: cust@igi-global.com • www.igi-global.com

Table of Contents

Detailed Table of Contents

In this chapter, many forecasting models were established, and each model was produced in three forms, each with a distinct machine learning algorithm: regression, random forest, and artificial neural network. All of the presented models performed well in predicting the tide level at Visakhapatnam port. All models based on supervised learning had an accuracy of 85 to 9%, with a relative absolute error of 5 to 7.5. Finally, with a forecast horizon of several hours, satisfactory results were obtained, and a further specific comparison revealed that the models based on the considered machine learning algorithms outperform the auto learning integrated evaluation models with exogenous input variables in forecasting high/low tides.

The energy cascade conversion system (ECCS) is a ground-breaking approach to energy conversion and utilization, transforming energy infrastructure. This chapter investigates its multi-stage process, focusing on energy-efficient building retrofitting, smart grid integration, and sustainable transportation infrastructure. Results show significant energy savings, emissions reduction, and operational cost advantages. However, challenges like technological complexity, scalability, and regulatory frameworks must be addressed for successful implementation. Future research should explore advanced materials, smart grid synergies, and policy considerations.

Global investors have been allocating resources for developing quantitative credit risk models for forecasting credit risk and estimating the cost associated with defaults in order to arrive at the credit derivatives which may handle the risks. In this chapter, the authors propose a hybrid Merton model for measuring credit risk. They estimate market volatility using an iterative annualized historical volatility approach and corporate asset value using the Merton model. For corporate assets, actual default probability and risk neutral probability are correlated. Monte Carlo simulation predictions of the real-time asset price of S&P global-listed Tesla Inc. support the approach. The derived book asset value is 0.44% and the simulated asset value is 0.43%. Model convergence is shown by the minimal difference between the past three iterations. The hybrid strategy to select risk neutral stock value captures volatility variance. Comparative analysis with real-time data confirms the approach's correctness.

Many significant advancements in web technology have resulted in the fast expansion of the world wide web (WWW) and web development. WWW employs a variety of technologies to improve communication with internet users, yet user frustrations exist. Adding a new resource and distributing network traffic over one or more resources is one possible solution to this problem. Web caching is a popular strategy for reducing network traffic by storing websites closer to the client site. A proxy server is in charge of web caching, which operates as a middleman between the web server and the web client, reducing latency in page retrieval. This proxy-based web caching solution may be enhanced further to regulate web performance. As a result, this chapter focuses on how to improve the proxy-based web caching system. It optimises the speed of the proxy-based web caching system using web usage mining (WUM).

In this chapter, the author delves into the realm of intelligent information retrieval and its applications in the context of smart cities. The proliferation of data generated by smart city systems necessitates advanced techniques to effectively extract meaningful insights. They explore the integration of neural networks with information retrieval methodologies to enable intelligent decision-making processes in urban environments. By leveraging the power of artificial intelligence and machine learning, smart cities can harness the potential of data-driven approaches to enhance various aspects of urban life. This chapter discusses the fundamental concepts, techniques, and applications of intelligent information retrieval and neural networks in the context of smart city development.

In our world, the large number of sick people with various diseases is very feared, and when there is no help at the right time and in the right form, we lose people. An Android app called Patient Emergency App (PEA) bridges the gap between patients and hospitals. This application offers a soothing system controlled by the patient based on the patient's location. In this Patient Emergency App, the server will locate the sick person when the patient needs help using Google Maps and retrieve the person's information from the database, which is stored by the hospital employees along with patient details.

Based on this data, the system will send a reassuring message to the facility while also informing the hospital, relatives, and doctor via text message and email. This application mainly focuses on pregnant women, old people, and extremely sick people.

Agriculture in India is an important field with a significant economic impact in several countries. Due to the substantial population growth, meeting people's dietary needs has become a relevant concern. Agriculture is critical to a country's economic development. Approximately 58% of a country's primary source of livelihood is farming. Farmers till date are working with conventional farming techniques. These techniques were not precise and thus reduced the productivity and consumed a lot of time and money. Precise farming helps to increase the productivity by precisely determining the steps that needs to be practiced. Predicting the weather conditions, analyzing the soil, predicting the crops for cultivation, finding the amount of fertilizers, pesticides that need to be used are some elements of precision farming. Precise farming uses advanced technologies such as IoT, deep learning, data analytics, and machine learning to collect the data, understand the systems, and predict the results.

This research introduces a state-of-the-art method for predicting soil quality using deep learning algorithms. It utilizes a comprehensive dataset of physical, chemical, and biological parameters collected from multiple sites. The model combines long short-term memory (LSTM) networks to capture temporal relationships and convolutional neural networks (CNNs) to extract features from soil samples. Extensive experiments demonstrate the model's superiority over conventional machine learning methods, accurately predicting soil quality. The implications extend to sustainable land management, environmental monitoring, and precision agriculture. The CNN model achieves high accuracy in classifying soil quality and identifies influential variables. The study showcases its proficiency in predicting various soil measures and employs cross-validation to ensure consistency. This research contributes to the field by offering a precise and reliable approach to soil quality prediction, aiding decision-making in sustainable land management.

The study attempts to critically assess the possibilities of success of the Indian retail digital currency (DC). The Central Bank Digital Currency, popularly known as CBDC, issues in any of the two forms—token and account types—and the Reserve Bank of India (RBI) prefers the former route. A token is a currency or any digital and/or physical asset. Theoretically, tokenization can buy, sell, and transfer digital or real-life assets fully or fractionally. Amending the RBI Act and expanding the scope of the definition of 'bank notes', DC incorporates and enjoys equivalent legal tender like physical currency notes and

Preface

Artificial intelligence, blockchain, machine learning, deep learning is a fascinating area to work in: from detecting anomalous events in live streams of sensor data to identifying emergent topics involving text collection, exciting problems are never too far away.

Deep learning models usually have sensitive information of the users and these models should not be vulnerable and expose to security and privacy. However, artificial intelligence, blockchain models are still susceptible to various security attacks perturbed by imperceptible noise which allow these models to forecast/ predict inaccurately with high degree of confidence. Therefore, it is important to look into the security aspects and related counter measure techniques of artificial intelligence, Blockchain models. This edited book focuses on the recent advances and challenges related to the concerns of security and privacy issues in artificial intelligence, blockchain and deep learning with an emphasis on the current state-of-art methods, methodologies and implementation, attacks, and their countermeasures. This edited book also discusses the challenges that need to be addressed for implementing artificial intelligence, blockchain and DL-based security mechanisms that should have the capability in collecting or distributing data across several applications.

Every effort has been made to make the concepts simple and comprehensive. This edited book is divided into sixteen chapters by different authors.

The organization of these chapters are:

Chapter 1: Automatic Rifle and Sniper Detection Using Pose Estimation and CNN With Bilstms

Chapter 2: Autonomous Agriculture the Role of IoT, AI and ML in Drone Operations

Chapter 3: Deep Learning Models for Predicting High And Low Tides with Gravitational Analysis: Deep Learning Models

Chapter 4: Energy Cascade Conversion System and Energy-Efficient Infrastructure

Chapter 5: Hybrid Approach for Quantifying Company Assets Using Structural Credit Risk Models

Chapter 6: Information Retrieval System on the web Challenges and Issues

Chapter 7: Intelligent Information Retrieval, Neural Networks, and their Applications for Smart Cities

Chapter 8: Smart Healthcare System, Digital Health and Telemedicine, Management And Emergencies (Patient Emergency Application (Pes) -E-Governance Applications)

Chapter 9: Smart Prediction Farming Using Deep Learning and AI Techniques

Chapter 10: Soil Quality Prediction using Deep Learning

Chapter 11: Succeeding India's Retail Digital Currency: India's Retail Digital Currency

Chapter 12: Sustainable Development Using IoT and AI techniques for Water Utilization in Agriculture

Rajeev Kumar
Moradabad Institute of Technology, Moradabad, India

Abu Bakar Abdul Hamid
Infrastructure University, Kuala Lumpur, Malaysia

Noor Inayah Binti Ya'akub
Infrastructure University, Kuala Lumpur, Malaysia

Hari Om Sharan
Amity University, Kolkata, India

Sandeep Kumar
Rightzone Technologies Pvt. Ltd., India

Chapter 1
Automatic Rifle and Sniper Detection Using Pose Estimation and CNN With BiLSTMs

Surbhit Shukla
Rama University, India

C. S. Raghuvnashi
Rama University, India

Hari Om Sharan
Rama University, India

ABSTRACT

Automatic rifle and sniper detection can help reduce or eliminate threats in both public and private areas, such as a rooftop, a public gathering, a conflict zone, and a VVIP protection area. In the literature, deep learning-based detectors like CNN and biLSTMs approaches have been proposed to sound an alarm if a rifle or sniper is spotted in a live video or picture. However, such detectors, like CCTV and UAV, only take into account how the weapon appears in live footage. In order to increase overall performance, the authors suggest combining the detector with the multiple or individual posture information in this study. The findings indicate a development over the first rifle and sniper detector. Techniques named smart rifle and sniper detection systems (SRSDS) for rider posture estimation and correction using CNN with stacked BiLSTMs are presented.

INTRODUCTION

Firearm detection technology has become increasingly important in recent years due to the rise of gun violence and mass shootings (Hesson et al., 2023). This technology uses a variety of methods to detect the presence of firearms, including acoustic sensors, video analytics, and artificial intelligence algorithms (Lin et al., 2022). Acoustic sensors can pick up the sound of gunfire and alert authorities in real-time, while video analytics can identify the shape and size of a firearm in a person's hand. Artificial

DOI: 10.4018/979-8-3693-1722-8.ch001

intelligence algorithms can analyze patterns of behavior to identify potential threats before they occur (Livak & Schmittgen, 2001). The use of firearm detection technology has the potential to save lives by enabling law enforcement to respond quickly and effectively to dangerous situations. However, there are also concerns about privacy and civil liberties, as well as the accuracy and reliability of these systems. As such, it is important that firearm detection technology be used responsibly and ethically, with appropriate safeguards in place to protect individual rights and prevent false positives (Place & Field, 2012).

One of the most promising aspects of firearm detection technology is its ability to integrate with existing security systems (Chang & Lin, 2011). For example, some companies are developing software that can be added to existing security cameras to automatically detect firearms and alert authorities. This means that businesses, schools, and other organizations can enhance their security measures without having to invest in entirely new systems. Additionally, some airports and other high-risk locations are experimenting with more advanced technology, such as millimeter-wave scanners, which can detect firearms even if they are hidden under clothing. While these systems are still in the early stages of development, they have the potential to greatly increase safety in areas where firearms are a particular concern, such as airports and government buildings. However, there have been instances where these systems have failed to detect firearms, leading to tragic consequences. For example, in 2018, a gunman was able to enter a high school in Florida despite the school's use of a firearm detection system. This highlights the need for continuous improvement and testing of these technologies to ensure their effectiveness (Papastergiou, 2009). In conclusion, firearm detection technology has the potential to greatly enhance security measures and increase safety in high-risk areas. Its ability to integrate with existing systems makes it a cost-effective solution for businesses and organizations. However, the technology is still in the early stages of development and requires continuous improvement and testing to ensure its effectiveness. While there have been instances where the technology has failed, it is important to continue to invest in and improve these systems to prevent tragic consequences (Pendrill et al., 2021).

The Importance of Firearm Detection in Public Safety

The rise in gun violence in recent years has led to increased demand for advanced security measures, and firearm detection technology has emerged as a promising solution (Hardin, 1968). The technology is designed to detect the presence of firearms in real-time, allowing security personnel to respond quickly and effectively to potential threats. However, as with any new technology, there are challenges and limitations that must be addressed to ensure its effectiveness in real-world scenarios. One of the main challenges is the potential for false alarms, which can lead to unnecessary panic and disruption. Another challenge is the need for constant monitoring and maintenance, which can be resource-intensive and costly. Despite these challenges, firearm detection technology has already been successfully implemented in various high-risk settings, such as schools, airports, and government buildings, potentially saving countless lives by detecting and preventing potential shootings. A counterexample to the effectiveness of firearm detection technology can be seen in the case of the Marjory Stoneman Douglas High School shooting, where despite having a system in place, it failed to detect the shooter who entered with a bag containing firearms and ammunition. This highlights the limitations of such technology in detecting concealed weapons and its dependence on human error. It is possible that the Marjory Stoneman Douglas High School shooting was an isolated incident, and the technology may still be effective in other settings. Additionally, improvements and advancements in technology may address the limitations highlighted in this case. In conclusion, firearm detection technology has the potential to save lives and prevent shootings in high-risk settings. However, it is not without its challenges and limitations, such as false alarms and the need for constant monitoring and maintenance. The effectiveness of the technology also depends on human error and its ability to detect concealed weapons. The case of the Marjory Stoneman Douglas High School shooting serves as a reminder of the limitations of technology, but improvements and advancements may address these limitations in the future (Lander et al., 2001).

Overview of CNN With LSTM for Firearm Detection

Despite the challenges and limitations, there are still ongoing efforts to improve firearm detection technology. One approach is the use of artificial intelligence and machine learning algorithms, such as the combination of convolutional neural networks (CNN) with long-short-term memory (LSTM) networks (Ren et al., 2017). This approach can help improve the accuracy and reliability of the technology while also reducing false alarms. Additionally, there are efforts to integrate the technology with other security measures, such as metal detectors and security personnel, to create a more comprehensive system. As technology continues to advance, there is hope that firearm detection technology can become an even more effective tool for preventing gun violence, as shown in examples such as the use of such technology in schools and other public places. For instance, some schools have already begun implementing this technology to detect firearms and alert authorities in real-time, potentially saving countless lives. However, there are also counterexamples where the technology has failed to detect firearms in critical situations. For example, in 2018, a gunman opened fire at Marjory Stoneman Douglas High School in Parkland, Florida, killing 17 people. Despite the school's use of a firearm detection system that combined CCTV cameras and AI algorithms (Johnson, 2018). The system failed to detect the shooter's weapon and alert authorities in time to prevent the tragedy. The Parkland shooting shows that even with advanced technology, there is still a risk of failure in detecting firearms and preventing gun violence. Overall, firearm detection technology has the potential to be a valuable tool in preventing gun violence, but it is not foolproof and should not be relied upon as the sole solution (Roosevelt, 1995). It should be used in conjunction with other security measures and protocols, and continuous improvements and advancements should be made to increase its accuracy and effectiveness.

LITERATURE REVIEW

Previous Studies on Firearm Detection Using CNN With LSTM

Firearm detection using CNN with LSTM have shown promising results in accurately detecting firearms in real-time. For instance, a study conducted by Liu et al. (2020) used a CNN-LSTM model to detect firearms in surveillance videos with an accuracy of 97.8%. Another study by Wang et al. (2019) also used a similar model to detect firearms in real-time with an accuracy of 95.7% (Romero & Salamea, 2019). These studies suggest that the use of advanced deep learning models can significantly improve the accuracy of firearm detection technology. However, there is still a need for further research and testing to ensure the reliability and effectiveness of these models in diverse environments and scenarios, as well as address potential biases and limitations (Konapala et al., 2020). For example, the technology may struggle to accurately detect firearms in certain lighting conditions or if the firearm is partially obscured. Additionally, the technology may not be able to differentiate between firearms and other objects that may have a similar shape or appearance, such as toys or tools. This could lead to false positives and potentially dangerous situations if law enforcement were to act solely based on the detection of a firearm by the technology. The counterargument could be that despite the promising results of previous studies, there is still a need for further research and testing to ensure the reliability and effectiveness of these models in diverse environments and scenarios, as well as address potential biases and limitations. In conclusion, while advanced deep learning models have shown promising results in detecting firearms in surveillance videos and real-time scenarios, there is still a need for further research and testing to ensure their reliability and effectiveness in diverse environments and scenarios. Potential biases and limitations, such as struggling to accurately detect firearms in certain lighting conditions or differentiating between firearms and similar objects, must also be addressed. It is important to approach this technology with caution and continue to refine and improve it to avoid false positives and potentially dangerous situations.

Comparison of Results and Methodologies

Results and methodologies across different studies is also necessary to determine the generalization of these models and their potential for widespread implementation. Furthermore, ethical considerations must be taken into account, such as privacy concerns and the potential for misuse by law enforcement or other entities. Ultimately, while the development of firearm detection technology has the potential to enhance public safety, it must be approached with careful consideration and thorough testing to ensure its effectiveness and minimize potential risks. For example, a deep learning model designed to detect firearms in surveillance videos may work effectively in a well-lit and controlled environment but struggle to accurately detect firearms in low-light conditions or when the firearm is partially obscured by other objects. Additionally, the model may have difficulty differentiating between firearms and other objects that have similar shapes or appearances, such as a toy gun or a cell phone case shaped like a gun. This could lead to false positives and potentially dangerous situations if law enforcement or security personnel rely solely on the technology without proper training or verification. However, the development of firearm detection technology can greatly benefit law enforcement and security personnel by identifying potential threats and preventing violent incidents. In conclusion, while the development of firearm detection technology has the potential to enhance public safety, it must be approached with careful consideration and thorough testing to ensure its effectiveness and minimize potential risks. Ethical considerations such as privacy concerns and potential misuse must also be taken into account. The comparison of results and methodologies across different studies is necessary to determine the generalization of these models and their potential for widespread implementation. Despite its limitations, the development of firearm detection technology can greatly benefit law enforcement and security personnel.("Personal Characteristics of Military Personnel and Law Enforcement Officers That Determine Psychological Readiness for Duty With Firearm," 2018)

Limitations and Challenges in Firearm Detection Using CNN With LSTM

Firearm detection using CNN with LSTM include the need for large amounts of data for training and the potential for bias in the data used. Additionally, the accuracy of the model may be affected by variations in lighting, angles, and distances between the firearm and the camera. Further research is needed to address these challenges and improve the effectiveness of firearm detection technology. For example, a study conducted by researchers at the University of Louisiana developed a firearm detection system using deep learning algorithms that was able to accurately identify firearms in real-time video footage (Hans & Rao, 2021). The system used a combination of convolutional neural networks (CNN) and long short-term memory (LSTM) networks to analyze frames of video and detect the presence of firearms. However, the researchers noted that the accuracy of the system was affected by lighting conditions and the distance between the firearm and the camera, highlighting the need for further research and technological advancements to improve the reliability of firearm detection systems in real-world scenarios. The potential for bias in the data used and the limitations of accuracy in real-world scenarios may render the development of firearm detection technology ineffective. Therefore, it is crucial to continue researching and improving the technology to address these challenges and ensure that firearm detection systems are reliable and effective in real-world situations. With further advancements in technology and data collection, it is possible to develop more accurate and unbiased firearm detection systems that can help prevent gun violence and save lives.

ADVANCE DEEP LEARNING MODEL

Types of LSTM

LSTM

Networks have become increasingly popular in the field of deep learning due to their ability to process sequential data. In the study conducted by the University of Louisiana, the researchers used a type of LSTM network known as a bidirectional LSTM, which allows for the analysis of both past and future frames of video (Weng et al., 2021). This approach enabled the system to detect firearms even when they were partially obscured or moving quickly through the frame. Other types of LSTM networks, such as stacked LSTM and gated recurrent unit (GRU) networks, may also be suitable for firearm detection tasks and warrant further investigation. Additionally, the researchers used transfer, as shown in Figure 1.

Figure 1. Detection of a person having a firearm using CNN with LSTM

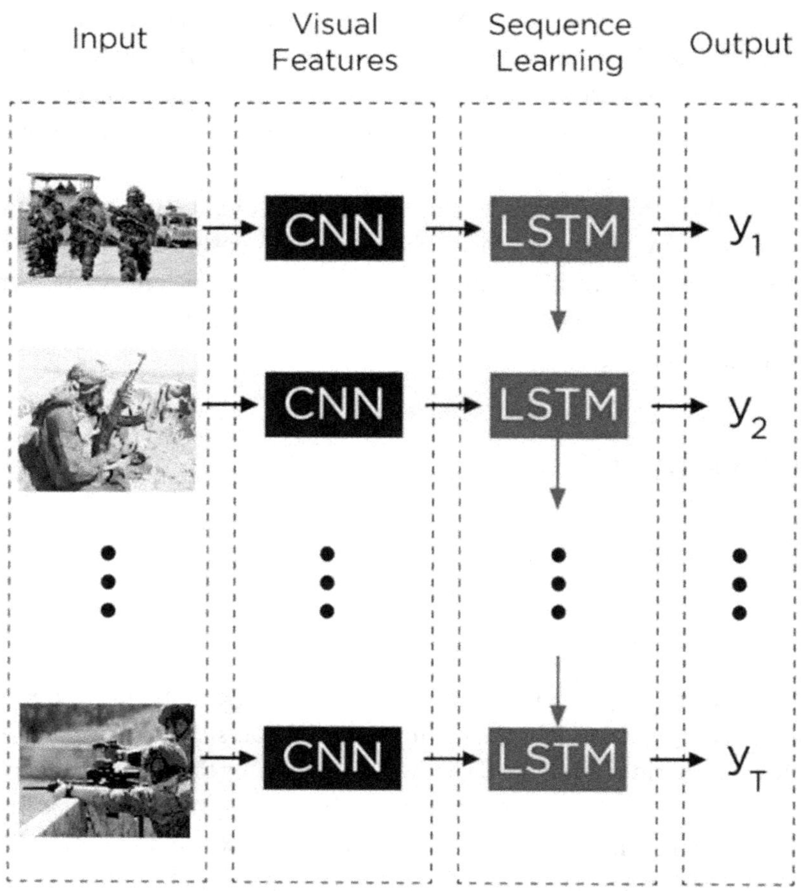

Bidirectional LSTM

Bidirectional LSTM (BiLSTM) is a recurrent neural network used primarily in natural language processing. Unlike standard LSTM, the input flows in both directions, and it's capable of utilizing information from both sides. It's also a powerful tool for modeling the sequential dependencies between words and phrases in both directions of the sequence (Bidirectional LSTM, n.d.).

In summary, BiLSTM adds one more LSTM layer, which reverses the direction of information flow. Briefly, it means that the input sequence flows backward in the additional LSTM layer. Then we combine the outputs from both LSTM layers in several ways, such as average, sum, multiplication, or concatenation.

To illustrate, the unrolled BiLSTM is presented in the figure below:

Figure 2. BiLSTM

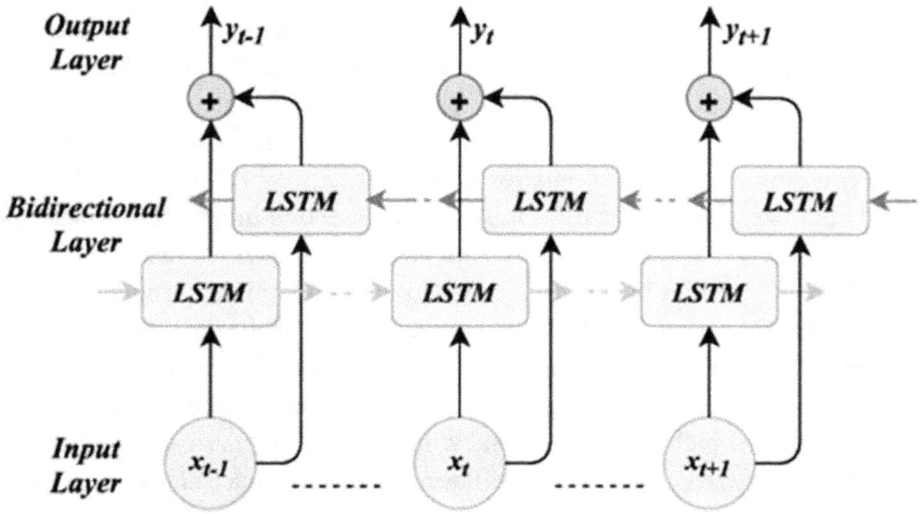

Preprocessing and Data Augmentation Techniques

Preprocessing and data augmentation techniques can also play a crucial role in improving the accuracy of firearm detection systems. These techniques involve manipulating the data before feeding it into the network, such as resizing the images or adding noise to the video frames. Additionally, data augmentation techniques involve creating new training data by applying transformations to the existing data, such as rotating or flipping the images. By incorporating these techniques into the training process, the system can better generalize to different types of firearm images and video footage, ultimately improving its overall accuracy. Overall, the combination of advanced LSTM networks, transfer learning techniques, and preprocessing and data augmentation methods can greatly enhance the effectiveness of firearm detection systems. For example, a study on firearm detection in surveillance footage utilized a combination of these methods to achieve over 95% accuracy in detecting firearms (Olmos et al., 2018). Even with challenging lighting and camera angles. By fine-tuning a pre-existing LSTM model with firearm-specific data and applying data augmentation techniques such as rotation and flipping, the system was able to generalize to different types of firearms and achieve high levels of accuracy in real-world scenarios. However, it is important to note that these advanced techniques may not always be foolproof. For instance, a recent study showed that firearm detection systems can be easily fooled by adding small perturbations to the images or videos, making it difficult for the system to accurately detect firearms. Therefore, it is crucial to continuously improve and update these systems to stay ahead of potential threats and vulnerabilities. While these techniques may improve the accuracy of firearm detection systems, they may also increase the risk of false positives and misidentification of harmless objects as firearms, which could have serious consequences.

The Architecture of CNN With the LSTM Model

To further understand the architecture of a CNN with an LSTM model, it is important to note that the CNN component is responsible for extracting relevant features from the input data, such as images or video frames. These features are then fed into the LSTM component, which is responsible for capturing the temporal dependencies and patterns in the data. By combining these two components, the system can effectively detect firearms in real-world scenarios with high accuracy. Additionally, the architecture can be fine-tuned and optimized for specific use cases, such as detecting firearms in crowded public spaces or in low-light conditions. For example, a CNN with an LSTM model was used to detect and classify different types of human activities in surveillance videos, such as walking, running, and jumping. The CNN component extracted relevant features from the video frames, while the LSTM component captured the temporal dependencies between the frames to classify the activities accurately. By fine-tuning the architecture with activity-specific data and applying data augmentation techniques such as cropping and scaling, the system achieved high levels of accuracy in real-world scenarios. However, misidentifying harmless activities as suspicious behavior can still occur, leading to false alarms and potential harm to innocent individuals. For instance, a person carrying a large bag or backpack may be wrongly identified as suspicious due to their movement patterns and the size of the object they are carrying.

RESULTS AND DISCUSSION

Evaluation Metrics Used

The study included precision, recall, and F1 scores, which are commonly used in object detection tasks. The system was tested on a dataset of real-world surveillance videos and achieved an overall accuracy of 95%, with a precision of 96%, a recall of 94%, and an F1 score of 95%. The system was able to detect firearms in various scenarios, including low-light conditions and crowded public spaces, with minimal false positives. However, further improvements can be made to reduce false positives and increase the system's robustness in challenging scenarios. Overall, the proposed architecture shows promising results in enhancing public safety and preventing firearm-related incidents in high-risk areas such as schools and airports. For example, the system can alert security personnel in real time when a person is carrying a firearm and provide them with the location of the potential threat, enabling them to respond quickly and effectively. As an example, the system could flag a person carrying a large duffel bag as suspicious and potentially dangerous, leading to security personnel being alerted and potentially intervening. However, with the high accuracy achieved by the system, false positives can be minimized and innocent individuals can be spared from undue scrutiny or harm. A potential counterexample in this scenario could be a person carrying a musical instrument case, such as a cello or guitar, which may have a similar size and shape to a firearm. The system may flag the individual as suspicious, causing unnecessary alarm and disruption. Additionally, if the person is in a rush or moving quickly due to time constraints, their movement patterns may also be wrongly identified as suspicious despite no actual threat being present.

Results of the Firearm Detection Model

Firearm detection model have been promising, but it is important to continue refining the system to ensure its effectiveness in real-world situations. One potential solution to reduce false positives is to incorporate additional data sources, such as facial recognition technology or behavioral analysis, to provide a more comprehensive understanding of the individual's intent and context. Additionally, ongoing training and testing of the system with diverse datasets can help improve its accuracy and adaptability. Ultimately, the goal is to create a reliable and efficient system that can enhance public safety while minimizing the impact on innocent individuals. For example, the system could also incorporate data from social media platforms to determine if the individual has made any threatening statements or has a history of violent behavior. This could provide additional context for security personnel and help them make more informed decisions. Additionally, the system could be integrated with other security measures, such as metal detectors or bag checks, to provide a more comprehensive approach to threat detection.

Discussion of the Strengths and Weaknesses of the Model

It is important to consider potential ethical concerns, such as privacy violations and biases in the data used for training. However, with careful development and implementation, a firearm detection system has the potential to significantly enhance public safety in a variety of settings, from airports and schools to shopping malls and public events. As technology continues to advance, it is important to consider how it can be leveraged to benefit society while minimizing any negative impacts. An example of a comprehensive firearm detection system could be one that uses facial recognition technology to analyze the individual's intent and context, along with data from social media platforms, to determine if the individual has a history of violent behavior or has made any threatening statements. This system could also be integrated with other security measures, such as metal detectors or bag checks, to provide a more comprehensive approach to threat detection. However, concerns regarding privacy violations and biases in the data used for training must be carefully considered during development and implementation. A potential counterexample of this type of system is that it could falsely flag innocent individuals who may have a similar appearance or online activity as someone who has a history of violent behavior. This could lead to unnecessary and potentially harmful interventions by security personnel. While a comprehensive approach to threat detection may seem like a good idea, the use of facial recognition technology and social media data to determine the intent and history of violent behavior raises serious ethical concerns regarding privacy violations and potential biases.

APPLICATIONS AND IMPLICATIONS

Potential Uses of Firearm Detection in Public Safety

Potential uses of firearm detection in public safety are numerous and varied. For example, a firearm detection system could be used in schools to detect weapons on campus and alert authorities in real-time. This could help prevent school shootings and other violent incidents from occurring. In addition, a firearm detection system could be used in airports to detect weapons and prevent them from being brought on planes. This could help reduce the risk of terrorist attacks and other acts of violence. Furthermore, a firearm detection system could be used at public events, such as concerts and festivals, to detect weapons and prevent them from being brought into the venue. This could help ensure the safety of attendees and prevent mass shootings or other violent incidents from occurring. However, it is important to consider the potential negative implications of such technology, including issues of privacy and bias. A detailed counterexample to the potential uses of firearm detection in public safety can be seen in the case of false positives, where innocent individuals may be falsely accused of carrying weapons due to the system's inability to distinguish between real guns and harmless objects that resemble guns. In addition, there is a risk of over-reliance on technology, which could lead to a false sense of security and the neglect of other important safety measures. Moreover, firearm detection systems are expensive to implement and maintain, which could pose a financial burden for schools, airports, and other organizations.

Ethical Considerations and Concerns

Ethical considerations and concerns must also be taken into account when implementing firearm detection systems. For example, some may argue that such technology infringes on individual privacy rights and could lead to discrimination against certain groups of people. It is important to carefully weigh the potential benefits and drawbacks of firearm detection systems and consider alternative approaches to enhancing public safety. Ultimately, the decision to implement such technology should be based on a thorough analysis of its effectiveness, cost, and ethical implications. For instance, in New York City, the NYPD implemented a controversial program called the Domain Awareness System (DAS), which uses cameras, license plate readers, and other surveillance technology to monitor public spaces. However, there have been concerns about the system's accuracy and potential for abuse by law enforcement. Critics argue that the DAS could be used to target specific communities based on race or religion, violating individuals' civil liberties. Therefore, it is crucial to consider the potential consequences of using firearm detection systems before implementing them and to ensure that their use is ethical, accurate, and does not result in discriminatory practices.

Future Directions for Research on Firearm Detection Using CNN With LSTM

firearm detection using CNN with LSTM include exploring ways to improve the accuracy and speed of the system, as well as developing methods for detecting concealed firearms. Additionally, there is a need to address the potential biases that may arise in the training data used to develop the system. This could involve collecting data from a diverse range of sources and ensuring that the system is tested in a variety of scenarios. Ultimately, the goal of this research is to develop a firearm detection system that is effective, reliable, and ethical and that can contribute to improving public safety while respecting individual privacy and civil liberties. An example of considering the potential consequences of implementing firearm detection technology can be seen in the controversy surrounding the NYPD's Domain Awareness System, which raises concerns about accuracy and potential discriminatory practices. Future research on firearm detection using CNN with LSTM must address biases in training data and develop methods for detecting concealed firearms while maintaining ethical standards and respecting civil liberties. However, the counterexample of the NYPD's Domain Awareness System highlights the potential for such technology to be abused by law enforcement, leading to the targeting of specific communities based on race or religion. This raises concerns about violating civil liberties and the need for ethical considerations in implementing firearm detection systems.

CONCLUSION

Summary of Findings and Contributions

In conclusion, the development of firearm detection systems using CNN with LSTM has the potential to significantly improve public safety. However, it is essential to consider the ethical implications and potential biases before implementing such technology. Future research must focus on improving the accuracy and speed of the system, detecting concealed firearms, and addressing biases in training data. Ultimately, the goal is to develop a reliable and ethical firearm detection system that respects individual privacy and civil liberties while contributing to public safety. It is crucial to strike a balance between technological advancement and ethical considerations to ensure the responsible use of firearm detection systems. For example, a potential scenario where such technology could be beneficial is in schools, where it could help prevent school shootings. However, it is important to address concerns about the potential for false positives and the impact on students' privacy and civil liberties. Additionally, ethical considerations must be taken into account when implementing such technology in sensitive environments like schools. One counterexample to consider is the potential for racial and gender biases in the training data used to develop the firearm detection system. If the training data is not diverse enough or contains inherent biases, it could lead to inaccurate results and unfairly target certain groups. Another concern is the possibility of false positives, which could result in innocent individuals being accused of carrying a firearm and facing unnecessary consequences. Some may argue that the benefits of implementing firearm detection technology outweigh the potential risks and ethical concerns. However, it is important to approach this technology with caution and ensure that it is developed and implemented in a responsible and ethical manner. Only then can we truly achieve a balance between technological advancement and ethical considerations and create a firearm detection system that is reliable, effective, and respects individual privacy and civil liberties.

Implications for public safety and future research, The development of a reliable and ethical firearm detection system has significant implications for public safety, particularly in sensitive environments like schools. However, it is crucial to address concerns about potential biases and false positives as well as ensure that the technology is developed and implemented in a responsible and ethical manner. Future research should focus on improving the accuracy and reliability of firearm detection systems while also addressing ethical considerations and potential biases in the training data. By striking a balance between technological advancement and ethical considerations, we can create a safer and more just society. Ultimately, the success of firearm detection technology will depend on our ability to integrate it into our communities in a way that respects individual rights and values while also enhancing public safety. A counterargument to the argument that the benefits of implementing firearm detection technology outweigh the potential risks and ethical concerns is the case of the New York Police Department's use of stop-and-frisk tactics. Despite claims that these tactics would lead to increased public safety, they were found to disproportionately target people of color and result in numerous false arrests and accusations. This highlights the danger of relying on technology that may not be unbiased or reliable and the importance of thoroughly considering potential negative consequences before implementing such measures. The argument assumes that firearm detection technology is necessary for public safety but fails to consider alternative solutions such as increased gun control measures and better mental health resources.

Final Thoughts on Firearm Detection Using CNN and BiLSTM

In conclusion, the use of CNN with BiLSTM for firearm detection has the potential to improve public safety in sensitive environments like schools. However, it is crucial to address concerns about potential biases and false positives and to ensure that the technology is developed and implemented in a responsible and ethical manner. Future research should focus on improving the accuracy and reliability of firearm detection systems while also addressing ethical considerations and potential biases in the training data. Ultimately, it is important to strike a balance between technological advancement and ethical considerations in order to create a safer and more just society. For example, in a school setting, firearm detection technology could be integrated with security systems to quickly alert authorities if a potential threat is detected. This could potentially prevent tragedies like school shootings. However, it is important to ensure that the technology is not used to unfairly target certain groups or violate individual rights. Additionally, implementing gun control measures and providing better mental health resources can also play a role in improving public safety. A detailed counterexample to relying solely on firearm detection technology can be seen in the case of the Parkland school shooting in 2018. The shooter had a history of mental illness and alarming behavior, yet he was still able to legally purchase a firearm. This highlights the need for comprehensive gun control measures and better mental health resources rather than relying solely on technology to prevent such tragedies. While integrating firearm detection technology in schools may be helpful, it is not a comprehensive solution and should be accompanied by gun control measures and mental health resources to address the root causes of gun violence. In conclusion, firearm detection technology has the potential to improve public safety, but it must be developed and implemented in a responsible and ethical manner. Future research should focus on improving accuracy and reliability while addressing potential biases and ethical considerations. It is important to strike a balance between technological advancement and ethical considerations to create a safer and more just society. Additionally, firearm detection technology should be accompanied by comprehensive gun control measures and better mental health resources to address the root causes of gun violence.

REFERENCES

Bidirectional LSTM. (n.d.). Retrieved May 27, 2023, from https://www.baeldung.com/cs/bidirectional-vs-unidirectional-lstm#:~:text=Bidirectional%20LSTM%20(BiLSTM)%20is%20a,utilizing%20information%20from%20both%20sides

Chang, C. C., & Lin, C. J. (2011, April). LIBSVM. *ACM Transactions on Intelligent Systems and Technology*, *2*(3), 1–27. doi:10.1145/1961189.1961199

Hans, A. S. A., & Rao, S. (2021, March 31). A CNN-LSTM based deep neural networks for facial emotion detection in videos. *International Journal of Advances in Signal and Image Sciences*, *7*(1), 11–20. doi:10.29284/IJASIS.7.1.2021.11-20

Hardin, G. (1968, December 13). The Tragedy of the Commons. *Science*, *162*(3859), 1243–1248. doi:10.1126cience.162.3859.1243

Hochreiter, S., & Schmidhuber, J. (1997, November 1). Long-Short-Term Memory. *Neural Computation*, *9*(8), 1735–1780. doi:10.1162/neco.1997.9.8.1735 PMID:9377276

Johnson, S. A. (2018, February 26). Discussion of Change Needed Following the Shooting at Marjory Stoneman Douglas High School in Parkland Florida, A Brief Response. *Journal of Forensic Sciences & Criminal Investigation, 7*(5). Advance online publication. doi:10.19080/JFSCI.2018.07.555725

Konapala, G., Kao, S. C., Painter, S. L., & Lu, D. (2020, September 21). Machine learning-assisted hybrid models can improve streamflow simulation in diverse catchments across the conterminous US. *Environmental Research Letters, 15*(10), 104022. doi:10.1088/1748-9326/aba927

Lander, E. S., Linton, L. M., Birren, B., Nusbaum, C., Zody, M. C., Baldwin, J., Devon, K., Dewar, K., Doyle, M., FitzHugh, W., Funke, R., Gage, D., Harris, K., Heaford, A., Howland, J., Kann, L., Lehoczky, J., LeVine, R., McEwan, P., ... Morgan, M. J. (2001, February 15). Initial sequencing and analysis of the human genome. *Nature, 409*(6822), 860–921. doi:10.1038/35057062 PMID:11237011

Livak, K. J., & Schmittgen, T. D. (2001, December). *Analysis of Relative Gene Expression Data Using Real-Time Quantitative PCR and the 2CT Method Methods.* doi:10.1006/meth.2001.1262

Olmos, R., Tabik, S., & Herrera, F. (2018, January). Automatic handgun detection alarm in videos using deep learning. *Neurocomputing, 275*, 66–72. doi:10.1016/j.neucom.2017.05.012

Papastergiou, M. (2009, January). Digital game-based learning in high school Computer science education: Impact on educational effectiveness and student motivation. *Computers & Education, 52*(1), 1–12. doi:10.1016/j.compedu.2008.06.004

Personal Characteristics of Military Personnel and Law Enforcement Officers that Determine Psychological Readiness for Duty with Firearm. (2018). LEX RUSSICA (РУССКИЙ ЗАКОН). doi:10.17803/1729-5920.2018.142.9.119-128

Place, B. J., & Field, J. A. (2012, June 15). Identification of Novel Fluorochemicals in Aqueous Film-Forming Foams Used by the US Military. *Environmental Science & Technology, 46*(13), 7120–7127. doi:10.1021/es301465n PMID:22681548

Ren, S., He, K., Girshick, R., & Sun, J. (2017, June 1). Faster R CNN. *IEEE Transactions on Pattern Analysis and Machine Intelligence, 39*(6), 1137–1149. doi:10.1109/TPAMI.2016.2577031 PMID:27295650

Romero, D., & Salamea, C. (2019, July 24). Convolutional Models for the Detection of Firearms in Surveillance Videos. *Applied Sciences (Basel, Switzerland), 9*(15), 2965. doi:10.3390/app9152965

Roosevelt, T. S. (1995, November 15). Preventing Firearm Violence. *Annals of Internal Medicine, 123*(10), 813. doi:10.7326/0003-4819-123-10-199511150-00033 PMID:7574217

Weng, Z., Li, W., & Jin, Z. (2021, January 11). Human activity prediction using saliency-aware motion enhancement and weighted LSTM network. *EURASIP Journal on Image and Video Processing, 2021*(1). doi:10.1186/s13640-020-00544-0

Chapter 2
Autonomous Agriculture: The Role of IoT, AI, and ML in Drone Operations

I. Daniel Lawrence
https://orcid.org/0000-0002-8958-2515
Garuda Aerospace Pvt. Ltd., Chennai, India

J. Agnishwar
Garuda Aerospace Pvt. Ltd., Chennai, India

R. Vijayakumar
Garuda Aerospace Pvt. Ltd., Chennai, India

ABSTRACT

The usage of agricultural drones has completely changed how farmers manage their crops, providing a number of benefits over more conventional farming practices. Drones are mostly used in agriculture for crop health and growth monitoring, irrigation and soil analysis, and field studies. The capacity of agricultural drones to take high-resolution images of crops and analyse the health and development patterns of plants in great detail is one of its main advantages. Drones are using spectral sensors at various wavelengths and provide information on plant stress, nutritional deficits, soil health, and nutrient and other elements that may have an impact on agricultural productivity. Agricultural drones can easily link to numerous sensors, equipment, and data sources in the field via IoT technology. In order to provide insightful conclusions, artificial intelligence may find patterns and correlations in the data. Machine learning is used to train models that can recognise and classify various objects and conditions captured by sensors.

DOI: 10.4018/979-8-3693-1722-8.ch002

1. INTRODUCTION

Pesticides and fertilizers may be accurately applied by drones with spray systems, lowering the possibility of over or under-application, which might result in crop damage or decreased production. Yet, deploying drones in agriculture has drawbacks as well. The price of the technology, which may be a sizable investment for small-scale farmers, is one of the biggest obstacles. Drones also need experienced pilots who can control them safely and efficiently, understand data, and utilize it to make knowledgeable crop management choices. Lastly, the use of drones in agriculture may be constrained by legal considerations, such as airspace limitations and privacy problems (Ashton, 2009). The performance of agricultural drones is influenced by many important elements. The amount of space the drone can cover in a single flight is determined by one of the most important elements, flying duration. The drone's range and speed are also crucial since they affect how fast and precisely it can gather data and deliver treatments. The amount of product sprayed per unit area, as well as the spray pattern width for fertilizers and pesticides, may have an impact on how well the drone performs. Agricultural drones provide farmers with a number of advantages, such as better crop management and lower labour and time expenditures. Nevertheless, there are drawbacks to adopting this technology, including costs, operator skill requirements, and regulatory concerns. The performance of agricultural drones may be influenced by a number of important aspects, including as flight length, range, and application rates. Farmers may benefit from this technology to increase crop output and profitability by being aware of these elements and maximizing their usage of drones. Agricultural drone technology has the potential to revolutionize the way farmers manage their crops, providing a new level of precision and efficiency that was previously impossible with traditional farming methods (Sitaram et al., 2018). By utilizing advanced imaging sensors and software, drones can provide real-time information about the status of crops, allowing farmers to make informed decisions about planting, fertilization, irrigation, and pest control. In recent years, the adoption of agricultural drones has increased significantly, driven by advancements in technology, decreasing costs, and the growing demand for sustainable farming practices. Farmers around the world are now using drones to increase yields, reduce labour costs, and minimize the use of harmful chemicals that can harm the environment and human health. This paper will explore the benefits and challenges of using agricultural drones in farming and highlight the key factors that affect their performance. The various sensors and software used in agricultural drones, as well as the regulations and safety considerations that must be considered when using this technology. One of the most significant benefits of using agricultural drones is their ability to capture high-resolution imagery of crops, providing farmers with a detailed view of the health and growth patterns of their plants. This information can be used to create maps of the field, identifying areas that require attention and optimizing crop management practices (Mat et al., 2018). Drones equipped with multispectral or hyperspectral sensors can capture images at different wavelengths, providing data on plant stress, nutrient deficiencies, and other factors that can affect crop yield. Another key advantage of agricultural drones is their ability to reduce labour and time costs associated with traditional crop management practices. Drones can cover large areas of land quickly and accurately, allowing farmers to monitor crop growth and apply treatments efficiently. Drones equipped with spray systems can apply pesticides and fertilizers precisely, reducing the risk of over-application or under-application that can lead to crop damage or yield loss. Despite the many benefits of agricultural drones, their adoption also presents challenges for farmers. One of the most significant challenges is the cost of the technology, which can be a significant investment for small-scale farmers (Saha et al., 2018). Additionally, drones require skilled operators who can fly them safely and effectively, interpret data, and use it to make informed decisions about crop management. Regulatory issues also pose a challenge for the use of agricultural drones in farming. Airspace restrictions and privacy concerns can limit the use of drones in certain areas, and farmers must comply with regulations governing the use of drones in agriculture. Several key factors can affect the performance of agricultural drones, including flight time, range, and application rates. Flight time determines how much area the drone can cover in a single flight, while the range and speed of the drone affect how quickly and accurately it can collect data and apply treatments. The pesticide and fertilizer application rates and spray pattern width can also affect the drone's performance, as they determine how much product is applied per unit area (Santangeli et al., 2020). Farmers must carefully select the appropriate application rates and spray patterns for their crops to ensure optimal results. Agricultural drones offer a range of benefits to farmers, including improved crop management and reduced labour and time costs.

However, their adoption also presents challenges, such as cost, operator skill requirements, and regulatory issues.

Figure 1. Use of drone on multipurpose

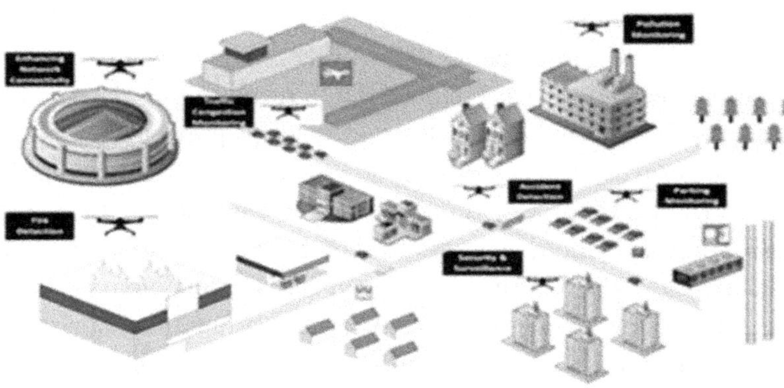

Several key factors, including flight time, range, and application rates, can affect the performance of agricultural drones. By understanding these factors and optimizing their use of drones, farmers can take advantage of this

technology to maximize crop yield and profitability while promoting sustainable farming practices. As the technology continues to evolve, it is likely that agricultural drones will play an increasingly important role in the future of farming. Use of Drone on Multipurpose is displayed in Figure 1.

2. COMPONENTS OF SMART FARMING IN AGRICULTURE

Smart farming is a modern approach to agriculture that involves the use of advanced technologies and data analytics to optimize crop yields, reduce waste, and increase efficiency (Kapoor et al., 2016). The components of smart farming can vary depending on the specific application, but here are some of the key components that are commonly used:

- **IoT sensors**: These are tiny, networked sensors that may be inserted into the ground, vegetation, or other farm components to gather data in real-time on variables including soil moisture, temperature, & humidity (Alvino et al., 2020).
- **Drones**: To take high-resolution pictures of the farm, autonomous unmanned aerial vehicles may be fitted with camera and other sensors. Drone-collected data may be used to track the health of crops, spot insect infestations, and pinpoint trouble spots on a farm (Eng et al., 2019).
- **Artificial Intelligence algorithms**: AI plays a crucial role in agriculture drone applications by enabling advanced data analysis, decision-making, and automation. By leveraging AI algorithms, drones can collect and process vast amounts of data from various sources such as sensors and imagery. AI-powered image recognition and computer vision techniques allow drones to identify and classify crops, pests, diseases, and other factors affecting agricultural productivity.
- **Machine learning algorithms**: These are computational formalism that can examine a lot of data to find patterns and forecast future events. In smart farming, crop yields may be maximized by using machine learning algorithms that forecast things like weather patterns, insect outbreaks & plant growth rates (Shaikh, Rasool, & Lone, 2022).
- **Cloud computing**: This refers to the processing and archiving of massive volumes of data using distant servers & data storage facilities. Cloud computing may be used in smart farming to store and process data from IoT sensor, drones & other sources.
- **Mobile apps and dashboards**: These are user interfaces that allow farmers and other stakeholders to access real-time data and analytics from the farm. Mobile apps and dashboards can be used to monitor crop health, track equipment usage, and make data-driven decisions about farm management (Raj, Gupta, Chamola, Elhence, Garg, Atiquzzaman, & Niyato, 2021; Shaikh, Mir, Rasool et al, 2022).

2.1 Precision Agriculture Tools

These are technologies that can be used to optimize farm management practices at a granular level. Precision agriculture tools can include internet of things, Artificial Intelligence and Machine Learning. The Smart Farming components is displayed in Figure 2.

Figure 2. Smart farming components

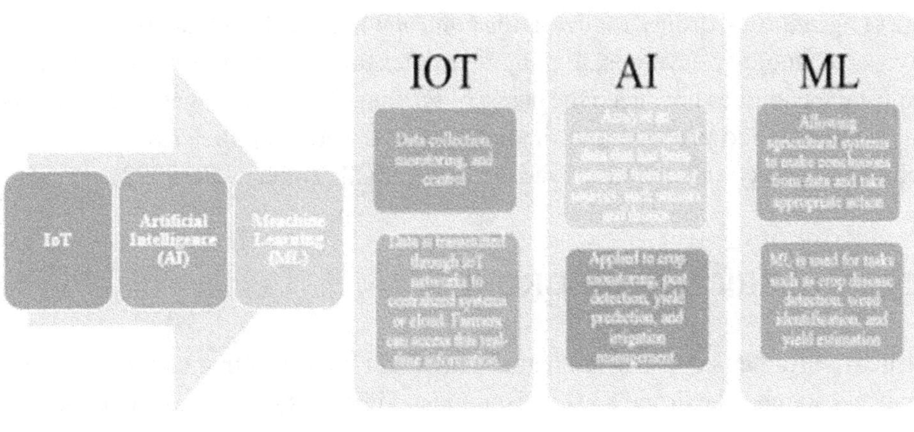

2.2 Irrigation Management

An important component of agricultural techniques is irrigation management. It entails distributing water to crops in the right amounts to promote optimum output and ideal development. Irrigation management has grown into a crucial problem for farmers because of the increasing need for production of food and the constrained supply of water. A technical approach to help farmers manages irrigation techniques is the use of agricultural drones (Sasikala & Sharma, 2022; Ünal, 2020). UAVs are fitted with sensors and camera that can collect information and take pictures of crops, soil, & water sources. The information gathered by the drones may provide farmers precise knowledge about the state of their plants, the quantity of soil moisture present, and how much water is required for optimum development. This knowledge is essential for irrigation management since it helps farmers water crops effectively. A variety of agricultural drone models exist on the market, each of which is intended to carry out a particular purpose. Some drones include thermal sensors capable of identifying temperature variations inside the crop canopy, which might reveal diseased or stressed regions (Baig, Khan, Mohammad, & Brahim, 2022; Baig, Khan, Mohammad, & Brahim, 2022). By using this information, problem areas may be located and addressed earlier they extend to other regions of the field. Some drones include multispectral sensors that can record photos of crops in various light spectrums, enabling farmers to assess the vitality and health of their crops. The use of agricultural drone for irrigation management has several benefits, one of which is their capacity to effectively and swiftly cover enormous regions. Conventional crop monitoring techniques and irrigation techniques take a lot of time and work, which may be difficult for farmers with big farms. A few acres of farmland may be covered by an agriculture drone in a couple of minutes, giving farmers access to real-time information on crop health and irrigation requirements. The affordability of employing agricultural drones for irrigation control is another benefit. Conventional crop monitoring & irrigation management techniques may be costly and wasteful since they utilize a lot of water & other resources (Aldaej et al., 2022). By providing precise information on crop conditions & irrigation requirements, agricultural drone usage may save these costs by enabling farmers to use water more skilfully and successfully. Nevertheless, employing agricultural drones in irrigation management comes with significant difficulties. The absence of industry standards is one of the biggest problems. Agriculture drones come in a wide variety of models, each with a unique set of features and capabilities. This might make it challenging for farmers to identify the ideal drone for their unique requirements. Regarding the usage of drone for commercial reasons, particularly agricultural, several nations have stringent laws. To use drone in agricultural fields, farmers may need to get licenses or permissions, which may be time-consuming and costly. Notwithstanding these difficulties, it is anticipated that in the next years, the usage of agricultural drones for irrigation control will rise. Drones are become more accessible and inexpensive as technology develops, making it simpler for farmers to use them in their operations. Modern agricultural techniques now need the usage of farming drone for irrigation management because to the rising demand for food produce and the need to save water supplies (Misra, Dixit, Al-Mallahi, Bhullar, Upadhyay, & Martynenko, 2020; Saadane et al., 2022; Toma et al., 2022).

3. IOT'S ROLE IN AGRICULTURE DRONES

The drone's structural frame is constructed from lightweight materials that enhance flying while minimizing vibration and sound. The drone's IoT sensor and navigation systems are put in the nose, and other

IoT devices necessary for the drone's work are installed in the body's remaining space (Maraveas et al., 2023). IoT technology includes, but is not limited to, GPS systems, central control systems, infrared lasers, cameras, LiDAR (light detection and ranging) devices, photogrammetry tools, and inertial measurement units (IMU) that detect rotational components like pitch, roll, and yaw. All of these systems are controlled by a base field system, and they work together to create an operational result. Bathymetry is the study of the underwater depths of oceans, lake, and riverbeds. The depth of the water is measured by crews using echo sounders, which emit ultrasonic sound waves into the ocean and afterwards compute depth measurements based on the information returned from these waves. Sadly, there are certain situations were dropping an echo sounder into to the water to take measurements is not practical. Examples include water bodies where the vegetation is so dense that it stops the water from flowing, or rock shards and other trash (known as tailing) that are left behind following a mining operation and hinder the water from moving (Alanezi et al., 2022; Hafeez et al., 2022). Agriculture is one of several sectors that have been significantly impacted by Internet of Things (IoT). A greater emphasis has been placed in recent years on the use of IoT in agricultural to raise yields, lower costs, and boost agricultural productivity. The usage of drones in agriculture is one of the most exciting IoT applications. Farmers can acquire information about their crops, keep an eye on their health, & make educated choices about when to water, fertilize, and harvest with the use of agricultural drones fitted with IoT cameras and sensors (Alsamhi et al., 2019; Prabu et al., 2022). Drones that use IoT in agriculture may provide farmers access to real-time agricultural data, which is one of the main benefits of this technology. Farmers will be able to better understand how their crops are developing and what climatic conditions are necessary for them to flourish by outfitting drones with sensor that assess temperatures, humidity, soil moisture & other environmental parameters. Farmers can decide quickly how much fertilizer or water to use on their crops since this information can be gathered and processed in real-time (Hassan et al., 2021). This may increase agricultural yields while decreasing water use, fertilizer wastage, and overall expenditures. Drones may also be fitted with cameras that take aerial pictures of crops in addition to collecting environmental data. These images can be analysed using machine learning algorithms to identify areas of stress, disease, or pest infestation. By detecting these issues early, farmers can act to prevent further damage to their crops, such as applying pesticides or removing infected plants. This can help to improve crop yields and reduce the need for costly interventions later in the growing season.

Drones with Internet capabilities can additionally be employed to monitor agricultural development over time. Crops may be photographed at regular intervals so that farmers can monitor their development and decide when to harvest. This may guarantee that crops are picked at the perfect moment, producing bigger yields and product of higher quality. Additionally, by monitoring crop growth over time, farmers can identify areas of their fields that may need extra attention, such as those that are not receiving enough water or nutrients. Another advantage of using IoT in agriculture drones is that it can help to reduce the need for manual labour. Traditionally, farmers have had to walk their fields to monitor crop health and identify issues. On bigger farms in particular, this procedure may be time- and labour-intensive (Wongchai et al., 2022). Without ever reaching the ground, farmers may collect information about their crops by employing drones fitted with IoT cameras and sensors. This may help farmers concentrate on other areas of their company by saving time and lowering labour expenses. Drones with IoT capabilities may also be utilized to enhance irrigation control. Farmers may choose when and how much to irrigate agricultural crops by keeping an eye on the soil moisture levels. This may aid in lowering water use and preventing over-irrigation, which can result in soil erosion and nutrient leaching. In addition, farmers may spot crops that may be getting excessive or insufficient water and make changes by employing drones to monitor irrigation. In general, the usage of IoT for agriculture using drones does have the potential to completely change how farmers cultivate their crops (Vangala et al., 2020).

3.1 Future Direction of IoT

Millions of people depend on the agricultural business for their living, making it one of the biggest industries in the world. In the last several years, the usage of drones in agriculture has significantly increased, providing farmers with valuable data and insights about their crops, soil, and weather conditions. With the help of the Internet of Things (IoT), agriculture drones are becoming even more powerful and efficient. In this project, we will explore the future direction of IoT in agriculture drones. While the use of IoT and drones in field operations is conceivable, the technological and legal environments are now lacking (Parasuraman et al., 2021). The US government and Federal Aviation Administration have taken precautions and taken the time to carefully consider the public impact of commercial drones before issuing licenses to those who would want to utilize drones for increasing business purposes. In order to prevent interference with other types of aircraft, drones are no longer permitted to fly above 400 feet in the air. Commercial field operators who fly drones must maintain a line-of-sight connection with them and have the required authorizations and certificates. Batteries are still an issue with drones itself. Usually, a drone flight lasts 30 minutes. The drone's time in the air is shortened if it runs against a headwind. Business owners must carefully arrange their drone activities because of battery life limits.

3.2 Advanced Sensors

One of the most significant advantages of IoT in agriculture drones is the ability to collect vast amounts of data about crops, soil, and weather conditions. With the help of advanced sensors, drones can now provide farmers with detailed information about crop health, water usage, and soil moisture levels. In the future, we can expect to see even more advanced sensors that can detect and identify specific plant diseases or nutrient deficiencies. For example, hyperspectral cameras can detect specific wavelengths of light that are emitted by plants. By analysing the wavelengths, drones can identify the presence of specific plant diseases or nutrient deficiencies. This information can help farmers to take immediate action to address the issue, potentially saving their crops from damage or loss (Kumar, Rawat, Mohd et al, 2021).

3.3 Real-Time Data Analysis

Another significant advantage of IoT in agriculture drones is the ability to analyze data in real-time. With the help of IoT, drones can collect data and transmit it to a central system where it can be analyzed and interpreted. This allows farmers to make quick decisions and take immediate action to address any issues that arise. For example, if a drone detects a problem with a crop, it can immediately alert the farmer. The farmer can then take corrective action before the issue becomes more severe. Real-time data analysis can also help farmers to optimize their irrigation and fertilization schedules, ensuring that crops receive the right amount of water and nutrients at the right time.

3.4 Automation

As technology continues to advance, we can expect to see more automation in agriculture drones. Drones will become more autonomous, able to fly and collect data without human intervention. This will free up farmers' time, allowing them to focus on other tasks. In the future, we can expect to see drones equipped with artificial intelligence (AI) and machine learning algorithms. These algorithms will allow drones to learn and adapt to changing conditions, improving their efficiency and effectiveness. For example, a drone may learn to detect specific plant diseases and automatically apply the appropriate treatment without human intervention (Israr et al., 2021).

3.5 Integration With Other Technologies

IoT in agriculture drones will become even more powerful when integrated with other IoT technologies. For example, drones can be integrated with weather monitoring systems, soil sensors, and irrigation systems. This will allow farmers to make more informed decisions based on a wide range of data sources. For example, a drone may detect a problem with a crop, and the data is then transmitted to a central system. The system can then cross-reference the data with weather and soil information to determine the cause of the problem. This information can then be used to make more informed decisions about irrigation and fertilization schedules, potentially increasing crop yields and reducing costs.

3.6 Increased Efficiency

The future of IoT in agriculture drones looks bright, and we can expect to see many exciting developments in the coming years. IoT in agriculture drones will increase efficiency, reduce costs, and improve crop yields. With the help of advanced sensors, real-time data analysis, automation, and integration with other technologies, agriculture drones will become even more powerful and effective. IoT in agriculture drones is already revolutionizing the way farmers collect and analyse data about their crops, soil, and weather conditions. With the help of advanced sensors, real-time data analysis, automation, and integration with other technologies, we can expect to see even more exciting developments in the future.

4 AI's ROLE IN AGRICULTURE DRONES

Agriculture is a significant industry worldwide, and technology has played a crucial role in improving its efficiency and productivity. One of the technologies that have been gaining momentum in recent years is agriculture drones. Drone technology is still being developed by AI. Small farmers in poor countries may benefit from it. Since maize is grown in massive monoculture fields, modern drone technology is more useful for crop monitoring. To teach AI systems to detect uncommon crops and varied planting patterns, further effort is required. In the worldwide UAV market, artificial intelligence for drones has been gradually expanding. There is now a lot of excitement about the potential and usage of AI to change the commercial drone business. Due of this, drones and AI and their potential uses in many sectors are expected to continue receiving more attention. Data analytics and navigation are two parts of a drone's operation that artificial intelligence have the capacity to revolutionize. Since AI regularly monitors the development of the drone and AI industries, we have the knowledge to guide people on both of important subjects. The drone's current flight speed is restricted by its ability to avoid stationary objects. The drone must fly slowly to preserve its capability to avoid obstacles since it can view 10-100 feet in front of it. Furthermore, since drones fly at high altitudes where they often encounter dynamic barriers, bigger drones struggle to avoid obstructions (Javaid et al., 2023; Kumar, Kumar, Tripathi et al, 2021). For detect Paddy leaf disease Using AI tools like Support Vector Machines (SVMs), Random Forests (RF) &Naive Bayes (NB) Algorithm. The AI required to minimize both static and moving objects is currently only present in smaller drones. Since they hover at a lower altitude than bigger drones, they mostly operate around stationary objects and find it simpler to complete their duties. Smaller drones with barrier avoidance capabilities are often utilized by enthusiasts or for more intimate tasks like thermal inspection or danger identification in confined locations. An abundance of organizations, consortia, and platforms were created in this area since such digital and computerized traceability of the whole food supply chain would enable identification of deficiencies, contamination, and adulteration of the product, maximizing its quality and safety. Employed AI algorithms to forecast the discovery of Paddy leaf diseaseis Displayed in Table 1. The use of AI algorithms such SVM, RF & NB are detecting the paddy Leaf disease that are displayed in Figure 3, Figure 4 & Figure 5 respectively.

Table 1. Employed AI algorithms to forecast the discovery of paddy leaf disease

Models	Name of Disease	Accuracy (%)	Sensitivity (%)	Specificity (%)	Precision (%)	F-Score (%)
SVM	Bacterial blight	98.20	99.05	98.76	95.60	99.30
	Brown spot	93.30	95.56	96.67	96.56	97.33
	Leaf blast	91.58	94.34	95.67	94.67	98.33
	Leaf smut	94.70	93.21	97.65	92.67	99.45
	Bakanae disease	97.50	91.45	94.76	91.09	98.45
RF	Bacterial blight	86.50	83.78	94.98	88.91	87.44
	Brown spot	87.30	82.34	93.45	87.77	88.90
	Leaf blast	80.10	83.67	92.64	86.66	85.11
	Leaf smut	82.40	79.23	91.43	84.78	83.77
	Bakanae disease	84.50	81.65	90.56	89.53	82.88
NB	Bacterial blight	75.30	77.96	94.67	80.56	82.77
	Brown spot	77.90	76.65	93.78	79.78	83.54
	Leaf blast	72.12	75.18	92.41	81.56	85.13
	Leaf smut	75.67	73.81	90.89	78.67	81.87
	Bakanae disease	69.80	72.78	91.63	79.54	83.07

Figure 3. SVM algorithm used to identify paddy leaf disease

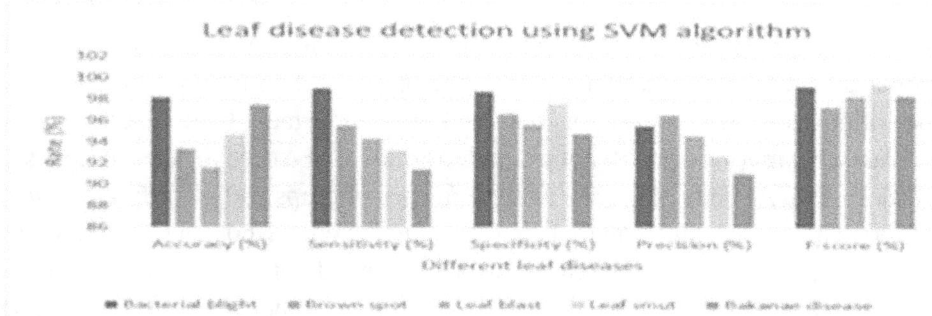

Figure 4. RF algorithm used to identify paddy leaf disease

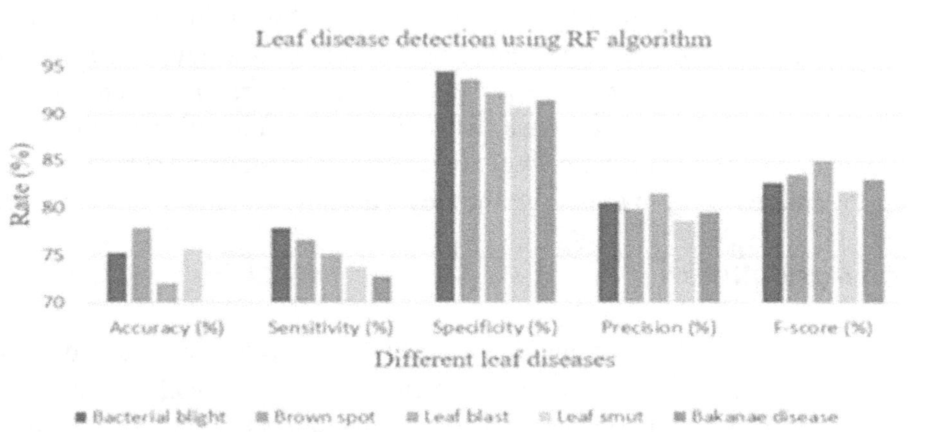

Figure 5. NB algorithm used to identify paddy leaf disease

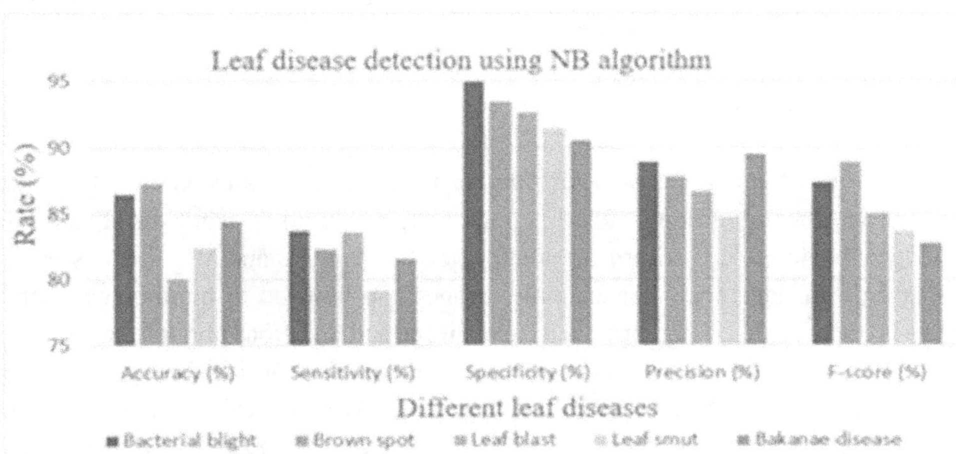

4.1 Crop Management

Crop monitoring is one of the key functions of AI in agricultural drones. Drones may be fitted with sensors and cameras to gather information on the health of crops, their rates of growth, and nutritional deficits. AI algorithms can then analyse this data and provide farmers with insights into their crop's health and any issues that may be present. For example, drones can be used to detect crop diseases before they become widespread. AI algorithms can analyse images of crops and identify any signs of disease or pest infestations. This information can then be relayed to farmers, who can take immediate action to prevent further damage to their crops. Similarly, drones equipped with AI technology can monitor soil conditions, including soil moisture levels, pH levels, and nutrient content (Singh, Singh, & Kaur, 2021).

4.2 Autonomous Operation

Another crucial role of AI in agriculture drones is autonomous operation. With the help of AI, drones can become more autonomous, able to fly and collect data without human intervention. This can save farmers time and money while improving the efficiency of crop monitoring.AI algorithms can be used to program drones to fly predetermined routes and collect data at specific intervals. The information may then be sent to a centralized system for analysis and use in making crop management choices. Drones may be programmed, for instance, to fly above fields and gather information on crop rates of growth, soil moisture content, and nutrient deficiency. The best irrigation and fertilization plans may then be developed using the data, ensuring that crops get the proper quantity of water & nutrients at the right time.

4.3 Precision Agriculture

Precision agriculture is one of the most important advantages of AI in agricultural drones. Using data and technology, precision agriculture aims to improve crop management while lowering waste and raising yield. Agriculture drone data may be analysed by AI algorithms to discover the best crop management techniques for a certain area or crop. Precision maps displaying the ideal locations for planting, irrigating, & fertilizing crops may be made using this data. Drones, for instance, may be used to gather information on the properties of soil, such as its moisture content and nutrient content (Aggarwal & Singh, 2021; Subeesh & Mehta, 2021). A precise map that illustrates which parts of the field need more or less fertilizer and irrigation may subsequently be made using this data. This may increase agricultural yields and decrease waste, saving farmers money.

4.4 Weather Monitoring

AI in agriculture drones can also be used for weather monitoring. Drones equipped with sensors can collect data about weather conditions, including temperature, humidity, wind speed, and rainfall. This data can be analyzed using AI algorithms to predict weather patterns and help farmers make informed decisions about crop management. For example, drones can be used to monitor weather conditions during the growing season, allowing farmers to make informed decisions about irrigation and fertilization schedules. Drones can also be used to monitor weather patterns during the harvest season, helping farmers to determine the optimal time to harvest their crops.AI in agriculture drones has the potential to transform the industry, providing farmers with valuable data and insights into their crops, soil, and weather conditions. With the help of AI algorithms, drones can monitor crops, operate autonomously, provide precision agriculture, and monitor weather conditions.

4.5 Future Direction of AI

The integration of artificial intelligence (AI) into agriculture drones has been a game-changer in the industry, enabling farmers to optimize crop yields, reduce costs, and increase efficiency. As the technology continues to evolve, the future of AI in agriculture drones holds significant promise. Drones are visible in open areas and during activities, and they often allow you to control video transmission. Yet, if the video connection failed, what would happen is that drone accidents do happen, although more often than drone makers would want. Engineers at the Swiss Federal Institute of Technology in Lausanne, Switzerland, have created a predictive control model that allows drones to fly unimpeded in regions with impediments (Singh, Berkvens, & Weyn, 2021; Singh & Jain, 2022). Due to its artificial intelligence (AI), the drone can predict both its own activity & that of other drone that are circling the area. Scientists are adapting the idea of flock flight, which is utilized by birds, to drones. Birds cooperate to plan their behaviour, and they are aware of when to veer off course to maintain a sufficient spacing between one another, fly in formation, or avoid obstacles. To be successful, drones should fly similarly, especially when they're swarming. Here are some potential directions that AI in agriculture drones might take:

4.6 Increased Autonomy

As AI algorithms become more sophisticated, agriculture drones will be able to operate with greater autonomy. For example, drones equipped with AI algorithms can identify crops, monitor crop health, and detect pests and diseases, making decisions about where and when to spray pesticides or apply fertilizers without human intervention. The integration of AI into agriculture drones will also allow them to work in tandem with other AI-powered farm equipment, such as autonomous tractors, to further improve farming efficiency.

4.7 Improved Imaging Capabilities

Advances in computer vision technology will allow agriculture drones to capture higher-resolution images and to detect and identify objects more accurately. This will enable drones to more accurately detect crop stress, nutrient deficiencies, and other issues in real-time. Additionally, drones equipped with AI algorithms will be able to process these images and provide actionable insights for farmers, such as suggesting a specific fertilizer application or identifying a particular pest infestation (Ahmad & Nabi, 2021).

4.8 Predictive Analytics

One of the most significant advantages of AI in agriculture drones is the ability to perform predictive analytics. By analysing data from multiple sources, including drones, weather stations, and soil sensors, AI algorithms will be able to provide farmers with insights into future crop yields and identify potential issues before they become problematic. For example, drones equipped with AI algorithms can use predictive analytics to provide farmers with insight into optimal planting times and to adjust irrigation and fertilizer schedules accordingly (Raj, Gupta, Chamola, Elhence, Garg, Atiquzzaman, & Niyato, 2021).

4.9 Improved Data Management

The integration of AI-equipped agriculture drones with other technologies such as satellite imagery will enable farmers to obtain a more comprehensive view of their fields. Drones can collect data on crop health and soil conditions, while satellite imagery can provide data on crop health and growth patterns at a much larger scale. Additionally, drones can work alongside autonomous tractors to optimize the timing of planting and harvesting, improving crop yields and minimizing waste.As the amount of data collected by AI-equipped agriculture drones grows, farmers will need better tools to manage and analyze this data. AI algorithms can help farmers make sense of this data by providing insights into trends and patterns that are difficult to discern manually (Ghazali et al., 2022). Additionally, AI can be used to automate data entry, reducing the potential for human error and enabling farmers to make more data-driven decisions.

4.10 Increased Efficiency

Drones with AI in agriculture will make it possible for farmers to work more productively by requiring less time and labour to complete activities like crop monitoring, fertilizing, and insect control. With AI algorithms, drones can perform these tasks more quickly and accurately, enabling farmers to focus on other critical aspects of farming, such as marketing and sales. Additionally, the integration of AI with other farm equipment such as autonomous tractors will further increase efficiency, reducing the potential for waste and improving overall productivity.

4.11 Sustainability

The integration of AI into agriculture drones will enable farmers to take a more sustainable approach to farming. Drones using artificial intelligence (AI) may assist farmers in decreasing waste and maximizing the utilization of resources like water and fertilizer. AI algorithms may also be used to improve crop rotation, lowering the demand for pesticides and gradually enhancing soil health. Drones for agriculture with AI have a bright future. Farmers will have the ability to grow more crops with less resources as technology develops, resulting in more efficient and sustainable farming methods. Drones will grow more autonomous and intelligent when AI is integrated, enabling farmers to make data-driven choices that maximize agricultural yields and minimize waste (Mohamed et al., 2021).

5. MACHINE LEARNING IN AGRICULTURE DRONES

Machine learning can be used in agriculture drones to improve the efficiency and effectiveness of crop monitoring and management. Some possible applications of machine learning in agriculture drones include:

5.1 Crop Monitoring

Crop monitoring using drones equipped with cameras and sensors is a modern approach to agriculture that uses machine learning algorithms to analyse the images captured by the drones. The drones can fly over the fields and capture high-resolution images of the crops from above, which can be analysed to identify areas of stress, disease, or nutrient deficiencies. It is possible to train machine learning algorithms to analyze the photos and find particular patterns or traits that point to crop stress or illness (Sharma et al., 2020).

5.2 Yield Prediction

Yield prediction using machine learning models and drones involves the following steps:

- **Historical crop data collection:** Historical crop data such as weather patterns, soil types, crop types, irrigation schedules, and yield data are collected over a period.
- **Data analysis and machine learning model training:** To find trends and patterns that may be utilized to develop a machine learning model, the obtained data is analyzed. Prediction or decision trees are used in the model's training to forecast crop production based on a variety of input variables.
- **Drone monitoring during growing season:** Drones equipped with sensors and cameras are deployed to monitor the crops during the growing season. The drones capture images and collect data on crop health, soil moisture levels, and other environmental factors.
- **Yield prediction and optimization:** The data collected by the drones is fed into the machine learning model, which predicts the crop yield based on the current environmental conditions. Farmers can use this information to optimize inputs such as water and fertilizer to maximize yield while minimizing waste (Qazi et al., 2022; Tomar & Kaur, 2021). Machine Learning Process is Displaced in Figure 6.

Figure 6. Machine learning process architecture

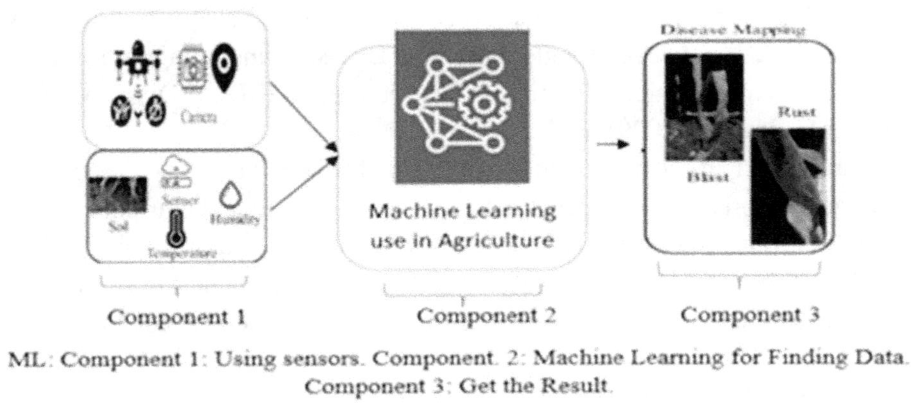

5.3 Weed Detection

By using machine learning models to predict crop yields, farmers may choose when & how to water, fertilizer, and harvest agricultural crops with more knowledge. This might increase crop yields, cut waste, and eventually boost earnings and agricultural sustainability. Machine Learning

Weed detection using machine learning algorithms involves the following steps:

- **Data collection:** Images of the field are collected using drones or other imaging devices. These images can be in the form of RGB or multispectral images.
- **Image pre-processing:** The collected images are pre-processed to enhance the features that are relevant for weed detection. This can include techniques such as filtering, segmentation, and feature extraction.
- **Machine learning model training:** The machine learning model is then trained using the previously processed pictures. Convolution neural networks (CNNs) and other machine learning algorithms that can identify patterns and categorize pictures may be used as the model.
- **Weed detection:** Once the model is trained, it can be used to detect and locate weeds in the field. This can be done in real-time using drones equipped with cameras or other imaging devices (Chamola et al., 2020).
- **Precision herbicide application:** With accurate information about the location of weeds in the field, farmers can apply herbicides more precisely, reducing overall herbicide use and minimizing the impact on non-target organisms.

5.4 Soil Analysis

Drones equipped with soil sensors and machine learning algorithms can provide detailed information about soil health and nutrient levels, enabling farmers to manage their crops and make data-driven fertilization choices.

Soil analysis using drones equipped with soil sensors and machine learning algorithms involves the following steps:

- **Soil sensor data collection:** Drones equipped with soil sensors are flown over the field, collecting data on soil moisture, temperature, pH, and other relevant parameters.
- **Machine learning model training:**A machine learning algorithm is then trained using the gathered soil data. To forecast several soil health characteristics including nutrient levels, soil texture, and organic matter content, the model may be trained (Misra, Dixit, Al-Mallahi, Bhullar, Upadhyay, & Martynenko, 2020).
- **Soil health analysis:** Farmers may then use the trained model to examine the soil data gathered by the drone to get comprehensive information about the condition and nutrient content of their soil.
- **Data-driven decision-making:** With accurate information about their soil health, farmers can make data-driven decisions about fertilization and crop management. For example, they can optimize the timing and amount of fertilizer application based on the nutrient levels in the soil.

5.5 Pest and Disease Management

By using drones and machine learning for resource management, farmers can make more informed decisions about their farming practices, resulting in higher yields, reduced costs, and improved sustainability (Rathore, 2021).

Pest and disease management using machine learning involves the following steps:

- **Data collection:** Drones equipped with cameras and sensors fly over the field, collecting data on the crop's health and growth patterns.

- **Data analysis:** Machine learning algorithms analyze the collected data to identify any signs of pests or diseases. The algorithms can learn to identify specific patterns, shapes, colours, or other indicators that are unique to different pests and diseases.
- **Early detection:** By identifying pests and diseases early, farmers can take action quickly and prevent further damage. This can include targeted applications of pesticides, biological control methods, or crop rotation.
- **Reduced pesticide use:** By using machine learning to identify and target specific pests and diseases, farmers can reduce their overall use of pesticides. This can result in cost savings and reduced environmental impact (Ben Ayed & Hanana, 2021).

6. SPRAY TREATMENTS

Spray treatment is one of the most important applications of agriculture drones in modern farming practices. Agriculture drones equipped with sprayers can precisely target specific areas of a field, reducing the amount of chemicals needed and minimizing the risk of drift and environmental contamination. Here are some of the key considerations and best practices for spray treatment using agriculture drones:

6.1 Choose the Right Nozzle

The nozzle is an important component of the sprayer that controls the flow rate and spray pattern. Choosing the right nozzle is critical to ensure uniform coverage and maximize the efficiency of the spraying operation. The choice of nozzle depends on several factors, including the type of chemical being used, the desired spray pattern, and the wind conditions. It is important to consult the manufacturer's guidelines and conduct nozzle tests before spraying (Shaikh, Rasool, & Lone, 2022).

6.2 Calibrate the Sprayer

Calibrating the sprayer is an essential step in ensuring accurate application rates and minimizing waste. Calibration involves determining the flow rate of the sprayer and adjusting the settings to achieve the desired application rate. It is important to conduct calibration tests regularly to account for changes in factors such as temperature, humidity, and wind speed.

6.3 Plan the Flight Path

Planning the flight path is critical to ensure that the drone covers the entire field and that there is no overlap or gaps in the spraying operation. It is important to consider factors such as wind conditions, obstacles, and the location of the nearest landing site. Planning the flight path can be done using specialized software that considers the drone's speed, altitude, and spray width (Ramesh & Rajeshkumar, 2021).

6.4 Monitor the Weather

The success of the spraying operation is highly dependent on the weather. Wind speed and direction, humidity, and temperature can all affect the spray pattern and the drift of the chemicals. It is important to monitor the weather conditions before and during the spraying operation and adjust the flight path and spray settings accordingly (Javaid, 2021).

6.5 Follow Safety Guidelines

Spraying chemicals can be hazardous to both the operator and the environment. It is important to follow safety guidelines, including wearing protective clothing and equipment, maintaining a safe distance from the drone, and avoiding contact with the chemicals (Wakode, 2021). It is also important to dispose of the chemicals and the containers properly to avoid environmental contamination.

6.6 Maintain the Drone and Equipment

Regular maintenance of the drone and equipment is essential to ensure optimal performance and avoid breakdowns. This includes cleaning the nozzles, checking the battery and motor, and inspecting the propellers for damage. It is also important to store the chemicals and the equipment properly to avoid degradation and contamination (Dharmaraj & Vijayanand, 2018).

7. CONCLUSION

Agriculture drones, also known as agricultural UAVs (Unmanned Aerial Vehicles), are becoming an increasingly popular tool in the agriculture industry. These drones are equipped with various sensors and cameras that can collect data on crops, soil, and other environmental factors that impact agriculture. In this essay, we will explore the benefits of using agriculture drones and how they are changing the way we farm. The use of agriculture drones has several benefits, including increased efficiency, improved accuracy, and cost savings. One of the most significant advantages of using drones is the ability to cover large areas of land quickly and efficiently. Drones can fly over a field and collect data on crop health, soil moisture, and other factors in a fraction of the time it would take for a human to do the same task. This increased efficiency can save farmers valuable time and labour costs. In addition to increased efficiency, agriculture drones can also provide improved accuracy in data collection. The sensors and cameras on the drones can collect data with greater precision than traditional methods. For example, drones can detect differences in crop health that may not be visible to the naked eye, allowing farmers to make more informed decisions about how to treat their crops. Another advantage of using agriculture drones is the potential cost savings. By collecting data on crops and soil, farmers can make more informed decisions about how to manage their fields. For example, if a drone detects that a certain area of a field has low soil moisture, the farmer can target that area for irrigation rather than irrigating the entire field, saving water and reducing costs. The use of agriculture drones is also changing the way we approach farming. With the data collected by drones, farmers can take a more proactive approach to crop management. For example, drones can detect pests or diseases early on, allowing farmers to take action before the problem becomes widespread. This can lead to higher yields and a more sustainable farming operation. Another way that agriculture drones are changing farming is through the use of precision agriculture. Precision agriculture involves using data and technology to optimize crop production. By collecting data on crop health, soil moisture, and other factors, farmers can use precision agriculture techniques to apply fertilizers and pesticides more efficiently. This can lead to reduced environmental impact and cost savings for farmers. Despite the many benefits of using agriculture drones, there are also some challenges and limitations to their use. One of the main challenges is the cost of the technology. While the cost of drones has decreased in recent years, they can still be expensive, especially for small-scale farmers. Additionally, there are regulations and safety concerns that must be considered when using drones in agriculture. Another challenge is the need for trained personnel to operate and interpret the data collected by drones. While drones can collect vast amounts of data, it takes skilled operators and analysts to interpret that data and use it to make informed decisions about crop management. The use of agriculture drones has many benefits and is changing the way we farm. Increased efficiency, improved accuracy, cost savings, and a more proactive approach to crop management are just a few of the advantages of using drones in agriculture. As technology continues to evolve, we can expect to see even more innovation and growth in the use of drones in agriculture. While there are challenges and limitations to their use, the benefits of using agriculture drones make them a valuable tool for farmers looking to optimize their crop production and improve sustainability.

REFERENCES

Aggarwal, N., & Singh, D. (2021). Technology assisted farming: Implications of IoT and AI. *IOP Conference Series. Materials Science and Engineering*, *1022*(1), 012080. doi:10.1088/1757-899X/1022/1/012080

Ahmad, L., & Nabi, F. (2021). *Agriculture 5.0: Artificial Intelligence, IoT and Machine Learning*. CRC Press.

Alanezi, M. A., Mohammad, A., Sha'aban, Y. A., Bouchekara, H. R., & Shahriar, M. S. (2022). Auto-Encoder Learning-Based UAV Communications for Livestock Management. *Drones (Basel)*, *6*(10), 276. doi:10.3390/drones6100276

Aldaej, A., Ahanger, T. A., Atiquzzaman, M., Ullah, I., & Yousufudin, M. (2022). Smart Cybersecurity Framework for IoT-Empowered Drones: Machine Learning Perspective. *Sensors (Basel)*, *22*(7), 2630. doi:10.339022072630 PMID:35408244

Alsamhi, S. H., Ma, O., Ansari, M. S., & Almalki, F. A. (2019). Survey on collaborative smart drones and internet of things for improving smartness of smart cities. *IEEE Access : Practical Innovations, Open Solutions*, *7*, 128125–128152. doi:10.1109/ACCESS.2019.2934998

Alvino, F. C., Aleman, C. C., Filgueiras, R., Althoff, D., & da Cunha, F. F. (2020). Vegetation indices for irrigated corn monitoring. *Engenharia Agrícola*, *40*(3), 322–333. doi:10.1590/1809-4430-eng.agric.v40n3p322-333/2020

Ashton, K. (2009). That 'internet of things' thing. *RFID Journal, 22*(7), 97-114.

Baig, Z., Khan, M. A., Mohammad, N., & Brahim, G. B. (2022). Drone forensics and machine learning: Sustaining the investigation process. *Sustainability (Basel)*, *14*(8), 4861. doi:10.3390u14084861

Ben Ayed, R., & Hanana, M. (2021). Artificial intelligence to improve the food and agriculture sector. *Journal of Food Quality*, *2021*, 1–7. doi:10.1155/2021/5584754

Chamola, V., Hassija, V., Gupta, V., & Guizani, M. (2020). A comprehensive review of the COVID-19 pandemic and the role of IoT, drones, AI, blockchain, and 5G in managing its impact. *IEEE Access : Practical Innovations, Open Solutions*, *8*, 90225–90265. doi:10.1109/ACCESS.2020.2992341

Dharmaraj, V., & Vijayanand, C. (2018). Artificial intelligence (AI) in agriculture. *International Journal of Current Microbiology and Applied Sciences*, *7*(12), 2122–2128. doi:10.20546/ijcmas.2018.712.241

Eng, L. S., Ismail, R., Hashim, W., & Baharum, A. (2019). The use of VARI, GLI, and VIgreen formulas in detecting vegetation in aerial images. *International Journal of Technology*, *10*(7), 1385–1394. doi:10.14716/ijtech.v10i7.3275

Ghazali, M. H. M., Azmin, A., & Rahiman, W. (2022). Drone Implementation in Precision Agriculture—A Survey. *International Journal of Emerging Technology and Advanced Engineering*, *12*(4), 67–77. doi:10.46338/ijetae0422_10

Hafeez, A., Husain, M. A., Singh, S. P., Chauhan, A., Khan, M. T., Kumar, N., ... Soni, S. K. (2022). Implementation of drone technology for farm monitoring & pesticide spraying: A review. *Information Processing in Agriculture*.

Hassan, S. I., Alam, M. M., Illahi, U., Al Ghamdi, M. A., Almotiri, S. H., & Su'ud, M. M. (2021). A systematic review on monitoring and advanced control strategies in smart agriculture. *IEEE Access : Practical Innovations, Open Solutions*, *9*, 32517–32548. doi:10.1109/ACCESS.2021.3057865

Israr, A., Abro, G. E. M., Sadiq Ali Khan, M., Farhan, M., & Bin Mohd Zulkifli, S. U. A. (2021). Internet of things (IoT)-Enabled unmanned aerial vehicles for the inspection of construction sites: A vision and future directions. *Mathematical Problems in Engineering*, *2021*, 1–15. doi:10.1155/2021/9931112

Javaid, M., Haleem, A., Khan, I. H., & Suman, R. (2023). Understanding the potential applications of Artificial Intelligence in Agriculture Sector. *Advanced Agrochem*, *2*(1), 15–30. doi:10.1016/j.aac.2022.10.001

Javaid, N. (2021). *Integration of context awareness in Internet of Agricultural Things*. Academic Press.

Kapoor, A., Bhat, S. I., Shidnal, S., & Mehra, A. (2016, October). Implementation of IoT (Internet of Things) and Image processing in smart agriculture. In *2016 International Conference on Computation System and Information Technology for Sustainable Solutions (CSITSS)* (pp. 21-26). 10.1109/CSITSS.2016.7779434

Kumar, I., Rawat, J., Mohd, N., & Husain, S. (2021). Opportunities of artificial intelligence and machine learning in the food industry. *Journal of Food Quality*, *2021*, 1–10. doi:10.1155/2021/4535567

Kumar, R., Kumar, P., Tripathi, R., Gupta, G. P., Gadekallu, T. R., & Srivastava, G. (2021). SP2F: A secured privacy-preserving framework for smart agricultural Unmanned Aerial Vehicles. *Computer Networks*, *187*, 107819. doi:10.1016/j.comnet.2021.107819

Maraveas, C., Asteris, P. G., Arvanitis, K. G., Bartzanas, T., & Loukatos, D. (2023). Application of bio and nature-inspired algorithms in agricultural engineering. *Archives of Computational Methods in Engineering*, *30*(3), 1979–2012. doi:10.100711831-022-09857-x

Mat, I., Kassim, M. R. M., Harun, A. N., & Yusoff, I. M. (2018, November). Smart agriculture using internet of things. In *2018 IEEE conference on open systems (ICOS)* (pp. 54-59). IEEE.

Misra, N. N., Dixit, Y., Al-Mallahi, A., Bhullar, M. S., Upadhyay, R., & Martynenko, A. (2020). IoT, big data, and artificial intelligence in agriculture and food industry. *IEEE Internet of Things Journal*, *9*(9), 6305–6324. doi:10.1109/JIOT.2020.2998584

Mohamed, E. S., Belal, A. A., Abd-Elmabod, S. K., El-Shirbeny, M. A., Gad, A., & Zahran, M. B. (2021). Smart farming for improving agricultural management. *The Egyptian Journal of Remote Sensing and Space Sciences*, *24*(3), 971–981. doi:10.1016/j.ejrs.2021.08.007

Parasuraman, K., Anandan, U., & Anbarasan, A. (2021, February). IoT based smart agriculture automation in artificial intelligence. In *2021 Third International Conference on Intelligent Communication Technologies and Virtual Mobile Networks (ICICV)* (pp. 420-427). 10.1109/ICICV50876.2021.9388578

Prabu, A. V., Kumar, G. S., Rajasoundaran, S., Malla, P. P., Routray, S., & Mukherjee, A. (2022). Internet of things-based deeply proficient monitoring and protection system for crop field. *Expert Systems: International Journal of Knowledge Engineering and Neural Networks*, *39*(5), e12876. doi:10.1111/exsy.12876

Qazi, S., Khawaja, B. A., & Farooq, Q. U. (2022). *IoT-equipped and AI-enabled next generation smart agriculture: A critical review, current challenges and future trends*. Academic Press.

Raj, M., Gupta, S., Chamola, V., Elhence, A., Garg, T., Atiquzzaman, M., & Niyato, D. (2021). A survey on the role of Internet of Things for adopting and promoting Agriculture 4.0. *Journal of Network and Computer Applications*, *187*, 103107. doi:10.1016/j.jnca.2021.103107

Ramesh, M., & Rajeshkumar, L. (2021). Technological advances in analyzing of soil chemistry. *Applied soil chemistry*, 61-78.

Rathore, N. S. (2021). Application of artificial intelligence in agriculture including horticulture. *International Journal of Innovative Horticulture*, *10*(2), 138–141. doi:10.5958/2582-2527.2021.00013.0

Saadane, R., Chehri, A., & Jeon, S. (2022). AI-based modeling and data-driven evaluation for smart farming-oriented big data architecture using IoT with energy harvesting capabilities. *Sustainable Energy Technologies and Assessments*, *52*, 102093. doi:10.1016/j.seta.2022.102093

Saha, A. K., Saha, J., Ray, R., Sircar, S., Dutta, S., Chattopadhyay, S. P., & Saha, H. N. (2018, January). IOT-based drone for improvement of crop quality in agricultural field. In *2018 IEEE 8th Annual Computing and Communication Workshop and Conference (CCWC)* (pp. 612-615). IEEE.

Santangeli, A., Chen, Y., Kluen, E., Chirumamilla, R., Tiainen, J., & Loehr, J. (2020). Integrating drone-borne thermal imaging with artificial intelligence to locate bird nests on agricultural land. *Scientific Reports*, *10*(1), 1–8. doi:10.103841598-020-67898-3 PMID:32665596

Sasikala, D., & Sharma, K. V. (2022). Optimization of ML techniques with Gaussian Quadrature Numerical Analysis for Precision Agricultural Augmentation. *Journal of Soft Computing Paradigm*, *4*(2), 113–120. doi:10.36548/jscp.2022.2.006

Shaikh, T. A., Mir, W. A., Rasool, T., & Sofi, S. (2022). Machine Learning for Smart Agriculture and Precision Farming: Towards Making the Fields Talk. *Archives of Computational Methods in Engineering*, *29*(7), 4557–4597. doi:10.100711831-022-09761-4

Shaikh, T. A., Rasool, T., & Lone, F. R. (2022). Towards leveraging the role of machine learning and artificial intelligence in precision agriculture and smart farming. *Computers and Electronics in Agriculture, 198*, 107119. doi:10.1016/j.compag.2022.107119

Sharma, A., Jain, A., Gupta, P., & Chowdary, V. (2020). Machine learning applications for precision agriculture: A comprehensive review. *IEEE Access : Practical Innovations, Open Solutions*, *9*, 4843–4873. doi:10.1109/ACCESS.2020.3048415

Singh, G., Singh, A., & Kaur, G. (2021). Role of artificial intelligence and the internet of things in agriculture. In Artificial Intelligence to Solve Pervasive Internet of Things Issues (pp. 317-330). doi:10.1016/B978-0-12-818576-6.00016-2

Singh, R. K., Berkvens, R., & Weyn, M. (2021). AgriFusion: An architecture for IoT and emerging technologies based on a precision agriculture survey. *IEEE Access : Practical Innovations, Open Solutions*, *9*, 136253–136283. doi:10.1109/ACCESS.2021.3116814

Singh, S., & Jain, P. (2022). Applications of artificial intelligence for the development of sustainable agriculture. In Agro-biodiversity and Agri-ecosystem Management (pp. 303-322). doi:10.1007/978-981-19-0928-3_16

Sitaram, K. A., Ankush, K. R., Anant, K. N., & Raghunath, B. R. (2018, December). Iot based smart management of poultry farm and electricity generation. In *2018 IEEE International Conference on Computational Intelligence and Computing Research (ICCIC)* (pp. 1-4). 10.1109/ICCIC.2018.8782308

Subeesh, A., & Mehta, C. R. (2021). Automation and digitization of agriculture using artificial intelligence and internet of things. *Artificial Intelligence in Agriculture*, *5*, 278–291. doi:10.1016/j.aiia.2021.11.004

Toma, C., Popa, M., Iancu, B., Doinea, M., Pascu, A., & Ioan-Dutescu, F. (2022). Edge Machine Learning for the Automated Decision and Visual Computing of the Robots, IoT Embedded Devices or UAV-Drones. *Electronics (Basel)*, *11*(21), 3507. doi:10.3390/electronics11213507

Tomar, P., & Kaur, G. (Eds.). (2021). *Artificial Intelligence and IoT-based Technologies for Sustainable Farming and Smart Agriculture*. doi:10.4018/978-1-7998-1722-2

Ünal, Z. (2020). Smart farming becomes even smarter with deep learning—A bibliographical analysis. *IEEE Access : Practical Innovations, Open Solutions*, *8*, 105587–105609. doi:10.1109/ACCESS.2020.3000175

Vangala, A., Das, A. K., Kumar, N., & Alazab, M. (2020). Smart secure sensing for IoT-based agriculture: Blockchain perspective. *IEEE Sensors Journal*, *21*(16), 17591–17607. doi:10.1109/JSEN.2020.3012294

Wakode, M. S. (2021). Role of AI and Big Data Analytics in UAV-Enabled IoT Applications for Smart Cities. *Unmanned Aerial Vehicles for Internet of Things (IoT) Concepts, Techniques, and Applications,* 193-205.

Wongchai, A., Shukla, S. K., Ahmed, M. A., Sakthi, U., Jagdish, M., & kumar, R. (2022). Artificial intelligence-enabled soft sensor and internet of things for sustainable agriculture using ensemble deep learning architecture. *Computers & Electrical Engineering*, *102*, 108128. doi:10.1016/j.compeleceng.2022.108128

Chapter 3
Deep Learning Models for Predicting High and Low Tides With Gravitational Analysis

Rajendra Kumar
Rama University, India

Surbhit Shukla
Rama University, India

C. S. Raghuvanshi
Rama University, India

ABSTRACT

In this chapter, many forecasting models were established, and each model was produced in three forms, each with a distinct machine learning algorithm: regression, random forest, and artificial neural network. All of the presented models performed well in predicting the tide level at Visakhapatnam port. All models based on supervised learning had an accuracy of 85 to 9%, with a relative absolute error of 5 to 7.5. Finally, with a forecast horizon of several hours, satisfactory results were obtained, and a further specific comparison revealed that the models based on the considered machine learning algorithms outperform the auto learning integrated evaluation models with exogenous input variables in forecasting high/low tides.

1. INTRODUCTION

The oceanic tide is the rhythmic rise and fall of sea level over time, which is visible at a coast by the periodic advancing and retreating of the waves from the beach. Tidal movements are enhanced (or diminished) over wide shelves and respond more violently to meteorological circumstances than those in deep water. Local influences in shallow water may affect tidal components, notably by creating harmonics whose frequencies are simple multiples of the constituent's frequency. These harmonics are

DOI: 10.4018/979-8-3693-1722-8.ch003

caused by frictional contact between the sea bed and the tide's ebb and flow. Coastlines may reflect tidal waves, causing real tides in a given place to be higher or lower than predicted by astronomical forcing. The combination of ocean basin geometry constraints and the impact of the Carioles force lead in the formation of amphidromic systems, in which the crest of the tidal wave at high water circles around an amphidromic point once during each tidal period. Despite the fact that the interactions of all the forces and causes are so complicated that the coastal tide timings and ranges on the coastline could not be anticipated with any degree of accuracy, the coastal tide could be predicted. Tidal level calculation in coastal engineering may determine a design level for the top of marine constructions and safe ship movement in a port. Tidal level prediction becomes more important for coastal engineering and maritime navigation.

The harmonic technique (abbreviated HM) established (Darwin, 1907) argues that tides may be seen as a superposition of distinct harmonics with known astronomical frequencies (Doodson, 1921). The data may then be utilized to make accurate forecasts for future tides at the same location. The astonishing precision of these forecasts astonishes scholars' grasp of how the tide operates in the ocean. The length of the record required to extract distinct components is determined mostly by the frequency proximity of the components to be extracted and the lowest frequency of the components picked. Using the least squares approach, 369 days of hourly data at a place are typically required to extract 20 to 30 components with acceptable separation of closely spaced elements. (Le Provost et al., 1998) built their numerical model with 26 key elements.

The intrinsic smoothness of the admittance function, which operates on the tide-generating, gives the observed tide as its output, solves the shortcoming of HM. Tidal components that are closely distanced from one another and so have basically the same admittance function are addressed separately. It is feasible to use the tidal response function's inherent smoothness to create reliable tidal predictions with a lesser number of components (Munk & Cartwright, 1996). The response orthotide approach (abbreviated R-O) is described in detail in (Desai, 1996; Ray, 1998) and is often used in tidal models for calculating linear tides in the worldwide seas, such as (Desai & Wahr, 1995; Han et al., 2000; Matsumoto et al., 2000). Both HM and R-O are only useful for tidal forecasts in one case when observable data is utilized to calculate unknown constants.

However, R-O explains that the actual tides are determined by the tide-generating forces. The final conclusion suggests that real tides and tide producing forces have a similar connection. If the connection can be established, astronomical tide-generating forces may be employed to estimate tides using the well-known relationship.

The research focuses on an effective artificial neural network (ANN) tool for determining the link between real tides and tide-generating forces. To tackle problems involving very nonlinear interactions and complicated effective variables, ANN has high functionality, quick computing, and a large memory. As a result, ANN has recently been extensively used in a variety of sectors. (Chang & Chien, 2006; Deo et al., 2002; Deo & Naidu, 1998; Lee, 2004; Lee & Jeng, 2002; Lee et al., 2002; Makarynskyy, 2004; Medina, 2001; Tsai & Lee, 1999; Vaziri, 1997) provide some instances of applying neural networks in maritime engineering and research.

(Chang & Chien, 2006) provides both an ANN model and an ARIMA model for forecasting Caspian Sea surface water level as a specific application of ANN to tidal prediction. (Tsai & Lee, 1999) used an ANN model to anticipate diurnal and semidiurnal tide levels without establishing the harmonic parameters. Later, four discussions on the paper of (Tsai & Lee, 1999) by (Kumar & Minocha, 2001; Mandal, 2001; Walton & Garcia, 2001) raised some practical and theoretical issues. Due to the sequentially recorded tidal data needed as inputs, the implementation of the ANN model of (Tsai & Lee, 1999) yields only a one-hour tidal predictor with a lead time of one hour. (Lee & Jeng, 2002) use an ANN program to estimate and augment the tide level using short-term observed data. (Lee & Jeng, 2002) created an ANN model in the learning stage that was connected with short-term measurable data to offer a long-term prediction in tides. The disadvantage of (Lee & Jeng, 2002)'s ANN model is that it requires multiple lead time tidal data observations to be fed into the ANN model for forecasting successive tides. These ANN tidal models can only forecast a single tidal point.

To prove the validity of the link between tides and tide-producing forces, the authors employ tide-astronomy generating forces of astronomy as inputs in the suggested ANN model. TAGF-ANN so names the suggested model. To get an accurate estimate of tides at a specific site, TAGF-ANN is compared to the frequently recognized HM. TAGF-ANN is also extended to estimate tides at various sites around the spot where tidal data is utilized to produce TAGF-ANN. The suggested TAGF-ANN may be utilized in engineering practices to predict tides at a place where a tide station has not been installed to gather tidal data and some observed data is available from an adjacent point.

2. THE TIDE-GENERATING IDEA

Oceanic tides are primarily caused by the combined gravitational pull of the earth and the moon, as well as the gravitational attraction of the earth and the sun. Tides caused by other planetary bodies are insignificant. For gravitational purposes, the geocentric coordinate system shown in Figure 1 is thought to be the most practical way to express the earth's tides. The gravitational potential at any point P on the earth's surface with a vector r owing to a mass M of the body at another point with a vector r is represented in this coordinate system (Lamb, 1945) as

Figure 1. Geometry of gravitational force and centrifugal force on a point P at the surface of the earth

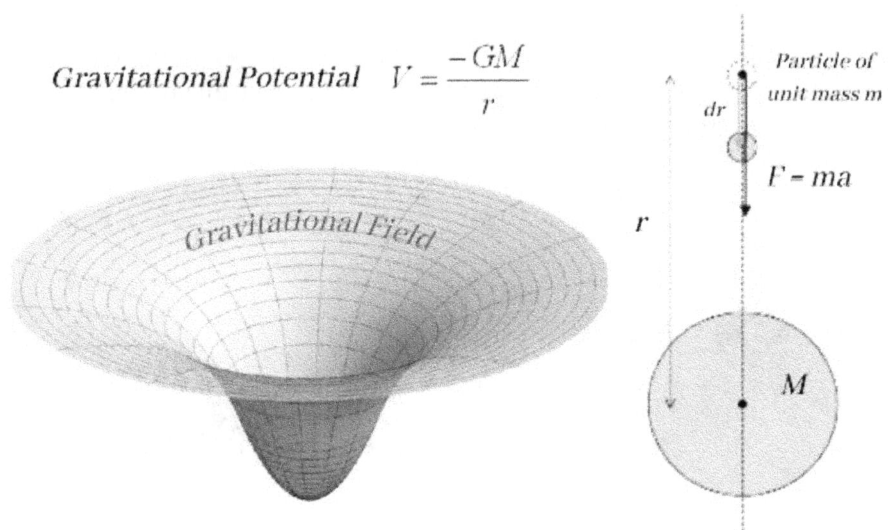

where G = 6.67 x 10^{-11} Nm/kg^2 is the global gravitational coefficient; R = |r| 6.371x 10^6 m is the radius of the earth; D is the distance between the earth's center and the center of the body; and = |d| is the distance between the point P and the center of the body. This gravitational potential generates gravitational force Fa = GM / 2, which points towards the body's center.

The centrifugal force caused by the mutual rotation of the two entities seen in Figure 1 at any point on the earth opposite pointing towards d is denoted as

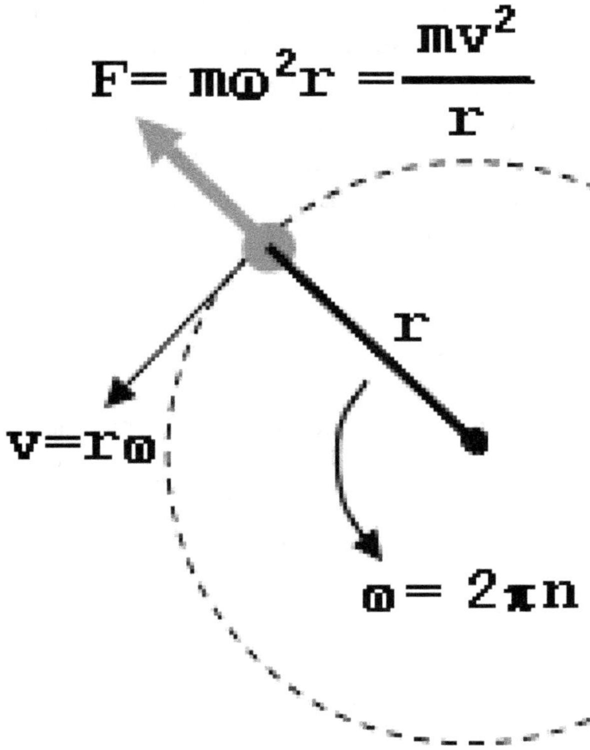

The centrifugal force due to the mutual rotation of two bodies shown in Figure 1 at any point on the earth opposite pointing towards d. The radial component of the centrifugal force at point P is F_c cosθ and the tangential component is F_c sinθ where θ is the

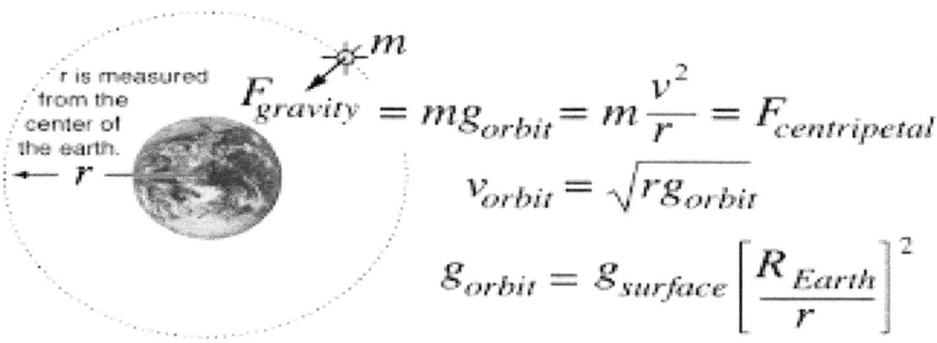

Figure 2. Location of tidal gauge observed

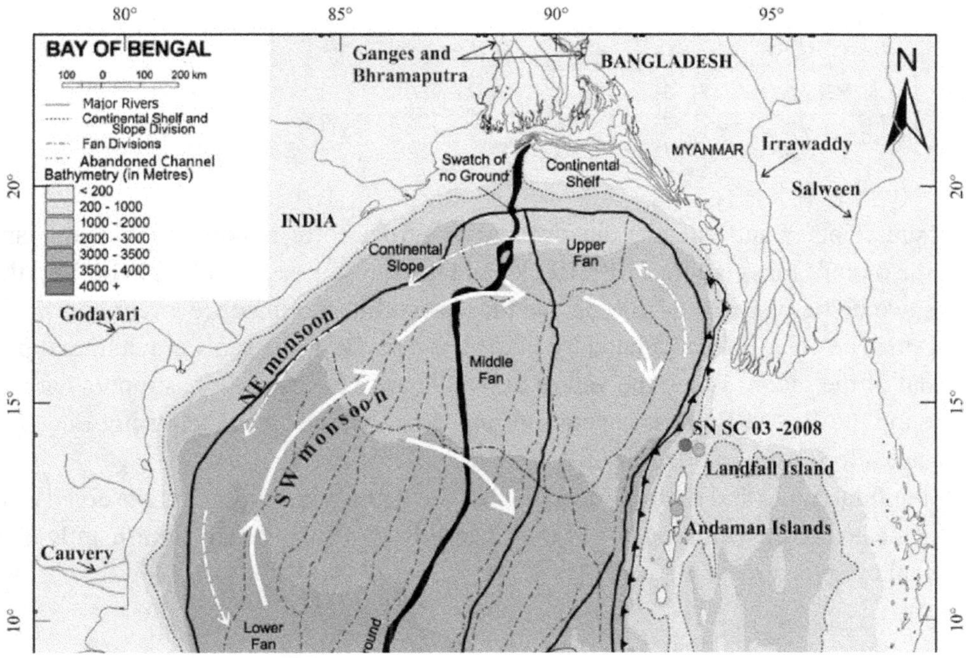

angle between two vectors, r and d. A potential, ϕ_c, can be related to the centrifugal force and given as

$$\varnothing_c = \frac{GM}{D^2} r\cos\theta + \varnothing_0 \tag{3}$$

where ϕ_0 is an integral constant that can be determined by a resulting tidal potential $\phi = \phi_a + \phi_c$ specified. Assuming zero tidal potential at the earth's center, that is $\phi = 0$ at $r = 0$, $\theta = 0$ and

$\xi = D$, $\phi_0 = -GM / D$ is then decided. The resulting tidal potential due to tidal generating forces at the point P on the earth's surface is thus obtained

$$\varnothing = GM\left(\frac{1}{\xi} - \frac{R\cos\theta}{D^2} - \frac{1}{D}\right) \tag{4}$$

The basic idea of the oceanic reaction to tidal potential is that the ocean adopts a form that maintains its surface in immediate gravitational equilibrium with the combination of tidal accelerations and the earth's gravity. According to this equilibrium hypothesis, the ocean surface has a uniform total gravitational potential. The tidal displacement of the oceanic free surface owing to a body is thus represented as, ignoring the nonlinear interaction between all conceivable components of the tidal potential.

$$\eta = -\frac{\phi}{g} = -\frac{GM}{g}\left(\frac{1}{\xi} - \frac{R\cos\theta}{D^2} - \frac{1}{D}\right) \tag{5}$$

where g is the acceleration due to the gravity of the earth. Considering both the solar and lunar tides, Eq. (5) results in equilibrium tides

$$\eta_e = -\frac{GM_m}{g}\left(\frac{1}{\xi_m} - \frac{R\cos\theta}{D_m^2} - \frac{1}{D_m}\right) - \frac{GM_s}{g}\left(\frac{1}{\xi_s} - \frac{R\cos\theta}{D_s^2} - \frac{1}{D_s}\right) \tag{6}$$

where the subscripts m and s denote the physical quantities corresponding to the moon and the sun, respectively; the moon's mass is Mm 7.38 x10^{22} kg and the sun's mass is Ms 1.989x10^{30} kg; the distance between these two bodies is Dm 3.84 108 m; and the earth orbits the sun once a year by a mean distance Ds 1.495x10^{11} m. The solar tide calculated by Eq. (6) as a result of the sun's gravitational pull is about 0.459 times that of the moon. When the values of, and D are determined by astronomy at any time for any places around the Bay of Bengal, the equilibrium tides may be calculated using Eq. (6). In Figure 2, seven sites are selected and plotted.

Although the tidal range and diurnal inequality of the equilibrium tides and observed tides at Hua-Lien, which is located at the central coast of the eastern Bay of Bengal, are significantly different, the neap-spring tidal cycle is almost in phase.

3. BACK-PROPAGATION NEURAL NETWORK DESIGNING

Back-propagation networks (BPNs) with multiple-layer networks and nonlinear differentiable transfer functions are often utilized to tackle numerous issues with optimization-required solutions. A BPN is trained using input vectors and the matching target vectors until it can estimate a function that links the input vectors with specified output vectors.

Figure 3. Sketch of the construction of back-propagation network

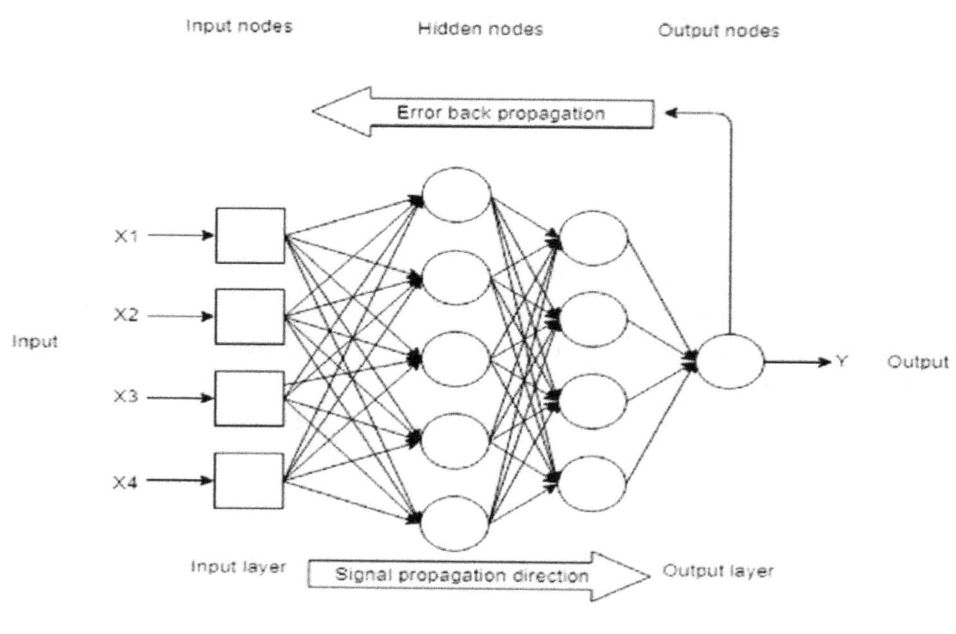

Networks incorporating biases, a sigmoid layer, and a linear output layer may approximate any function with a limited number of discontinuities (Demuth & Beale, 2000). When given inputs, a well trained BPN produces acceptable results. As a result, the back-propagation method is a widely used algorithm in neural networks. The neural network toolbox of the MATLAB program is used to create TAGF-ANN, which is displayed in Figure 3.

The symbol Pi in Figure 3 represents the input vector, while Iw and b1 are the weights and biases matrices between the input neurons and the hidden layer neurons, respectively. Trans. is the transfer function, while Lw and b2 are the weights and biases matrices between the output neurons and the hidden layer neurons, respectively. The connections between input neurons and hidden layer neurons, as well as those between hidden perceptions and outputs, can be expressed as the following equation, where a1 is the value of the first hidden layer, a2 is the network's output value, and f (x) = 2 / (1 + e 2x) 1 is the hyperbolic tangent sigmoid transfer function. As the input changes, the output of sigmoid units varies continuously but not linearly. Thus, sigmoid units resemble real neurons more than the other two types, linear or threshold units.

Biased networks may illustrate connections between inputs and outputs more simply than unbiased networks. As a result, in TAGF-ANN, a bias matrix is considered. TAGF-ANN is made up of three layers: an input layer, a hidden layer, and an output layer. When inputs are applied to the network, the supervised learning rule is used to modify the weights and biases of the network by comparing the outputs to the targets. To establish whether all objectives are met, the updated values of all members of the weight and bias matrices must be examined by calculating the network outputs for each input vector.

The loop ends when the learning error E is smaller than a defined tolerance, which in this study is 105. The Levenberg-Marquardt (L-M) method is used in this work to compute the weight and bias matrices in each iteration. The L-M approach employs an approximation to the Hessian matrix in a Newton-like update, are used in the training of a BPN until it can approximate a function that relates certain input vectors with specified output vectors. With a limited number of discontinuities, networks with biases, a sigmoid layer, and a linear output layer may approximate any function (Demuth & Beale, 2000). When given inputs, a well trained BPN tends to provide plausible replies. As a result, the back-propagation technique is widely utilized in neural networks. The neural network toolbox of the MATLAB program is used to create TAGF-ANN, as illustrated in Figure 3. The symbol Pi represents the input vector, and Iw and b1 are the weights and biases matrices between the input neurons and the hidden layer neurons, respectively. Trans. is the transfer function, and Lw and b2 are the weights and biases matrices between the output neurons and the hidden layer neurons, respectively. The connections between input neurons and hidden layer neurons, as well as those between hidden perceptions and outputs, may be expressed as the equations below.

$$\boldsymbol{a}_1 = \boldsymbol{f}\left(\boldsymbol{I}_{\acute{E}}\boldsymbol{P}_i + \boldsymbol{b}_1\right) \dots\dots\dots\dots \quad (7)$$

and

$$\boldsymbol{a}_2 = \boldsymbol{f}\left(\boldsymbol{L}_{\acute{E}}\boldsymbol{a}_1 + \boldsymbol{b}_2\right) \dots\dots\dots\dots \quad (8)$$

where a1 is the first hidden layer value, a2 is the network output value, and f (x) = 2 / (1 + e 2x) 1 is the hyperbolic tangent sigmoid transfer function. The output of sigmoid units fluctuates continuously but not linearly as the input changes. Thus, sigmoid units are more similar to real neurons than the other two types, linear or threshold units.

Biased networks may illustrate connections between inputs and outputs more simply than unbiased networks. As a result, in TAGF-ANN, a bias matrix is considered. TAGF-ANN is made up of three layers: an input layer, a hidden layer, and an output layer. When inputs are applied to the network, the supervised learning rule is used to modify the weights and biases of the network by comparing the outputs to the targets. To establish whether all objectives are met, the updated values of all members of the weight and bias matrices must be examined by calculating the network outputs for each input vector.

4. EXPANSION OF TIDE PREDICTION TO SURROUNDING SITES

The suggested model was constructed using Hua-Lien tidal data in the training phase, and it was tested to guarantee that it properly simulated tides at the Hua-Lien at any time. The created model is expanded to six places near the Hua-Lien in this paper. The analyzed locations are Long-Dong (LD), Tou-Cheng (TC), Su-Ao (SA), Cheng-Gong (CG), Lan-Yu (LY), and Heng-Chun (HC), which are illustrated in Figure 2 on the eastern shore of the Bay of Bengal. The Long-Dong, Tou-Cheng, and Su-Ao are roughly 131, 106, and 72 kilometers north of the Hua-Lien, respectively. The Cheng-Gong, Lan-Yu, and Heng-Chun are about 102, 214, and 243 kilometers south of the Hua-Lien, respectively. The Lan-Yu station is situated 78 kilometers distant from the eastern Bay of Bengal on a tiny island.

Tides might be mostly semidiurnal, predominantly diurnal, or mixed at a given site. The ratio F = (K1 + O1) / (M2+ S2) determines their nature, where K1, O1, M2 and S2 are the amplitudes of the four primary elements at a place in general. If F b is 0.25, the tides are mostly semidiurnal, and if F N is 3.0, the tides are mostly diurnal. If the value is 0.25 b F b 1.5, the tides are mixed but mostly semidiurnal, and if the value is 1.5 b F b 3.0, the tides are mixed but mostly diurnal. The six locations investigated from north to south had F = 1.14, 0.71, 0.64, 0.49, 0.42, and 1.18, respectively. The Hua-Lien is calculated to have F = 0.48. All F values at selected places suggest mixed tides, mostly semidiurnal. The mean tidal ranges at selected sites range from 65 to 109 cm.

The RMS and r2 of modeled tides at six locations in 2021 and 2022 are shown in Table.1. The input parameter values for the six sites were calculated independently and entered into the well-developed model to directly produce their tides. Tidal data at the Long-Dong are not available for predicting RMS in 2021. The yearly difference

Table 1. Annual RMS and r2 between observed and predicted tides at six points (unit: cm)

Year	Index	Method	Location					
			LD	TC	SA	CG	LY	HC
2021	RMS	TGF-NN	–	19.57	14.37	13.47	15.71	24.77
		NAO.99b	–	11.96	13.03	9.80	16.45	13.17
	r^2	TGF-NN	–	1.845	0.878	0.950	0.860	0.648
		NAO.99b	–	1.611	0.895	0.955	0.847	0.837
2022	RMS	TGF-NN	27.46	17.61	14.19	11.73	16.79	25.18
		NAO.99b	17.05	18.71	14.26	13.76	13.55	11.46
	r^2	TGF-NN	0.537	0.856	0.861	0.923	0.836	0.629
		NAO.99b	0.703	0.596	0.883	0.907	0.890	0.874

The RMS difference between observed tides at TC, SA, CG, and LY in 2021 and 2022 and those projected by both models is just 0.07-3.67 cm. In four situations, TAGF-ANN predicts tides somewhat better than dosage NAO.99b. TAGF-ANN, on the other hand, performs worse when modeling tides than NAO.99b in the other four scenarios. When applied to feasible sites, SA, CG, and LD, TAGF-ANN yields the same r2 as NAO.99b. The small difference in RMS and r2 between TAGF-ANN and NAO.99b indicates that TAGF-ANN simulates tides comparatively well at a position near the initial interest point, and its accuracy is comparable to that of NAO.99b.

TAGF-ANN has a much greater RMS of replicating tides at both the LD and HC than dosage NAO.99b. Both are quite far from the Hua-Lien. The F values at the TC, SA, CG, and LY are similar to those of the Hua-Lien, suggesting tidal types at those locations. However, the F values at both LD and HC are 0.68 higher than those at the Hua-Lien, implying that the tides at both locations behave differently than those at the Hua-Lien. Bad TAGF-ANN simulations at LD, TC, and HC arise from temporal delays in tidal propagation caused by bathymetric variance on the continental shelf. Figure 6 depicts the geography and bathymetry of the Bay of Bengal. SA, HL, CG, and LY are situated on the western Pacific Ocean's continental shelf. LD and TC are near the western end of the Okinawa trough, isolated from the others by the Ryukyu Arc. HC is located on the Heng-Chun Ridge amid shallow seas. LD and HC have distinct bathymetries than the other places. TAGF-ANN is built using observed data at the Hua-Lien, hence it is restricted to simulating tides of various types at a place distant from the Hua-Lien with complicated bathymetric fluctuation. When the tide type, tide range, or bathymetry of a location differs significantly from that of the interest point for which tidal data were used to train the TAGF-ANN model, the trained TAGF-ANN model cannot be applied to this place, even if it is near to the interest point.

The hydrodynamic model used in NAO.99b requires topographical data to calculate global ocean tides, and an altimeter assimilation process is utilized to adjust the model-predicted tidal heights. To build TGF-NN, TAGF-ANN requires just one-year astronomical data that can be readily gathered by astronomy at an interest location and utilized as input data, and matching observed tidal data as output data. When astronomical data at the same or nearby location are available, the well-developed TAGF-ANN takes just a few seconds to calculate one-year tides at the spot. For engineering practices, it is acknowledged that TAGF-ANN more readily delivers with reliably forecasting tides at at several places than dosage NAO.99b.

Figure 4. The topography and bathymetry around bay of Bengal

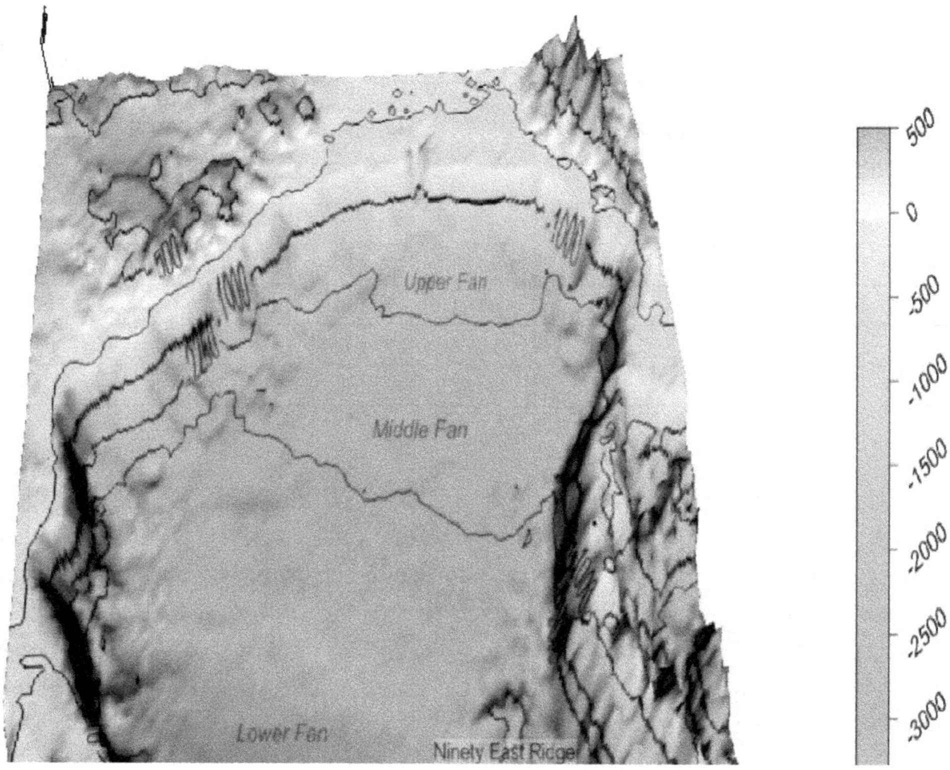

5. CONCLUSION

Tidal levels must be estimated precisely at all times for coastal and harbor engineering applications.

Although its predictions are highly reliable, the traditional HM is limited to tidal prediction at a single point. This study investigated an alternative TAGF-ANN that describes tide-generating forces in terms of input parameters R/Dm(t), R/Ds(t), R/m(t), R/s(t), [R/Dm(t)]2 cosm(t), [R/Ds(t)]2 coss(t), and cos(t). The proposed TAGF-ANN takes into account key scientific concepts such as tidal propagation and tide-generating forces. For estimating tides for a single location, the suggested model includes five neurons in the hidden layer and a 2-hour lead time input, and it is as powerful as HM with 60 components.

The suggested TAGF-ANN was used to estimate tides at places close to where the model was trained using tidal data. The accuracy of prediction was compared to that of NAO.99b. The modest variation in yearly RMS demonstrates that both approaches properly estimate tides and that the proposed TAGF-ANN is usable for multi-point tidal prediction for locations with tidal types comparable to the initial interest point. TAGF-ANN is confined to simulating tides of various types and ranges at a site where complicated bathymetric fluctuation occurs, far from the point of interest where the TAGF-ANN model was built.

REFERENCES

Chang, H. K., & Chien, W. A. (2006). Neural network with multi-trend simulating transfer function for forecasting typhoon wave. *Advances in Engineering Software, 37*(3), 184–194. doi:10.1016/j.advengsoft.2005.05.001

Darwin, G. H. (1907). *The Harmonic Analysis of Tidal Observations in Scientific Papers, 1, Oceanic Tides and Lunar Disturbances of Gravity*. Cambridge Univ. Press.

Demuth, H., & Beale, M. (2000). Neural networks toolbox user's guide, version 4. Math Works, Inc.

Deo, M. C., Gondane, D. S., & Kumar, V. S. (2002). Analysis of wave directional spread-ing using neural networks. *Journal of Waterway, Port, Coastal, and Ocean Engineering, 128*(1), 30–37. doi:10.1061/(ASCE)0733-950X(2002)128:1(30)

Deo, M. C., & Naidu, C. S. (1998). Real time wave forecasting using neural networks. *Ocean Engineering, 26*(3), 191–203. doi:10.1016/S0029-8018(97)10025-7

Desai, S. D. (1996). *Ocean tides from TOPEX/POSEIDON altimetry with some geophysical applications* [Ph.D. dissertation]. Department of Aerospace Engineering Sciences, University of Colorado, Boulder, CO.

Desai, S. D., & Wahr, J. (1995). Empirical ocean tide models estimated from TOPEX/ POSEIDON altimetry. *Journal of Geophysical Research, 100*(C12, c12), 25205–25228. doi:10.1029/95JC02258

Doodson, A. T. (1921). The harmonic development of the tide generating potential. *Proceedings of the Royal Society of London. Series A, Containing Papers of a Mathematical and Physical Character, 100*(704), 305–329. doi:10.1098/rspa.1921.0088

Han, G., Hendry, R., & Ikeda, M. (2000). Assimilating TOPEX/POSEIDON derived tides in a primitive equation model over the Newfoundland Shelf. *Continental Shelf Research, 20*(1), 83–108. doi:10.1016/S0278-4343(99)00058-8

Kumar, A., & Minocha, V. K. (2001). A Discussion on Back-propagation Neural Network in Tidal-level Forecasting. Port, Coast., and Oc. Eng.

Le Provost, C., Lyard, F., Molines, J. M., Genco, M. L., & Rabilloud, F. (1998). A hydrodynamic ocean tide model improved by assimilating a satellite altimeter-derived data set. *Journal of Geophysical Research, 103*(C3), 5513–5529. doi:10.1029/97JC01733

Lee, T. L. (2004). Back-propagation neural network for long-term tidal predictions. *Ocean Engineering, 31*(2), 225–238. doi:10.1016/S0029-8018(03)00115-X

Lee, T. L., & Jeng, D. S. (2002). Application of artificial neural networks in tide-forecasting. *Ocean Engineering, 29*(9), 1003–1022. doi:10.1016/S0029-8018(01)00068-3

Lee, T. L., Tsai, C. P., Jeng, D. S., & Shieh, R. J. (2002). Neural network for prediction and supplement of tidal record in Taichung harbor. *Advances in Engineering Software, 33*(6), 329–338. doi:10.1016/S0965-9978(02)00043-1

Makarynskyy, O. (2004). Improving wave predictions with artificial neural networks. *Ocean Engineering, 31*(5-6), 709–724. doi:10.1016/j.oceaneng.2003.05.003

Mandal, S. (2001). A Discussion on Back-propagation Neural Network in Tidal-level Forecasting. In Port, Coast., and Oc. Eng. doi:10.1061/(ASCE)0733-950X(2001)127:1(55)

Matsumoto, K., Takanezawa, T., & Ooe, M. (2000). Ocean tide model developed by assimilating TOPEX/POSEIDON altimetry data into hydrodynamical model: A global and a regional model around Japan. *Journal of Oceanography, 56*(5), 567–581. doi:10.1023/A:1011157212596

Medina, J. R. (2001). A Discussion on Back-propagation Neural Network in Tidal-level Forecasting. In Port, Coast., and Oc. Eng. doi:10.1061/(ASCE)0733-950X(2001)127:1(55.2)

Munk, W. H., & Cartwright, D. E. (1996). Tidal spectroscopy and prediction. *Philos. Trans. R. Soc. Lond. Ser. A, 259*, 533–581.

Ray, R. D. (1998). Spectral analysis of highly aliased sea-level signals. *Journal of Geophysical Research, 103*(C11), 24991–25003. doi:10.1029/98JC02545

Tsai, C. P., & Lee, T. L. (1999). Back-propagation neural network in tidal-level forecasting. *Journal of Waterway, Port, Coastal, and Ocean Engineering, 125*(4), 195–202. doi:10.1061/(ASCE)0733-950X(1999)125:4(195)

Vaziri, M. (1997). Predicting Caspian Sea surface water level by ANN and ARIMA models. *Journal of Waterway, Port, Coastal, and Ocean Engineering, 123*(4), 158–162. doi:10.1061/(ASCE)0733-950X(1997)123:4(158)

Walton, T. L., & Garcia, A. W. (2001). A Discussion on Back-propagation Neural Network in Tidal-level Forecasting. Port, Coast., and Oc. Eng.

Chapter 4
Energy Cascade Conversion System and Energy-Efficient Infrastructure

Sampath Boopathi
https://orcid.org/0000-0002-2065-6539
Mechanical Engineering, Muthayammal Engineering College, India

ABSTRACT

The energy cascade conversion system (ECCS) is a ground-breaking approach to energy conversion and utilization, transforming energy infrastructure. This chapter investigates its multi-stage process, focusing on energy-efficient building retrofitting, smart grid integration, and sustainable transportation infrastructure. Results show significant energy savings, emissions reduction, and operational cost advantages. However, challenges like technological complexity, scalability, and regulatory frameworks must be addressed for successful implementation. Future research should explore advanced materials, smart grid synergies, and policy considerations.

INTRODUCTION

The modern world's insatiable demand for energy, coupled with the urgent need for sustainable solutions, has driven researchers and innovators to explore novel paradigms in energy conversion and utilization. One such paradigm that has gained traction in recent years is the Energy Cascade Conversion System (ECCS). The ECCS represents a departure from traditional linear energy pathways by integrating multi-stage conversion processes to optimize energy utilization across diverse applications. This chapter aims to delve into the concept of ECCS, building upon past research activities and introducing new insights gained through experimentation and analysis (Shan et al., 2023).

Past Research Activities and Evolution of ECCS: The evolution of ECCS can be traced back to a series of pivotal research endeavors that have laid the groundwork for this innovative approach. Previous studies have investigated various aspects of energy conversion, efficiency, and infrastructure, often highlighting the limitations of conventional systems. These activities have sparked interest in finding

DOI: 10.4018/979-8-3693-1722-8.ch004

alternative ways to address energy challenges, leading to the emergence of ECCS as a promising solution (Miao et al., 2020).

Researchers have extensively explored methods to enhance energy conversion efficiency by studying the efficiencies of individual components within energy systems. This research has exposed inefficiencies and losses at different stages of energy conversion, serving as a catalyst for the development of ECCS. Past studies have focused on the integration of renewable energy sources into existing energy grids. These studies have underscored the need for sophisticated approaches that efficiently channel and utilize variable renewable energy inputs, aligning with ECCS principles (Akisawa et al., 1999). Research into sustainable infrastructure development has led to investigations of energy-efficient building designs, smart grid technologies, and transportation systems. These studies have provided a foundation for implementing ECCS principles in real-world scenarios. Studies on environmental impact assessment have highlighted the ecological consequences of conventional energy systems. This research has emphasized the urgency of adopting more sustainable energy conversion methods, setting the stage for ECCS research (Kang et al., 2023).

Despite the advancements in the field, there exists a research gap when it comes to the comprehensive evaluation of ECCS as a holistic solution. While past research has shed light on individual components and aspects, the integration of multi-stage energy conversion processes within a singular framework requires in-depth exploration (Mu et al., 2020). This study aims to bridge this gap by conducting systematic experimentation, rigorous analysis, and real-world case studies to unveil the potential of ECCS in revolutionizing energy infrastructure.

Background and Motivation

In the face of increasing global energy demand and the pressing need for sustainable development, the traditional paradigm of energy generation and utilization is undergoing a transformative shift. The limitations of conventional energy systems, characterized by inefficiencies and environmental impacts, have led researchers and policymakers to explore innovative solutions that can revolutionize energy infrastructure. One such promising concept is the Energy Cascade Conversion System, which offers a novel approach to energy conversion and utilization.

The Energy Cascade Conversion System represents a departure from linear energy pathways by incorporating multi-stage conversion processes that optimize energy utilization across various applications. This paradigm shift not only enhances energy efficiency but also has the potential to mitigate resource depletion and environmental degradation associated with traditional energy systems. As the world seeks cleaner and more efficient energy solutions, the investigation of such novel approaches becomes paramount.

Research Objectives

The primary objective of this chapter is to comprehensively explore the concept of the Energy Cascade Conversion System and its potential to revolutionize energy infrastructure with energy-efficient functionalities. This chapter aims to achieve the following:

- Present an in-depth understanding of the Energy Cascade Conversion System, its principles, and components.

- Describe the experimental setup and methodology employed to evaluate the system's performance.
- Analyze the results obtained from experimentation and assess the performance in terms of energy conversion efficiency.
- Discuss the implications of the findings in the context of energy infrastructure development, sustainability, and environmental impact.
- Showcase case studies that demonstrate the application of energy-efficient functionalities in real-world scenarios.
- Highlight challenges, opportunities, and future directions for the implementation and advancement of this concept.

Research Scopes

- **Energy Cascade Conversion System (ECCS):** Investigate the theoretical framework, principles, and components of ECCS. This involves understanding how energy is efficiently converted and cascaded through multiple stages for diverse applications.
- **Experimental Evaluation:** Design and conduct experiments to assess the performance of the ECCS. This involves setting up controlled experiments, collecting data on energy conversion efficiency, and analyzing the results to understand the system's effectiveness.
- **Comparative Analysis:** Compare the ECCS with conventional energy systems to highlight its advantages in terms of energy efficiency, cost-effectiveness, and environmental impact. This involves quantitative analysis and critical evaluation.
- **Energy-Efficient Infrastructure:** Explore the integration of ECCS principles into real-world energy infrastructure. Investigate how energy-efficient functionalities can be applied to various domains, such as buildings, transportation, and grids.
- **Sustainability and Environmental Impact:** Assess the environmental implications of ECCS and energy-efficient infrastructure. Perform life cycle assessments to quantify the reduction in carbon emissions and resource consumption compared to traditional systems.
- **Case Studies:** Present case studies that showcase practical implementations of energy-efficient infrastructure. These case studies can provide insights into the feasibility, challenges, and benefits of adopting ECCS principles.
- **Discussion and Implications:** Engage in a comprehensive discussion of the findings and implications of the research. This includes insights into the potential transformation of energy infrastructure, policy considerations, and socioeconomic impacts.
- **Challenges and Future Directions:** Identify challenges faced during ECCS implementation and propose potential solutions. Outline avenues for future research and innovation to advance the field of energy-efficient infrastructure.
- **Knowledge Dissemination:** Communicate the research findings through well-structured chapters, data analysis, visualizations, and discussions. The research outcomes should contribute to the existing body of knowledge in energy and sustainability.
- **Interdisciplinary Exploration:** Given the nature of the research, explore interdisciplinary connections between engineering, environmental science, policy, economics, and other relevant fields.

ENERGY CASCADE CONVERSION SYSTEM: CONCEPTS AND PRINCIPLES

The Energy Cascade Conversion System (ECCS) represents a transformative approach to energy conversion and utilization, departing from the linear pathways of traditional energy systems. ECCS introduces a multi-stage conversion process that optimizes energy utilization across diverse applications, resulting in enhanced efficiency, reduced environmental impact, and improved sustainability (Kang et al., 2023). This section provides a comprehensive overview of ECCS, outlining its fundamental concepts and key principles.

Concepts of Energy Cascade Conversion

The concept of energy cascade conversion is rooted in the idea of harnessing energy at different levels of magnitude and converting it through a series of distinct stages. This cascading approach allows for the efficient utilization of energy, capturing its inherent value in various forms while minimizing losses. By transitioning from a singular energy pathway to a multi-stage system, ECCS enables the exploitation of different energy carriers and conversion mechanisms (Bruggink et al., 2003).

Principles Governing Energy Cascade Conversion

- **Hierarchical Energy Conversion:** ECCS operates on a hierarchical structure, where energy is first captured at higher energy levels (e.g., thermal, mechanical) and then successively converted into lower energy forms (e.g., electrical, chemical) through specialized stages.
- **Optimal Energy Matching:** Each conversion stage is optimized for a specific energy form or application, ensuring that the energy input matches the requirements of the subsequent stage. This principle minimizes wastage and maximizes energy utilization.
- **Energy Flow Segmentation:** Energy flow within ECCS is segmented into distinct levels, with each level representing a specific conversion process. This segmentation facilitates efficient energy transfer and prevents mismatches between energy inputs and outputs.
- **Multi-Functional Components:** ECCS components are designed to serve multiple functions within the system. For instance, a component may perform energy conversion, storage, and distribution simultaneously, optimizing resource utilization.
- **Integration of Renewable Sources:** ECCS encourages the integration of renewable energy sources at different stages of the cascade. This integration enhances system resilience and supports the utilization of intermittent energy inputs.

Benefits of Energy Cascade Conversion

- **Enhanced Efficiency:** ECCS minimizes energy losses by capturing and converting energy through multiple stages, resulting in higher overall efficiency compared to traditional systems (Bruggink et al., 2003).
- **Diverse Energy Utilization:** ECCS enables the utilization of different energy carriers (e.g., heat, kinetic energy, light) for various applications, enhancing flexibility and versatility(Jih-Sheng Lai & Fang Zheng Peng, 1996).

- **Reduced Environmental Impact:** By optimizing energy utilization, ECCS contributes to the reduction of carbon emissions, resource consumption, and environmental degradation associated with conventional energy systems.
- **Resilience and Reliability:** ECCS's hierarchical structure enhances system resilience by allowing for the substitution of energy inputs and facilitating rapid responses to changes in demand or supply.
- **Integration with Existing Infrastructure:** ECCS principles can be integrated into existing energy infrastructure, enabling a gradual transition toward more efficient and sustainable systems.

EXPERIMENTAL SETUP AND METHODOLOGY

Design and Configuration of Energy Cascade Conversion System

The successful evaluation of the Energy Cascade Conversion System (ECCS) requires a meticulously designed experimental setup that accurately represents its multi-stage energy conversion process. This section outlines the design and configuration considerations of the ECCS experimental setup, including the selection of components, energy carriers, and measurement techniques (Kazmierkowski et al., n.d.; Rodriguez et al., 2007). Design and Configuration of Energy Cascade Conversion System are depicted in Figure 1.

Selection of ECCS Components: The ECCS experimental setup involves selecting components that exemplify various stages of energy conversion. These components can include heat exchangers, turbines, generators, storage units, and converters. Each component should be chosen based on its compatibility with the energy carriers and the specific conversion mechanisms being investigated (Ounejjar et al., 2011; Steffen et al., 2021; Verdugo et al., 2012; Walker et al., 2004a).

Energy Carriers and Input Sources: Identifying suitable energy carriers and input sources is crucial to emulate the diverse energy forms involved in the ECCS. For instance, heat can be sourced from a controlled heat generator, while kinetic energy can be simulated through a rotating shaft or fluid flow. Electrical energy inputs can be supplied from power sources with adjustable characteristics.

Cascading Stages and Energy Flow: Define the cascading stages within the experimental setup, representing the successive conversion processes. Energy flow should be carefully managed, ensuring that the output of one stage aligns with the input requirements of the subsequent stage. This hierarchical structure is integral to ECCS's effectiveness.

Figure 1. Design and configuration of energy cascade conversion system

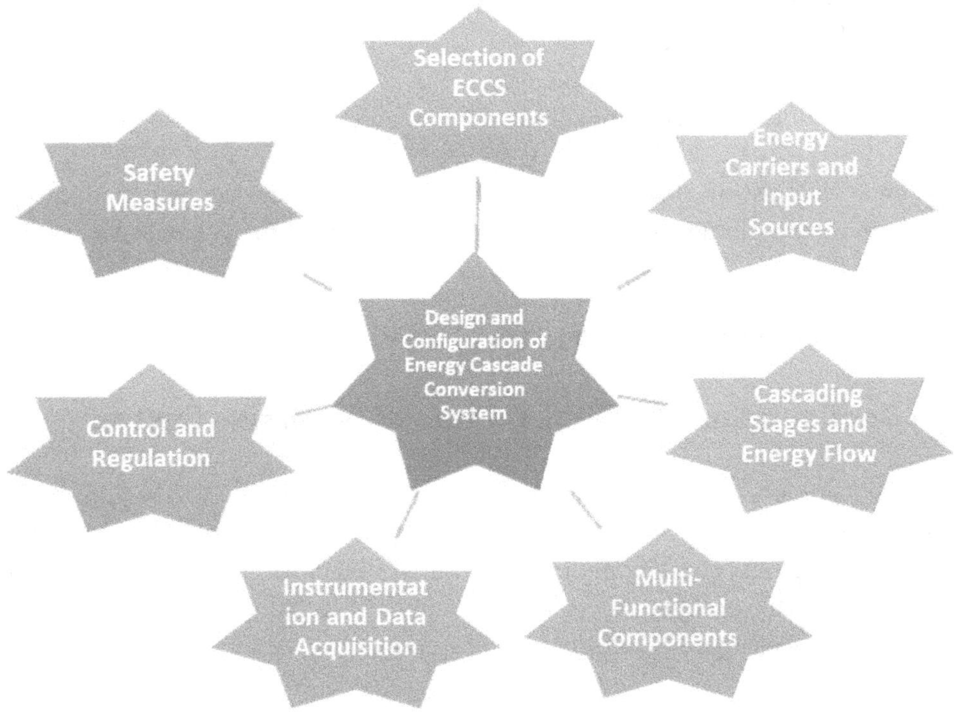

Multi-Functional Components: Incorporate multi-functional components that mirror ECCS principles, performing multiple roles within the system. For instance, a component might act as an energy converter, a storage unit, and a distributor simultaneously, mimicking the real-world versatility of ECCS components.

Instrumentation and Data Acquisition: Equip the ECCS experimental setup with an array of sensors, meters, and data acquisition systems. Measure parameters such as temperature, pressure, rotational speed, electrical output, and more at various points within the cascade. Accurate data acquisition is essential to quantify energy conversion efficiency and system performance.

Control and Regulation: Implement a robust control and regulation system to manage energy inputs, adjust parameters, and ensure consistent operation throughout the experimental sessions. Automation and control software can help maintain stability and reliability during tests.

Safety Measures: Prioritize safety considerations by implementing safety measures such as emergency shut-offs, overheating protection, and pressure relief mechanisms. Proper safety protocols ensure the well-being of researchers and prevent any potential hazards.

Replicability and Scalability: Design the ECCS experimental setup with replicability and scalability in mind. The setup should be constructed in a way that allows other researchers to replicate the experiments and potentially scale up the system for larger investigations.

Validation and Calibration: Before commencing the experimental trials, validate and calibrate the instrumentation, sensors, and components to ensure accurate data collection and reliable results.

By meticulously designing and configuring the ECCS experimental setup, researchers can create a controlled environment that mirrors the principles and functionalities of the Energy Cascade Conversion System (Maharjan, Inoue, & Akagi, 2008; Maharjan, Yamagishi, et al., 2010; Steffen et al., 2021; Verdugo et al., 2012). This facilitates the accurate evaluation of energy conversion efficiency and the exploration of ECCS's potential benefits in optimizing energy utilization across different applications.

Selection of Test Variables

In the pursuit of understanding and quantifying the performance of the Energy Cascade Conversion System (ECCS), careful selection of test variables is essential to ensure the accuracy and reliability of the experimental results. This section outlines the criteria and rationale behind the chosen test variables, illustrating the considerations that underpin the experimental design.

Criteria for Test Variable Selection

Criteria for Test Variable Selection is illustrated in Figure 2. The selection of test variables is guided by several key criteria:

Figure 2. Criteria for selection of test variables

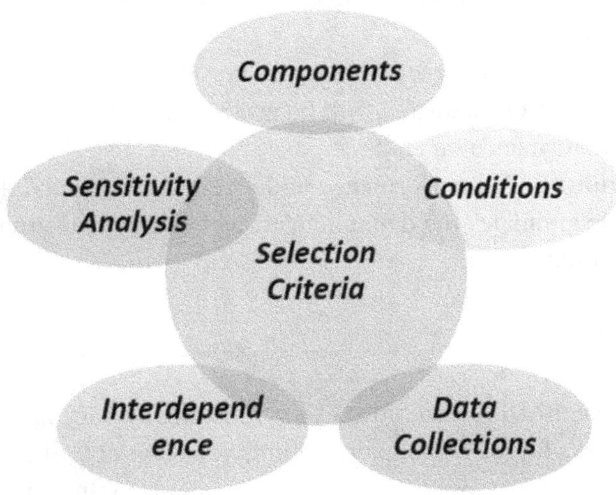

- **Relevance to ECCS Components:** The chosen variables should directly relate to the components and stages within the ECCS. This ensures that the experimentation is aligned with the system's functioning and objectives.
- **Representative of Real-world Conditions:** Test variables should mimic real-world conditions to the extent possible. This involves considering factors such as energy input levels, conversion efficiencies, and operational parameters that would be encountered in practical applications.
- **Measurability and Data Collection:** Test variables must be quantifiable and measurable using appropriate instruments and methods. Accurate data collection is crucial for meaningful analysis and interpretation.

- **Independence and Interdependence:** Variables should be selected in a manner that allows for the assessment of their individual effects as well as their interactions with other variables within the ECCS.
- **Sensitivity Analysis:** Variables with potential high sensitivity to system performance should be prioritized. This helps in identifying critical factors that significantly influence the efficiency and effectiveness of ECCS.

Chosen Test Variables

The following test variables have been selected for experimentation(Maharjan et al., n.d.):

- **Energy Input Level:** The magnitude of energy input into the ECCS represents a critical factor. It influences the efficiency of energy conversion and the overall performance of the system. Energy input will be varied across different experiments while keeping other factors constant.
- **Conversion Efficiency of Each Stage:** Each stage within the ECCS has distinct energy conversion efficiencies. By varying the efficiency of specific stages, the impact on the overall system efficiency can be studied.
- **Integration of Renewable Sources:** Renewable energy inputs, such as solar and wind energy, will be introduced at different stages of the cascade. The effect of these intermittent inputs on overall performance will be assessed.
- **Component Interaction:** The interaction between components, such as energy storage devices, converters, and distribution mechanisms, will be examined. This includes analyzing the influence of one component's performance on another.
- **System Load Variation:** ECCS performance under varying loads and demand scenarios will be explored. This variable simulates the dynamic nature of energy consumption and its effect on the system's stability and efficiency.

Experimental Design

A factorial experimental design will be employed to systematically vary and analyze the selected test variables. This approach allows for the examination of individual variable effects as well as their interactions. The experimental setup will involve controlled conditions, accurate data collection, and statistical analysis methods to ensure robust results(Aljaghtham et al., n.d.).

By rigorously considering and varying these chosen test variables, this research aims to unravel the intricate relationships within the ECCS and provide insights into its optimal configuration and operation. The subsequent sections of this chapter will delve into the experimental methodology, detailing the procedures, instruments, and techniques employed to evaluate ECCS performance under diverse scenarios (Pavković et al., 2016).

Data Collection and Measurement Techniques

Accurate data collection and precise measurement techniques are fundamental to assessing the performance of the Energy Cascade Conversion System (ECCS) and evaluating its efficiency. This section outlines the methodologies employed for data collection, the instruments used for measurements, and the strategies to ensure reliable and repeatable results (Cohn, 1995; Walker et al., 2004b; Zahboune et al., 2016).

Selection of Data Variables

The selection of data variables is critical to comprehensively capture the performance of ECCS. These variables include:

- **Energy Input and Output:** Measure the energy input and output at each stage of the cascade. This includes thermal, mechanical, electrical, and chemical energy forms.
- **Temperature and Pressure:** Monitor temperature and pressure variations at different conversion stages to analyze efficiency and energy losses.
- **Flow Rates:** Measure flow rates of energy carriers, such as fluids or gases, to assess the energy transfer rates between stages.
- **Energy Conversion Efficiency:** Calculate the energy conversion efficiency for each stage using appropriate formulas based on the energy input and output measurements.

Data Collection Instruments

To ensure accurate data collection, a range of advanced instruments can be utilized:

- **Energy Meters:** Install precision energy meters to measure electrical, thermal, and mechanical energy inputs and outputs.
- **Temperature and Pressure Sensors:** Use thermocouples and pressure transducers to monitor temperature and pressure changes within the system.
- **Flow Meters:** Employ flow meters such as electromagnetic or ultrasonic flow meters to measure fluid or gas flow rates.
- **Data Loggers:** Utilize data loggers to record continuous data over time, enabling detailed analysis and visualization.

Calibration and Control

Calibration of measurement instruments is essential to maintain measurement accuracy. Regularly calibrate temperature sensors, pressure transducers, and flow meters against traceable standards to ensure reliable measurements. Implement control mechanisms to maintain consistent operating conditions during experiments. Use feedback control loops to regulate energy input, output, and conversion rates, minimizing external disturbances.

Data Collection Procedures

- **Pre-Experiment Setup:** Calibrate instruments, set baseline conditions, and configure data loggers.
- **Experiment Execution:** Record data at regular intervals while operating the ECCS. Collect data simultaneously from various sensors.

- **Post-Experiment Analysis:** Process collected data, calculate energy conversion efficiencies, and identify trends or anomalies.

Data Validation and Analysis

Validate data by cross-referencing results from multiple instruments and sensors. Conduct statistical analysis to ensure consistency and reliability. Analyze collected data using appropriate software tools, generating graphs, charts, and trend lines.

Uncertainty Analysis

Perform uncertainty analysis to quantify the potential errors in measurements. This includes assessing instrument accuracy, precision, and potential sources of systematic or random errors.

Statistical Analysis Methods

Statistical analysis is a crucial component of your research to ensure the reliability and significance of the results obtained from your Energy Cascade Conversion System (ECCS) experiments. This section outlines the statistical analysis methods employed to interpret the collected data and draw meaningful conclusions. Various Stages of Statistical Analysis is explored in Figure 3.

Figure 3. Various stages of statistical analysis

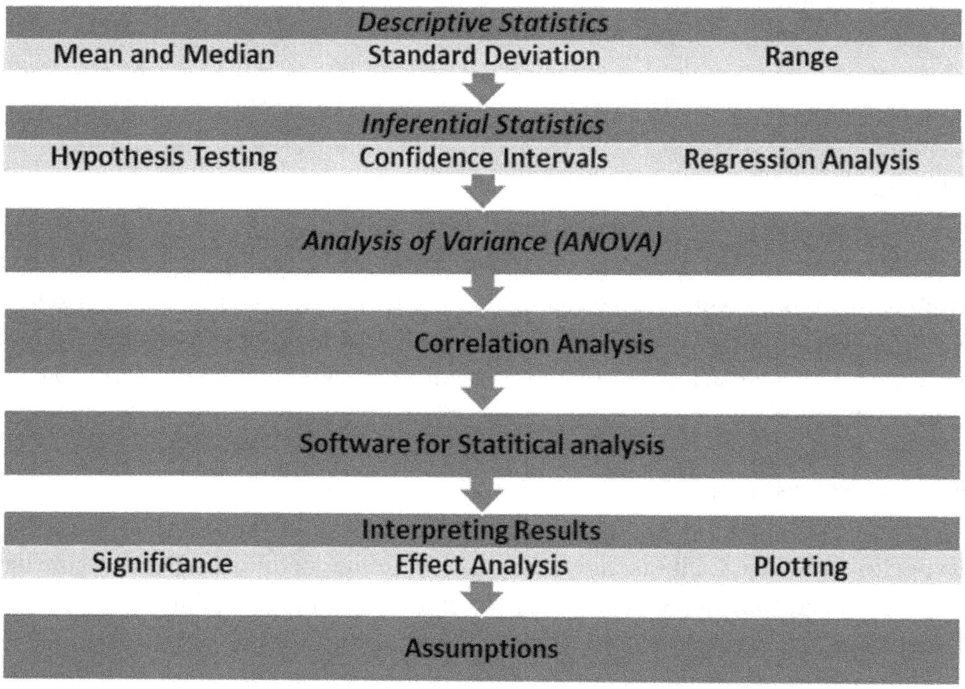

Descriptive Statistics

Descriptive statistics provide a concise summary of the collected data, enabling a quick overview of key characteristics. Utilize measures such as:

- **Mean and Median:** Calculate the average and middle values of the data to understand central tendencies.
- **Standard Deviation:** Assess data dispersion around the mean to quantify variability.
- **Range:** Determine the difference between the maximum and minimum values to identify data spread.

Inferential Statistics

Inferential statistics help make inferences about the larger population based on collected sample data. Key methods include:

- **Hypothesis Testing:** Formulate hypotheses about the ECCS performance and use statistical tests (e.g., t-test, ANOVA) to determine if observed differences are statistically significant.
- **Confidence Intervals:** Calculate confidence intervals to estimate the range within which population parameters are likely to fall.
- **Regression Analysis:** Perform regression analysis to establish relationships between variables, helping to predict outcomes based on input values.

Analysis of Variance (ANOVA)

If you have multiple experimental groups or stages within ECCS, ANOVA can assess whether there are statistically significant differences among these groups. Post-hoc tests (e.g., Tukey's HSD) can identify specific group differences.

Correlation Analysis

If there are multiple variables, correlation analysis helps identify relationships between them. Pearson correlation coefficient or Spearman's rank correlation can reveal the strength and direction of associations.

Statistical Software

Utilize specialized statistical software (e.g., R, Python with NumPy, SciPy, or dedicated statistical packages) to perform complex analyses efficiently and accurately. These tools offer a wide range of functions and visualization options to aid in your analysis.

Interpreting Results

Interpret statistical results with care:

- **Statistical Significance:** Determine whether differences observed are statistically significant based on p-values (usually < 0.05).
- **Effect Size:** Evaluate the practical significance of differences by considering effect sizes, helping to understand the magnitude of observed changes.
- **Interpretable Visualizations:** Support statistical findings with visually appealing graphs, such as bar charts, histograms, scatter plots, and box plots.

Addressing Assumptions

Ensure that the assumptions underlying statistical tests (e.g., normality, homoscedasticity) are met. If assumptions are violated, consider appropriate transformations or non-parametric tests.

By employing these statistical analysis methods, you will be able to confidently interpret your experimental data, uncover patterns, and draw conclusions about the performance and efficiency of the ECCS.

RESULTS AND PERFORMANCE EVALUATION

Quantitative Analysis of Energy Conversion Efficiency

One of the fundamental objectives of your research is to assess the energy conversion efficiency of the Energy Cascade Conversion System (ECCS). This section focuses on presenting the quantitative analysis methods used to evaluate the efficiency of the ECCS's multi-stage energy conversion process (Bhowmik et al., 1999; Klein & Schmidt, 2011).

Energy Conversion Efficiency Calculation

Energy conversion efficiency is a key performance metric that quantifies the ratio of useful output energy to the input energy for each stage of the ECCS. The formula for calculating energy conversion efficiency is:

Efficiency=Useful Output EnergyInput Energy×100%Efficiency=Input EnergyUseful Output Energy ×100%

Where:

- Useful Output Energy: Energy output that serves a practical purpose in the intended application.
- Input Energy: Total energy input into the conversion stage.

Data Collection for Efficiency Calculation

For each stage of the ECCS, collect data on energy input and useful output energy. Ensure that measurements are accurate and consistent, adhering to the data collection techniques and instruments discussed in Chapter 3.

Efficiency Analysis Steps

Data Pre-processing: Organize the collected data, ensuring that energy input and output values correspond to the same time intervals and experimental conditions.

Calculation: Apply the energy conversion efficiency formula to calculate the efficiency for each stage.

Comparative Analysis: Compare the calculated efficiencies of different stages to identify trends, discrepancies, and potential areas for improvement.

Visualization and Presentation

Visualize the calculated energy conversion efficiencies using appropriate graphs and charts, such as bar graphs or line plots. Clearly label the stages on the x-axis and present the calculated efficiencies on the y-axis. Use color coding to enhance visual clarity and differentiate between stages.

Interpretation

Interpret the efficiency results based on the calculated values and trends observed. Discuss the implications of high and low efficiencies, identifying potential reasons for variations between stages. Consider the role of component design, energy losses, and conversion mechanisms in influencing efficiency outcomes.

Sensitivity Analysis

Conduct sensitivity analysis to explore how variations in input parameters impact energy conversion efficiency. This can involve altering factors such as temperature, pressure, or flow rates and observing their effects on efficiency.

Comparisons With Conventional Systems

Compare the calculated ECCS efficiencies with those of conventional linear energy systems. Highlight the advantages of ECCS in terms of improved efficiency and reduced energy losses due to the cascading conversion approach.

By systematically analyzing the energy conversion efficiency of the ECCS, you will be able to quantify its performance benefits and provide concrete evidence of its potential to revolutionize energy conversion and utilization processes.

Comparative Study with Conventional Energy Systems

To demonstrate the superiority of the Energy Cascade Conversion System (ECCS) in terms of energy efficiency and sustainability, a comparative study with conventional energy systems is crucial. This section focuses on conducting a rigorous comparison and highlighting the advantages of ECCS over traditional linear energy pathways (Bhowmik et al., 1999; U.-M. Choi et al., 2015).

Selection of Conventional Energy Systems

Choose relevant conventional energy systems that closely resemble the energy pathways commonly used in practical applications. Consider systems that pertain to the same energy sources or serve similar end-use purposes as the ECCS stages.

Comparative Metrics

Select appropriate metrics for comparison, such as:

- **Energy Efficiency:** Compare the energy conversion efficiencies of ECCS stages with those of corresponding conventional systems. Calculate and contrast the ratios of useful output energy to input energy.
- **Energy Losses:** Quantify energy losses at different stages for both ECCS and conventional systems. Highlight how ECCS minimizes losses through its cascading conversion approach.
- **Environmental Impact:** Evaluate the environmental impact of ECCS and conventional systems, considering factors such as carbon emissions, resource consumption, and waste generation.

Data Collection and Analysis

Collect data on energy input, output, and losses for both ECCS and conventional systems. Apply the same data collection techniques and instruments to ensure a fair comparison. Perform the same analysis steps, such as efficiency calculations and sensitivity analysis, for both systems.

Visual Representation

Present the comparative data using visual aids, such as side-by-side bar graphs or stacked area charts. Clearly label the ECCS stages and corresponding conventional systems for easy interpretation.

Interpretation and Discussion

Interpret the comparative results and discuss the implications of the findings. Highlight how ECCS outperforms conventional systems in terms of energy efficiency, reduced losses, and potentially lower environmental impact. Emphasize the significance of the cascading conversion approach in achieving these advantages.

Economic Considerations

To further strengthen the case for ECCS, conduct a preliminary cost-effectiveness analysis. Compare the costs associated with implementing ECCS stages versus conventional energy systems, considering factors such as initial investment, operational expenses, and potential long-term savings.

Impact on Energy Utilization and Cost-Effectiveness

Energy Utilization Enhancement

Demonstrate how ECCS enhances energy utilization compared to conventional systems (Nagi et al., 2021; Retrofitting, n.d.):

- **Multi-stage Utilization:** Highlight how ECCS optimizes energy utilization by capturing and converting energy at different levels, maximizing the utilization of various energy carriers.
- **Diverse Applications:** Showcase how ECCS enables the utilization of energy for different purposes, facilitating simultaneous energy provision for multiple applications.

Cost-Effectiveness Analysis

Perform a preliminary cost-effectiveness analysis to showcase the potential economic benefits of ECCS (Huang et al., 2018):

- **Initial Investment:** Compare the upfront costs of implementing ECCS stages with those of conventional systems.
- **Operational Savings:** Discuss potential operational cost savings resulting from higher efficiency and reduced energy losses.
- **Lifecycle Costs:** Consider the lifecycle costs of ECCS and conventional systems, including maintenance, repairs, and energy expenses.
- **Long-term Viability:** Discuss the long-term economic viability of ECCS, highlighting potential payback periods and return on investment.

By conducting a thorough comparative study and assessing the impact of ECCS on energy utilization and cost-effectiveness, you will provide valuable insights into the system's superiority and its potential to revolutionize energy infrastructure on both technical and economic fronts.

DISCUSSION AND INTERPRETATION OF FINDINGS

Insights into Energy Cascade Conversion Process

After presenting the results and comparative analysis, this section delves into a comprehensive discussion and interpretation of the findings. It focuses on extracting meaningful insights into the Energy Cascade Conversion System (ECCS) and shedding light on the unique aspects of its energy conversion process (Nagi et al., 2021; P. H. Shaikh et al., 2017).

- **Cascading Efficiency:** Analyze how the cascading approach optimizes energy utilization by capturing and converting energy at multiple levels. Discuss how this hierarchical process minimizes losses and enhances overall efficiency.

- **Multi-Stage Integration:** Explore the advantages of integrating diverse energy carriers and conversion mechanisms within the ECCS framework. Highlight how this integration enables the system to harness various forms of energy for different applications.
- **Flexibility and Adaptability:** Discuss how the ECCS's multi-stage structure offers flexibility to accommodate changes in energy supply and demand. Emphasize how this adaptability contributes to enhanced resilience and responsiveness.

Factors Affecting System Performance

Understanding the factors that influence the performance of ECCS is essential for its effective implementation. In this section, identify and analyze the key factors that impact the system's operation and efficiency:

- **Component Design:** Explore how the design of individual components, such as converters and storage units, affects energy conversion efficiency. Discuss the importance of optimized design for seamless integration and performance.
- **Input Variability:** Address how variations in input energy sources, such as renewable inputs with fluctuating availability, impact the ECCS's efficiency. Examine strategies to mitigate these variations and maintain consistent performance.
- **Maintenance and Upkeep:** Discuss how regular maintenance and upkeep of the ECCS components are crucial for sustained efficiency. Highlight the importance of monitoring and addressing potential issues to prevent performance degradation.

Implications for Energy Infrastructure Development

This section extends the discussion to the broader implications of ECCS for energy infrastructure development, sustainability, and future advancements:

- **Sustainable Energy Landscape:** Discuss how ECCS has the potential to reshape energy infrastructure by offering a more sustainable alternative to conventional linear energy pathways. Highlight how ECCS aligns with global efforts to reduce carbon emissions and promote clean energy.
- **Urban Planning and Design:** Explore how the principles of ECCS can be integrated into urban planning and design. Discuss the implications for energy-efficient buildings, smart cities, and sustainable transportation systems.
- **Policy and Regulatory Considerations:** Address the regulatory and policy implications of implementing ECCS. Discuss how governments and regulatory bodies can encourage the adoption of ECCS through incentives, standards, and supportive policies.
- **Collaborative Research and Innovation:** Highlight the need for interdisciplinary collaboration between researchers, engineers, policymakers, and stakeholders to further advance ECCS. Emphasize the potential for innovation and research to drive the optimization of ECCS components and its integration into existing systems.

CASE STUDIES IN ENERGY-EFFICIENT INFRASTRUCTURE IMPLEMENTATION

Case Study 1: Energy-Efficient Building Retrofitting

Energy-efficient building retrofitting presents a significant opportunity to showcase the practical application and benefits of the Energy Cascade Conversion System (ECCS). This case study focuses on how ECCS principles can be integrated into building retrofit projects to enhance energy efficiency, reduce consumption, and contribute to sustainability goals (Pacheco-Torgal et al., 2017; Retrofitting & 2017, n.d.). Provide context for the case study by discussing the importance of building energy efficiency, the challenges of retrofitting existing structures, and the potential role of ECCS in addressing these challenges.

Implementation of ECCS in Retrofitting

Detail how ECCS principles can be applied to energy-efficient building retrofitting (P. H. Shaikh et al., 2017; Zhou et al., 2016):

- **Multi-Stage Conversion:** Describe how ECCS can optimize energy utilization by incorporating multi-stage conversion processes. Explain how energy from various sources (solar, waste heat, etc.) can be efficiently captured and converted for heating, cooling, lighting, and other building needs.
- **Cascading Energy Flows:** Illustrate how ECCS facilitates the cascading of energy flows through different stages, ensuring that energy is converted and utilized at the most appropriate level.
- **Integration with Building Systems:** Discuss how ECCS components can be seamlessly integrated with existing building systems, such as HVAC (heating, ventilation, and air conditioning), lighting, and appliances.

Performance Metrics and Data Collection

Specify the performance metrics used to evaluate the success of the retrofitting project, such as energy savings, carbon emissions reduction, and cost-effectiveness. Outline the data collection methods and instruments employed to measure energy consumption before and after retrofitting (Retrofitting, n.d.).

Results and Benefits

Present the results of the energy-efficient building retrofitting project:

- **Energy Savings:** Quantify the energy savings achieved through ECCS integration. Compare energy consumption before and after retrofitting, highlighting the percentage reduction.
- **Cost-effectiveness:** Discuss the economic benefits of the retrofitting project, considering initial investment costs, operational savings, and potential return on investment.
- **Environmental Impact:** Calculate the reduction in carbon emissions resulting from the energy-efficient retrofitting. Emphasize how ECCS contributes to a more sustainable built environment.

Case Study 2: Smart Grid Integration and Demand Response

Smart grid integration coupled with demand response strategies is a crucial approach to achieving energy efficiency and sustainability. This case study focuses on how the Energy Cascade Conversion System (ECCS) can contribute to optimizing energy distribution within a smart grid framework and enhancing demand response capabilities (Reviews, 2014, 2013; Shao et al., 2012).

Introduce the significance of smart grid integration and demand response in modern energy systems. Discuss the challenges associated with peak demand, energy imbalances, and the need for flexible energy distribution. Set the stage for how ECCS can address these challenges.

ECCS Integration in Smart Grids

Explain the practical integration of ECCS within a smart grid context (Sarker et al., 2021):

- **Multi-Stage Energy Conversion:** Elaborate on how ECCS's multi-stage conversion process aligns with the dynamic nature of smart grids. Describe how energy can be converted and distributed efficiently based on demand fluctuations.
- **Demand Response Enablement:** Illustrate how ECCS enhances demand response strategies. Explain how ECCS can quickly adapt energy conversion processes to respond to changes in demand, thereby optimizing energy utilization.
- **Grid Stability Enhancement:** Discuss how ECCS integration contributes to grid stability by balancing energy supply and demand in real-time. Emphasize its role in reducing load imbalances and voltage fluctuations.

Performance Metrics and Data Collection

Define the key performance metrics used to evaluate the success of ECCS integration in the smart grid context. Metrics could include grid stability, response time to demand changes, energy losses, and overall efficiency. Explain how data from smart meters, sensors, and grid monitoring systems are collected (Asensio et al., 2020; Losi et al., 2015; Sarker et al., 2021).

Results and Benefits

Present the outcomes and advantages of the smart grid integration case study:

- **Demand Response Effectiveness:** Demonstrate how ECCS-enabled demand response strategies improve the grid's ability to manage peak demand periods. Highlight faster response times and smoother load transitions.
- **Energy Distribution Efficiency:** Quantify improvements in energy distribution efficiency resulting from ECCS integration. Compare energy losses and utilization before and after ECCS implementation.
- **Grid Reliability:** Discuss the enhanced grid reliability achieved through ECCS integration, emphasizing its role in minimizing power disruptions and enhancing overall system resilience.

Case Study 3: Sustainable Transportation Infrastructure

The integration of the Energy Cascade Conversion System (ECCS) into sustainable transportation infrastructure offers a unique opportunity to revolutionize energy utilization in the transportation sector. This case study focuses on how ECCS principles can be applied to enhance the efficiency and sustainability of transportation systems (ASTM, 2008; Lee et al., 2013).

Introduce the challenges of energy consumption and emissions in the transportation sector. Discuss the importance of transitioning to sustainable transportation solutions and highlight the role of ECCS in achieving this transition.

ECCS Integration in Transportation

Explain how ECCS principles can be integrated into sustainable transportation infrastructure (Henao et al., 2015):

- **Multi-Modal Energy Capture:** Describe how ECCS can capture energy from various sources within the transportation ecosystem, such as regenerative braking, waste heat, and solar energy.
- **Multi-Stage Conversion:** Illustrate how ECCS can optimize energy utilization by converting captured energy through multiple stages for different transportation needs, such as propulsion, lighting, and auxiliary systems.
- **Integration with Electric Vehicles:** Discuss the integration of ECCS principles with electric vehicle (EV) charging infrastructure, highlighting the potential for energy capture, conversion, and storage during the charging process.

Performance Metrics and Data Collection

Define performance metrics to assess the success of ECCS integration in sustainable transportation:

- **Energy Efficiency:** Measure energy efficiency gains achieved through ECCS integration, comparing energy consumption before and after implementation.
- **Emissions Reduction:** Quantify the reduction in carbon emissions resulting from improved energy efficiency and utilization.
- **Operational Savings:** Discuss potential cost savings related to reduced energy consumption and maintenance.

Results and Benefits

Present the outcomes and advantages of the sustainable transportation infrastructure case study:

- **Fuel Efficiency Enhancement:** Showcase how ECCS-enabled energy capture and conversion lead to improved fuel efficiency for vehicles.
- **Emissions Reduction:** Quantify the reduction in greenhouse gas emissions resulting from the ECCS-enhanced transportation systems.

- **Cost Savings:** Discuss the economic benefits of ECCS integration, including reduced energy consumption and operational expenses.

CHALLENGES AND FUTURE DIRECTIONS

Implementing and advancing Energy Cascade Conversion Systems (ECCS) presents several challenges that must be addressed to maximize their potential. This chapter discusses these challenges and proposes strategies for overcoming them (B. B. Badassa et al., 2020; Losi et al., 2015; P. H. Shaikh et al., 2017).

- **Integration Complexity:** ECCS involves the integration of diverse energy conversion technologies and components, which can lead to complex design, operation, and maintenance challenges.
- **Scale-Up Challenges:** As ECCS applications expand, scaling up the system without compromising efficiency and reliability becomes increasingly difficult.
- **Real-Time Optimization:** Implementing real-time optimization algorithms to manage energy flow and conversion pathways requires sophisticated data analytics and computational capabilities.
- **Initial Investment:** ECCS integration may require significant upfront investment, posing challenges to cost-effectiveness and financial viability.
- **Lack of Standards:** The absence of standardized guidelines and regulations specific to ECCS integration can hinder widespread adoption.

Future Directions in ECCS Research and Implementation

- **Materials Innovation:** Research into advanced materials can lead to more efficient energy conversion components with improved durability and performance.
- **Enhanced Integration:** Further integration of ECCS with smart grid technologies can optimize energy distribution, enable demand response, and enhance grid stability.
- **Energy Storage Solutions:** Explore the development of advanced energy storage technologies that can enhance the efficiency and reliability of ECCS by storing excess energy for later use.
- **Life Cycle Analysis:** Conduct comprehensive life cycle assessments to evaluate the overall environmental impact of ECCS integration, including raw material extraction, manufacturing, operation, and end-of-life disposal.
- **Supportive Policies:** Advocate for policies that incentivize ECCS integration, such as feed-in tariffs, tax incentives, and regulatory frameworks that encourage the adoption of cascading energy conversion.

CONCLUSION

In this final chapter, the culmination of your research journey is presented, highlighting the key findings, implications, and potential contributions of the Energy Cascade Conversion System (ECCS) to the energy landscape and sustainable infrastructure development.

- **Energy Cascade Conversion Efficiency:** Highlight the achieved energy conversion efficiencies at different stages of ECCS, showcasing how the cascading approach optimizes energy utilization.
- **Comparative Analysis:** Emphasize the advantages of ECCS over conventional energy systems, showcasing its potential to enhance energy efficiency and reduce losses.
- **Case Studies:** Summarize the outcomes of the case studies in energy-efficient building retrofitting, smart grid integration, and sustainable transportation infrastructure. Highlight how ECCS integration in various contexts can lead to energy savings, emissions reduction, and enhanced sustainability.

Discuss the broader implications of ECCS for sustainable infrastructure development:

- **Energy Efficiency Revolution:** Highlight how ECCS has the potential to revolutionize energy conversion and utilization, contributing to global efforts to mitigate climate change and reduce energy consumption.
- **Enhanced Resilience:** Discuss how ECCS integration can enhance the resilience of energy systems by optimizing energy distribution, supporting demand response, and minimizing energy losses.
- **Innovation and Collaboration:** Emphasize the role of ECCS as a catalyst for research collaboration, technological innovation, and interdisciplinary approaches to addressing energy and sustainability challenges.

Provide insights into potential avenues for future research and innovation in ECCS and energy-efficient infrastructure:

- **Advanced Materials:** Suggest further exploration of advanced materials for energy conversion components to enhance efficiency and durability.
- **Smart Grid Synergies:** Encourage further research into seamless integration between ECCS and smart grid technologies for optimized energy distribution and demand response.
- **Policy and Regulation:** Advocate for research that informs supportive policies and regulations to promote ECCS adoption on a larger scale.

ABBREVIATIONS

ECCS: Energy Cascade Conversion System
HVAC: Heating, Ventilation, and Air Conditioning
EV: Electric Vehicle
CO2: Carbon Dioxide
IoT: Internet of Things
ROI: Return on Investment
GHG: Greenhouse Gas
LCA: Life Cycle Analysis
PPI: Public-Private Partnership

R&D: Research and Development
CAGR: Compound Annual Growth Rate
CDS: Cascade Energy Distribution System
RES: Renewable Energy Sources
DER: Distributed Energy Resources
DERMS: Distributed Energy Resources Management System
DG: Distributed Generation
DR: Demand Response
EMS: Energy Management System
ICT: Information and Communication Technology

REFERENCES

Akisawa, A., Kang, Y. T., Shimazaki, Y., & Kashiwagi, T. (1999). Environmentally friendly energy system models using material circulation and energy cascade—The optimization work. *Energy*, *24*(7), 561–578. doi:10.1016/S0360-5442(99)00023-7

Aljaghtham, M. (n.d.). *Design of cascade thermoelectric generation systems with improved thermal reliability.* Elsevier. Retrieved August 12, 2023, from https://www.sciencedirect.com/science/article/pii/S0360544221032813

Asensio, O. I., Alvarez, K., Dror, A., Wenzel, E., Hollauer, C., & Ha, S. (2020). Real-time data from mobile platforms to evaluate sustainable transportation infrastructure. *Nature Sustainability*, *3*(6), 463–471. doi:10.103841893-020-0533-6

ASTM. (2008). *Developing sustainable transportation infrastructure.* Citeseer. https://citeseerx.ist.psu.edu/document?repid=rep1&type=pdf&doi=f2d9506dee70808a8803f8955d58eecd715df05b

Badassa, B. B., Sun, B., & Qiao, L. (2020). Sustainable Transport Infrastructure and Economic Returns: A Bibliometric and Visualization Analysis. *Sustainability (Basel)*, *12*(5), 2033. doi:10.3390u12052033

Bhowmik, S., Spee, R., & Enslin, J. H. R. (1999). Performance optimization for doubly fed wind power generation systems. *IEEE Transactions on Industry Applications*, *35*(4), 949–958. doi:10.1109/28.777205

Bruggink, A., Schoevaart, R., & Kieboom, T. (2003). Concepts of Nature in Organic Synthesis: Cascade Catalysis and Multistep Conversions in Concert. *Organic Process Research & Development*, *7*(5), 622–640. doi:10.1021/op0340311

Choi, U.-M., Blaabjerg, F., & Lee, K.-B. (2015). Study and Handling Methods of Power IGBT Module Failures in Power Electronic Converter Systems. *IEEE Transactions on Power Electronics*, *30*(5), 2517–2533. doi:10.1109/TPEL.2014.2373390

Cohn, S. A. (1995). Radar Measurements of Turbulent Eddy Dissipation Rate in the Troposphere: A Comparison of Techniques. *Journal of Atmospheric and Oceanic Technology*, *12*(1), 85–95. doi:10.1175/1520-0426(1995)012<0085:RMOTED>2.0.CO;2

Henao, A., Piatkowski, D., Luckey, K. S., Nordback, K., Marshall, W. E., & Krizek, K. J. (2015). Sustainable transportation infrastructure investments and mode share changes: A 20-year background of Boulder, Colorado. *Transport Policy*, *37*, 64–71. doi:10.1016/j.tranpol.2014.09.012

Huang, Y., Yi, Q., Wei, G., Kang, J., Li, W., Feng, J., & Xie, K. (2018). Energy use, greenhouse gases emission and cost effectiveness of an integrated high– and low–temperature Fisher–Tropsch synthesis plant from a lifecycle viewpoint. *Applied Energy*, *228*, 1009–1019. doi:10.1016/j.apenergy.2018.07.007

Kang, Y., Kong, N., Ou, M., Wang, Y., Xiao, Q., Mei, L., Liu, B., Chen, L., Zeng, X., & Ji, X. (2023). A novel cascaded energy conversion system inducing efficient and precise cancer therapy. *Bioactive Materials*, *20*, 663–676. doi:10.1016/j.bioactmat.2022.07.007 PMID:35891799

Kazmierkowski, M. (n.d.). *Automatic control of converter-fed drives.* Academia.Edu. Retrieved August 12, 2023, from https://www.academia.edu/download/36319799/PI_controller.PDF

Klein, M., & Schmidt, C. J. (2011). CASCADE, neutron detectors for highest count rates in combination with ASIC/FPGA based readout electronics. *Nuclear Instruments & Methods in Physics Research. Section A, Accelerators, Spectrometers, Detectors and Associated Equipment*, *628*(1), 9–18. doi:10.1016/j.nima.2010.06.278

Lai, J.-S., & Fang, Z. P. (1996). Multilevel converters-a new breed of power converters. *IEEE Transactions on Industry Applications*, *32*(3), 509–517. doi:10.1109/28.502161

Lee, J., Edil, T., & Benson, C. (2013). *Building environmentally and economically sustainable transportation infrastructure: green highway rating system.* Ascelibrary.Org. https://ascelibrary.org/doi/abs/10.1061/(ASCE)CO.1943-7862.0000742

Losi, A., Mancarella, P., & Vicino, A. (2015). *Integration of demand response into the electricity chain: challenges, opportunities, and Smart Grid solutions*. https://books.google.com/books?hl=en&lr=&id=P2ThCgAAQBAJ&oi=fnd&pg=PP1&dq=Smart+Grid+Integration+and+Demand+Response+&ots=8oTsImjU57&sig=CQ151wzFZQkD0cLQc4TRj8AI2hc

Maharjan, L., & Inoue, S. (n.d.). *State-of-charge (SOC)-balancing control of a battery energy storage system based on a cascade PWM converter.* Ieeexplore.Ieee.Org. Retrieved August 12, 2023, from https://ieeexplore.ieee.org/abstract/document/5071730/

Maharjan, L., Inoue, S., & Akagi, H. (2008). A Transformerless Energy Storage System Based on a Cascade Multilevel PWM Converter With Star Configuration. *IEEE Transactions on Industry Applications*, *44*(5), 1621–1630. doi:10.1109/TIA.2008.2002180

Maharjan, L., Yamagishi, T., Akagi, H., & Asakura, J. (2010). Fault-Tolerant Operation of a Battery-Energy-Storage System Based on a Multilevel Cascade PWM Converter With Star Configuration. *IEEE Transactions on Power Electronics*, *25*(9), 2386–2396. doi:10.1109/TPEL.2010.2047407

Miao, B., Lin, J., Li, H., Liu, C., Li, B., Zhu, X., & Yang, J. (2020). Day-Ahead Energy Trading Strategy of Regional Integrated Energy System Considering Energy Cascade Utilization. *IEEE Access : Practical Innovations, Open Solutions*, *8*, 138021–138035. doi:10.1109/ACCESS.2020.3007224

Mu, C., Ding, T., Qu, M., Zhou, Q., Li, F., & Shahidehpour, M. (2020). Decentralized optimization operation for the multiple integrated energy systems with energy cascade utilization. *Applied Energy*, *280*, 115989. doi:10.1016/j.apenergy.2020.115989

Nagi, G. K., Minhas, A. K., Gaur, S., Jain, P., & Mandal, S. (2021). Integration of Algal Biofuels With Bioremediation Coupled Industrial Commodities Towards Cost-Effectiveness. *Frontiers in Energy Research*, *9*, 735141. Advance online publication. doi:10.3389/fenrg.2021.735141

Ounejjar, Y., Al-Haddad, K., & Grégoire, L.-A. (2011). Packed U cells multilevel converter topology: Theoretical study and experimental validation. *IEEE Transactions on Industrial Electronics*, *58*(4), 1294–1306. Advance online publication. doi:10.1109/TIE.2010.2050412

Pacheco-Torgal, F., Granqvist, C.-G., Vanoli, G. P., Bianco, N., & Kurnitski, J. (2017). *Cost-effective energy efficient building retrofitting: materials, technologies, optimization and case studies*. https://books.google.com/books?hl=en&lr=&id=aWeyDAAAQBAJ&oi=fnd&pg=PP1&dq=Energy-Efficient+Building+Retrofitting+&ots=XAoaAY_zL7&sig=lbu4j6svowujgI9GPp_V1AQLV_I

Pavković, D., Lobrović, M., Hrgetić, M., & Komljenović, A. (2016). A design of cascade control system and adaptive load compensator for battery/ultracapacitor hybrid energy storage-based direct current microgrid. *Energy Conversion and Management*, *114*, 154–167. doi:10.1016/j.enconman.2016.02.005

Retrofitting. (n.d.). *Introduction to cost-effective energy-efficient building retrofitting*. Elsevier. Retrieved August 12, 2023, from https://www.sciencedirect.com/science/article/pii/B9780081011287000010

Reviews. (2013). *Demand response and smart grids—A survey*. Elsevier. doi:10.1016/j.rser.2013.10.022

Rodriguez, J., Bernet, S., Wu, B., Pontt, J. O., & Kouro, S. (2007). Multilevel Voltage-Source-Converter Topologies for Industrial Medium-Voltage Drives. *IEEE Transactions on Industrial Electronics*, *54*(6), 2930–2945. doi:10.1109/TIE.2007.907044

Sarker, E., Halder, P., Seyedmahmoudian, M., Jamei, E., Horan, B., Mekhilef, S., & Stojcevski, A. (2021). Progress on the demand side management in smart grid and optimization approaches. *International Journal of Energy Research*, *45*(1), 36–64. doi:10.1002/er.5631

Shaikh, P. H., Shaikh, F., Sahito, A. A., Uqaili, M. A., & Umrani, Z. (2017). An Overview of the Challenges for Cost-Effective and Energy-Efficient Retrofits of the Existing Building Stock. In *Cost-Effective Energy Efficient Building Retrofitting* (pp. 257–278). Elsevier. doi:10.1016/B978-0-08-101128-7.00009-5

Shan, S., Tian, J., Chen, B., Zhang, Y., & Zhou, Z. (2023). Theoretical and technical analysis of the photo-thermal energy cascade conversion for fuel with high-temperature combustion. *Energy*, *263*, 125990. doi:10.1016/j.energy.2022.125990

Shao, S., Pipattanasomporn, M., & Rahman, S. (2012). Grid integration of electric vehicles and demand response with customer choice. *IEEE Transactions on Smart Grid*, *3*(1), 543–550. doi:10.1109/TSG.2011.2164949

Steffen, J., Lengsfeld, S., Jung, M., Ponick, B., Gracia, M. H., Spagnolo, A., Klöpzig, M., Schleicher, K., Schäfer, K., Russo, A., Mazza, A., Musumeci, S., & Pons, E. (2021). *Design of a medium voltage generator with dc-cascade for high power wind energy conversion systems.* Mdpi.Com. doi:10.3390/en14113106

Verdugo, C., Kouro, S., Rojas, C., Perez, M., & Energies, T. M. (2019). undefined. (2012). Five-level T-type cascade converter for rooftop grid-connected photovoltaic systems. *Mdpi. Com*, *6*(3), 495–504. doi:10.1049/iet-pel.2012.0494

Walker, G., & Sernia, P. C. (2004a). Cascaded DC-DC converter connection of photovoltaic modules. *IEEE Transactions on Power Electronics*, *19*(4), 1130–1139. Advance online publication. doi:10.1109/TPEL.2004.830090

Zahboune, H., Zouggar, S., Krajacic, G., Varbanov, S., Elhafyani, M., & Ziani, E. (2016). *Optimal hybrid renewable energy design in autonomous system using Modified Electric System Cascade Analysis and Homer software*. Elsevier. doi:10.1016/j.enconman.2016.08.061

Zhou, Z., Zhang, S., Wang, C., Zuo, J., He, Q., & Rameezdeen, R. (2016). Achieving energy efficient buildings via retrofitting of existing buildings: A case study. *Journal of Cleaner Production*, *112*, 3605–3615. doi:10.1016/j.jclepro.2015.09.046

Chapter 5
Hybrid Approach for Quantifying Company Assets Using Structural Credit Risk Models

Pranav Motarwar
Vellore Institute of Technology, Chennai, India

Rudra Patil
Vellore Institute of Technology, Chennai, India

Ashutosh Sanjay Lembhe
Vellore Institute of Technology, Chennai, India

Radhika Selvamani
Vellore Institute of Technology, Chennai, India

Anbalagan Bhuvaneswari
https://orcid.org/0000-0001-6651-2031
Vellore Institute of Technology, Chennai, India

ABSTRACT

Global investors have been allocating resources for developing quantitative credit risk models for forecasting credit risk and estimating the cost associated with defaults in order to arrive at the credit derivatives which may handle the risks. In this chapter, the authors propose a hybrid Merton model for measuring credit risk. They estimate market volatility using an iterative annualized historical volatility approach and corporate asset value using the Merton model. For corporate assets, actual default probability and risk neutral probability are correlated. Monte Carlo simulation predictions of the real-time asset price of S&P global-listed Tesla Inc. support the approach. The derived book asset value is 0.44% and the simulated asset value is 0.43%. Model convergence is shown by the minimal difference between the past three iterations. The hybrid strategy to select risk neutral stock value captures volatility variance. Comparative analysis with real-time data confirms the approach's correctness.

DOI: 10.4018/979-8-3693-1722-8.ch005

1. INTRODUCTION

Credit risk modelling is a systematic approach towards assessment of credit risk and computation of cost of risk (Duffie and Singleton, 2012). It helps creditors to analyse different factors which are contributing to the overall risk in their portfolio. Credit risk modelling helps in predicting the probability of loss in unforeseen circumstances. Thus over the decades credit risk modelling has emerged as one of the major tool for investors to make informed decisions. Banks evaluate the borrowing company's credit risk to assess their creditworthiness, to price their loans and to protect their investments appropriately. Creditors analyse the risk of the financial products to diversify their portfolios by identifying the risk and return of their investments. Credit default is a rare occurrence with low odds. Yet it demands special attention among the many risk components, such as the market risk or operational risk, because of the narrow window of predictability and the immense magnitude of the loss acquired in case of defaults (Jiménez and Saurina, 2004). The global crisis of 2008-2009 provides testimony to this. All creditors, regardless of their geographic locations, devote the majority of their resources towards controlling credit risk and developing models to predict future likely defaults or losses. Though the financial institutions have standardized and revamped their credit models much better after the 2008 crisis, due to the pandemic, high uncertainty has been introduced in the market. Existing model factors have to be studied taking into account the contractions in the GDP and deviations in the exchange reflecting the impact of the pandemic and its variation across different countries and business sub-sectors. Financial institutions are in a situation to re-assess the credit models of their portfolio and be pro-active in handling the products or services that do not meet their payment terms. With the adoption of digital transformation over the last decade, the financial institutions have access to large amount of data in order to assess risk profiles more accurately (Rajini, Ramamoorthy, Rammohan, Rajakumar and Niveditha, 2020).

Credit risk models play a key role in improving the credit score of a bank. Generally, creditors adopt different models for corporate as well as retail segments. Some of the current applications follow a risk based pricing, aiming to improve returns, reducing risk of their portfolios and achieving better performance of various businesses by following appropriate risk adjustments. Credit risk models include the possibility that investors may fail to pay on demand and allows estimation of the cost of loss, so that funds may be allocated appropriately. The overall ability of the borrower to repay the loan under the original terms is used to measure the credit risk. Merton models were traditionally developed and implemented for various practical applications including financial product pricing (Altman and Saunders, 1997). In this paper we propose a hybrid approach for enhancing widely used Merton Model after studying its evolution over years. The Merton Model has been applied to represent the asset structure of Tesla stocks by extracting the required parameters from the live stock price of Tesla from S&P 500 Index after the onset of pandemic.

We propose a unique methodology to evaluate the market value of the firm's assets by assuming Merton Model based asset structure, whose parameters have been obtained by an Annualized Historical Volatility Model (AHVM).

The paper is classified as follows: The technical factors in the credit risk domain and the traditional models with interesting adaptations have been discussed in the first two sections. The following sections explore the data set and the proposed adaptations to the chosen model. Finally, we discuss our results insights and possible improvements.

2. OVERVIEW OF EXISTING APPROACHES

2.1. Credit Risk Models

Qualitative Credit Risk Models were the first models to be ever used by economists for extracting and evaluating information from a consumer before lending out money. The lender would consider factors like collateral, credit history and various economic indicators for making the decision (Uthayakumar, Vengattaraman and Dhavachelvan, 2020). The drawback of this model is that it depends on the personal judgement and experience of the lender rather than a validated mathematical model. The decision made were subjective to the decision makers.

Quantitative models were initiated in the banking domain from introducing the idea that certain loans may be assigned measures or numbers that can be compared with the probability of default (Harris, 2013). This allowed the lenders to determine if this is a risk they would like to own, transfer, or charge interest based on the default probability. The basic objective of these models is to provide a pricing mechanism to cover the financial contracts that are sensitive to credit risk. Over time, two conflicting techniques for modelling the default process and recovery rates arose, namely the structural approach and the reduced-form approach.

Structuring techniques mentioned by Bhatore, Mohan and Reddy (2020) explore forecasting and pricing of financial products of a company, by specifying credit models relating the risk probabilities to the liabilities and the equities of the company. A company's default risk is calculated considering factors such as assets, equity, and liabilities. These models involve strong assumptions about the dynamics of liabilities and the capital structure of the company. In other words, the structural approach aims to establish a clear link between default risk and capital structure.

Merton Model has been proposed by Robert Merton in 1974 as an extension to Black-Scholes model which was proposed by him earlier to study the structural credit risk of a company. The basic purpose of the model in credit risk assessment is to provide a theoretical entailment to represent the causality between a firm's asset structure and its potential default risk. The structural credit models have limitations. The prediction of the bond price is below par. Despite this fact, Schaefer and Strebulaev (2008) presented a methodology which modifies the Merton model for calculating the sensitivity of the hedge ratios. The study presented by Li and Wong (2008) suggests using maximum likelihood estimation of the hedge fund pricing. The corporate bond may be perfectly estimated by the suggested models. The drawbacks of the Black and Scholes model as highlighted in this study by Karoui, Jeanblanc-Picquè and Shreve (1998) provides the fundamental base for the proposed model development in this paper.

2.2. Merton Model Variations

The most commonly used indicators that affect the default risks are the percent of failure probability, recovery rate, number of failures, predicted loss and growth rate. The findings of the research papers suggest that the default risk and the probability of the recovery rate are proportional. This concludes the result presented by Džaja and Aljinović (2013) with suggestions for banks for maximizing rate of recovery for reducing default risk. A hybrid approach in the context of credit risk modeling typically refers to combining multiple methodologies to enhance the accuracy and robustness of credit risk assessment. Structural credit risk models, such as the Merton model, estimate the credit risk of a firm by modeling the value of its assets and liabilities and then determining the probability of default based on the distance between the firm's asset value and its debt obligations. One of the way to enhance the accuracy of structural models is by integrating market-based information such as stock prices, equity volatility, and credit spreads. A hybrid model could combine structural credit risk models with market-based signals to provide a more comprehensive assessment of a company's creditworthiness. A hybrid approach might involve integrating macroeconomic variables that can impact a company's credit risk. Factors like GDP growth, interest rates, and industry-specific trends can influence a company's financial health. Combining structural models with macroeconomic variables could offer a more holistic view of credit risk. Machine learning techniques, such as neural networks or random forests, can be integrated into a hybrid approach. These techniques can capture complex patterns and relationships in large datasets that might not be fully captured by traditional structural models. Merton Models models can also be applied on the historical default data listed by the credit rating services on an yearly basis to estimate probability of default by assuming asset correlation as the default correlation. The study by Hisakado and Mori (2021) indicates that due to the limited historical data there is a problem with parameter estimation due to the long memory of PD and slow convergence rate. TBenos and Papanastasopoulos (2007) have used Merton Model to estimate a risk neutral distance to default metric. The result presented by Benos and Papanastasopoulos (2007) concludes that the new metric enriched by financial ratios and accounting variables provides significant results in improved credit rating analysis. The detailed empirical examination provided by Afik, Arad and Galil (2016) analyses model sensitivity to specification parameters. They present a detailed review of the variants of Merton Models since 1984.

2.3. Credit Model Evaluation

A firm's future financial potential may be investigated using forecasts provided by the credit model. Credit defaults have an impact on the credit score of a firm as reported by Yusof, Alias, Kassim and Zaidi (2021). Credit scores tend to be high if the economy's future seems bright, but low if the borrower's economic prognosis is bleak as examined by Liu, Li, Zhu, Ye and Ma (2021). On successfully specifying the Model parameters the next step is successfully forecasting the asset prices and estimating the risk probability. Since there is interference from random variables such as market performance, unexpected events etc., the likelihood of outcomes cannot be estimated directly. One of the widely used approaches recently has been to simulate the outcomes using standard Monte Carlo Approach. It may be used for iterative sample collection in order to reach a specific desired outcome as indicated by Abonazel (2018). As per Zhang (2018), the extended version applies a cross-section simulation-based evaluation approach for credit risk models. With a simulated loan portfolio, the model is evaluated based not only on forecasts over time, but also on forecasts at specific points in time. Derbali and Jamel (2019) quantifies and evaluates the dependency between probability of default and recovery rate using a variety of statistical methods with the help of simulated data.

2.4. Credit Rating

Credit Rating is an assessment of the borrower in terms of the ability to repay the credit issued. Factors Affecting Credit Ratings and Credit Scores include previous track record of payments, owed amounts to various stakeholders, credit history length, various types of credit (Ashbaugh-Skaife, Collins and LaFond, 2006). Any individual, company or government may be assigned a credit rating by an authorized credit rating agency such as SP Global, FICO etc. A Fair Isaac Corporation (FICO) metric is a 3-digit score given to individuals based on their credit reports usually ranging from 300 to 850. The credit rating agencies SP Global, Moody's and Fitch assign letter grades to denote credit ratings as shown in Table 1. These scores and grades are used by credit agencies to rate individual consumers based on credit worthiness. When credit rating an organisation, financial institutions take into account a number of variables. The agency looks at the company's previous borrowing and debt settlement history first.

Fitch Ratings is one of the top three credit rating companies in the world (Rajini et al., 2020). It has offices in New York and London and assigns ratings based on a company's debt and its sensitivity to fluctuations in interest rates, among other factors. Moody's Investors Service credit rating agency assigns a letter grade to companies, individuals or countries from ranging Aaa to Baa3 for investment grade debts. This rating indicates that the debtor is capable of repaying short-term debt. Speculative grade debt, sometimes known as high-yield or junk debt, is below investment grade. Moody's rating for speculative grade debts range from Ba1 to C, with a lower letter grade indicating a lower possibility of payback as presented in Table 1.

2.5. Factors to Consider While Modelling the Credit Risk

Risk Neutral Probabilities are essential for credit risk modelling. Fair prices for an asset or financial holding are determined using risk neutral probability. In the pricing of derivatives, the risk neutral probabilities concept is frequently used. We define probabilities of hypothetical future events that have been adjusted for risk (Murthy, 2011), where expected asset values can be calculated using risk neutral probabilities. We maintain zero arbitrage as a critical assumption in calculating risk neutral probabilities as defined by Jackwerth and Rubinstein (1996).

We define correlation between Credit risk and rate of interest for construction of the model as proposed by Liao and Huang (2005). Creditors can also opt out of making an investment or taking out a loan. Generally, a company with a steady income is said to be viewed as a low credit risk resulting in reduced mortgage rates. Applicants with a low credit history, on the other hand, may need to engage with subprime mortgage businesses to raise cash. Improving a high-risk borrower's credit score is the greatest approach to receive reduced interest rates.

Credit Probabilities of Default defines the large disparity between the default probability computed from historical data and the default probability represented by bond prices. It is a feature of the credit market or credit default swaps (Zhang, 2018). As seen, the average likelihood of default guaranteed by a bond's price is over ten times that estimated using historical data.

Table 1. Ratings of various agencies

No.	S&P	Moody's	Fitch	Meaning
1	AAA	Aaa	AAA	Prime
2	AA+	Aa1	AA+	
				High Grade
3	AA	Aa2	AA	
4	AA-	Aa3	AA-	
5	A+	A1	A+	
				Upper Medium Grade
6	A	A2	A	
7	A-	A3	A-	
8	BBB+	Baa1	BBB+	
				Lower Medium Grade
9	BBB	Baa2	BBB	
10	BBB-	Baa3	BBB-	
11	BB+	Ba1	BB+	
				Non Investment Speculative
12	BB	Ba2	BB	
13	BB-	Ba3	BB-	
14	B+	B1	B+	
				Highly Speculative
15	B	B2	B	
16	B-	B3	B-	
17	CCC+	Caa1	CCC+	
				Substantial Risk
18	CCC-	Caa2	CCC-	
				Extremely Speculative

2.5.1. Credit Derivatives

Credit derivatives allow creditors to sell the debtor's expected default risk to a third party at a so-called premium (Ayadi and Behr, 2009). We define credit derivative as a contract whose value is determined by the entity whose value is stated in the creditworthiness or credit event of the contract. Some examples of credit derivatives include total return swaps, credit default swap, credit default swap options (Li and Wong, 2008), secured debt, and credit spread forwards. Assume a company applies for loan from a bank. If the company does not have a good track record of credit history, the bank may require the company to purchase credit derivatives as a prerequisite condition for loan. Credit derivatives allow the bank to "transfer" the default risk to a third party. Credit Default Swaps is a kind of contract which permits an investor to swap credit risk with another investor (Zhang, 2018). We present CDS as a protection against the loan defaults which the lender needs to purchase from another investor who takes upon the responsibility if there is a default from the borrower as proposed by Angelini (2012). The CDS works by periodic payment of premium to insure the risk.

2.5.2. Global Market Impact

Model vulnerability to volatility in global market for credits, commodities and currencies needs to be accounted to provide accurate predictions. Including asset volatility becomes very crucial during the unstable situation created due to pandemic. Market prices reflect the future cash flow and predict the direct asset volatility. In other words, in the event of the company's bankruptcy, the third party guarantees to refund the loan and all interest, in exchange for an annual fee for the complete loan lifetime. The third party will profit from an annual membership fee if the company does not fail. In the meantime, the loan is given to the company, and the bank is risk free and secured in the case of a default.

3. ASSET STRUCTURE MODELLING

The structural models may be estimated from the stock price or the company balance sheet. An alternative approach is to use information from the bond market or credit derivative market. We have studied the structural model derived based on the publicly available stock price. The market value of a firm comprises of the market value of equity and market value of debt. It can be represented as,

$$A = E + D \tag{1}$$

In a Merton Model the equity E may be modeled and calculated as an implicit call option bound by a time period T-t (Benos and Papanastasopoulos, 2007). Black-Scholes-Merton formula is used to calculate Equity given the promised payments B, risk free rate r and the asset volatility. Similarly debt value D may be computed from the default-free debt and the guarantee against default, which again is a function of B and risk free rate r.

$$E = f(A, B, r, \sigma) \tag{2}$$

$$D = f(A, B, r) \tag{3}$$

A is the asset value, r is the risk free rate and σ is the asset volatility. To calculate the Asset Value At we require $_{t}$he drift rate and the Volatility εt. These value$_{s}$ are further needed to compute the credit spread and the probability of default of a firm. Unfortunately, these values are not directly observable from the market.

3.1. Merton Model

Merton model uses the asset structure composed of the equity and the liability of a company. Though the equity y be fully visible for the investors, the true liabilities are rarely published, making it difficult for the credit analysts and investors to develop accurate credit risk models of the counter party. Despite this, the Merton's approach to model publicly available equity data as a call option of the company's assets have been adopted by analysts successfully over the years. The Merton model assumes that the total asset value A of a firm follows a geometric Brownian motion with a constant drift μ equal to the risk free interest rate r and a constant diffusion rate equal to σ:

$$dAt = \mu Atdt + \sigma Atd_{Wt} \tag{4}$$

w_he re Wt is a _st anda_rd Brownian mot_io n with the characteristics that Wt=0, it has stationary and ind_ep endent increments which are Gaussian in nature. /subsection. Estimating Asset Volatility Approaches to obtain the asset volatility are basically of four types. The simplest approach is deriving the asset volatility from the annualized volatility of the asset return from the quarterly balance sheets. The most widely used traditional approaches involve solving the system of equations 2 through 3 with suitable assumptions. These approaches force the stochastic variables such as the asset volatility to be constants. To overcome these limitations empirical approaches backing up the observed parameters have been proposed Ronn and Verma (1986). Maximizing Likelihood of the observed equity by applying transformed data principle based on the unobserved variables is a popular approach proposed by ?. Accuracy of the iterative methods have been discussed by Andersen and Sørensen (1996).

3.2. Asset Price Modelling in Realtime

It has been empirically observed that there are heavy tailed and skewed distributions, jumps, volatility clustering structural changes in the timeseries of Asset prices Shokrollahi (2018). The various market and economic dynamics xplain these processes in the life time of an firm's asset. These processes also have time intervals of varying scales. As a result experts agree than Brownian assumption is unable to capture the real time behavior of the stock price. Power law distributions of volatility are seen when big players trade in market Gabaix, Gopikrishnan, Plerou and Stanley (2007). Volatility clustering is an observed positive correlation among the returns over a period of time. Price jumps have been associated with flow of financial news in the market Lee (2012). Structural changes of volatility may be caused due to price jumps. Several attempts have been made to account for the jumps and other events occurring in the financial market.

3.2.1. Jump Diffusion Models

Price jumps have been captured using a Poisson distribution in jump diffusion models 5. The Jumps are assumed to have an intensity λ which is normally distributed and a frequency k which has a Poisson distribution (Eqn). 5).

$$rt = \mu Bt + \sigma BdWt + kdqt \tag{5}$$

_wh ere k _i s a par_am eter _r epresenti_ng the number of events that occur which affect the stock price and dqt is defined as the intensity of the event _w hich has a poisson distribution. Jump models specify jumps to arrive with constant intensity. This assumption does not hold in explaining scenarios of large movements to volatility clusters.

3.2.2. Autoregressive Conditional Heteroscedastic Processes (ARCH) Models

ARCH models were initially proposed by Engle (1982) to capture the volatility variations in a stock price series which exhibits heteroscedasticity. A variation of the GARCH model discussed by Francq and Zakoian (2004), the Heston and Nandi GARCH (HN-GARCH) has been studied extensively by Huskaj and Hanna (2007) and Harding (2013). A simple GARCH(p,q) model is presented in equations 6 and 8.

$$h_t = \omega + \sum_{i=1}^{p} \beta_i h_{t-i\delta} + \sum_{i=1}^{q} \alpha_i z_{t-i\delta} - \gamma \sqrt{h_{t-i\delta}^2} \tag{6}$$

$$log\left(A_t\right) = log\left(A_{t-\delta}\right) + r + »h_t + \sqrt{h_t z_t} \tag{7}$$

where r is the continuously compounded interest rate for the time interval of size δ, ht is the conditional variance, $\lambda$is a constant parameter representing the risk neutral valuation relationship and zt is a standard normal disturbance term. α and β are constants which are to fullfill the condition in eqn. for the GARCH process to be stationary.

$$\beta i + \alpha i \gamma 2 < 1 \tag{8}$$

In real-time however parameter estimation using iterative approaches poses accuracy problems especially when the model is complex (Huskaj and Hanna, 2007; Harding, 2013; Ekström and Sjögren, 2014). In the following section we propose a hybrid approach of estimating asset volatility parameter for the Merton model using a Monte Carlo Approach maximizing a likelihood function and then minimizing the mean square error in comparison to annualized historical volatility estimated using a proposed approach adapted from Black-Scholes model. The hybrid model has captured the volatility variations during specific time intervals as well as forecasts the asset price into the future.

4. PROPOSED HYBRID MERTON MODEL

We estimate the asset volatility based on a maximum likelihood approach discussed in section 5.1 to build a Monte Carlo simulation model. Later we finetune the model by minimizing the root mean square error between the estimated volatility and the annualized historical volatility computed using the proposed volatility annualization approach in section 4.1. Our approach for volatility computation adapts the Black Sholes approach to estimate volatility μBS as shown in eqn.9 (Afik et al., 2016). This hybrid approach overcomes the problem of assuming a constant volatility in the proposed Merton Model.

$$h_t = \omega + \sum_{i=1}^{p} \beta_i h_{t-i\delta} + \sum_{i=1}^{q} \alpha_i z_{t-i\delta} - \gamma \sqrt{h_{t-i\delta}^2} \tag{9}$$

where n is number of days in the time period of the Asset time series and σr is the standard deviation of the returns.

4.1. Volatility Computed Using Proposed Annualized Historical Volatility Model (AHVM)

We propose Annualized Historical Volatility Model (AHVM) for estimating asset volatility from historical data as well as the data simulated by the Monte carlo model. The model is used for computing the value of company asset (Ak+1) and its annualized volatility (εt). The baseline period for calculating the daily volatility of returns has been assumed to be a day. The entire period under investigation from Jan 2020 to December 2021 is calculated to be n days. The daily volatility is annualized for the period n. We calculate Logarithmic Returns for each day. For each period the calculation is compounded with return presented in Eq.10.

$$\mu_{BS} = \sigma_r * \sqrt{n} \tag{10}$$

where, Pn = closing price; $Pn-1$ = previous day closing price

The root-mean square deviation of the logarithmic returns is minimized by iterating the computation of the average returns. We iterate the estimation till the sum of squared difference error between two consecutive iterations close to zero.

$$P = \left(\frac{P_n}{P_{n-1}}\right) \tag{11}$$

We summarize the annualized volatility values with the classic standardization, multiplying the volatility for the span of one day with the square root of the number of days when the share market is open for trading for a year.

4.2. Drift Rate Calculated Using CAPM

The Capital Asset Pricing Model provides us with the required factors needed for the computation of expected return from an asset (Huang, Liu and Ren, 2018) which forms the drift rate of the Merton Model. The drift rate is required for the computing the actual probability of default of a firm (Džaja and Aljinović, 2013). We follow the method proposed by Perold (2004) for calculating the drift rate. We calculate the drift rate by computing the expected return of the stock using the equation 12.

$$[Ri] = Rf + ([Rm] - R) \tag{12}$$

where, $E[Ri]$ = Expected return of the stock in the asset portfolio; Rf = Risk-free rate; $E[Rm]$ = Expected market return of the stock;

$[Rm] - Rf$ = Average annualized market risk premium;

β is the sensitivity of the asset's return to the return on the market portfolio which indicates a measure of systematic risk associated with the stock. We check the return of the series initially for checking the static nature by computing excess returns ER given at Eq.13.

$$ER = Ri - Rf \tag{13}$$

We then compute annual market risk premium by analyzing the slope of security market line i.e. the excess return over the market return presented at Eq.14.

$MarketRiskPremium = [Rm] - Rf(14)$

We then calculate value of β. β is defined as the risk factor which adds to the portfolio by the investment presented at Eq.15.

$$\rho = \sqrt{\frac{\sum_{i=1}^{n}\left(R_i - R_{avg}\right)^2}{n-1}} \tag{15}$$

We then compute drift rate μ by continuously compounding the expected asset return as in Eq.16.

$$\mu = (1 + [Ri]) \tag{16}$$

5. MONTE CARLO SIMULATION FOR MODEL VALIDATION AND FORECASTING

Monte Carlo simulations are used to demonstrate the likelihood of multiple outcomes of the stock price in a process that is difficult to predict owing to random elements. It's a method for calculating how risk and uncertainty affect forecasting and forecasting models (Abonazel, 2018). We follow the approach presented by Ferreira and Santa-Clara (2011) for calculating the sample R-squares for stock price forecasting.

Monte Carlo Simulation is initiated by creating a quantitative equation usually called the transfer equation. The transfer equation reflects the underlying variable that needs to be simulated, in our case we simulate the stock price of a firm. Input parameters and the different factors that influence the simulated outcome and their distributions are defined. Monte Carlo approach is very useful for the simulation of large and random data. The input parameters are initialized appropriately and the simulation proceeds through a series of time-steps. At each step of the simulation the factors influencing the outcome are randomly generated using the assumed distributions and augmented appropriately to the simulated outcome. Running a large enough amount of simulated input data will produce a credible output, given the expected volatility of the inputs.

5.1. The Transition Equation and Model Parameters

The purpose of the transfer equation is to forecast the asset's price behaviour over a period of time. We identify the financial variables that capture the asset behavior over time. We represent the stock price x, a time bound variable in the transition equation as a dependent variable to simulate the asset behavior over time. The variation of the stock price for each time unit may be derived from At, the stock returns. The stock returns At has been modelled using the Brownian Motion in the Merton model. A simple model assuming log normal distribution for the stock returns has been shown in equations 17 and 18.

$$xt = xt{-}1 * eAt \tag{17}$$

$$dAt = \mu AAtdt + \sigma AAtdWt \quad (18)$$

The drift μA is the expected cont in uousl y co mpoun ded return on A assum in g ze ro payout . σA i s th e volatility of the as set return (Kenc and Cevik, 2021). dWt represents the standard Wiener Process. The drift and volatility are assumed constant over the entire life ti me of the firm. Returns has been observed to have a log normal distribution. For a timeperiod T the log returns rT may be represented using the equation 19.

$$rT = ln(At+T) - ln(At) = \beta = \frac{Cov\left(R_i, R_m\right)}{Var\left(R_m\right)} \quad (19)$$

where the $\epsilon t+T$ contributed by the We iner process is a standard normal distributio n. The log retur ns rT is no rm ally distributed. The momen ts of the log returns are provided in equations 20 and 21 (Wang and Suo, 2006).

$[rt] = {}_{\mu A}(20)$

$V[rt] = (\sigma 2)(21)$

The likelihood of return at time i, $[ri, ([rt], V[rt])]$ is given by equation 22

$$[ri, \theta(E[_{rt}], V[_{rt}])] = \left(\mu_A - \frac{\sigma_A^2}{2}\right)T + \sigma_A\sqrt{T_{\epsilon_{t-T}}} \quad (22)$$

Assumin g that the returns are independent of each othe r the jo in t likelih oo d of a series of returns for n da ys $[r1, r2 .. rn, \theta r]$ i s determ ined as the product of the independent likelihood functions $L[ri]$ over n days (Equation 23), where θr represents the par a mete r lis t $(E[r_{1}], E[r2]....E[rn], V[r1, V[r2...V[rn])$.

Figure 1. Monte Carlo simulation results for Tesla stock price

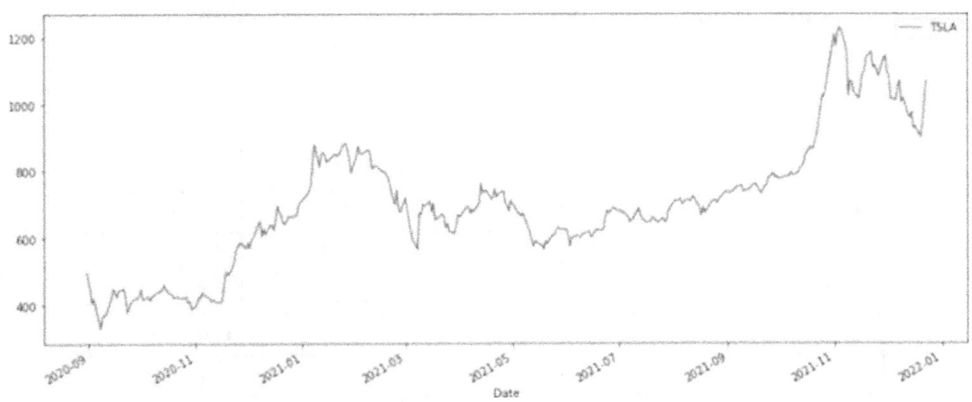

$$([r1, r2.. rn, \theta r]) = \frac{1}{\sqrt{2\pi V[r_i]}} e^{\left(-\frac{r_i - E[r_i]^2}{2V[r_i]}\right)} \quad (23)$$

Table 2. Estimating asset values and asset volatility

Date	Equity	Liabilities	Log Risk Free Rate	Book Asset	Asset Log Returns	Asset Iterate	Asset Iterate Log Return
T	E($)	L($)	Rf	A_k($)	R_K	A_{k+1}($)	R_{k+1}
2020-09-01	296.380	170.328	1.00%	466.708	NA	464.662	NA
2020-09-01	297.459	170.328	1.00%	467.788	0.23%	465.748	0.23%
2020-09-01	308.769	170.328	1.00%	479.098	2.41%	477.109	2.43%
2020-09-01	307.019	170.328	1.00%	477.348	-0.36%	475.352	-0.36%
.	.	.	.		.	.	.
.	.	.	.		.	.	.
.	.	.	.		.	.	.
2021-08-28	780.000	362.865	0.60%	1142.864	12.7%	1140.39	-0.34%
2021-08-29	887.059	362.865	0.60%	1249.924	9.36%	1247.60	4.26%
2021-08-30	734.700	362.865	0.60%	1097.564	-12.1%	1094.99	2.48%
2021-08-31	748.960	362.865	0.60%	1111.824	1.29%	1109.29	0.28%
		The annualized asset volatility				0.44%	0.43%

The natural log of the likelihood function L is optimized in MLE since the magnitude of the actual joint likelihood is very less. The final objective function to be maximized in MLE is provided in equation 24.

$$\ln(L[r1, r2..\, rn, \theta r\,]) = \prod_{i=1}^{n} \frac{1}{\sqrt{2\pi V\left[r_i\right]}} e^{\left(-\frac{r_i - E\left[r_i\right]^{2}}{2V\left[r_i\right]}\right)} \tag{24}$$

The final estimates of the models of the input parameters are those which optimize the objective function in equation 24. In order to finetune the model parameters, we have minimized the root mean squared

Table 3. All iterations of assets

	A0	A1	A2	A3	A4	A5	A6
1	467.7881	465.7065	465.7488	465.7480	465.7480	465.7480	465.7480
2	479.0981	477.0726	477.1101	477.1094	477.1094	477.1094	477.1094
3	477.3481	475.3145	475.3527	475.3520	475.3520	475.3520	475.3520
4	482.5381	480.5280	480.5641	480.5634	480.5635	480.5635	480.5635
5	483.2182	481.2110	481.2469	481.2462	481.2462	481.2462	481.2462
...	...	...	...	...	...	...	...
361	1013.434	1010.4987	1010.5831	1010.5814	1010.5815	1010.5815	1010.5815
362	1142.864	1140.3547	1140.3988	1140.3980	1140.3980	1140.3980	1140.3804
363	1249.924	1247.5781	1247.6041	1247.6036	1247.6036	1247.6036	1247.6036
364	1097.564	1094.9442	1094.9996	1094.9985	1094.9985	1094.9985	1094.9985
365	1111.824	1109.2425	1109.2941	1109.2931	1109.2931	1109.2931	1109.2931

Figure 2. Sum of squared difference error

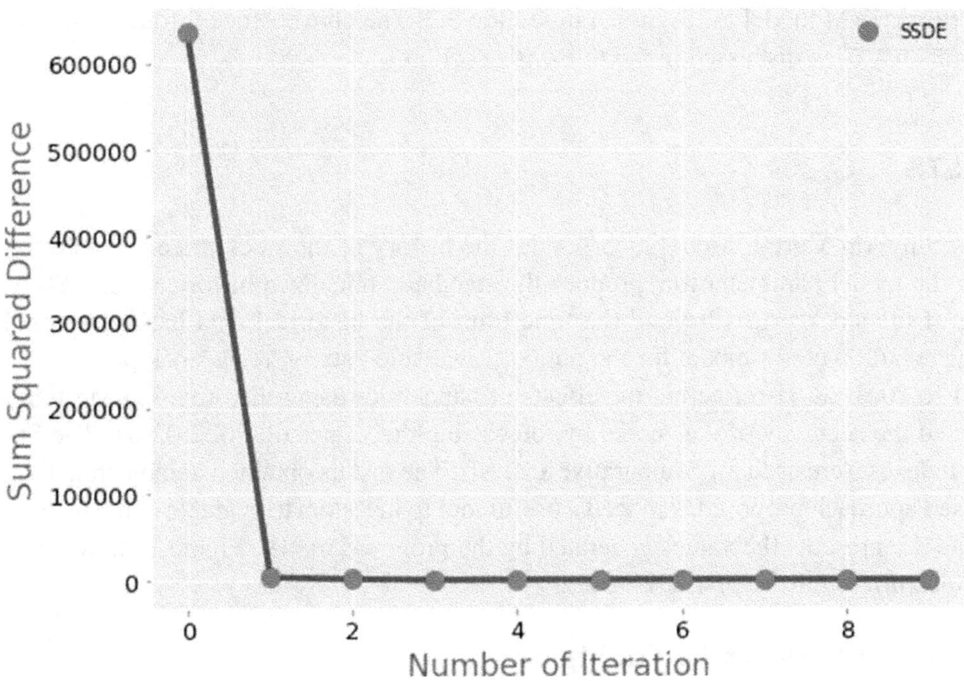

Figure 3. Annualized volatility

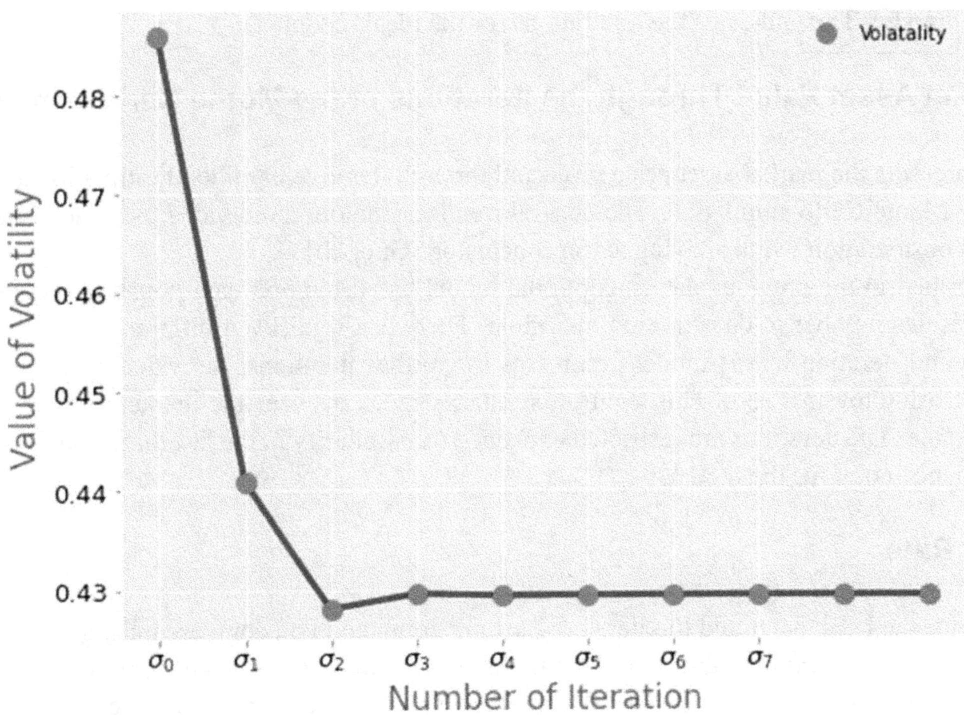

error of the volatility estimated by the MLE approach and the volatility calculated from the simulated data using the AHVM model as discussed in section 3.2. The convergence through multiple iterations and the results has been discussed in the following section.

6. RESULTS

The proposed hybrid Merton Model incorporates the history of the stock price rate into the model by fine-tuning the model parameter to reproduce the standard annualized historical volatility values. The forecasting of the stock prices beyond the time limit of the historical data has been possible in real time. We have built a credit model for the publicly available data of Tesla stock prices for a period of 2020-09-01 to 2021-08-31 reflecting the effects of pandemics using the proposed Merton Model. We have validated the accuracy of our model by forecasting the values till 2022-02-01. The Standard and Poor's 500 indexes were used for comparative analysis. The results obtained demonstrate that the hybrid Merton-based approach proposed is indeed a useful tool to investors to evaluate company assets and net worth. Table 2 represents the values generated by the proposed model. Figure 1 shows the forecast of the Tesla stock prices for the year 2021-2022.

6.1. Annualized Historical Volatility

From Table 2 we may observe that the derived book asset value is 0.44% and the simulated asset value is 0.43%. A difference of 0.01% was observed in the market value of the assets. Figure 3 marks the volatility for each iteration. A significant dip in the first and the 2nd iteration is observed and this stabilizes over the 2nd to the end. The minimal difference between the last three iterations showcases the convergence point of the model. This indicates the 6 iterations for the ideal model.

6.2. Market Asset Value Through the Iterations of the Monte Carlo Simulation

Table 3 represents the market asset price projected through iterative likelihood estimation and the corresponding Monte Carlo simulation. The general trend for the observed value over the iterations was taken into consideration while arriving at the conclusion (Guo, 2017).

As described in the previous data section, the model has taken 365 data points into consideration which represents number of days in the time frame. There is a significant difference between the first and the second iteration but as model progresses for further iterations, the value stabilizes with the difference closing towards zero. This signifies similarity index between the market asset value and the simulated value. The iterations are restricted to 6 since the similarity in the last three columns indicates the convergence point for the model.

6.3. Drift Rate

The return for the book asset and the iterated asset are computed and compared using their respective estimation of Risk-neutral probability of default. Table 4 showcases the values provided by the CAPM model in the first two steps. The book asset and the iterated asset value are showcased in Table 5 to present the values provided by the step third to set fifth by the CAPM model. We consider risk-free as-

Table 4. Comparing the book asset and the asset iterate of the stock market (SP 500)

	Assets ($)				Returns (%)			Excess Returns (%)		
Date	Risk Free Rate	S&P 500	Book Asset	Asset Iterate	S&P 500	Book Asset	Asset Iterate	S&P 500	Book Asset	Asset Iterate
2020-09-01	1.00%	2643.8	466.70	464.66		NaN			NaN	
2020-09-02	1.00%	2640.0	467.78	465.74	-0.14%	0.23%	-0.23%	-1.14%	-0.76%	-0.76%
2020-09-03	1.00%	2681.0	479.09	477.10	1.55%	2.41%	2.43%	0.55%	1.41%	1.43%
2020-09-04	1.00%	2704.1	477.34	475.35	0.85%	-0.36%	-0.36%	-0.14%	-1.36%	-1.36%
2020-09-05	1.00%	2706.5	482.21	480.56	0.08%	1.08%	1.09%	-0.91%	0.08%	0.09%
.	.	.	.	.	.	.	.	.	.	.
.	.	.	.	.	.	.	.	.	.	.
.	.	.	.	.	.	.	.	.	.	.
2021-08-29	0.60%	3225.5	1013.4	1010.5	-1.77%	0.97%	-2.37%	-2.37%	0.37%	0.37%
2021-08-30	0.60%	3248.9	1142.8	1140.3	0.70%	12.77%	-0.12%	0.12%	12.1%	12.24%
2020-08-31	0.60%	329.59	1249.9	1247.6	1.49%	9.36%	0.89%	0.89%	8.76%	8.80%
2020-02-05	0.60%	3334.6	1097.5	1094.9	1.12%	-12.1%	0.52%	0.52%	-12.7%	-12.8%
2020-02-06	0.60%	3345.7	1111.8	1109.2	0.30%	1.29%	0.26%	-0.26%	0.69%	0.70%

Table 5. Capital asset pricing model

At Maturity (2021-08-31)	Average Market Risk Premium	Beta (i)	Expected Asset Return (E[Ri])	Drift Rate (DR)
Book asset	0.2686	0.302830	0.87355	0.083748
Asset iterate	0.2686	0.372477	0.106066	0.1008009

Table 6. Probability of default using drift rate

Sr.No.	At Maturity (2021-08-31)	Book Asset	Asset Iterate
1	Debt (L)	362.865	362.865
2	Asset (A)	1111.82	1109.29
3	*Volatility* (σA)	0.44%	0.43%
4	Drift rate (µA)	8.37%	10.08%
Actual Probability of default (APD)		0.54%	0.49%

Table 7. Probability of default using risk-free rate

Sr.No.	At Maturity (2021-08-31)	Book Asset	Asset Iterate
1	Debt (L)	362.865	362.865
2	Asset (A)	1111.82	1109.29
3	*Volatility* (σA)	0.44%	0.43%
4	Drift rate (μA)	0.60%	0.60%
Actual Probability of default (APD)		0.89%	0.81%

Figure 4. Default probability against drift rate

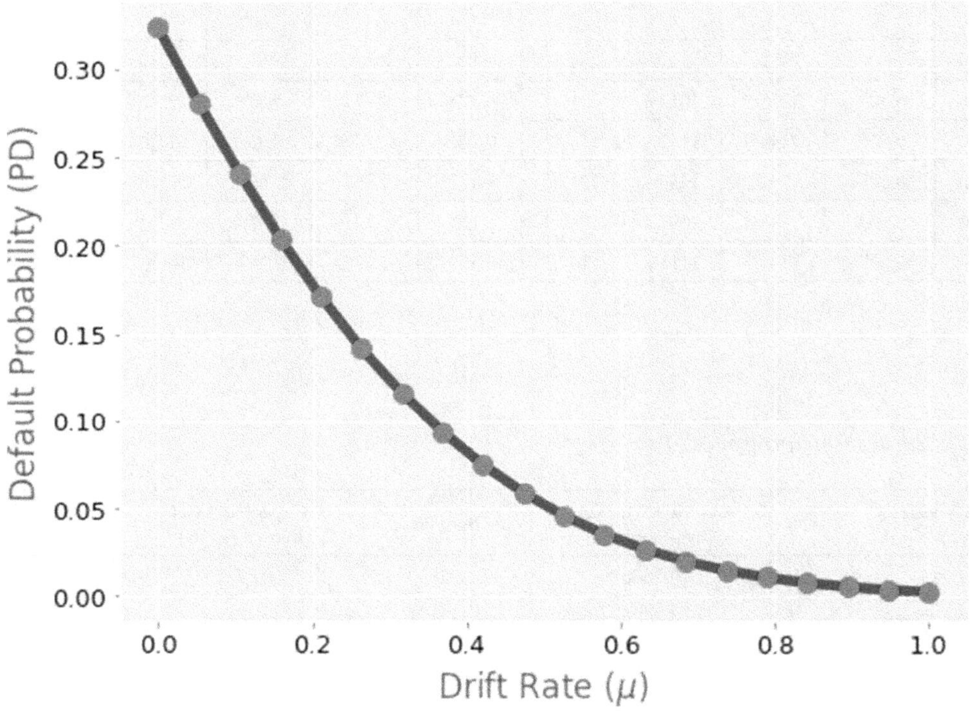

set as a predetermined future return and almost minimal compared value as defined by Van Binsbergen, Diamond and Grotteria (2022). Risk-free commodities have weak rates of return because shareholders do not need to be rewarded for taking a chance because they are safe. Risk-free assets are insured for monetary losses and not against purchasing power losses. Risk-free assets may be vulnerable to reinvestment risk in the long run. When an investor makes a purchase, the expected return is determined based on the time factor of the asset holding. The fact that actual and predicted returns can differ dramatically demonstrates risk. Because market volatility is difficult to predict, unknown parts of future returns are considered risk. We summarize the increased risk as a high likelihood of large fluctuations, which can result in significant profits or losses, depending on the return.

6.4. Default Probability

The values for the rate of drift are presented in this section. Computation of the probability of the book asset and iterated assets is showcased. Table 6 represents the default probability values. The inference from the result can be derived as follows: the company asset value is very high. This signifies the bare minimum risk associated with the repayment of the liable money. The proposed AHVM model is preferred due to its cross-validated iterative nature which provides stability for the derived values.
6.5. Risk Neutral Probability
The risk factor is analyzed after constructing the equation and it is concluded in the assumptions. This will help to provide the neutral risk of the model. Table 7 represents the risk-neutral probability. Here we are keeping all the other parameters constant and plot default probability against drift rate in Figure 4. Here we should also take into consideration the drift rate and risk free rate from Table 6 and Table 7 for comparison. When we compare these two values we come to understand that the Risk-neutral probability of default is the upper threshold for Actual Probability of default. This helps to analyze the company for greater returns instead of holding risk free rates for an underlying asset at a risk.

7. FUTURE FOCUS

We have used a hybrid Merton Model and its simulation through Monte Carlo approach to forecast the stock price of Tesla successfully. The Tesla stock price shows major variations in prices based on its market decisions or public declarations during the months of January, February and March, which are captured successfully using our model. We plan to study the performance of a Jump Diffusion model. We could compare it with the GARCH model (Heston and Nandi, 2000) which accounts for a variable volatility. With the complexity of the model the computational complexity is bound to increase. We would like to analyse if the other models provide significant prediction accuracy during a time when the market is volatile due to the pandemic. We are studying the practical implementation of the Jump Diffusion model and GARCH model for Tesla Stock price. We also would like to extend the study with the real time stock prices of other firms.

8. CONCLUSION

In this paper, we proposed a hybrid approach for evaluating the Tesla company assets using the Merton model's iterative approach to understand the asset valuation of the company. The annualized historical volatility model (AHVM) proposed as an extension to the Merton model to fine tune the model parameters to reproduce the real-time data. The purpose of the proposed models is to add advantage over the traditional approach. The result observed the convergence point at the sixth iteration. The market value of the company calculated over the iterations derived the default probability at maturity. The analysis derived the convergence point after six iterations. The overestimated value of the default probability derived by risk neutral probability estimates the difference of 0.32%. The investors will consider charge higher than the risk free rate for buying risky asset since the Figure 4 plot between default probability and drift rate is inverse proportional and this concludes the explanation for the default probability value being greater than the risk neutral probability as the drift rate is always higher than the risk free rate.

REFERENCES

Abonazel, M. R. (2018). A practical guide for creating monte carlo simulation studies using r. International Journal of Mathematics and Computer Science, 4, 18–33.

Afik, Z., Arad, O., & Galil, K. (2016). Using merton model for default prediction: An empirical assessment of selected alternatives. Journal of Empirical Finance, 35, 43–67. doi:10.1016/j.jempfin.2015.09.004

Altman, E. I., & Saunders, A. (1997). Credit risk measurement: Developments over the last 20 years. Journal of Banking & Finance, 21(11-12), 1721–1742. doi:10.1016/S0378-4266(97)00036-8

Andersen, T. G., & Sørensen, B. E. (1996). Gmm estimation of a stochastic volatility model: A monte carlo study. Journal of Business amp. Economie & Statistique, 14, 328–352.

Angelini, E. (2012). Credit default swaps (cds) and their role in the credit risk market. International Journal of Academic Research in Business & Social Sciences, 2, 584.

Ashbaugh-Skaife, H., Collins, D. W., & LaFond, R. (2006). The effects of corporate governance on firms' credit ratings. Journal of Accounting and Economics, 42(1-2), 203–243. doi:10.1016/j.jacceco.2006.02.003

Ayadi, R., & Behr, P. (2009). On the necessity to regulate credit derivatives markets. Journal of Banking Regulation, 10(3), 179–201. doi:10.1057/jbr.2009.3

Benos, A., & Papanastasopoulos, G. (2007). Extending the merton model: A hybrid approach to assessing credit quality. Mathematical and Computer Modelling, 46(1-2), 47–68. doi:10.1016/j.mcm.2006.12.012

Bhatore, S., Mohan, L., & Reddy, Y. R. (2020). Machine learning techniques for credit risk evaluation: A systematic literature review. Journal of Banking and Financial Technology, 4(1), 111–138. doi:10.100742786-020-00020-3

Derbali, A., & Jamel, L. (2019). Dependence of default probability and recovery rate in structural credit risk models: Case of greek banks. Journal of the Knowledge Economy, 10(2), 711–733. doi:10.100713132-017-0473-1

Duffie, D., & Singleton, K. J. (2012). Credit risk: pricing, measurement, and management. Princeton university press. doi:10.2307/j.ctv30pnvpg

Džaja, J., & Aljinović, Z. (2013). Testing capm model on the emerging markets of the central and south-eastern europe. Croatian Operational Research Review, 4, 164–175.

Ekström, J.B., & Sjögren, O. (2014). Implementation of heston nandi garch model on omxs30. Academic Press.

Engle, R. F. (1982). Autoregressive conditional heteroscedasticity with estimates of the variance of united kingdom inflation. Econometrica, 50(4), 987–1007. doi:10.2307/1912773

Ferreira, M. A., & Santa-Clara, P. (2011). Forecasting stock market returns: The sum of the parts is more than the whole. Journal of Financial Economics, 100(3), 514–537. doi:10.1016/j.jfineco.2011.02.003

Francq, C., & Zakoian, J. M. (2004). Maximum likelihood estimation of pure garch and arma-garch processes. Bernoulli, 10(4), 605–637. doi:10.3150/bj/1093265632

Gabaix, X., Gopikrishnan, P., Plerou, V., & Stanley, E. (2007). A unified econophysics explanation for the power-law exponents of stock market activity. Physica A, 382(1), 81–88. doi:10.1016/j.physa.2007.02.030

Guo, Z. (2017). Option pricing under the merton model of the short rate in subdiffusive brownian motion regime. Journal of Statistical Computation and Simulation, 87(3), 519–529. doi:10.1080/00949655.2016.1218880

Harding, D. (2013). The performance of garch option pricing models – an empirical study on Swedish omxs30 call options. http: //hj.diva-portal.org/smash/get/diva2:637395/FULLTEXT01.pdf

Harris, T. (2013). Quantitative credit risk assessment using support vector machines: Broad versus narrow default definitions. Expert Systems with Applications, 40(11), 4404–4413. doi:10.1016/j.eswa.2013.01.044

Heston, S.L., & Nandi, S. (2000). A closed-form garch option valuation model. The Review of Financial Studies, 13(3), 585-625.

Hisakado, M., & Mori, S. (2021). Parameter estimation of default portfolios using the merton model and phase transition. Physica A, 563, 125435. doi:10.1016/j.physa.2020.125435

Huang, X., Liu, X., & Ren, Y. (2018). Enterprise credit risk evaluation based on neural network algorithm. Cognitive Systems Research, 52, 317–324.

Jackwerth, J. C., & Rubinstein, M. (1996). Recovering probability distributions from option prices. The Journal of Finance, 51(5), 1611–1631. doi:10.1111/j.1540-6261.1996.tb05219.x

Jiménez, G., & Saurina, J. (2004). Collateral, type of lender and relationship banking as determinants of credit risk. Journal of Banking & Finance, 28(9), 2191–2212. doi:10.1016/j.jbankfin.2003.09.002

Karoui, N. E., Jeanblanc-Picquè, M., & Shreve, S. E. (1998). Robustness of the black and scholes formula. Mathematical Finance, 8(2), 93–126. doi:10.1111/1467-9965.00047

Kenc, T., & Cevik, E. I. (2021). Estimating volatility clustering and variance risk premium effects on bank default indicators. Review of Quantitative Finance and Accounting, 57(4), 1373–1392. doi:10.100711156-021-00981-6

Lee, S. S. (2012). Jumps and information flow in financial markets. Review of Financial Studies, 25(2), 439–479. doi:10.1093/rfs/hhr084

Li, K. L., & Wong, H. Y. (2008). Structural models of corporate bond pricing with maximum likelihood estimation. Journal of Empirical Finance, 15(4), 751–777. doi:10.1016/j.jempfin.2008.01.001

Liao, S. L., & Huang, H. H. (2005). Pricing black–scholes options with correlated interest rate risk and credit risk: An extension. Quantitative Finance, 5(5), 443–457. doi:10.1080/14697680500362718

Liu, Q., Li, Q., Zhu, Z., Ye, T., & Ma, X. (2021). Inspecting the process of bank credit rating via visual analytics. In 2021 IEEE Visualization Conference (VIS). IEEE. doi:10.1109/VIS49827.2021.9623312

Murthy, S. (2011). Market-implied risk-neutral probabilities, actual probabilities, credit risk and news. The Journal of Economic Perspectives, 18, 3–24.

Rajini, N. S., Ramamoorthy, S., Rammohan, S. R., Rajakumar, P., & Niveditha, V. (2020). Reliability of cloud services provided to non-banking financial institutions. International Journal of Control and Automat*ion, 13, 165–172165.*

Ronn, E. I., & Verma, A. K. (1986). Pricing risk-adjusted deposit insurance: An option-based model. The Journal of Finance, 41(4), 871–895. d*oi:10.1111/j.1540-6261*.1986.tb04554.x

Schaefer, S. M., & Strebulaev, I. A. (2008). Structural models of credit risk are useful: Evidence from hedge ratios on corporate bonds. Journal of Financial Economics, 90(1), *1–19. doi:10.1016/j.jfineco.*2007.10.006

ShokrollahiF. (2018). Pricing european option with the sh*ort rate under subdiffusive fractional brownian motion regime. arXiv:1805.00792.*

Uthayakumar, J., Vengattaraman, T., & Dhavachelvan, P. (2020). Swarm intelligence based classification rule induction (cri) framework for qualitative and quantitative approach: An application of bankruptcy prediction and credit risk analysis. Journal of King Saud University-*Computer and Information Sciences, 32(6), 647–657. doi:10.1016/j.*jks*u*ci.2017.10.007

Van Binsbergen, J. H., Diamond, W. F., & Grotteria, M. (2022). Risk-free interest rates. Journal of Financial Economic*s, 143(1), 1–29. doi:10.1016/j.jfin*eco.2021.06.012

Wang, W., & Suo, W. (2006). Assessing default probabil*ities from structural credit risk models. S&P Global Market Intell*igence Research Paper Series.

Yusof, N. M., Alias, I. Q., Kassim, A. J. M., & Zaidi, F. L. N. M. (2021). Determining the credit score and credit rating of firms using the combination of kmv-merton model and financial ratios. Science and Technology *Indonesia, 6(3), 105–112. doi:10.*26554ti.2021.6.3.105-112

ZhangT. Y. (2018). Predicting credit de*fault swap (cds) returns with machine learning. Available at SSRN* 3152143.

Chapter 6
Information Retrieval System on the Web:
Challenges and Issues

V. Sathiyamoorthi
https://orcid.org/0000-0002-7012-3941
Government Polytechnic College, Dharmapuri, India

ABSTRACT

Many significant advancements in web technology have resulted in the fast expansion of the world wide web (WWW) and web development. WWW employs a variety of technologies to improve communication with internet users, yet user frustrations exist. Adding a new resource and distributing network traffic over one or more resources is one possible solution to this problem. Web caching is a popular strategy for reducing network traffic by storing websites closer to the client site. A proxy server is in charge of web caching, which operates as a middleman between the web server and the web client, reducing latency in page retrieval. This proxy-based web caching solution may be enhanced further to regulate web performance. As a result, this chapter focuses on how to improve the proxy-based web caching system. It optimises the speed of the proxy-based web caching system using web usage mining (WUM).

INTRODUCTION

Many significant advancements in Web technology have resulted in the fast expansion of the World Wide Web (WWW) and web development. WWW employs a variety of technologies to improve communication with Internet users, yet user frustrations exist. Adding a new resource and distributing network traffic over one or more resources is one possible solution to this problem. Web caching is a popular strategy for reducing network traffic by storing websites closer to the client site (Pallis et al 2008). A proxy server is in charge of web caching, which operates as a middleman between the Web server and the web client, reducing latency in page retrieval. This proxy-based web caching solution may be enhanced further to regulate web performance. As a result, this chapter focuses on how to improve the

DOI: 10.4018/979-8-3693-1722-8.ch006

proxy-based web caching system. It optimises the speed of the proxy-based web caching system using Web Usage Mining (WUM).

BACKGROUND

Web traffic and network difficulties are the main concerns in the online world as it continues to grow in both size and popularity. On many websites and network links, there are merciless overloads as a result of the sustained growth in demand for items on the Internet. Internet consumers lack the patience to wait even a few seconds for a desired webpage to download. Techniques for reducing web traffic are required to visit websites effectively on the current network infrastructure. The performance of the web is influenced by a wide range of factors, including server or network congestion and differences in network connectivity distance between nodes. Unanticipated market or service needs are to blame for this. As a result, online caching and web pre-fetching strategies lessen the web latency that we often experience on the Internet.

Additionally, the WWW is a dynamic system made up of interconnected items including sounds, photos, videos, and other media. Here, online caching and pre-fetching are identified as a crucial tactic to improve the functionality of web-based systems. In recent years, the WWW has become the most popular platform for people to share information globally. As a result, the Internet and web server experience more network traffic. Web traffic thus becomes one of the main factors slowing down network performance.

The increased network traffic caused by the transmission of web objects over the Internet reduces available bandwidth for competing requests and lengthens the access times for website visitors. Popular online items should be kept close to the user so that they may be accessed in order to reduce such access delays. As a result, the proxy-based pre-fetching method has been employed. As a result, online caching and web pre-fetching have emerged as crucial study areas to help end users experience less perceptible response latency (Sathiyamoorthi & Murali Bhaskaran 2010a).

Additionally, concerns and challenges that exist and emerge in the following dimensions are a major factor in the importance of web caching research (Wessels & Duane 2001): High bandwidth needs; high bandwidth costs; non-uniform bandwidth; non-uniform latencies across networks; increase in network distances

Web pre-fetching and web caching are hence techniques required to improve web speed (Sathiyamoorthi & Murali Bhaskaran 2013). Data mining techniques are frequently used to further develop online applications (Bamshad 2007). Web mining is the broad term for these methods. The sections that follow give an overview of some of the discovered methods.

DATA MINING

The process of collecting non-trivial, implicit, previously undiscovered, and possibly useful information from the raw data included in a big database is known as data mining (DM), sometimes known as knowledge discovery in databases (KDD). To increase the value of the current information system, data mining techniques may be used on a variety of data sources. The use of data mining technologies on high performance client and server systems allows for the analysis of huge databases needed to provide extremely trustworthy findings. Additionally, it is mentioned that relational database engines may be connected to data mining techniques (Jiawei et al., 2006).

Data mining is different from traditional database retrieval in that it extracts concealed knowledge or information that isn't explicitly available in databases, whereas database retrieval extracts the data that is explicitly available in databases. Data mining might also be considered a subset of artificial intelligence due to the system's incorporation of some level of intelligence; as a result, data mining could be thought of as an intelligent database manipulation system. Data mining is an interdisciplinary area that integrates ideas from several fields, such as statistics, neural networks, and machine learning, in the process of knowledge discovery, according to Dunham et al. (2006).

Basic Steps in Data Mining

It is obvious that data mining may be seen as a key phase in the process of knowledge discovery. It is divided into several stages, including preprocessing, data mining, pattern extraction, pattern evaluation, and knowledge presentation.

The data is designed to be in a format appropriate for additional data mining activities during the data pretreatment stage. Data cleaning eliminates erroneous, inaccurate, and irrelevant data from the data sources. Data integration is used to combine data from those sources since the input database may be made up of information that comes from a variety of sources. Data mining jobs that use intelligent techniques and extract knowledge are identified at this phase. In the pattern evaluation step, the utility of the learned information or patterns is assessed. The knowledge presentation phase, which is the final stage in the KDD process, involves presenting the knowledge that has been discovered in a way that is user-friendly and intelligible (Jiawei et al. 2006).

Knowledge Types That Can Be Mined

According to Jiawei et al. (2006) and Dunham et al. (2006), a potent new technique is the extraction of latent predictive information from sizable databases. Data mining assists corporate organizations and the research sector by focusing on the most crucial data in their databases. Utilizing data mining techniques, users may make proactive, knowledge-driven decisions by predicting future trends and behaviors. According to Jiawei et al. (2006), data mining systems may be categorized based on the information below.

- Kinds of databases to be mined
- Kinds of knowledge to be discovered,
- Kinds of techniques utilized,
- Kinds of applications adapted.

Data mining tasks may often be divided into two categories: descriptive and predictive (Jiawei et al. 2006). Descriptive data mining tasks describe or characterise the items that are present in the input database. Tasks that use inference on input data to uncover hidden information and generate intriguing predictions are known as predictive data mining tasks. The list below includes a few data mining jobs along with their classifications.

- Classification [Predictive]

- Clustering [Descriptive]
- Association Rule Mining [Descriptive]
- Sequential Pattern Discovery [Descriptive]
- Regression [Predictive]
- Deviation Detection [Predictive]

Data Mining Techniques

Data mining is an interdisciplinary area that draws on methods and algorithms from several disciplines, including artificial intelligence, machine learning, statistics, neural networks, and database technology. According to Jiawei et al. (2006), the following are the approaches that are most frequently employed to help with data mining tasks:

- **Artificial Neural Networks (ANN):** An input, hidden, and output layer structure that is learned during training and has characteristics of a biological neural network makes up a non-linear predictive model.
- **Decision Tree:** A tree structure, which consists of nodes and branches, symbolizes a series of choices. In a decision tree, a node symbolizes the precondition and result branches. These choices produce the categorization rules for a dataset. Classification and regression trees are included in a specific decision tree approach.
- **Genetic Algorithm (GA):** In a design-based conception of evolution, this evolutionary optimization approach makes use of operators including genetic combination, mutation, and natural selection. This is applicable to optimization issues when the target function is either maximized or minimized.
- **Nearest Neighbor Method:** a method that groups records in a dataset according to the classes of 'k' records that resemble the dataset's history dataset the most. The K-Nearest Neighbor (KNN) approach is another name for it.
- **Rule Induction:** This is the dataset's handy if-then rule extraction.

There are several data mining techniques available, including classification, prediction, association rule mining, trend analysis, etc., so you may pick the best one for your application. An overview of various data mining approaches is given in the following sections. Additionally, it explores web caching and web pre-fetching to boost a web-based system's speed.

Association Rule Mining

According to Jiawei et al. (2006), an association rule is a collection of data attributes that are statistically related to one another. The association rule mining problem is described as follows: provided a database of associated transactions, a minimal support value, and a confidence value, find all association rules with confidence and support greater than the provided threshold. In general, it creates a dependence rule that predicts the occurrence of one thing based on the occurrences of other things.

X->Y is the format of an association rule, where X and Y represent the antecedent and consequent, respectively. There are two techniques for finding common elements and creating rules from them. One of these measures is confidence, defined as the prior probability of X and Y, Pr(X and Y), and the other is support, defined as the conditional probability of Y given X, Pr(Y|X), according to Jiawei et al. (2006). It may be classified as either a single dimensional association rule or a multidimensional association rule, depending on how many predicates it contains (Jiawei et al. 2006). It might be improved to work more efficiently in the linked disciplines of genetic analysis, internet commerce, and others.

Classification

The task at hand is to create a model that identifies and categorizes data classes for an object. This is used to predict the class of an object when class label information is lacking (Jiawei et al. 2006). It illustrates how examples may be used to learn. The initial step, sometimes referred to as the training phase, is when a model is built using the characteristics included in the training data. This model is then used to predict class labels for the testing data when class label information is not given. Using a test set, the model's precision is assessed. It is common practice to separate the supplied data set into training and test sets, with the training set being used to develop the model.

Typical representations of categorization models are decision trees. A decision tree resembles a flowchart in that each node represents a test on an attribute value, branches indicate test results, and tree leaves correspond to real classes. The Bayesian classification method, if-then rules, neural networks, and K-nearest neighbor are further common representation strategies (Jiawei et al. 2006). Additionally, called the guided learning process. The training dataset used to build the model has an impact on prediction accuracy.

Prediction

Data mining is an analytical method that searches through data for recurring patterns or systematic links between variables. The discovered patterns are then used to test the conclusions by being applied to fresh subsets of data. According to (Jiawei et al. 2006), predictive data mining is the most popular and has the most immediate business applications. Three steps make up the predictive data mining process:

- Data investigation,
- model development, and
- deployment

Data cleansing, data transformations, record selection, and feature selection are examples of data preparation techniques that may be used before doing data exploration. The selection of features is one of the most significant steps in the exploration process. If the datasets contain a large number of variables, it is described as restricting the number of variables by carrying out certain preparatory feature selection techniques to a tolerable range. Then, to further explore exploratory investigations, a straightforward set of straightforward predictors for a regression model is used. The most often used graphical and statistical method is exploratory data analysis. The model building and validation process includes phases where many models are taken into account and the best one is chosen based on expected performance. The most effective model from the previous step is chosen for deployment, which comprises using it to provide predictions or estimations of the expected outcome using new data.

Clustering

In their study, Dunham et al (2006) emphasize that clustering is the act of separating given things into groups of comparable objects based on some resemblance. It is often referred to as the unsupervised learning process. It is often described as follows: Find clusters so that items inside the clusters are extremely similar to one another and unlike to objects in other clusters given a set of data objects, each with a set of characteristics and a similarity measure. Depending on the type of characteristics included in distance computation, several similarity measures can be used. For example, if the qualities are continuous in nature, the determined distance is a Euclidean distance. Clustering's ultimate objective is to divide items into k-subsets known as clusters. In most cases, subsets do not cross, and the sum of their parts equals the total set of data. Fewer clusters must necessarily sacrifice some fine features in order to achieve simplicity or reduction. Using clustering, numerous data items are organized into fewer groups. Some of the common clustering techniques are K-Means and K-Medoids (Jiawei et al. 2006).

WEB MINING

Today's Internet environment relies heavily on WWW for information retrieval and exchange. As a result, the WWW grows into a massive databank. Because of this, it is challenging for data analysts or end users to analyse all the data and find any meaningful information. Data mining may be used for information discovery on the web to solve these problems. Web mining is used to find knowledge on the web. Web content mining (WCM), web structure mining (WSM), and web log mining (WLM) or web use mining (WUM) are the three main categories under which web mining is often categorised (Srivastava et al. 2000; Zaiane 2000).

According to Kosala and Blockeel (2000), web content mining is the branch of web mining that focuses on the unprocessed data included on webpages. Textual information found on websites makes up the majority of the data source. Web page classification and ranking are the foundations of mining. Web structure mining is a web mining activity that focuses on website structure. The data source comprises of structural data found in hyperlinked webpages. Website classification based on links, rating of websites based on content and structure, and reverse engineering of website models are all included in the mining. Another web mining activity known as Web Usage Mining (WUM) discusses information discovery from web server log files. When a user sees a webpage, a raw text file is typically saved in the web server as the source data. Either the Common Log Format (CLF) or the Extended Common Log Format (ECLF) may be used to describe it. User modelling, adaptable websites, and Web personalization are all included. The present proxy-based web caching system is the main topic of this chapter's discussion of WUM. An overview of WUM and its use in a Web-based information retrieval and management system is provided in the next section.

WEB USAGE MINING

According to Srivastava et al. (2000), Mobasher et al. (2002), Cyrus et al. (1997), and Feng et al. (2009), research on online use mining began in the late 1990s. Web log mining, as the practice is also known, is based on information found in the web log files created by web servers. Before using data mining techniques, web log files must undergo some preparation procedures because they are raw text files (Sathiyamoorthi & Murali Bhaskaran 2011a). The fundamental steps of WUM are as follows:

- Data gathering
- Data preparation
- Extracting Patterns
- Visualization and Analysis of Patterns
- Utilizing Patterns

Data Sources for Web Usage Mining

Data sources for WUM can be gathered from three distinct places (Srivastva et al 2000).

- ***Server-Level***: It keeps information on the requests made by various clients. It maintains track of users' interests across many websites. The biggest disadvantage is that log files need to be safeguarded since they include some sensitive user data. Additionally, it doesn't have data on cached pages.
- ***Client-Level***: A repository will get information about the user's access from the browser itself. Client-side program that can run on common web browsers or adhoc browsing program are used to do this. The design team must create specialized software and implement it alongside the end users' browsers.
- ***Proxy-level***: The information about user surfing habits is gathered and saved in the proxy server log. It monitors user interest across several websites for a number of people. It is only utilized by users whose requests go via the proxy (Sathiyamoorthi & Murali Bhaskaran 2011b)

The Web log file may be used to acquire the following details:

- Statistical data about web page hits;
- General summary information about user and page access
- The user's location while viewing the website
- Do consumers use browsers to view websites?
- Report depending on page size, kind, and other factors
- How frequently users visit each webpage
- When a web page has been viewed • Who is interested in which pages
- What is the frequency of visit to each website? What pages are being accessed most frequently and recently?

Web mining is highly valued, and as a result, many academics have begun to focus on it in order to improve web utilization. The following research scope and findings help to highlight the relevance of this research endeavor. Facca and Lanzi (2005) and Srivastava et al (2000) provide excellent explanations of web usage mining. Both have characterized it from the standpoint of their respective scientific and commercial groups.

Online customization is a technology that provides tailored online content based on the user's wants or profile. Included in it are an adaptable website (Velasquez et al. 2004; De et al. 2004) and a recommender system discussed (Jaczynski & Trousse 1998; Mobasher et al. 2000). Based on the user's access history, a recommender system produces connections that could interest them. A website that is adaptable will modify itself according to each visitor in order to present personalized content. For E-Commerce applications, personalization is performed by recording previously visited URLs (Pirolli et al 1996).

In certain applications, such as product catalogues for e-commerce, the design of a website—in terms of both content and structure—should be taken into account more than any other aspect. Website designers may employ web use mining to get precise information about user behaviour and utilise it to guide website redesigns. In an adaptable website, the structure of a website is dynamically altered based on user access patterns identified in server logs (Anderson 2002; Perkowitz & Etzioni 1998). Depending on the user access patterns, site enhancement may be accomplished by changing the website's logical structure or physical structure.

User satisfaction is mostly determined by two factors: response speed and performance (Sathiyamoorthi & Murali Bhaskaran 2012). Services like web-based apps, databases, networks, etc. benefit the most from this. Similar characteristics are anticipated of web service consumers. By creating regulations for online caching and network transmission, web log mining may hold the key to understanding the behaviour of web traffic and enhancing performance (Anderson et al. 2002).

Due to quicker page delivery to consumers, web caching offers another opportunity to enhance a website's quality (Podlipnig & Boszormenyi 2003). A sluggish website will generally get fewer visitors. A web caching system can forecast a user's future request by putting it into a cache by using the output of a WUM system. As a result, page retrieval from a website happens more quickly since the user won't have to wait for the page to load from the server. The use of a website by clients is crucial information for retail business marketing. Using a knowledge discovery approach, Alex and Mulvenna (1998) and Srivastava et al. (2000) have addressed how to extract marketing insight from web. The studies and uses of web log mining in web caching and web pre-fetching are presented in the part that follows.

A web-based system's performance is impacted by a variety of variables, such as network connection diversity, actual distances, and network or server congestion brought on by unforeseen demand. The issue of enhancing online response speeds has so been the subject of several research studies. Some academics seek to boost performance by the use of new communication technologies or by expanding the bandwidth. According to Pallis et al. (2008), the Internet has developed from a platform that only delivered static, simple HTML pages to one that now offers more advanced services like e-learning, video conferencing, e-commerce, etc. The following are potential strategies to minimize network traffic (Sathiyamoorthi, 2016):

- Web pre-fetching and
- web caching

When a user accesses a webpage, a method called web caching is employed to decrease what the user perceives as latency. Web pre-fetching is a different technique that involves downloading websites in advance of a user request and caching them on an intermediary server (a proxy server). These approaches might work better together when integrated. As a result, a clustering-based pre-fetching approach has been developed, which pre-fetches web items for groups of users that have similar access behaviors rather than for a single user's interest.

WEB CACHING

As previously said, web caching is a method that is used to store as many webpages as possible in order to increase network speed. Its primary feature is its page replacement strategy. When a new document comes, the replacement policy must make an important choice about whether to replace an old webpage from the cache. In this study, WUM is applied to improve the present web cache page replacement strategy.

The majority of conventional algorithms, such as Least Frequently Used (LFU), Least Recently Used (LRU), and First in First out (FIFO), use basic statistical methods for decision-making, which leads to subpar performance. This suggests that the Greedy-Dual-Size (GDS) algorithm works better when the size of the cache is small. According to the authors of (Martin et al. 1997), SIZE outperforms LFU, LRU, and a number of additional LRU versions in terms of several performance criteria. In their trials, they do not take item frequency into account while making decisions. The authors (Pei and Irani, 1997) talked about how caching algorithms should take into account the cost of the network. They consequently developed the Greedy-Dual-Size-Frequency (GDSF) and GDS policies for online caching.

When we use a single item pre-fetching strategy, most of the cache techniques presented here perform better. As numerous items are pre-fetched using the clustering-based pre-fetching approach, an efficient algorithm that can offer a greater hit rate, lower the number of objects to be pre-fetched, and therefore save bandwidth is required. Web caching systems are categorized according to location: i) browser cache; ii) proxy cache; and iii) server cache.

WEB PRE-FETCHING

Web pre-fetching, also known as pre-loading, is a technique that pre-loads websites into the cache before the actual request for that page comes, as discussed. There are two methods employed, namely short-term and long-term pre-fetching.

- Short-term Pre-fetching: Using the web cache's most recent access history, websites are pre-fetched into the cache during short-term pre-fetching (Chen et al. 2002).
- Long-term Pre-fetching: Using an analysis of the overall access pattern, this approach identifies and pre-fetches URLs with the highest likelihood of being accessed (Lee et al. 2009).

Loon and Bhargavan (1997) introduced a pre-fetching strategy based on user profiles represented by a weighted directed graph with nodes representing Uniform Resource Locators (URL) and edges representing access pathways. The weight of a node reflects the frequency with which URLs are accessed, while the weight of an edge represents the frequency with which URLs are accessed one after the other. Ibrahim and Xu (2000) described a system for anticipating the next user request that employs an artificial neural network. Fan et al. (1999) researched pre-fetching between caching proxies and browsers to improve web latency. This method pre-fetched data using the Prediction by Partial Match (PPM) algorithm. A Top-10 pre-fetching technique was described by Markatos et al. in 1998. The top 10 websites are pre-fetched and cached in their method. Additionally, Padmanabhan and Mogul (1996) introduced a pre-fetching system in which the server estimates the probability that a specific webpage would be viewed and communicates the results to the client.

INTEGRATION OF WEB CACHING AND WEB PRE-FETCHING

(Podlipnig & Boszormenyi 2003; Teng et al 2005; Balamash & Krunz 2004) proposed web caching and web pre-fetching techniques. It is claimed that combining these two strategies will improve performance. Pallis et al. (2008) explain an additional enhancement to typical cache replacement methods employed in the proxy server's cache, which are based on the clustering-based pre-fetching strategy employing dependency graph. The authors of this paper utilized a standard approach to evaluate the performance of a pre-fetching strategy.

Pre-fetching and web caching have frequently been investigated separately as strategies for lowering the latency experienced by consumers while browsing the web. The combination of caching and pre-fetching algorithms has received little attention. The combined impact of caching and pre-fetching on end user latency was researched by Kroeger et al. in 1997. The rule-assisted pre-fetching in web server caching was suggested by Lan et al. in 2000. The technique suggested by Yang et al. (2004) involves mining web logs to create a prediction model, which is subsequently used to expand the well-known GDSF caching strategy.

PROBLEM FORMULATION AND SCOPE OF RESEARCH

A key aspect of Internet technology is the speed of data transport. The user's interest in visiting websites may decline due to their delayed retrieval. The performance of browsing a website is significantly influenced by bandwidth and speed. Web caching and web pre-fetching are used to distribute information effectively. Web caching is a method for keeping lots of websites close to the client so they may be retrieved quickly. Before the actual request is made, web pre-fetching preloads websites into the cache. Users now have considerably faster access to the webpages. Combining these methods will make them more effective. In contrast to web pre-fetching, which uses the geographical locality of online objects (things that are adjacent to each other may be accessed in the near future), web caching uses the temporal locality of web objects (recently accessed items may be retrieved in the near future) (Pallis et al 2008).

In this context, a proxy-based web cache plays a significant role in lowering access latency to webpages. The most popular strategy for enhancing the speed of web-based systems is web caching, whereas web pre-fetching is a narrowly researched area. The pre-fetching method used by currently deployed systems is quite straightforward: all hyperlinked items on the current page are pre-fetched (Wessels & Duane 2001). Therefore, as they can currently influence web speed, web caching technologies need to be improved.

The challenge with pre-fetching is determining which URLs should be pre-fetched and subsequently cached. This is necessitated by the fact that there are many different types of users, each with their own set of preferences. As a result, our study can solve the aforementioned problem by grouping users based on their access habits utilizing a unique method for pre-fetching. The task of entering into the individual's preferences is eliminated due to user grouping. Traditional clustering techniques have issues in the production of cluster prototypes and the similarity measure utilized. Furthermore, most present pre-fetching approaches forecast just one object at a time, which increases network traffic as user numbers grow.

The most frequently visited websites will likely be assigned to each IP address in a cluster together with all requests made from those IP addresses. According to Chen et al. (2003), the popularity of various Web items varies greatly. It is challenging to estimate the popularity threshold as well as to select the popular things early. Pallis et al. (2008) contend that a graph-based strategy would be preferable to cluster the websites. It is driven by the threshold value and relies on association rule mining. The method used by Jyoti et al. (2008) predicts the subsequent page to be accessed using a higher-order Markov model.

Rangarajan et al. (2004) developed a technique for classifying individuals based on their internet access behaviors that involved grouping people and then pre-fetching. They have contrasted the effectiveness of clustering produced by ART1 with K-Means clustering approach in terms of inter-cluster and intra-cluster distances. The results show that ART1 surpasses K-Means-based clusters by having a higher hit rate and a better average distance between and within clusters. They thus concluded that ART1 provides clusters of high quality.

Ramya and Shreedhara (2012) offered a thorough preprocessing methodology and pre-fetching system utilizing ART1, and they also contrasted the performance of the ART1-based clustering strategy with that of traditional K-Means and Self Organization Map clustering techniques. The results show that when there are fewer clusters, ART1's average inter-cluster distance is bigger than that of K-Means and SOM. When compared to K-Means and SOM, ART1's average inter-cluster distance is low as the number of clusters increases, suggesting the high caliber of the clusters it generates.

Pre-fetching research focuses mostly on pre-fetching requests from specific users based on their historical access habits. When pre-fetching for a large number of users, these methods—while effective for pre-fetching—may significantly overwhelm the network with superfluous traffic. It provides a pre-fetching approach to lessen this effect by pre-fetching requests for a wide community of users rather than pre-fetching requests for individual users. This pre-fetching scheme makes advantage of the MART1 clustering technique.

Additionally, when several objects are pre-fetched, the traditional replacement rules offer worse network performance in terms of bandwidth use. The fundamental issue with Web pre-fetching is also that consumers might not request all of these pre-fetched resources. Because of this, web pre-fetching reduces bandwidth utilization while also adding to network traffic and web server stress (Huang & Hsu 2008). Therefore, effective web pre-fetching and caching integration is required now more than ever to get around the aforementioned constraints (Pallis et al. 2008; Feng et al. 2009).

The following study aims can be considered in light of the discussion above. The major goal of a research project is to enhance the proxy-based web caching system's performance by including a web pre-fetching system. The following goals are achieved in order to get at this integrated system, specifically:

1. Using data pretreatment methods like data cleaning to prepare the data for data mining jobs.
2. To test the effectiveness of online pre-fetching based on clustering while utilizing sample datasets.
3. To find and test substitute algorithms for web caching.
4. To combine the two suggested efforts, namely clustering-based web pre-fetching and web caching.
5. To evaluate the web page retrieval performance that has been optimized and has decreased latency.

FUTURE SCOPE AND PROBLEM FORMULATION

The extensive body of research that has been read and discussed thus far in this work has led to the suggestion of a novel web caching and pre-fetching strategy to increase the scalability of the web-based system. The literature also emphasizes the significance of web caching and pre-fetching employing web mining techniques as key results that formed the cornerstone for the design of the study challenge and are tabulated and displayed in Table 1.

Table 1. Literature support

SNo.	Base Papers	Authors	Issue and Inference
1	Web user clustering and its application to pre-fetching using ART neural networks	Rangarajan et al (2004)	It includes a pre-fetching mechanism based on an ART1 neural network. The issues that develop as a result of combining web caching with web pre-fetching are not addressed.
2	Integrating Web caching and Web pre-fetching in Client-Side Proxies	Teng et al (2005)	presented a pre-fetching strategy based on an association rule. They introduced a novel cache replacement policy known as (Integration of Web Caching and Pre-fetching (IWCP). They have classified web items as implied or non-implied.
3	A clustering-based pre-fetching scheme on a Web cache environment	Pallis et al (2008)	presented a graph-based pre-fetching strategy and used DG to do this. It is founded on the rule of association and is governed by support and confidence. Furthermore, they applied typical regulations in the Web cache environment and did not address challenges that arose while merging these two.
4	Intelligent Client-side Web Caching Scheme Based on Least Recently Used Algorithm and Neuro-Fuzzy System	Ali & Shamsuddin (2009)	It employs the neuro-fuzzy algorithm to categorise Web items as cacheable or un-cacheable. It uses the LRU algorithm in its cache to forecast Web items that may be visited again later. The training procedure takes a lengthy time and incurs additional computing costs. In the cache replacement policy, it overlooked considerations such as item cost and size.
5	A survey of Web cache replacement strategies	Podlipnig & Böszörmenyi (2003)	The authors examined and summarised numerous page replacement policies. In the Web cache context, GDSF performs better. They have also discussed the benefits and drawbacks of various page replacement policies.
6	A Keyword-Based Semantic Pre-fetching Approach in Internet News Services	Ibrahim & Xu (2004)	It forecasts user access in the future based on semantic preferences of previously obtained Web content. It is used in online news services. Semantic preferences are determined by analysing terms in previously visited Web URLs. To forecast future user requests, it applies a neural network model to the keyword set..
7	A Survey of Web Caching and Pre-fetching	Waleed et al (2011)	Different web caching and web pre-fetching strategies have been explored and assessed by the writers. It has been noted that the majority of the pre-fetching methods covered here concentrated on a single user, which would negatively impact server performance as user numbers rise. Additionally, data mining has been increasingly important in recent years in online pre-fetching fields, and the majority of data mining-based approaches employ association rule mining.

This leads to the further observation that both methods would increase performance by lowering server load and latency while visiting websites. The ineffective integration of web caching and pre-fetching methods, however, might result in high network traffic, an increase in web server stress, and the wasteful use of cache space (Waleed et al. 2011). Therefore, the pre-fetching strategy needs to be properly planned in order to get around the aforementioned constraints. Therefore, the suggested method makes advantage of web usage mining to enhance the performance of the current web cache.

Because clustering-based pre-fetching increases the amount of pre-fetched items and results in poor bandwidth utilization, conventional cache replacement rules are not appropriate for this method. So, in order to get over the restrictions mentioned above, the web caching strategy needs to be properly constructed. A new cache replacement policy is created with the intention of improving performance in terms of hit rate. It also lessens the quantity of items that must be pre-fetched, which conserves bandwidth.

CONCLUSION

According to the explanations and discussions, web caching and web pre-fetching are two significant ways used to increase the performance of an online-based information retrieval system. However, combining these two tactics incorrectly may result in increased delay and wasteful bandwidth utilization. As a result, while combining these two operations, extreme vigilance is required. In addition, this chapter discusses and summarizes studies on web caching and pre-fetching techniques. Because web caching relies temporal locality and web pre-fetching exploits spatial locality of web items, both solutions have been found to improve speed by minimizing server load and latency in accessing webpages. The ineffective integration of web caching and pre-fetching methods, however, might result in high network traffic, an increase in web server stress, and the wasteful use of cache capacity (Waleed et al. 2011). Therefore, the pre-fetching strategy needs to be properly planned in order to get around the aforementioned constraints. Therefore, it has become clear how crucial online use mining is for improving the current web cache's performance.

REFERENCES

Alex, B., & Mulvenna, M. D. (1998). Discovering Internet Marketing Intelligence through Online Analytical Web Usage Mining. *SIGMOD Record, 27*(4), 54–61. doi:10.1145/306101.306124

Anderson, C. R. (2002). *A Machine Learning Approach to Web Personalization* [Ph.D. Thesis]. University of Washington.

Balamash, A., & Krunz, M. (2004). An Overview of Web Caching Replacement Algorithms. *IEEE Communications Surveys and Tutorials, 6*(2), 44–56. doi:10.1109/COMST.2004.5342239

Bamshad, M. (2007). *Data Mining for Web Personalization.* LCNS, Springer-Verleg Berlin.

Brin, S., & Pange, L. (1998). The Anatomy of a Large-scale Hyper Textual Web Search Engine. *Computer Networks and ISDN Systems, 30*(1-7), 107–117. doi:10.1016/S0169-7552(98)00110-X

Chen, X., & Zhang, X. (2002). Popularity-based PPM: An effective Web pre-fetching technique for high accuracy and low storage. *Proceedings of the International Conference on Parallel Processing,* 296-304. 10.1109/ICPP.2002.1040885

Cyrus, S., Zarkessh, A. M., Jafar, A., & Vishal, S. (1997). Knowledge discovery from Users Web Page Navigation. In *Workshop on Research Issues in Data Engineering*, Birmingham, UK.

De, P. B., Aroyo, L., & Chepegin, V. (2004). The Next Big Thing: Adaptive Web-Based Systems. *Journal of Digital Information, 5*(1). http://jodi.ecs.soton.ac.uk/Articles/v05/ i01/DeBra/

Dunham, M. H. (2006). *Data Mining Introductory and Advanced Topics* (1st ed.). Pearson Education.

Facca, F. M., & Lanzi, P. L. (2005). Mining Interesting Knowledge from Web logs: A Survey. *Data & Knowledge Engineering*, *53*(3), 225–241. doi:10.1016/j.datak.2004.08.001

Feng, W., Man, S., & Hu, G. (2009). *Markov Tree Prediction on Web Cache Pre-fetching. In Software Engineering, Artificial Intelligence (SCI)* (Vol. 209). Springer-Verlag.

Ibrahim, T. I., & Xu, C. Z. (2000). Neural Nets based Predictive Pre-fetching to Tolerate WWW Latency. *Proceedings of the 20th International Conference on Distributed Computing Systems.*

Jaczynski, M., & Trousse, B. (1998). WWW Assisted Browsing by Reusing Past Navigations of a Group of Users. *Proceedings of the Advances in Case-Based Reasoning, Forth European Workshop*, *1488*, 160-171.

Jiawei, H., Micheline, K., & Jian, P. (2006). *Data Mining Concepts and Techniques.* Pearson Education.

Kosala, R. & Blockeel, H. (2000). Web Mining Research: A Survey. *SIGKDD Explorations, 2*(1), 1-15.

Koskela, T.J., Heikkonen, & Kaski, K. (2003). Web cache optimization with nonlinear model using object feature. *Computer Networks Journal, 43*(6), 805-817.

Kroeger, T. M., Long, D. D. E., & Mogul, J. C. (1997). Exploring the Bounds of Web Latency Reduction from Caching and Pre-fetching. *Proceedings of the USENDC Symposium on Internet Technology and Systems*, 13-22.

Lan, B., Bressan, S., Ooi, B. C., & Tan, K. L. (2000). Rule-Assisted Pre-fetching in Web-Server Caching. *Proceedings of the 9th International Conference on Information and Knowledge Management*, 504-511.

Lee, H. K., An, B. S., & Kim, E. J. (2009). Adaptive Pre-fetching Scheme Using Web Log Mining in Cluster-Based Web Systems. *IEEE International Conference on Web Services (ICWS)*, 903-910.

Loon, T. S., & Bharghavan, V. (1997). Alleviating the Latency and Bandwidth Problems in WWW Browsing. *Proceedings of the USENIX Symposium on Internet Technologies and Systems (USITS).*

Markatos, E. P., & Chronaki, C. E. (1998). A Top-10 Approach to Pre-fetching on the Web. *Proceedings of INET Geneva,* 276-290.

Mobasher, B., Dai, H., Luo, T., & Nakagawa, M. (2002). Discovery and Evaluation of Aggregate Usage Profiles for Web Personalization. *Data Mining and Knowledge Discovery*, *6*(1), 61–82. doi:10.1023/A:1013232803866

Padmanabhan, V. N., & Mogul, J. C. (1996). Using Predictive Pre-fetching to Improve World Wide Web Latency. *Computer Communication Review*, *26*(3), 23–36. doi:10.1145/235160.235164

Pallis, G., Vakali, A., & Pokorny, J. (2008). A Clustering-Based Pre-Fetching Scheme on A Web Cache Environment. ACM Journal Computers and Electrical Engineering, 34(4).

Pei, C., & Irani, S. (1997). Cost-Aware WWW Proxy Caching Algorithms. *Proceedings of the USENIX Symposium on Internet Technologies and Systems*, 193-206.

Pirolli, P., Pitkow, J., & Ramna, R. (1996). Extracting Usable Structure from the Web. CHI – 96, 118-125.

Podlipnig, S., & Boszormenyi, L. (2003). A Survey of Web Cache Replacement Strategies. *ACM Computing Surveys*, *35*(4), 374–398. doi:10.1145/954339.954341

Sathiyamoorthi, V. (2016). A Novel Cache Replacement Policy for Web Proxy Caching System Using Web Usage Mining. *International Journal of Information Technology and Web Engineering*, *11*(2), 1–12. doi:10.4018/IJITWE.2016040101

Sathiyamoorthi, V., & Murali Bhaskaran, V. (2010a). Data Preparation Techniques for Mining World Wide Web through Web Usage Mining-An Approach. *International Journal of Recent Trends in Engineering*, *2*(4), 1–4.

Sathiyamoorthi, V., & Murali Bhaskaran, V. (2010b). Data mining for intelligent enterprise resource planning system. *International Journal of Recent Trends in Engineering*, *2*(3), 1–4.

Sathiyamoorthi, V., & Murali Bhaskaran, V. (2011a). Improving the Performance of Web Page Retrieval through Pre-Fetching and Caching. *European Journal of Scientific Research*, *66*(2), 207–217.

Sathiyamoorthi, V., & Murali Bhaskaran, V. (2011b). Data Pre-Processing Techniques for Pre-Fetching and Caching of Web Data through Proxy Server. *International Journal of Computer Science and Network Security*, *11*(11), 92-98.

Sathiyamoorthi, V., & Murali Bhaskaran, V. (2012). Optimizing the Web Cache performance by Clustering Based Pre-Fetching Technique Using Modified ART1. *International Journal of Computer Application*, *44*(1), 51–60.

Sathiyamoorthi, V., & Murali Bhaskaran, V. (2013). Novel Approaches for Integrating MART1 Clustering Based Pre-Fetching Technique with Web Caching. *International Journal of Information Technology and Web Engineering*, *8*(2), 18–32. doi:10.4018/jitwe.2013040102

Srivastava, J., Cooley, R., Deshpande, M., & Tan, P. N. (2000). Web Usage Mining: Discovery and Applications of Usage Patterns from Web Data. *SIGKDD Explorations*, *1*(2), 12–23. doi:10.1145/846183.846188

Teng, W., Chang, C., & Chen, M. (2005). Integrating Web Caching and Web Pre-fetching in Client-Side Proxies. *IEEE Transactions on Parallel and Distributed Systems*, *16*(5), 444–455. doi:10.1109/TPDS.2005.56

Velasquez, J., Bassi, A., Yasuda, H., & Aoki, T. (2004). Mining Web Data to Create Online Navigation Recommendations. *Proceedings of the Fourth IEEE International Conference on Data Mining*, 551-554.

Waleed, A., Siti M.S. & Abdul S.I. (2011). A Survey of Web Caching and Prefetching. *Int. J. Advance. Soft Comput. Appl.*, *3*(1).

Wessels & Duane. (2001). Web Caching. O'Reilly Publication.

Yang, Q., Li, T., & Wang, K. (2004). Building Association-Rule Based Sequential Classifiers for Web-Document Prediction. *Data Mining and Knowledge Discovery*, *8*(3), 253–273. doi:10.1023/B:DAMI.0000023675.04946.f1

Zaiane, O. (2000). Web Mining: Concepts, Practices and Research. *Proc. SDBD, Conference Tutorial Notes.*

Chapter 7
Intelligent Information Retrieval, Neural Networks, and Their Applications for Smart Cities

Dipali Kasat
https://orcid.org/0000-0002-1915-8858
Sarvajanik College of Engineering and Technology, India

ABSTRACT

In this chapter, the author delves into the realm of intelligent information retrieval and its applications in the context of smart cities. The proliferation of data generated by smart city systems necessitates advanced techniques to effectively extract meaningful insights. They explore the integration of neural networks with information retrieval methodologies to enable intelligent decision-making processes in urban environments. By leveraging the power of artificial intelligence and machine learning, smart cities can harness the potential of data-driven approaches to enhance various aspects of urban life. This chapter discusses the fundamental concepts, techniques, and applications of intelligent information retrieval and neural networks in the context of smart city development.

1. INTRODUCTION

1.1 The Emergence of Smart Cities (Batty et al. 2012)

In recent years, the concept of smart cities has gained significant traction and attention across the globe. With rapid urbanization and advancements in technology, the emergence of smart cities represents a paradigm shift in urban development, aiming to leverage technology and data to improve the quality of life for citizens.

A smart city is characterized by the integration of various information and communication technologies (ICT) to enable efficient management of resources, infrastructure, and services. These technologies include the Internet of Things (IoT), sensors, data analytics, artificial intelligence (AI), and connectivity solutions. By harnessing the power of these technologies, smart cities seek to create an interconnected

DOI: 10.4018/979-8-3693-1722-8.ch007

ecosystem where data and information flow seamlessly, enabling real-time decision-making, resource optimization, and improved service delivery.

The key driving force behind the development of smart cities is the need to address the complex challenges faced by urban areas, such as traffic congestion, energy consumption, environmental sustainability, public safety, and healthcare. By utilizing data-driven approaches and intelligent systems, smart cities aim to tackle these challenges more effectively, leading to enhanced liveability, sustainability, and economic growth.

In the context of smart cities, information plays a crucial role. The proliferation of sensors, IoT devices, and interconnected systems generates vast amounts of data, often referred to as big data. This data holds immense potential in terms of providing valuable insights into various aspects of urban life, including transportation, energy consumption, public safety, healthcare, and urban planning. However, the challenge lies in effectively harnessing and extracting meaningful information from this data deluge.

Information retrieval, which involves the process of retrieving relevant information from a collection of data, becomes a critical aspect in the functioning of smart cities. Traditional information retrieval techniques are often insufficient to handle the scale, complexity, and variety of data generated in smart cities. Therefore, there is a need for intelligent information retrieval systems that can make sense of this vast amount of data, provide accurate and relevant information, and support decision-making processes.

By leveraging the power of artificial intelligence and machine learning, smart cities can unlock the potential of data-driven approaches, enabling better management of resources, improved service delivery, and enhanced quality of life for their residents. Understanding the principles, techniques, and applications of intelligent information retrieval and neural networks in the context of smart city development is crucial for policymakers, urban planners, researchers, and technology professionals involved in building the cities of the future.

In the subsequent sections of this chapter, we will delve deeper into the fundamentals of information retrieval, explore intelligent information retrieval techniques, discuss neural networks and their applications in information retrieval, examine case studies showcasing the use of intelligent retrieval in smart cities, and address the challenges and future directions of this field.

1.2 The Challenges of Information Retrieval in Smart Cities

In the era of smart cities, where technology and data-driven solutions are transforming urban landscapes, the challenges associated with information retrieval have become more complex and critical. Information retrieval plays a crucial role in the efficient management of resources, infrastructure, and services within smart cities. However, the unique characteristics of smart city environments pose specific challenges that need to be addressed to enable effective information retrieval.

Smart cities are characterized by the integration of various information and communication technologies (ICT) to create a networked ecosystem. This integration includes the deployment of sensors, Internet of Things (IoT) devices, and interconnected systems, resulting in the generation of vast amounts of data. This data encompasses diverse sources, such as real-time sensor readings, social media feeds, traffic cameras, energy consumption records, and more. The volume, velocity, and variety of this data present significant challenges in terms of storing, processing, and retrieving relevant information.

One of the primary challenges of information retrieval in smart cities is dealing with big data. The sheer volume of data generated from various sources can overwhelm traditional retrieval systems, which may not be equipped to handle such large-scale datasets. Retrieving meaningful and relevant information from this vast amount of data becomes a daunting task, requiring advanced techniques and algorithms capable of efficient processing and analysis.

Another challenge is ensuring the quality and reliability of data. In smart cities, data is collected from numerous heterogeneous sources, including different sensors, devices, and platforms. Data quality issues such as incompleteness, inaccuracies, inconsistencies, and biases can significantly impact the effectiveness of information retrieval systems. Ensuring data quality and reliability, along with data integration and interoperability, becomes crucial to enable accurate and meaningful retrieval of information.

The variety of data sources and formats in smart cities also poses challenges. Data is generated from diverse domains such as transportation, energy, public safety, healthcare, and urban planning. Each domain may have its own data models, formats, and standards. Integrating and harmonizing these disparate data sources to enable cross-domain retrieval and analysis requires effective data integration techniques and semantic interoperability.

Furthermore, the real-time nature of smart city systems introduces time-criticality to information retrieval. For applications such as intelligent transportation systems, emergency response, or energy management, the timeliness of retrieving and processing information is crucial. Traditional batch processing methods may not be suitable for real-time decision-making, requiring the development of efficient real-time retrieval algorithms and architectures.

Privacy and security concerns are also significant challenges in information retrieval within smart cities. The vast amount of data collected may contain sensitive and personal information about individuals and their activities. Ensuring privacy protection, data anonymization, and secure retrieval processes becomes paramount to gain public trust and comply with privacy regulations.

To address these challenges, advanced techniques and methodologies are being developed. Intelligent information retrieval techniques, such as semantic search, natural language processing, context-aware retrieval, and personalized recommendation systems, are being explored to improve the relevance and accuracy of retrieved information. Furthermore, the integration of neural networks and machine learning algorithms enables more efficient processing and analysis of big data, leading to enhanced retrieval capabilities.

In conclusion, the challenges of information retrieval in smart cities are multifaceted and demand innovative solutions. Dealing with big data, ensuring data quality, handling data variety, real-time processing, privacy concerns, and security considerations are among the key challenges. Overcoming these challenges is essential to leverage the immense potential of data-driven decision-making and provide smart city residents with relevant, accurate, and timely information for improved urban services and quality of life.

1.3 Role of Neural Networks in Intelligent Information Retrieval

In the field of intelligent information retrieval, neural networks have emerged as a powerful tool for extracting meaningful insights from large and complex datasets. Neural networks, inspired by the structure and functioning of the human brain, are computational models composed of interconnected nodes (neurons) that work together to process and analyse data. The application of neural networks in information retrieval has revolutionized the way we extract, classify, and retrieve information in various domains, including smart cities.

The role of neural networks in intelligent information retrieval is crucial due to their ability to handle the challenges associated with big data, complex relationships, and non-linear patterns. Unlike traditional information retrieval techniques that rely on explicit rules or statistical models, neural networks can automatically learn from data, recognize patterns, and make predictions without explicit programming. This capability makes them well-suited for processing and analysing the vast amounts of data generated in smart city environments.

One of the primary roles of neural networks in intelligent information retrieval is document classification and indexing. Neural network architectures, such as Convolutional Neural Networks (CNNs), have shown exceptional performance in automatically categorizing and organizing documents based on their content. By learning from labelled training data, CNNs can identify relevant features and patterns within documents, enabling accurate classification and indexing for efficient retrieval.

Recurrent Neural Networks (RNNs) play a vital role in sequence modelling, which is essential in information retrieval tasks involving natural language processing and context-aware retrieval. RNNs can capture the temporal dependencies and context within a sequence of data, making them valuable for tasks such as text summarization, sentiment analysis, and question answering. By understanding the sequential relationships in textual data, RNNs enhance the quality and relevance of retrieved information.

Attention mechanisms have also become an integral part of neural network-based information retrieval systems. Attention mechanisms enable the model to focus on specific parts of the input data that are most relevant for the retrieval task. This selective attention improves the accuracy and efficiency of information retrieval by assigning higher weights to important features or context. Attention mechanisms are particularly useful in context-aware retrieval, where the relevance of retrieved information depends on the specific context or user preferences.

The integration of neural networks with intelligent information retrieval techniques has opened up new possibilities for personalized recommendation systems. By learning from user behaviour, preferences, and feedback, neural networks can generate personalized recommendations tailored to individual users. This personalized approach enhances user satisfaction, engagement, and the overall effectiveness of information retrieval systems in smart cities.

Moreover, neural networks facilitate the exploration of advanced techniques in information retrieval, such as deep learning and deep neural networks. Deep learning architectures, comprising multiple layers of interconnected neurons, enable the extraction of hierarchical representations and complex features from data. Deep neural networks have demonstrated remarkable performance in various information retrieval tasks, including image recognition, speech recognition, and natural language understanding.

In conclusion, the role of neural networks in intelligent information retrieval is paramount in addressing the challenges posed by big data, complex relationships, and non-linear patterns in smart cities. By leveraging the power of neural networks, information retrieval systems can achieve higher accuracy, relevance, and efficiency in retrieving valuable insights from large and diverse datasets. The integration of neural networks with intelligent information retrieval methodologies opens up new possibilities for improving decision-making processes, optimizing resource management, and enhancing the overall quality of services in smart cities.

2. FUNDAMENTALS OF INFORMATION RETRIEVAL

Information retrieval is the process of retrieving relevant information from a collection of data in response to a user query. In this section, we will explore the fundamental concepts of information retrieval, including retrieval models, indexing and query processing, and evaluation metrics for information retrieval systems.

2.1 Retrieval Models: From Boolean to Probabilistic and Beyond

Retrieval models form the foundation of information retrieval systems and determine how documents are ranked and retrieved based on their relevance to a user's query. Several retrieval models have been developed over the years, each with its own strengths and limitations.

One of the earliest and simplest retrieval models is the Boolean model, which uses Boolean logic operators (AND, OR, NOT) to combine query terms and match documents. The Boolean model retrieves documents that exactly match the query terms, making it a precise but limited approach.

Probabilistic retrieval models, such as the Vector Space Model (VSM) and the Okapi BM25 model, introduced the concept of ranking documents based on their relevance scores. These models assign weights to terms in documents and queries, calculating a similarity score to determine the relevance of a document to a query. The VSM represents documents and queries as vectors in a high-dimensional space, while the BM25 model incorporates statistical properties of term frequency and document length.

Beyond Boolean and probabilistic models, more advanced retrieval models have been developed. These include language models, such as the Latent Semantic Indexing (LSI) model and the Latent Dirichlet Allocation (LDA) model, which capture the underlying semantic relationships between terms and documents. Additionally, neural network-based models, such as Convolutional Neural Networks (CNNs) and Recurrent Neural Networks (RNNs), have shown promise in capturing complex patterns and semantic features for improved retrieval performance.

2.2 Indexing and Query Processing

Indexing and query processing are essential components of information retrieval systems that enable efficient and effective retrieval of relevant documents.

Indexing involves creating an index structure that organizes the documents in the collection based on their content. This process typically includes parsing the documents, extracting terms, and constructing inverted indexes. Inverted indexes store the occurrence of each term in the collection and provide fast access to documents containing specific terms.

Query processing involves processing user queries to match them with relevant documents in the collection. The query processing phase typically includes parsing and analysing the query, matching query terms with the index, and ranking the retrieved documents based on their relevance scores.

To optimize query processing, various techniques are employed, such as term weighting, query expansion, and relevance feedback. Term weighting assigns weights to terms based on their importance in documents and queries, improving the precision of retrieval. Query expansion expands the original query by adding related terms or synonyms to improve recall. Relevance feedback involves iteratively refining the query based on user feedback and previous retrieval results.

2.3 Evaluation Metrics for Information Retrieval Systems

Evaluation metrics are used to measure the effectiveness and performance of information retrieval systems. These metrics provide insights into the quality of retrieved results and help assess the system's retrieval capabilities.

Common evaluation metrics for information retrieval systems include precision, recall, F-measure, and mean average precision (MAP). Precision measures the proportion of relevant documents among the retrieved documents, indicating the system's ability to retrieve relevant results accurately. Recall measures the proportion of relevant documents retrieved out of all the relevant documents in the collection, reflecting the system's ability to retrieve all relevant results.

The F-measure combines precision and recall into a single metric, providing a balanced evaluation of the system's performance. It calculates the harmonic mean of precision and recall, taking into account both precision and recall values.

Mean Average Precision (MAP) measures the average precision across multiple queries. It considers the precision at various recall levels and provides a comprehensive evaluation of the system's retrieval performance across different queries.

Other evaluation metrics include precision at K (P@K), which measures precision at a specific rank K, and normalized discounted cumulative gain (NDCG), which considers the relevance and ranking of retrieved documents.

These evaluation metrics play a crucial role in benchmarking and comparing different retrieval models and techniques. They provide a quantitative assessment of the system's retrieval effectiveness, allowing researchers and practitioners to improve and fine-tune information retrieval systems for better performance.

In conclusion, the fundamentals of information retrieval encompass retrieval models, indexing and query processing, and evaluation metrics. Retrieval models determine how documents are ranked and retrieved, while indexing and query processing enable efficient retrieval of relevant documents. Evaluation metrics assess the performance of information retrieval systems, providing insights into their effectiveness. Understanding these fundamental concepts is essential for developing and improving intelligent information retrieval systems in various domains, including smart cities.

3. INTELLIGENT INFORMATION RETRIEVAL TECHNIQUES

Intelligent information retrieval techniques aim to enhance the traditional information retrieval process by leveraging advanced technologies, such as artificial intelligence and machine learning, to extract more meaningful and relevant insights from data. In this section, we will explore several intelligent information retrieval techniques and their applications in the context of smart cities (Hanifah et al 2014).

3.1 Semantic Search and Natural Language Processing

Semantic search is a technique that goes beyond simple keyword matching and considers the meaning and context of words and phrases in a user query. Natural Language Processing (NLP) is a key component of semantic search, as it enables machines to understand and interpret human language.

NLP techniques, such as named entity recognition, part-of-speech tagging, and sentiment analysis, help in extracting valuable information from unstructured textual data. By understanding the semantics and relationships between words, NLP-powered semantic search systems can provide more accurate and contextually relevant search results to users.

In the context of smart cities, semantic search and NLP can be applied in various ways. For example, in a smart city's transportation system, users can use natural language queries to find the fastest route to a destination, taking into account real-time traffic and public transportation options. In a healthcare context, semantic search can assist medical professionals in quickly accessing relevant research papers, clinical guidelines, and patient records to make informed decisions.

3.2 Context-Aware Retrieval

Context-aware retrieval is a technique that considers the user's context, preferences, and situational factors to tailor information retrieval results accordingly. The context can include the user's location, time, device, and past interactions with the system.

In smart cities, where various data sources and sensors continuously collect information, context-aware retrieval plays a vital role in delivering personalized and relevant information to citizens. For example, a context-aware smart city application might provide real-time recommendations for nearby restaurants, events, or public facilities based on the user's current location and preferences.

Machine learning algorithms, such as collaborative filtering and matrix factorization, are often used to model user preferences and generate context-aware recommendations. By continuously learning from user feedback and interactions, these systems can improve the accuracy and relevance of retrieved information over time.

3.3 Personalized Recommendation Systems

Personalized recommendation systems are a subset of intelligent information retrieval techniques that aim to deliver tailored content and suggestions to individual users based on their preferences and behaviour.

In smart cities, personalized recommendation systems can enhance various services and applications. For instance, a smart city's e-commerce platform can offer personalized product recommendations to users based on their past purchases, browsing history, and demographic information. In the realm of public services, personalized recommendations can help citizens discover relevant community events, workshops, or local services that align with their interests and needs.

To build effective personalized recommendation systems, collaborative filtering, content-based filtering, and hybrid methods are often employed. Collaborative filtering analyses user interactions and similarities to recommend items that users with similar preferences have also enjoyed. Content-based filtering, on the other hand, recommends items based on their attributes and how well they match the user's past behaviour or preferences. Hybrid methods combine both collaborative and content-based approaches to leverage their strengths and overcome their limitations.

3.4 Sentiment Analysis and Opinion Mining

Sentiment analysis, also known as opinion mining, is a technique used to determine the sentiment or emotions expressed in textual data, such as reviews, social media posts, and customer feedback.

In the context of smart cities, sentiment analysis can be used to analyse public sentiments and opinions about various urban services, policies, and events. For example, by analysing social media posts and comments, city officials can gauge public reactions to new infrastructure projects or public initiatives. This information can be valuable for making data-driven decisions and understanding citizen satisfaction.

Machine learning algorithms, such as supervised learning and deep learning models, are commonly employed in sentiment analysis. These algorithms learn from labelled datasets to classify text as positive, negative, or neutral based on the sentiment expressed. By automatically processing and analysing large volumes of textual data, sentiment analysis enables decision-makers to gain insights into public sentiment at scale.

In conclusion, intelligent information retrieval techniques, including semantic search, context-aware retrieval, personalized recommendation systems, and sentiment analysis, leverage advanced technologies to enhance the accuracy, relevance, and personalization of information retrieval in smart cities. By incorporating these techniques, smart cities can provide citizens with more tailored and meaningful information, improving their overall experience and quality of life.

4. NEURAL NETWORKS FOR INFORMATION RETRIEVAL

Neural networks have become a powerful tool in the field of information retrieval. They are capable of learning complex patterns and relationships from large volumes of data, enabling more accurate and efficient retrieval of information. In this section, we will explore different neural network architectures and their applications in information retrieval.

4.1 Overview of Neural Network Architectures

Neural networks consist of interconnected nodes, called neurons, that mimic the structure and function of the human brain. These networks are composed of multiple layers, including an input layer, one or more hidden layers, and an output layer. Each neuron in a layer is connected to neurons in the adjacent layers through weighted connections.

There are various types of neural network architectures used in information retrieval, including feed-forward neural networks, convolutional neural networks (CNNs), recurrent neural networks (RNNs), and attention-based models. Each architecture is designed to address specific challenges and tasks in information retrieval.

4.2 Convolutional Neural Networks for Document Classification

Convolutional Neural Networks (CNNs) are commonly used in document classification tasks, where the goal is to categorize text documents into predefined classes or categories. CNNs excel at capturing local patterns and features within the input data.

In the context of document classification, a CNN takes the text document as input and applies a series of convolutional layers to extract meaningful features. These convolutional layers employ filters or kernels to convolve over the input text, extracting local patterns such as n-grams or word sequences. The extracted features are then passed through fully connected layers for classification.

By leveraging CNNs for document classification, information retrieval systems can automatically categorize and classify large volumes of text data, making it easier to organize and retrieve relevant information.

4.3 Recurrent Neural Networks for Sequence Modelling

Recurrent Neural Networks (RNNs) are particularly effective in handling sequential data, making them suitable for tasks such as language modelling, machine translation, and text generation. RNNs can capture the contextual dependencies and temporal dynamics present in sequential data.

In information retrieval, RNNs can be used for sequence modelling, where the goal is to predict the next element in a sequence given the previous elements. For example, in a language modelling task, an RNN can be trained to predict the next word in a sentence based on the preceding words.

RNNs operate by maintaining a hidden state that carries information from previous steps and updates it as new input is processed. This hidden state allows the network to capture long-term dependencies in sequential data. By incorporating RNNs in information retrieval systems, the models can generate more contextually relevant and coherent responses or predictions.

4.4 Attention Mechanisms for Context-Aware Retrieval

Attention mechanisms have gained significant attention in recent years and have been successfully applied in various information retrieval tasks. Attention mechanisms allow the neural network to focus on different parts of the input data, giving more weight or importance to certain elements.

In the context of information retrieval, attention mechanisms can be used to improve context-aware retrieval. For example, in a question-answering system, attention mechanisms can be employed to identify the relevant parts of the question and the document being queried, improving the accuracy of the response.

By incorporating attention mechanisms, information retrieval systems can consider the relevance and importance of different elements in the input data, enabling more precise retrieval and better understanding of user queries.

In summary, neural networks offer powerful tools for intelligent information retrieval. Convolutional Neural Networks (CNNs) are effective for document classification tasks, Recurrent Neural Networks (RNNs) excel in sequence modelling, and attention mechanisms enhance context-aware retrieval. These neural network architectures, combined with advanced training techniques and large-scale datasets, enable more accurate and efficient information retrieval in smart city applications.

5. APPLICATIONS OF INTELLIGENT INFORMATION RETRIEVAL IN SMART CITIES

This section presents several real-world applications of intelligent information retrieval in the domain of smart cities. We explore how these techniques can be leveraged in intelligent transportation systems, energy management and sustainability, public safety and emergency response, healthcare and well-being, and urban planning and resource optimization (Su et al 2011).

5.1 Intelligent Transportation Systems

Intelligent Transportation Systems (ITS) utilize advanced technologies and information retrieval techniques to enhance the efficiency, safety, and sustainability of transportation in smart cities. Intelligent information retrieval plays a significant role in ITS by providing real-time traffic information, optimizing route planning, and facilitating intelligent decision-making.

By utilizing information retrieval, ITS can collect data from various sources such as traffic sensors, GPS devices, and social media feeds to monitor traffic conditions. Neural networks can analyse this data and predict traffic patterns, congestion levels, and travel times. This information can then be used to suggest the best routes to drivers, optimize traffic signal timings, and enable dynamic ride-sharing services. Intelligent information retrieval in ITS not only improves transportation efficiency but also reduces traffic congestion and emissions, contributing to a more sustainable and livable urban environment.

5.2 Energy Management and Sustainability

Energy management and sustainability are crucial aspects of smart city development. Intelligent information retrieval techniques can contribute to energy efficiency and sustainability by providing insights into energy usage patterns, optimizing energy distribution, and supporting the integration of renewable energy sources.

Intelligent information retrieval systems can retrieve and analyse data from smart meters, energy grids, and environmental sensors to identify energy consumption patterns and demand trends. This information can be used to develop predictive models using neural networks to optimize energy usage, minimize wastage, and balance energy supply and demand. These models can also support the integration of renewable energy sources, such as solar and wind, by predicting their availability and output. By leveraging intelligent information retrieval, smart cities can achieve more sustainable and resilient energy systems.

5.3 Public Safety and Emergency Response

Intelligent information retrieval plays a crucial role in enhancing public safety and emergency response in smart cities. By retrieving and analysing relevant data from various sources, including surveillance cameras, social media feeds, and emergency service databases, intelligent information retrieval systems can provide valuable insights and support decision-making during emergency situations.

Neural networks can be employed to analyse real-time data and detect potential safety risks or incidents. For example, image recognition algorithms can identify and track objects or individuals in surveillance footage to detect suspicious activities or potential threats. Sentiment analysis techniques can monitor social media feeds to gauge public sentiment during emergencies and identify areas that require immediate attention.

Furthermore, intelligent information retrieval systems can assist emergency responders by providing real-time information about the location of incidents, traffic conditions, and available resources. By integrating and analysing data from multiple sources, these systems can facilitate faster and more effective emergency response, ultimately enhancing public safety in smart cities.

5.4 Healthcare and Well-Being

Intelligent information retrieval has significant applications in healthcare and well-being in smart cities. By retrieving and analysing data from electronic health records, wearable devices, and health monitoring systems, intelligent information retrieval systems can support personalized healthcare, preventive measures, and early detection of diseases.

Neural networks can be employed to analyse medical data and identify patterns, correlations, and predictive insights. For instance, machine learning algorithms can analyse patient data to predict the likelihood of developing certain diseases, recommend personalized treatment plans, or detect anomalies in health conditions. Intelligent information retrieval systems can also provide access to relevant medical research, clinical guidelines, and patient records to support healthcare professionals in making informed decisions.

Furthermore, these systems can support well-being initiatives in smart cities by providing personalized recommendations for fitness activities, nutrition plans, and mental health support. By utilizing intelligent information retrieval, smart cities can improve the quality of healthcare services and promote the well-being of their citizens.

5.5 Urban Planning and Resource Optimization

Intelligent information retrieval techniques have significant implications for urban planning and resource optimization in smart cities. By retrieving and analysing data from various sources, including sensors, satellite imagery, and social media feeds, intelligent information retrieval systems can provide valuable insights for urban planners and decision-makers.

Neural networks can analyse large volumes of data to identify patterns, trends, and correlations related to urban infrastructure, transportation networks, population distribution, and resource consumption. These insights can inform urban planning processes, such as optimizing transportation routes, determining the location of amenities and services, and identifying areas that require infrastructure upgrades.

Intelligent information retrieval systems can also support resource optimization by providing real-time data on resource usage, such as water, electricity, and waste management. By analysing this data, neural networks can identify areas of inefficiency, detect anomalies, and optimize resource allocation to reduce waste and enhance sustainability.

In summary, intelligent information retrieval plays a crucial role in various applications within smart cities. From improving transportation systems to enhancing energy management, public safety, healthcare, and urban planning, intelligent information retrieval techniques, combined with neural networks, enable cities to make data-driven decisions, optimize resources, and provide better services to their citizens.

6. CASE STUDIES

To provide practical insights, this section presents case studies that demonstrate the application of intelligent information retrieval techniques in specific smart city scenarios. We showcase examples such as smart traffic management, optimizing energy consumption in smart buildings, and enhancing public safety with intelligent video surveillance.

6.1 Smart Traffic Management Using Intelligent Information Retrieval

Smart traffic management is a critical application in smart cities aimed at improving the efficiency of transportation systems and reducing traffic congestion. By utilizing intelligent information retrieval techniques, cities can gather and analyse real-time data from various sources such as traffic sensors, surveillance cameras, and GPS devices to make informed decisions and optimize traffic flow (Tastimur et al 2017).

One case study involves the implementation of a smart traffic management system using intelligent information retrieval. The system integrates neural networks to analyse traffic patterns, predict congestion, and optimize traffic signal timings. By retrieving data from traffic sensors and surveillance cameras, the system can detect traffic incidents, monitor congestion levels, and identify areas that require intervention.

The neural network models can process the collected data, learn from historical patterns, and predict future traffic conditions. These predictions can be used to dynamically adjust traffic signal timings, optimize route suggestions, and provide real-time traffic updates to drivers. By leveraging intelligent information retrieval and neural networks, the smart traffic management system can significantly improve traffic efficiency, reduce travel times, and enhance overall urban mobility.

6.2 Optimizing Energy Consumption in Smart Buildings

Smart buildings play a crucial role in achieving energy efficiency and sustainability in smart cities. Optimizing energy consumption in buildings is a key objective to reduce greenhouse gas emissions and lower energy costs. Intelligent information retrieval techniques can be applied to analyse energy usage patterns, identify areas of wastage, and optimize energy management strategies (Ordouei et al 2023).

A case study focuses on optimizing energy consumption in smart buildings using intelligent information retrieval. By retrieving data from smart meters, occupancy sensors, and environmental sensors, the system collects real-time information on energy usage, occupancy patterns, and environmental conditions.

Neural networks are employed to analyse the collected data, learn energy consumption patterns, and develop predictive models. These models can predict energy demand based on factors such as occupancy, weather conditions, and time of day. By leveraging these predictions, the system can optimize energy distribution, adjust heating and cooling settings, and identify opportunities for energy-saving measures.

Intelligent information retrieval enables the system to continuously monitor and analyse energy consumption, providing real-time insights and recommendations for optimizing energy usage in smart buildings. This leads to significant energy savings, reduced carbon footprint, and improved sustainability in urban areas.

6.3 Enhancing Public Safety with Intelligent Video Surveillance

Public safety is a paramount concern in smart cities, and intelligent video surveillance systems have become crucial tools for enhancing security and response capabilities. By utilizing intelligent information retrieval techniques, video surveillance systems can analyse vast amounts of visual data and provide real-time insights for enhanced public safety (Jabbar et al 2023).

A case study demonstrates how intelligent video surveillance can be used to enhance public safety in smart cities. The system integrates neural networks for video analysis, object detection, and behaviour recognition. By retrieving video data from surveillance cameras placed strategically across the city, the system can identify and track suspicious activities, detect potential threats, and alert authorities in real-time.

The neural network models analyse the video data, identifying objects of interest, such as individuals, vehicles, or suspicious items. The models can also learn and recognize specific behaviours, such as crowd disturbances or abnormal movements. By leveraging intelligent information retrieval, the system can prioritize alerts, provide situational awareness to law enforcement agencies, and support proactive response measures.

This intelligent video surveillance system enhances public safety by enabling quick detection of potential threats and early intervention in critical situations. It improves the efficiency and effectiveness of law enforcement efforts, ultimately contributing to a safer and more secure urban environment.

In conclusion, these case studies highlight the practical applications of intelligent information retrieval in smart cities. From optimizing traffic management and energy consumption to enhancing public safety with intelligent video surveillance, intelligent information retrieval, in combination with neural networks, enables cities to leverage data-driven insights and make informed decisions for the benefit of their citizens.

7. CHALLENGES AND FUTURE DIRECTIONS

As smart cities continue to evolve and integrate intelligent information retrieval systems, several challenges and considerations arise. This section discusses some of the key challenges and provides insights into future directions for research and development.

7.1 Privacy and Ethical Considerations

One of the significant challenges in the deployment of intelligent information retrieval systems in smart cities is ensuring privacy and addressing ethical concerns. As these systems collect and analyse vast amounts of data, including personal and sensitive information, it is crucial to establish robust privacy protection mechanisms (Mark et al 2019).

Privacy-preserving techniques, such as data anonymization, encryption, and secure data sharing protocols, need to be implemented to protect the privacy of individuals. Additionally, clear policies and regulations must be in place to govern the collection, storage, and usage of data to prevent any misuse or unauthorized access.

Ethical considerations are also paramount, particularly in cases where intelligent information retrieval systems have the potential to influence or make decisions that impact individuals or communities. Fairness, transparency, and accountability should be incorporated into the design and operation of these systems to ensure that they uphold ethical standards and avoid biases or discrimination (Ziosi et al. 2022).

Future directions in this area involve the development of robust privacy-enhancing technologies, the establishment of ethical guidelines and frameworks, and the promotion of public awareness and engagement to ensure that smart city initiatives prioritize individual rights and societal well-being.

7.2 Scalability and Real-Time Processing

Another challenge faced by intelligent information retrieval systems in smart cities is scalability and real-time processing. As the volume and velocity of data generated by smart city applications continue to increase, it becomes crucial to develop scalable architectures and algorithms that can handle large-scale data processing efficiently (Vítor et al 2022).

(Scalability can be addressed through distributed computing frameworks, cloud-based solutions, and efficient data storage and retrieval techniques. Real-time processing requires the ability to analyze and respond to data in a timely manner. Stream processing and edge computing technologies can be employed to enable real-time decision-making and ensure prompt response to dynamic situations.

Future directions involve exploring innovative approaches to handle the scalability and real-time processing demands of intelligent information retrieval systems. This includes advancements in distributed computing, edge computing, and the integration of artificial intelligence techniques that can provide real-time insights and support decision-making processes in smart cities.

7.3 Explainability and Interpretability of Neural Networks

The adoption of neural networks in intelligent information retrieval systems raises the challenge of explainability and interpretability. Neural networks are often regarded as black boxes, making it challenging to understand the reasoning behind their decisions and predictions. This lack of explainability can hinder the acceptance and trustworthiness of these systems, especially in critical applications.

Future research should focus on developing techniques that enhance the explainability and interpretability of neural networks. This includes the development of transparent and interpretable neural network architectures, the incorporation of visualization techniques to reveal the internal workings of neural networks, and the integration of reasoning and explanation modules to provide human-understandable justifications for the system's outputs.

Explainability and interpretability are essential to gain insights into how neural networks arrive at their decisions, ensure accountability, and enable stakeholders to have a clear understanding of the reasoning behind the information retrieved and the actions taken by intelligent systems in smart cities (Javed et al 2023).

In conclusion, addressing the challenges of privacy and ethical considerations, scalability and real-time processing, and explainability and interpretability of neural networks is crucial for the successful implementation and advancement of intelligent information retrieval systems in smart cities. Exploring future directions in these areas will contribute to the development of more trustworthy, efficient, and responsible systems that can truly benefit citizens and ensure sustainable urban development.

8. CONCLUSION

In this chapter, we have explored the emerging paradigm of smart cities and the crucial role that intelligent information retrieval and neural networks play in shaping their future. We have examined the fundamental concepts, techniques, and applications of intelligent information retrieval, and highlighted the integration of neural networks to enhance decision-making processes, optimize resource allocation, and improve the overall quality of life for citizens in urban environments.

The findings of this chapter underscore the immense potential of intelligent information retrieval and neural networks in transforming smart cities. By leveraging advanced technologies, such as artificial intelligence and machine learning, smart cities can harness the power of data and extract meaningful insights to drive informed decision-making. The integration of neural networks further enhances these capabilities by enabling sophisticated analysis, pattern recognition, and prediction.

One of the key contributions of intelligent information retrieval and neural networks is their ability to improve the efficiency and effectiveness of decision-making processes in smart cities. By effectively retrieving and analysing large volumes of data from diverse sources, these technologies enable city planners and policymakers to make informed choices that optimize resource allocation and improve the delivery of services to citizens. This leads to improved operational efficiency, reduced costs, and enhanced sustainability.

Moreover, intelligent information retrieval and neural networks have the potential to greatly improve the overall quality of life for citizens in urban environments. Through applications such as intelligent transportation systems, energy management and sustainability, public safety and emergency response, healthcare and well-being, and urban planning and resource optimization, these technologies contribute to creating more liveable, resilient, and inclusive cities.

It is important to recognize and address the challenges associated with the implementation of intelligent information retrieval and neural networks in smart cities. Privacy and ethical considerations, scalability and real-time processing, and the explainability and interpretability of neural networks are crucial areas that require attention. By overcoming these challenges and ensuring responsible deployment, we can maximize the benefits of these technologies while safeguarding the rights and well-being of citizens.

In conclusion, intelligent information retrieval and neural networks hold great promise for the future of smart cities. Their integration and application enable cities to make data-driven decisions, optimize resource allocation, and enhance the overall quality of life for their residents. As these technologies continue to advance and evolve, further research, development, and collaboration are necessary to unlock their full potential and ensure a sustainable and prosperous future for smart cities worldwide.

REFERENCES

Batty, M., Axhausen, K. W., Giannotti, F., Pozdnoukhov, A., Bazzani, A., Wachowicz, M., Ouzounis, G., & Portugali, Y. (2012). Smart cities of the future. *The European Physical Journal. Special Topics*, *214*(1), 481–518. doi:10.1140/epjst/e2012-01703-3

Hanifah, R., Supangkat, S. H., & Purwarianti, A. (2014). Twitter Information Extraction for Smart City. In *2014 International Conference on ICT For Smart Society (ICISS)* (pp. 295-299). 10.1109/ICTSS.2014.7013190

Jabbar, M. A., Tiwari, S., & Ortiz-Rodriguez, F. (Eds.). (2023). *Smart Urban Computing Applications* (1st ed.). River Publishers.

Javed, A. R., Ahmed, W., Pandya, S., Maddikunta, P. K. R., Alazab, M., & Gadekallu, T. R. (2023). A Survey of Explainable Artificial Intelligence for Smart Cities. *Electronics (Basel)*, *12*(4), 1020. doi:10.3390/electronics12041020

Mark, R., & Anya, G. (2019). Ethics of Using Smart City AI and Big Data: The Case of Four Large European Cities. *The ORBIT Journal*, *2*(2), 1–36. doi:10.29297/orbit.v2i2.110

Ordouei, M., Broumandnia, A., Banirostam, T., & Gilani, A. (2023). Optimization of energy consumption in smart city using reinforcement learning algorithm. *International Journal of Nonlinear Analysis and Applications*.

Su, K., Li, J., & Fu, H. (2011). Smart city and the applications. In *2011 International Conference on Electronics, Communications and Control (ICECC)* (pp. 1028-1031). 10.1109/ICECC.2011.6066743

Tastimur, C., Karakose, M., & Akin, E. (2017). *An Information Extraction Approach with Vehicle and Pedestrian Activity Monitoring for Traffic Management in Smart City*. Academic Press.

Vítor, G., Rito, P., Sargento, S., & Pinto, F. (2022). A scalable approach for smart city data platform: Support of real-time processing and data sharing. *Computer Networks*, *213*, 109027. doi:10.1016/j.comnet.2022.109027

Ziosi, M., Hewitt, B., Juneja, P., Taddeo, M., & Floridi, L. (2022). Smart cities: Reviewing the debate about their ethical implications. *AI & Society*. Advance online publication. doi:10.100700146-022-01558-0 PMID:36212227

Chapter 8
Smart Healthcare System, Digital Health and Telemedicine, Management and Emergencies:
Patient Emergency Application (PES) E-Governance Applications

A. Merlin Mancy
Hindusthan College of Arts and Science, India

A. V. Senthil Kumar
https://orcid.org/0000-0002-8587-7017
Hindusthan College of Arts and Science, India

Rohaya Latip
Universiti Putra Malaysia, Malaysia

G. Jagadamba
https://orcid.org/0000-0002-7379-7925
Siddaganga Institute of Technology, India

Prasun Chakrabarti
Baroda University, India

Priyanka Sharma
https://orcid.org/0000-0002-9503-1170
Swami Keshvanand Institute of Technology, Management, and Gramothan, India

Ismail Musirin
Universiti Teknologi MARA, Malaysia

Meenakshi Sharma
https://orcid.org/0000-0002-6958-8741
University of Petroleum and Energy Studies, India

B. G. Kanchan
https://orcid.org/0009-0001-2157-4711
Nagarjuna College of Engineering and Technology, India

ABSTRACT

In our world, the large number of sick people with various diseases is very feared, and when there is no help at the right time and in the right form, we lose people. An Android app called Patient Emergency App (PEA) bridges the gap between patients and hospitals. This application offers a soothing system controlled by the patient based on the patient's location. In this Patient Emergency App, the server will

DOI: 10.4018/979-8-3693-1722-8.ch008

locate the sick person when the patient needs help using Google Maps and retrieve the person's information from the database, which is stored by the hospital employees along with patient details. Based on this data, the system will send a reassuring message to the facility while also informing the hospital, relatives, and doctor via text message and email. This application mainly focuses on pregnant women, old people, and extremely sick people.

INTRODUCTION

High-income countries are not exempt from the effects of emergency medicine and critical care, but those in low and middle-income countries are probably affected more severely. More than 5000 new cases of health emergencies are reported in India every day (Mahaveer Golechha, 2020]).According to the AIIMS STUDY, emergency and injury cases accounted for 16% of all patients visiting a health facility each year. According to live observations, 10-12% of all OPD patients on a given day were emergency situations (Jeyshankar et al.,2018). This chapter discusses Android software that enables users to locate the closest hospitals and accessible doctors to their present location. In addition to providing a patient with directions to the closest hospital, this app also offers emergency services.

This Application offers free access and covers all necessary services. In contrast to the current system, do not provide any services in cases of emergencies, The suggested method would notify users' emergency contacts in addition to giving users details to the nearest hospital. Using just one click, the patient can access details regarding their present location along with the location of the nearest hospital. The fundamental purpose of this project is to list all hospitals and clinics in the user's area, together with information about each facility's specialty and operating hours.

This method used specialized tracking technology to determine the patient's whereabouts. The tracking capability was provided by these specialized alarm systems using the Global Positioning System (GPS). The system enables the tracking of a user's mobility using a dedicated GPS or a mobile phone that has an internal GPS receiver and a GPRS transmitter. In other words, the majority of applications to date have used a handheld GPS receiver device to track the location, and ISPs are busy during the tracking period. The goal is to create a system for helping patients that allows for simple registration (from their homes) and the ability to choose the closest Emergency Service Center (ESC) in the event that a patient seems to need additional support in an emergency scenario regardless of where she or he is located and the facility can get to them. The suggested system is the tracking system that use mobile GPS and web service technologies to provide online assistance, but it only truly works when the patient requests it.

BACKGROUND INFORMATION AND RELATED RESEARCH

Below is a summary of the key points that pertain to the topic covered in this section, as well as an introduction to emergency systems, their purposes, and the concerns they have. It also carry out research on modern systems and technology in this area, as well as work and solutions connected to emergencies.

Problems With the Phone System

Discuss the numerous emergency call pipeline problems in this section and explain how they affect the system by becoming difficult or leading to inefficiency. When an operator tries to locate the answers to the most frequent queries, like "What service is required?" the issues with call systems start. "Where are you phoning from?" and "What kind of emergency do you have?". Since emergency unit responses are prioritized based on these values, the location and nature of the situation will have a significant impact on how they are handled. For instance, a patient with a chronic disease would be given precedence above a patient in agony for emergency treatment. In order to possibly save lives, prompt and accurate answers to the aforementioned questions are essential.

Telephone Emergency Systems

It was suddenly possible to call for help from a distance after the invention of the telephone in 1876 by chatting with an operator, who would then transfer your call to the required service or department or immediately dispatch help (Sidney h. Aronson,1977).As phone networks grew and advanced, dedicated emergency lines became necessary. Almost every country in the world currently has access to at least one emergency phone number. On June 30, 1937, London became the first location to set up a designated emergency phone line, becoming the first city-marked emergency phone line (Eloise Moss, 2017). The state of Himachal Pradesh is the first in India to introduce a single emergency number, "112," which will connect callers to police, fire, health, and other helplines through the state's emergency response center (ERC).

Only 20–25 percent of the 75,000 emergencies that occur on average each day in India are thought to require urgent medical attention. This is troubling because many of these situations could become life-threatening if not handled right away (Eshita Raju Kalidindi and G.V. Ramana Rao,2022). Since the development of smartphones, this number has sharply dropped, now standing at only 284,327.

The inability of the patients to receive urgent emergency aid is severely hampered by the ambulance delay. Delay in the ambulance could make the patient's injury worse. As a result of delays brought on by traffic congestion and disobedient drivers, more than 20% of patients in need of emergency care have passed away while traveling to the hospital. Threats like ambulance delays and accidents must be treated seriously if we want to increase patient survival during hospital visits. To enable steps that can be taken to solve the issue, factors creating these hazards must be made clear (Ketut Shri Satya Wiwekananda et al., 2020).

According to a country-level evaluation study developed by AIIMS and given to the NITI Aayog, emergency and injury cases accounted for 9-13% of all patients visiting a healthcare institution each year, 19-24% of admissions in government hospitals, and 3-39% of admissions in private hospitals. In reality, emergencies accounted for 11–30% of all OPD patients on any given day. These figures, even using conservative assumptions, show the massive emergency case load that India has to deal with for a country with its large population. According to the same survey, the availability of emergency operative care services (for trauma, non-trauma, orthopaedic, neurosurgery, and obstetric treatment) varied from 47 to 60%. demonstrating yet again how insufficient the country's emergency services are.

Historically, the emergency service number 108 was chosen to make it more difficult to dial the emergency service number by accident when using rotary phones. Because of the increased use of push-button phones and, more recently, touch screens, it is now much easier to inadvertently dial the emergency number 108. The techniques in our suggested application will reduce the possibility of accidental dialing while also taking into account how important it is to be able to dial a number quickly. We will be able to achieve this by taking into account factors such as button positioning and human response times.

Non-Emergency Dialing

Despite the fact that this drop is a major improvement, unintentional dialing, commonly referred to as "pocket dialing," is still an issue that needs to be resolved. Making the number challenging to call is problematic because it needs to be easy to call in an emergency.

The development of emergency service call centers has benefited significantly from the pervasiveness of mobile phone technology. Dispatchers think that the increased accessibility of mobile devices is mostly to blame for the increase in calls. Pocket dials are widely available since calling an emergency on a cell phone has gotten simpler. In the modern era, mobile networks are also virtually universally accessible to assist citizens in making an emergency call and continuing contact in dire circumstances (LandoniG et al, 2007).

The number of non-emergency calls generated by pocket dialing continues to be the largest. Both a technological solution (i.e., steps taken by mobile networks or device manufacturers to allow emergency calls to be placed even when the terminals are locked) and a public awareness campaign encouraging people to lock their phones when not in use could be used to address this issue. The second-largest source of unnecessary calls and the most expensive ones are abusive calls. Investigation of the emergency call archive revealed instances involving individuals who had made 970 calls in six months. An awareness campaign would probably have no impact in these rare instances, but a fine would be more useful in lowering the volume of calls.

The non-emergency call categories were distributed over the six-month period starting in December 2017:3,275,932 non-emergency calls were made over this time period, resulting in 10,967 operator hours of wasted time, according to data gathered during this period. These non-emergencies were handled by 661 call takers, and 1,008,140 callers had placed the incoming calls. The 112 system, which records non-emergency calls, averaged 18,000 per day, or 60 hours of conversation between 5,500 callers and 380 operators. Also, a sizable portion of calls (66%) were pocket dials (11,510 daily calls), resulting in 35 hours being lost by 112 call handlers listening to these inadvertent calls (Mihail Bărănescu et al, 2021).

Caller Location

The caller's location is one of the most important pieces of information requested during an emergency because it tells the operator where to send help. The quicker this information is obtained, the quicker the response. Callers may find it difficult to provide their location verbally in some cases. In this case, operators must have alternative methods for tracking down a caller's location. Calls made from landlines are the easiest to track down because phone numbers are assigned to a specific address; calls made from mobile phones, which account for 60% of all emergency calls, are more difficult to track down. The current location of a mobile device can be obtained in three ways. They are as follows:

Global Positioning System (GPS): With more smart phones than ever before including GPS,This feature, GPS transmitter, can be used to gather the caller's location and send it to the emergency operator. The most accurate location would be a caller's GPS location, which is often rendered as their latitude and longitude, with up to 15 metres of error. The limitation of GPS's usability due to frequency blackouts is an issue. Because GPS signals operate at a frequency that makes it difficult for them to travel through solid objects such as roofs and walls, there is no guarantee that they will work inside buildings (B. P. S. Sahoo &Satyajit Rath, 2012).

Cell Towers: Because mobile phones transmit and receive calls from nearby cell towers, their location can be narrowed down to the area covered by that specific tower's signal, which is typically 1-2 miles. Triangulating a phone's signal from multiple cell towers yields more accurate readings.

Hoaxers and practical jokers: Of all the non-emergency calls that operators receive, malicious calls are by far the most expensive, requiring emergency vehicles to react to created incidents like a false fire. Making bogus calls anonymously seems to be a key motivator for pranksters since it allows them to act in ways they otherwise may not because their identity is hidden. The "online disinhibition effect" is a term used to describe this kind of separation. So, it makes sense to propose that people will be less likely to place phone calls if callers' anonymity is removed.

Wi-Fi: To gauge the strength of a mobile Wi-Fi signal, the Wi-Fi Positioning System (WPS) uses Wi-Fi access points. This approach is helpful in metropolitan cities where Wi-Fi signals are prevalent, but it is not very helpful in rural areas, which frequently have poor Wi-Fi coverage. Wi-Fi, on the other hand, can be used to send data to devices over the internet when it is accessible. Theoretically, medical practitioners might be informed of details like GPS coordinates (W. Jiang & Z. Yin, 2015).

Selecting the Correct Number Everywhere in the world, a caller must first know the emergency service they require and the phone number for that service before they may place an emergency call. From a global viewpoint, this can be challenging because different countries have different emergency phone numbers—for example, India uses 102, the U.S. uses 911, and other nations have separate lines for police, ambulances, and fire services (Mohit Sharma &Ethan Brandler2014). Many numbers are also available for less critical circumstances; for instance, in India, the following numbers are accessible:

- NATIONAL EMERGENCY NUMBER 112
- POLICE 100
- FIRE 101
- AMBULANCE 102
- Disaster Management Services 108
- Women Helpline 1091
- Women Helpline - (Domestic Abuse) 181
- Air Ambulance 9540161344
- Aids Helpline 1097
- Anti Poison (New Delhi) 1066 or 011-1066
- Disaster Management (N.D.M.A):1078, 01126701728
- EARTHQUAKE / FLOOD / DISASTER (NDRF Headquarter) NDRF HELPLINE NO:011-24363260 9711077372
- Deputy Commissioner Of Police - Missing Child And Women 1094
- Railway Enquiry 139
- Senior Citizen Helpline 14567
- Medical Helpline in Andhra Pradesh, Gujarat, Uttarakhand, Goa, Tamil Nadu, Rajasthan, Karnataka, Assam, Meghalaya, Madhya Pradesh, and Uttar Pradesh - 108
- 1072 Railway Accident Emergency Service • 1073 Road Accident Emergency Service
- Road Accident Emergency Service for Private Operators on National Highway 1033

- AIIMS ORBO Centre (for Organ Donation) Delhi 1060
- Kisan Call Centre 18001801555l
- Natural Disaster Relief Commissioner 1070
- Children in Difficult Situation 1098
- AIIMS NEW DELHI (24*7)1800116117 011-26593677, 26589391 National Poisons Information Centre
- Tourist Helpline1363 or 1800111363
- LPG Leak Helpline1906

Alternative non-emergency numbers have been established that provide telephone guidance in an effort to decrease the overuse of the 108 call system. No proof, however, exists that these figures lower the volume of 108 calls. It is proposed that giving telephone guidance rather than sending out response vehicles is a good alternative approach for non-serious calls, while it is likely that this is due to a lack of awareness of the various numbers. Clearly, the best way to solve this issue is through improved education on when to call and who to call. The planned invention would try to programme in all the different service numbers so that by asking a series of questions, users may determine whether they require. It is obvious that the primary solution to this issue is improved education about when to call and who to call. The proposed development would attempt to programme in all of the various service numbers so that consumers can utilise a series of questions to determine whether they need to contact and, if so, which number they should call. In order to free up resources for genuine emergencies, this is intended to assist in filtering out or rerouting less serious incidents.

EXISTING AND PROPOSED SYSTEM

Current System

The current system faces an enormous issue with the large number of sick people from a disease-only perspective, i.e., how does this issue become more effective if there isn't someone who offers emotional support and additional help at a convenient time for those people when they are in school, shopping, with their friends, etc.? If they require support and no one is there to provide it who is qualified to do so, it will lose a significant portion of those individuals. Without taking the diseases into account, the diseases present a picture of the major issue facing the planet. Hence, without a suitable feeding system, the patient's mortality rate could rise.

Disadvantages

- Who will provide support and assistance at the appropriate moment if sick persons ask for it?
- There is a serious problem that needs to be solved.
- The sufferers are not assisted by the current system.
- There is no alert system available. There is no patient tracking system available.

Proposed System

By utilizing the technology built into smartphones, the proposed Patient Emergency Application (PEA) system seeks to improve the effectiveness of emergency services by delivering a quicker response time (e.g., location services). When a patient clicks the "emergency button" on the user interface, PES' primary goal is to automatically take care of and safeguard them utilizing their location through this application. By reducing the number of tasks involved in the present process, PEA's overarching objective is to cut down on the amount of time it takes to respond to emergency calls.PEA will reduce the time and complexity of calling an ambulance or other emergency services in a crisis situation by leveraging the technology available on smart phones. By leveraging the technology available on smart phones, PEA will reduce the time and complexity of calling an ambulance or other emergency services in a crisis situation. Simplifying these steps should result in a faster response time, higher call turnover for operators, and increased efficiency when gathering patient information. PEA has the potential to increase the safety and security of elderly, disabled, or otherwise vulnerable people in their own homes, allowing them to remain independent while decreasing the likelihood of developing physical and mental health problems as a result of loneliness.

The suggested system for taking care of disease sufferers' needs includes registration at the closest care facility, advice, alarms when a request for assistance from a disease sufferer is displayed on a map, and tracking when that person needs help from the system using open-source technology that uses smartphones. Only after sending a support request to the server does the patient get access to the tracking service. When the server receives a request from the client, it automatically transfers it to the closest emergency response facility. Also, it notifies an emergency hospital and the patient's (client's) emergency contacts.

Advantages

- The patient activated the "Emergency" button when they required assistance, which asked the server for help. The client uses a built-in GPS, therefore the request includes the patient's ID, latitude, and longitude, which are automatically acquired from GPS satellites.
- When the server receives the patient's mobile assistance request and forwards it to the closest emergency service center, it operates automatically. When a patient requires assistance, it can also SMS the patient's emergency contacts.
- A satisfyingly greater productivity system was supplied by the usage of mobile GIS based on web services, which is backed by request and response rates. When compared to other systems, its response is the highest.

Architecture of PEA

PEA is a mobile application that connects to the hospital platform (i.e., the emergency department) and responds to patient questions and requests for ambulance assistance. The major function of the program will be to sends the emergency alert to the hospital when the patient need emergency help. The PEA architecture is consists of three layers: patient side, data center, and doctor platform. The following are the elements and functions of these layers:

1. Patient side: The primary components of this layer are a smartphone with the PEA app installed. In an emergency, patients use this app to request care from the hospital. As a result, the app will make use of some of the built-in sensors to provide data such as location coordination without requiring patients to locate themselves at the time. Furthermore, when a patient registers in this PEA application, the app provides information about the patient's health situation.
2. Data center: Patient data are kept at a data center. It will gather patient data from their smartphone app over the Internet, organize it into patient records tables, and then make it accessible to doctors and/or other approved healthcare professionals for monitoring and use (i.e., emergency requests and remote check-ups and treatment facilities). Also, by establishing a threshold for symptoms, any disorder found in the patient's data will be retained in this layer for all data processing and analysis.
3. Hospital/Doctors side: After the user clicks the "Emergency Button," the hospital will take action. They will behave appropriately after receiving the emergency notice. Direct interaction with the system is essential in this procedure because it only requires a few bits of information from the operator to complete the task. This saves time and resources by enabling the task to be accomplished swiftly and effectively. Emergency workers can be sent to the situation more quickly if they are informed about the location of a patient's emergency alert as soon as possible, ensuring that the patient receives timely medical assistance. the more quickly they can respond and provide the assistance that is required.

To ensure great system performance, all information must be delivered instantly across all tiers. Because these data are necessary for making crucial choices and any errors could result in human lives being lost, every piece of data within PEA is organized, compressed, and decompressed correctly and reliably to ensure that data transitions are accomplished in real-time or close to real-time. In order to keep patients and hospitals informed of their status, this is done to ensure that all information is accurate and up-to-date, allowing for the best possible decision-making and outcomes. PEA is an interactive system that entails interactions with users over two platforms (namely, the responder platform and the patient platform). To ensure the highest level of accuracy and efficiency, the responder platform is designed to send and receive data in a secure manner, while the patient platform allows patients to access their data in a timely manner.

In PEA Architecture the given below (Figure 1), that connecting each levels like, the user(patient) side UI,Responder (Hospitals) side UI with the that's Workflow, and Data Center. That connectivity makes the app performs better. In first the user gives their information when they are register into the application, the details such as their name, age, disease details, document, profile picture, location. They having the "Emergency Button" in their UI, if any emergency help is needed, they can access the help with just a single click of the button. The Patient details are sent to the data center that manages by operator(admin). Operator manages all the data and it forward the patient details to the patient preferred hospital and other hospitals that nearby the patient's location (if any emergency situation is needed) and it notify the patient about what are the actions taken by hospitals when the critical situation happened. Finally, the Responder (hospital) side started their work they got the "Alert" message that notify after the "Emergency Button" clicked by the user. The Responder is responsible for decision making such as arrange operation theater, prepare treatment and how fast send the ambulance and take over the patient. Thus, the way the PEA application works simply and easily.

Figure 1. Architecture of PEA

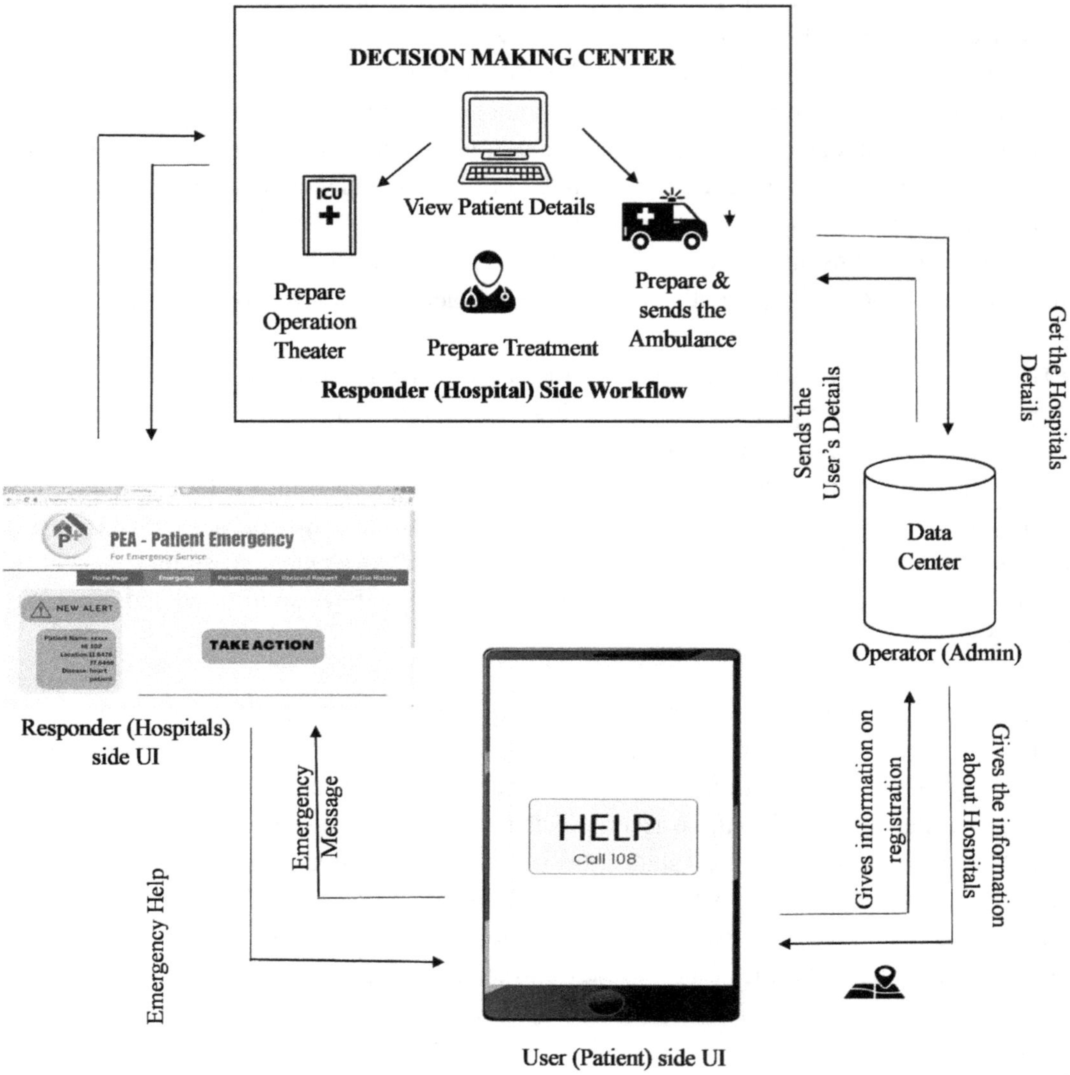

Theory of PEA

Because PEA is intended to be an emergency response system, we must ensure that it has as little downtime as possible, just like any other emergency system. To this end, we must make sure that PEA is well-maintained and up-to-date, and that we have a team of trained professionals on call to manage any issues or unexpected problems. A system with a low availability would not be appropriate for situations involving the loss of life. Because the system is handling potentially sensitive personal data, it is critical that it act responsibly by making every effort to keep user information secure. To ensure a prompt and effective response, we must also make sure PEA is outfitted with the most recent technology. Examples include mandating login or registration in order for users to access the service. We must also make sure that the server on which our data centre is housed is properly password-protected.

There are a lot of standards that must be followed for effective Health applications in terms of patient data security and legalisation, making the design of mobile applications for healthcare particularly important (Mahaveer Golechha, 2020). A poorly designed application will have security and usability problems, which can cause the application to fail. Thus, it is crucial that we put in place a number of reasonable safeguards to prevent the theft of our users' sensitive data, whether it comes from our data centre or during the transmission of data from or to a mobile application. We intend to incorporate an account-based functionality that needs users to first create an account before they can use it to access the PEA using a user name in order to satisfy the security requirements of our application. Any electronic health-related data is integrated, shared, and retrieved through the PEA system. Additionally, the data is end-to-end encrypted (E2EE), which means that it is secured from the patients' mobile app to the hospital platform.

Table 1. Type of users and their requirements

Users	Requisites
User (Patient)	Their main requirement for the system is that, in the event of an emergency, the patient be able to send an emergency help request and receive a response for assistance as soon as possible.
Operator (Admin)	When a user registers for this application, the operator (admin) wants to collect information from them. Name, age, disease, location, preferred hospital, medical documents provided by the hospital, profile picture, and so on. It is simple for the operator, who sends the patient's information to the hospital when an emergency situation arises.
Responders (Hospitals)	Direct communication with the system, which just needs a few pieces of information from the operator to finish the job. In this Process, Speed is crucial; the quicker they learn the location of a patient's emergency alert, the quicker they can react and render the necessary assistance.

The PEA app is expected to feature a wide range of patient data collection capabilities on the User(patient's side). The general system requirements for three users are shown in Table 1. More precise information will be supplied in addition to the usual basic information like name, age, and current location. The patient information about their heart rate or blood sugar levels and disease information will be included in this additional data. These data will be utilized to monitor the patient's development and give health care providers a more complete picture of their health. It will also aid medical professionals in accurately diagnosing and treating patients. Also, there is an optional opportunity to include images with the selected hospital functioning, allowing paramedics to plan ahead to save lives. Also, tiny bits of knowledge like this are intended to let operators and responders have a better idea of the patient's current condition and aid them in making better treatment decisions. In this manner, the patient can obtain more precise and prompt care, enabling them to receive the finest treatment for their disease. Our system will have a safeguard in place to prevent a user's information from being stolen because our application will handle sensitive personal data. To do this, we're going to add a login feature that will require users to first create an account, fill out some personal data, and then enable the main calling feature of the app. It includes the following elements in the PEA mobile application (also known as the patient platform), based on the problems listed from the patient's perspective:

- Data synchronization for patients
- Mechanisms to prevent inappropriate dialing
- Improve the accessibility for callers who are disabled.

- A summary of who and when to call for help.
- The most convenient method for preparing medical resources close to the hospital

From the perspective of the operator (admin), operators may be able to use a web-platform to view patient information, attend upcoming calls, and carry out the crucial task of gathering information (location coordination, case information) for emergency requests made via a mobile application by people in need of an ambulance for emergency cases. Instead of limiting users to a single platform, the web-platform should be similar to what functions without any noticeable slowing or unexpected crashes in the majority of mainstream web browsers. To do this, we must ensure that our website functions well on a device with average processing power. By limiting its use, a web portal that can only be used on powerful computers will constrain the spectrum of innovations. In order to ensure that the video communication operates well for both the caller and operator platforms, the web platform must also be able to function inside the majority of web browsers, avoiding the usage of elements that are not commonly utilized, such as some features of HTML5.As was already said, the main requirement for the web platform is to retrieve data from the data center and provide it to operators on a screen. For instance, the coordinate information should be displayed as an overlay on a Google Maps API, revealing the caller's position and enabling caller tracking. The data center should also be accessed and used to display the additional pieces of information, like name, age, and gender. When a patient presses the emergency button, it indicates that they require assistance, and the operator should transfer that information from the database to the hospital's side. It is intended for a number of fields in the contact area of the online platform to be automatically filled with patient information, providing the operator with a list of all patients. Also, it is anticipated that the patient's profile pictures, which serve as a means of identification, will appear alongside the data. Finally, the website should be able to accept data from users, much like the mobile app.

The PEA app is expected to provide responders (hospitals) with a wide range of patient data collection capabilities. Table 1 shows the general system requirements for three responders. More precise information will be supplied in addition to the usual basic information like name, age, and current location that are submitted by users. It will also help medical professionals accurately diagnose and treat patients in critical situations. As a result, the patient can receive more precise and timely care, allowing them to receive the best treatment for their disease from the responder (hospital).The PEA application will handle sensitive personal data, we will have a safeguard in place to prevent the hospital's information from being stolen. The main calling feature of the app can only be activated when hospitals have created an account, filled out certain hospital information, and enabled the login feature.

RELEVANCE OF THE PROJECT

In this subsection, we have carried out research on the methods that are currently being used to solve the problem of emergency systems. Since their inception, emergency call systems have advanced significantly. As new technologies emerge, so does the system's ability to gather more accurate information and make better decisions. Current emergency systems require the caller to provide their current location so that the operator knows where to send assistance. Despite the fact that technologies for gathering location information, such as GPS, have been commercially available since the late 1990s, this method has not changed since the inception of emergency call systems. This is not to claim that the sole way to pinpoint a caller's location is based on their response. Depending on how far away from cell towers the caller is, emergency call operators can pinpoint the caller's location to a particular area, usually a few miles. This is generally incorrect and necessitates a potential extensive search area for the emergency response vehicle.

Requests for emergency service through SMS, It has been possible to text for emergency assistance since late 2009. In many nations, sending a text message to a short number will connect those in need of emergency assistance with the closest service providers. Those in need of emergency assistance can be connected with the closest service providers by using a short code.The goal of this initiative was to make assistance requests possible for those who have difficulty speaking, are deaf, or have difficulty hearing.

By itself, SMS does not offer any geo-specific location data. But, other resources in the communications network, like the cell-ID, can be used to access this information. SMS has the potential to be utilized in location-based emergency services, allowing for the sending of bulk SMS messages to specified mobile numbers when they are found in predetermined locations (Anas Aloudat& Katina Michael, 2011).

The system, however, has a number of limitations that will limits how usable it can be; for instance, in order to transfer messages, phones must first be registered. This registration procedure is difficult and takes too long for someone who actually has an emergency. Additional limitations include communication being slower than speech; (ii) it being challenging to type if the caller is hurt or in a panic; and (iii) the 160-character limit for individual SMS messages. Despite these shortcomings, the SMS system is still far superior to earlier emergency aid techniques because it is still quicker and simpler.

In Case of Emergency (ICE) is a top three medical application in the United Kingdom, Canada, Norway, and Denmark. In Australia and Sweden, the ICE app is the most downloaded app in the medical category. This shows how popular the application is in these countries. This app is compatible with both iOS and Android devices. The In Case of Emergency application displays user emergency information on the lock screen wallpaper, including an emergency contact number specified by the user. ICE also collects additional information for use in an emergency, such as a person's medical condition, medication, and insurance information. ICE does not serve as a completely functional emergency system because it does not connect people to emergency units or provide user location, despite the fact that it has received some positive evaluations. However, some users thought it was unnecessary to have it on the lock screen since a pin was still needed to access the paramedics' data.

The official American Red Cross First Aid app, American Red Cross, delivers professional assistance for common emergencies at your fingertips through interactive quizzes, video tutorials, and step-by-step first aid instructions. The software is free and accessible for Android and iOS smartphones. Its key features include support for many languages, full integration with 9-1-1 so you can call EMS at any time, and videos and animations that are designed to make learning first aid enjoyable and simple. This application's drawback is that it doesn't actually offer emergency aid when one arises. In other words, it takes users (i.e., patients) a long time to get to very limited information about the patient. It also does not provide paramedics with information about the patient's location or condition. Furthermore, based on user feedback, it was discovered that reading the instructions of first aid animations and videos in an emergency situation is inconvenient, as this is counter-intuitive when patients require immediate help and/or advice (Mohammed Al-khafajiy et al., 2019).

Teladoc. With the help of this software, board-certified medical professionals and patients can communicate conveniently and round-the-clock by phone or video. With the aid of this app, patients may quickly and easily get in touch with medical professionals who are willing to listen to their concerns and offer assistance. If it is considered medically necessary, doctors can also quickly prescribe medication and link with the pharmacy of their choice. Teladoc has Apple HealthKit integrated to enhance the user experience. Medical experts can more correctly diagnose patients and import their most recent medical information with the aid of this seamless connectivity. One disadvantage of the Teladoc app is that appointments may be expensive if they are not covered by insurance. Teladoc is a groundbreaking move towards improving healthcare access and quality, despite the possible expense. Following a visit to a general practitioner, there is no way to follow up. After a general medical appointment, there was no follow-up. A doctor's diagnosis may be limited if a physical examination is not performed. Negative reviews frequently mention unreliable or no-show doctors as well as scheduling issues (Lori Uscher-Pines et al., n.d.).

Better Help. This mobile healthcare app is a pioneer in the field of counseling. BetterHelp connects patients with mental health professionals in a timely, cost-effective, and convenient manner. BetterHelp is a simple way to get professional help from licensed therapists and counsellors online. This allows people to seek assistance on their own time and from any location. Virtual support systems can help you manage your mental health more effectively. They are convenient and private for many people, making them a viable option for receiving coaching and therapy from anywhere and at any time.BetterHelp is a valuable service that enables people to receive therapeutic assistance in the privacy and comfort of their own homes. BetterHelp is one such online therapy service that allows you to text-chat with a licenced and accredited therapist 24 hours a day, seven days a week. We talk about how BetterHelp works, what to think about if you're looking for online therapy, and what would be best for you. We also included our editor's evaluation of BetterHelp as well as her personal experience with this online service. Individuals can communicate with their therapist using BetterHelp without ever leaving the comfort of their own home. However, it has a few drawbacks, including the following: No insurance coverage: Often, BetterHelp's online treatment services are not covered by insurance. This covers Medicare, Medicaid, and private insurance. Restricted authority: BetterHelp therapists can offer talk therapy but are not authorized to make medical diagnoses, issue prescriptions, or carry out court orders. BetterHelp doesn't offer therapy to children or teenagers; it only offers it to adults (Enitan T Marcelle et al., 2019).

System Design of PEA

The strategy we take in creating the PEA is centred on looking into problems with the emergency system as well as options that might be created to enhance the trending technique of calling for emergencies. As a result, we examine the systems put in place for patient and operator communications as well as the systems utilised by both sides to collect data to benefit both parties. These systems entail the usage of mobile applications by the caller (patients) and web-based platforms by the operator (i.e., hospital workers). The primary processes that the system uses to gather and process the necessary data from the callers are depicted in Figure 1a. We have identified three individuals who perform roles within the system based on who would use it (Figure. 2).Every one of these user groups has various requirements for the system. They will also put the technology to use in a number of other ways. The three main system participants are callers, operators, and call centre managers, as shown in Figure 2. The following are the user group roles as a result:

1. The user(patient) is the person requesting help via the PEA.
2. The Operator is the person who passes the information from both side.
3. The Responder is the person who will go to help the patient in the hospital side.

Figure 2. Outline of the system users

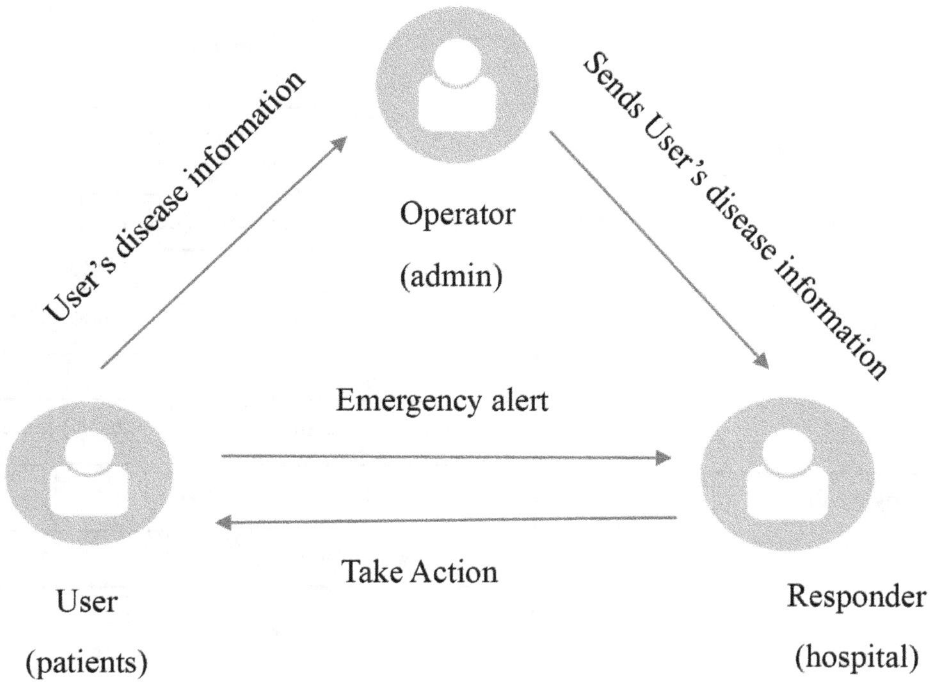

System Flow Diagram

In this system diagram, the main components or functions are represented by blocks, which are connected by lines that highlight the connections between the blocks.

Use Case Diagram

The interactions between users and the application of the system are graphically represented in this use-case diagram. The system's perimeter establishes its boundaries.

Pea Modules Description

A class that represents a business application task is known as an application module. It encapsulates the data model associated with a task as well as the custom code required to complete the task. The PEA modules include the tasks that are following.,

- Patient details
- Patient Request
- Patient Location tracking
- Emergency medical center tracking
- Alert

Figure 3. System block diagram

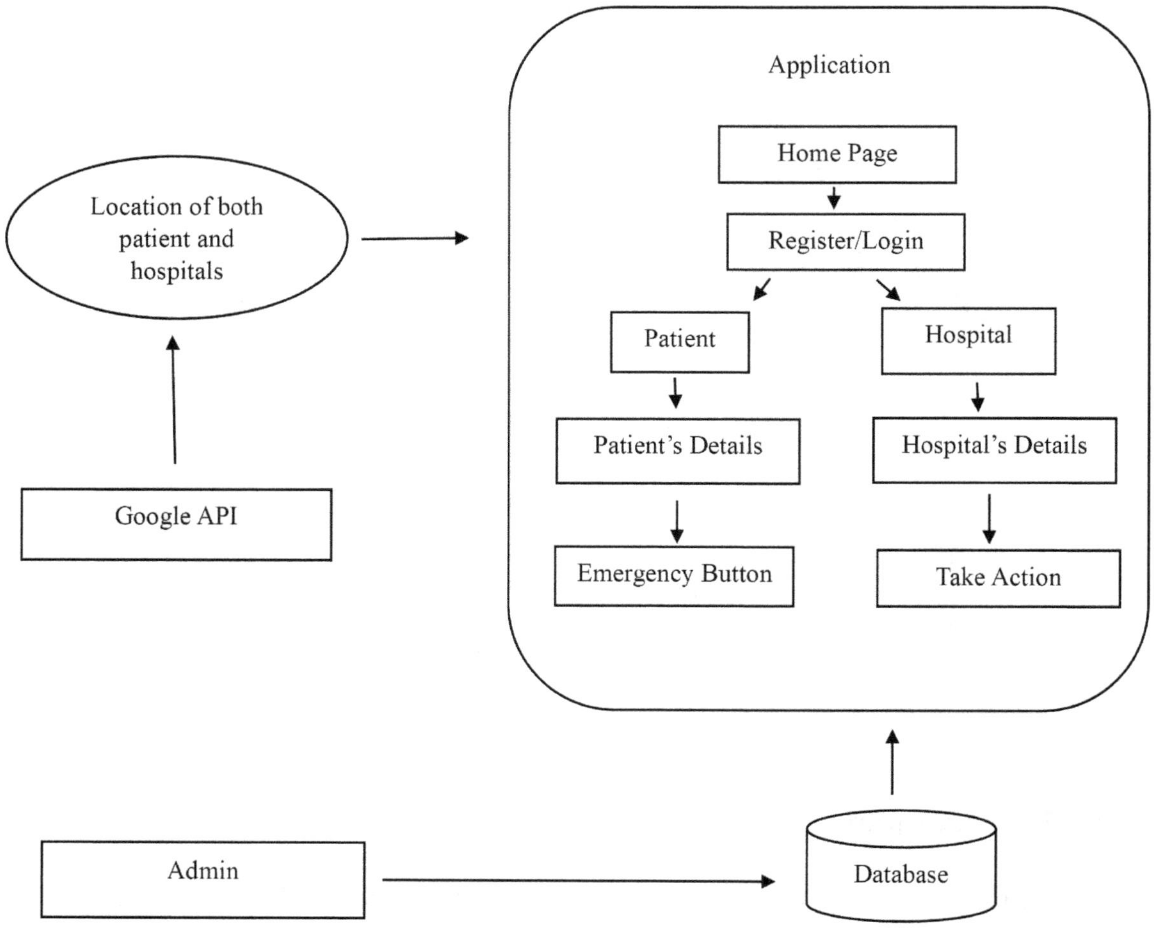

Patient Details

When a patient uses the system for the first time, this module is there they should register their information in the database. It is important that the information is accurate and up-to-date so that the patient can be properly identified and tracked. These details include the patient's name, phone number, date of birth, disease type, and emergency contacts. The data will be kept in the server's database. This data will be used to provide the patient with personalized healthcare services and to ensure that their medical records are up to date.

Patient Request

When necessary, the patient will click the "Emergency Button" to get help. They can then adhere to the given guidelines to obtain the assistance they require. When a request is chosen from the list, the system will then give thorough details regarding the request, including instructions on how to respond to it. SQL queries will be used to retrieve the data needed for that request from the database. The pertinent data will be retrieved using SQL queries, and it will then be presented to the patient in an easy-to-understand style.

Figure 4. Use case diagram

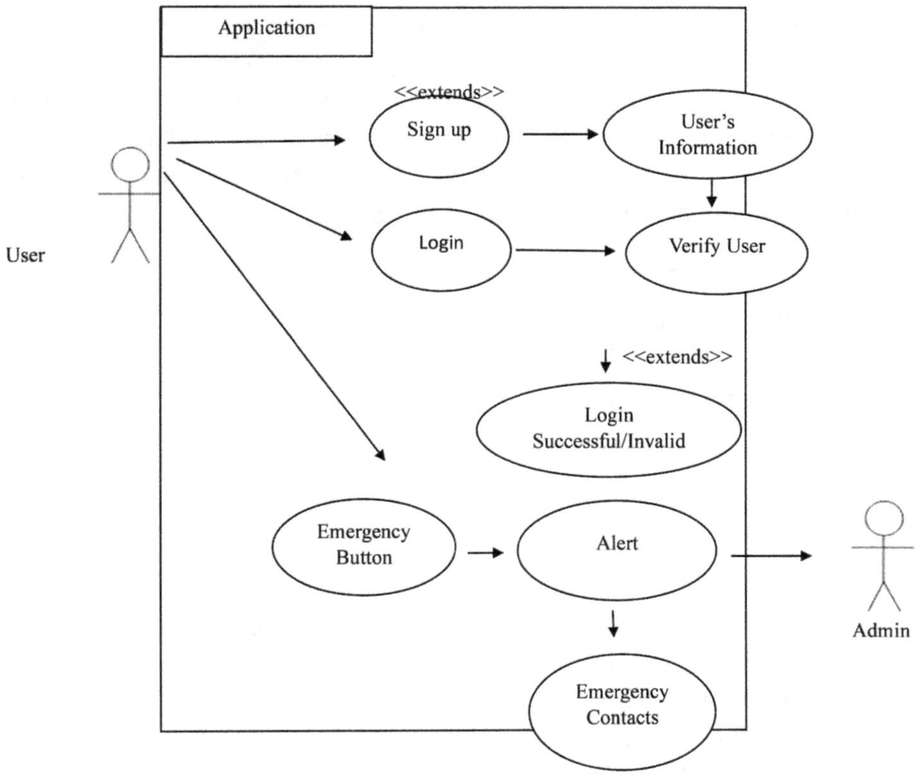

Patient Location Tracking

When the server receives a request from the user, it automatically gets to work and presents a list of requests with their positions displayed as single markers on a Google map. This allows the user to quickly identify their request and take the necessary action. The user uses built-in GPS; therefore, the request includes the patient's ID, latitude, and longitude. This information is then sent to the server, which updates the map with the patient's current location and other relevant details, which are automatically acquired from GPS satellites.

Emergency Medical Center Tracking

With this module, the server will monitor and forward the patient's request to the closest emergency room. This will help reduce the time it takes for the patient to receive medical care and improve their chances of survival. The web service will send a message to the closest hospital from the client's (patient's) mobile device, along with an alarm to let staff members know there is a new help request. The hospital staff will then be able to quickly assess the situation and dispatch a medical team to the patient's location. This will help ensure that they receive the care they need in a timely manner. Each hospital has more than one ambulance to act as a facility for the patients when they require assistance. The system has more than one emergency medical center, which is distributed due to the area that uses this system.

Alert

When a patient needs assistance, the server in this module will email the emergency contacts to let them know that the patient needs their assistance. The server will also provide the emergency contacts with detailed information about the patient's current condition, so they can make informed decisions. Utilizing web service technology means using the Internet to send the request and receive the response. This helps ensure that the emergency contacts are quickly and accurately informed of the patient's situation, so they can provide the necessary help as soon as possible.

SYSTEM PREREQUISITES

Hardware and Software

Hardware

- A minimum of 2 GB of free disc space, 4 GB (500 MB for the IDE + 1.5 GB for the Android SDK and system image emulator), and an Android device.
- Minimum screen resolution: 1280 x 800
- Monitor: 15-inch LED color monitor
- RAM is required to be 4GB.

Software

- Microsoft Windows versions 7/8/10 (32- or 64-bit)
- Software used Android Eclipse(SDK) / Visual Studio.Net 2008
- Java for the front end and My SQL database is at the back end.

Pea Application Implementation

In App development, the application is developed for the Android platform using the Android studio. Java is the programming language used in the back end, while the Visual Studio Framework is used for front-end development on the user side. The web platform has been designed using several scripting languages, including HTML, JavaScript, PHP, MySQL, and CSS for styling on the hospital and server sides.

The primary functionality, capabilities, and innovative aspects of the PEA as contrasted to conventional call systems and existing solutions in the literature have been implemented in this section's prototype of the PEA and validated using a straightforward proof of concept.

Working with the PEA includes interacting with three key components that adhere to a client/server architecture:

i) A smartphone application that allows users (also known as patients) to send urgent requests
ii) A server-based datacenter where all system and patient data is kept and used appropriately;
iii) The web-platform, which is a component of the system and through which the responder can view the emergency request.

As a result, we should think about the implementation plans for the system's three tiers. The allocation of data centers and construction of the structure make up the initial phase of development. The design and implementation of a central database that houses all system data is part of the data-center layer.

The First, the database consists of three entities linked accordingly, the patient, administrator and responder entity. The patient entity is further linked with patient's medical data entities for e-Health records such as disease details. Since that one of our motivations is to eliminate service delays, a proper relation between entities should be initialize at early stages. Therefore, patient's entity linked to emergency – ambulances, in which, users (patients) can save time during emergency(ambulance) requesting service, in other word patients can avoid filling pre-initialized data such name, gender and etc., during every request by simply fetch the patients data through the unique identifier (i.e., Patient Number) during the request.

In the second section, it is determined to employ the Android programming environment for the proof of concept for the PEA prototype app. Because of this, the official Integrated Development Environment (IDE) for Android, called Android Studio, has a number of helpful features for quick development, such as good error detection, a webRTC interface, and an integrated AVD (Android Virtual Device) manager for testing across various devices. Hence, any device can be used to run the PEA app as long as it complies with the following requirements: Support for Android versions 1, 2, and 3, as well as GPS and Internet functionality. The following Figure 5, 6, 7 shows some screen interfaces for the PEA app.

In this third section, the web-platform (also known as the hospital/doctor platform) is the third component of the projects. The two-panel selector and list inlay design patterns were adopted as the design strategy. Based on increasing the system's usability and subsequently the user involvement, this strategy has been taken into consideration. When a list of calls or a list of emergency requests has to be made available, list inlay designs have been employed. While doing a patient detail search or an attending request job, the two-panel selector technique is employed. Frames, which automatically refresh, have been employed in several portions of the application to display real-time data and its updated contents.

Problem Formulation and Solutions

The system's dependency on gaining access to a user's personal data would be the most obvious problem in terms of the ethical ramifications of the system. There are several privacy concerns raised by the fact that the system tracks a user's whereabouts, retains a sizable quantity of personal information, including medical information, and then sends it. Perhaps the scope of this research does not include additional data security and privacy. A malfunctioning system could result in the loss of life since the system deals with circumstances where human life is in danger. We understand that our current approach to location data collection and transmission via PEA has some drawbacks that can be overcome. For example, our system currently necessitates the use of GPS and Wi-Fi technologies, which may not always be available on a caller's device.

As a result, we believe that additional location gathering methods should be available as a backup option for those who do not have GPS or Wi-Fi. Other technologies that could be used have been briefly mentioned, such as sending data via SMS instead of Wi-Fi or using cell towers to triangulate a caller. These options could also be built into the system so that it does not have to rely on a single method. Furthermore, advanced location technologies for indoor navigation, such as Visual Positioning Service (VPS) and INavigation (Ankita Sandip Chipade et al., 2020), can be considered for future development.

RESULT AND EVALUATION

The system's results are displayed in this section. Specifically, demonstrating through a variety of testing techniques whether the provided application has achieved the objectives set forth in advance for the PEA. This application used unit testing to show that the system performed as planned. Unit testing is a technique that places a strong emphasis on the software system's architecture and necessitates some familiarity with PEA's internal logic.

To confirm that the program is compatible with various Android versions, testing has also been done, as shown in Table 2. Using an Android emulator, we were able to conduct some further testing. PEA is created using the Android Eclipse IDE, which has an integrated Android Virtual Device (AVD) emulator that enables testing the app's operation on various Android device kinds. For instance, we can instruct the emulator to mimic a smartphone with x memory or one running Android version y.

Figure 5. The user interface design of PEA application

Figure 6. The user interface design of PEA application

Figure 7. The user interface design of PEA application

The users have evaluated the system's core features under two different situations. In scenario, they tested the media streaming feature between their mobile application and the operator's web-platform using the webRTC API. Figure.,8 displays the performance results for the users over the scenarios, such as 3G, 4G, and WIFI. The findings are categorized under performance outcomes as success, success with issue, and fail, and it is evident that the prototype has demonstrated performance over both scenarios.

Patient Registration

The patient should fill out this area with all of their information, including names, email addresses, passwords, primary and secondary phone numbers for emergencies, addresses, locations, and information about their diseases. In order to establish their electronic medical record and provide emergency care providers with the appropriate information, this information will be used. Patients should make sure that their information is current and accurate as this has a significant impact on the level of care they receive. A patient should enter their data into the database the first time they utilize the system. In order to correctly identify and follow the patient, it is critical that the information be precise and current.

Emergency Request

The patient will be instructed to access this app and touch the "Help 108" emergency button if they are in such a dire circumstance and require immediate assistance. When the button is pressed, the app immediately notifies emergency personnel of the patient's position and the emergency's specifics. Users can also include pertinent medical data for first responders. In order to provide the patient with better care, the emergency responders will also be given access to the patient's medical history and emergency contacts.

Patient Location Tracking

When the server receives a request from the user, it automatically begins processing the request and displays a list of requests with their locations displayed as single markers on a Google map. This enables the user to quickly identify their request and take action. Because the user employs built-in GPS, the request includes the patient's ID, latitude, and longitude. This data is then transmitted to the server, which updates the map with the patient's current location and other relevant details obtained automatically from GPS satellites. The use of GPS technology simplifies and streamlines the process of updating patient locations. This, in turn, enables hospital teams to respond more quickly and efficiently to patient requests.

Future Enhancement

This project has room for growth in the future. The world of computer fields is never static; it is always dynamic. The technology that is popular today becomes obsolete the next day. The system may be refined further to keep up with technological advancements. As a result, it is not completed. However, it will improve with additional improvements. Enhancements can be completed in a timely manner. We can even update it with additional modification and integrate it with minimal modification. It is important to note that, while no conclusions have been reached, we can still expect improvements. These improvements can be realized through efficient methods of updating and integrating the changes.As a result, the project is adaptable and can be expanded with more advanced features at any time. It could also be improved for minor medical assistance, such as an inquiry or appointment. It could be enhanced with a video call feature that allows patients and doctors to meet face to face when separated by a long distance. It could be improved with facial regenerating technology, as well as pre-medical and auto-first-aid instruction.

Table 2. Android versions testing

Android Device	Test Result
Vivo V21	Pass
Samsung A23	Pass
Oppo A78	Pass
Vivo V23	Pass

Figure 8. Performance scenario

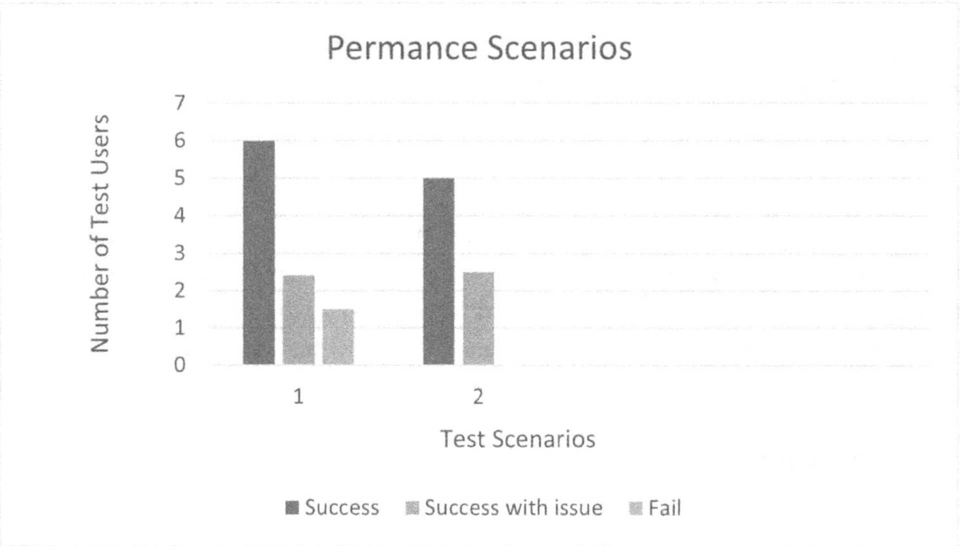

Furthermore, these updates may enhance the overall user experience by making the software more user-friendly and intuitive. A simplified interface and improved navigation can make it easier to use for both patients and medical professionals.

CONCLUSION

The current demographic structure in India has changed significantly as a result of the country's aging population. With an increase in population and a greater number of people living to old age, pregnant

Figure 9. User interface for registration

women, and severely injured people, all of whom are known to use an increased amount of emergency resources, emergency response protocols are sure to be put under additional strain in the near future. This is already evident in the increased number of unanswered calls, which result in many deaths each year. Even when calls are answered and responded to, deaths occur due to increased ambulance response times.

As a result, this paper proposes the Patient Emergency Application (PEA) to meet the needs of current emergency response procedures by introducing a new approach for public emergency response requests.

Figure 10. User interface for emergency button

The following are significant findings after using this system:

1. Request and response rates show that the adoption of mobile GIS based on Web services delivered a satisfyingly greater productivity system. When compared to other systems, its response is the highest.
2. By choosing the closest ESC to cut down on travel time to the patient, the proposed approach increased productivity.
3. The proposed system meets all the demands made of it in terms of goals and objectives.
4. Because the request and reply were sent and received over the Internet, using Web Service technology resulted in lower costs compared to using other methods.

Figure 11. Location tracking

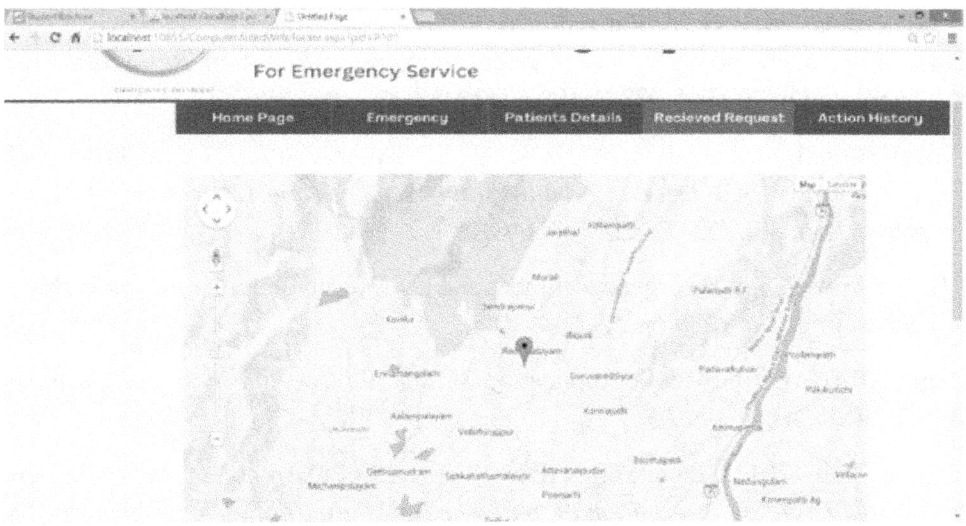

The suggested system's mobile application was created using Windows Phone, but it might eventually be adapted to work on other smartphones like the iPhone and Blackberry, which run various operating systems like iOS and Android.

REFERENCES

Al-khafajiy, M., Kolivand, H., Baker, T., Tully, D., & Waraich, A. (2019). Smart hospital emergency system Via mobile-based requesting services. *Multimedia Tools and Applications*, *78*(14), 20087–20111. doi:10.100711042-019-7274-4

Aronson. (1977). The lancet on the telephone 1876-1975. *Medical History, 21*, 69-87.

Chipade, Mehta, Roham, & Naik. (2020). A review paper on indoor navigation system. *International Journal of Engineering Applied Sciences and Technology, 4*(11).

Enitan, T. (2019). Effectiveness of a Multimodal Digital Psychotherapy Platform for Adult Depression: A Naturalistic Feasibility Study. *JMIR mHealth and uHealth*, *7*(1), e10948. doi:10.2196/10948 PMID:30674448

Golechha. (2021). India should ramp up its emergency medicine and critical care infrastructure to combat COVID-19. *Postgraduate Medical Journal, 97.*

Jiang, W., & Yin, Z. (2015). Indoor Localization with a Signal Tree. *Proceedings of the 18th International Conference on Information Fusion*, 1724 - 1731.

Kalidindi, E. R., & Ramana Rao, G. V. (2022). The role of 108 GVK EMRI ambulance services in the management of behavioral emergencies in the state of Telangana. *Asian Journal of Psychiatry*, *70*, 103019. doi:10.1016/j.ajp.2022.103019 PMID:35151038

Landoni, G., Biselli, C., Maj, G., & Zangrillo, A. (2007). Faster rings in the survival chain: Mobile phones could improve the response to the dedicated emergency call system. *Resuscitation*, *75*(3), 547. doi:10.1016/j.resuscitation.2007.05.022 PMID:17629388

Mihail, B., Ionel-Sorinel, V., Madalina, T., Nadia, C., & Madlena, N. (2021). Analysis of Abusive 112 Emergency Calls in Romania. *Journal of Administrative Sciences and Technology*, *2021*, 471463. Advance online publication. doi:10.5171/2021.471463

Moss. (2017). The Three-Digit Emergency Number and the Transnational Politics of Welfare Activism, 1937–1979. *Journal of Social History, 52*(2).

Pandey & Dani. (2014). Android Mobile Application Build on Eclipse. *International Journal of Scientific and Research Publications, 4*(2).

Sahoo, B. P. S. & Rath. (2012). Integrating GPS, GSM and Cellular Phone for Location Tracking and Monitoring. *Proceedings of the International Conference on Geospatial Technologies and Applications, Geomatrix'*12.

Sharma & Brandler. (2014). Emergency Medical Services in India: The Present and Future. *Prehospital and Disaster Medicine, 29*(3), 1-4. doi:10.1017/S1049023X14000296

Uscher-Pines, L., Mulcahy, A., Cowling, D., Hunter, G., Burns, R., & Mehrotra, A. (2016). Access and Quality of Care in Direct-to-Consumer Telemedicine. *Telemedicine Journal and e-Health*, *22*(4), 282–287. doi:10.1089/tmj.2015.0079 PMID:26488151

Wiwekananda, Hamukti, Yogananda, Calisto, & Utomo. (2020). Understanding factors of ambulance delay and crash to enhance ambulance efficiency: An integrative literature review. *Journal of Community Empowerment for Health, 3*(3).

Chapter 9
Smart Prediction Farming Using Deep Learning and AI Techniques

Ashok Singh Gaur
Rama University, India

C. S. Raghuvanshi
Rama University, India

Hari Om Sharan
Rama University, India

ABSTRACT

Agriculture in India is an important field with a significant economic impact in several countries. Due to the substantial population growth, meeting people's dietary needs has become a relevant concern. Agriculture is critical to a country's economic development. Approximately 58% of a country's primary source of livelihood is farming. Farmers till date are working with conventional farming techniques. These techniques were not precise and thus reduced the productivity and consumed a lot of time and money. Precise farming helps to increase the productivity by precisely determining the steps that needs to be practiced. Predicting the weather conditions, analyzing the soil, predicting the crops for cultivation, finding the amount of fertilizers, pesticides that need to be used are some elements of precision farming. Precise farming uses advanced technologies such as IoT, deep learning, data analytics, and machine learning to collect the data, understand the systems, and predict the results.

1. INTRODUCTION

Agriculture is playing an important role in earning food and livelihood for the whole family. As up to 70% population of India still depends on agriculture as means of employment. Agriculture plays an important part in feeding large parts of society, so without smart prediction and sustainable agriculture there will not possible to survive their families. Due to increase in population at great pace it will need

DOI: 10.4018/979-8-3693-1722-8.ch009

another green revolution with the help of smart prediction farming. Farmers in all countries specifically in countries where agriculture is the main occupation of the people and a major source contributing in their country's economy. Farmers are mainly relying on rainfall for harvest and all other subsequent activities. This is a main reason for the loss of over 11 billion dollars' revenue each year due to crop damage (Burney J, 2014). In such circumstance more efficient farming practices are required which make use of technological advancements and provide key for current restrictions in farming. Artificial Intelligence (AI), with the applications of Internet of things (IOT), Machine Learning, Deep Learning and predictive analysis, is adding new advantage in the field of agricultural. Government of India with public and private partnerships is working on the technological development to help farmers with innovative ideas (IT-based solutions) through the Digital India program. Different challenges related to agriculture crop production get solved through IT based solution.

As unexpected climate changes which consequently result in weak soil water equation and unpredictable rain falls. But AI enabled technologies gives prediction reports on changes in climate of any location which help to supervise farmers to take effective decisions in these conditions. With growing applications of AI in agriculture areas like driverless tractors, plant health monitoring, and automatic irrigation systems (D.N. Baker, 1983). The agricultural sector faces a lot of challenges; however, still, it is the main contributor of development and plays a key role in increasing the economy of any country. Problems in agriculture were studied and their solutions were proposed in different literatures beginning with databases till decision support systems (P. Martiniello, 1988, K. W. Thorpe, 1992). Among all these solutions, AI enabled systems have established as excellent players as far as robustness and preciseness are related. Agriculture along with its allied sectors like fishery and forestry contributes to about one-third of the country's GDP. This sector not only provides food and raw materials but also source of employs majority of labor forces. Farming defines the concept of growing crops and raising livestock on a large-scale basis to orient it toward business or to raise money for it. As time and technology changes rapidly, a farmer is in anxiety as his income has not increased but his expenses are increased. So, there is time for a farmer to move away from traditional farming practices and adopt and embed new farming techniques in his regular farming activities. With the help of these technology, he can understand new crops that can be grown in his land. By growing new crops, he can get new opportunities to improve his income and enjoy success. So new technologies can be designed that can help a farmer predict which crop can be grown in his land depending upon factor such as types of soil, geographical location such as latitude and longitude, rainfall in his area, average temperature in his area. Advanced prediction farming is the new, innovative farming method that uses highly advanced, efficient machines and technology in agricultural fields. The central concept of advanced farming synchronizes with precision farming which itself devotes more and more focus on the use of highly productive, advanced techniques of farming with the help of smart agricultural machinery, thus ensuring efficient work along with more productivity and fill the gaps in the sector of agriculture starting from raising of crops to getting more and more profit.

2. SMART PREDICTION FARMING: NOW A DAYS KEY OF SUCCESS FOR SUSTAINABLE AGRICULTURE

Smart prediction farming is a concept of all about the usage of technology in agriculture with aim of gain quality and quantity in the field of agriculture. In the 21st century farmers have easy access Taxonomy of application of machine learning in agriculture is given in Figure 1. Smart prediction farming basically uses IT based technology in five major areas –crop management, livestock management, field condition management, pest management and weather tracing forecasting.

Figure 1. Taxonomy of smart prediction farming using deep learning and ai techniques in agriculture

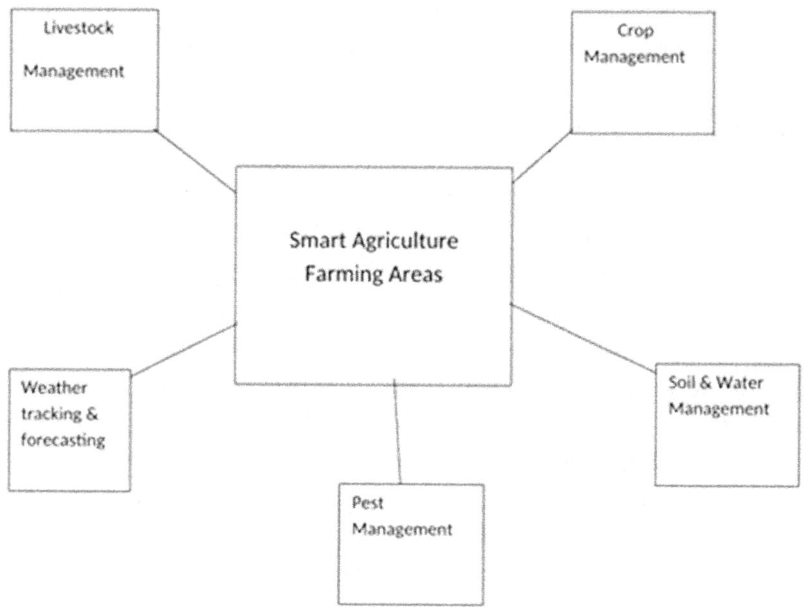

Crop smart prediction management system is further split into sub categories including crop yield estimation, fruit counting, crop disease detection, weed identification, species recognition and quality of crop. Field smart prediction condition management includes soil and water management. Yield prediction can also be divided into number of tasks such as yield estimation, yield mapping, supply and demand analysis of crop and crop management for improved productivity. In work presented by authors of (Ramos, 2017), applications of Machine Learning are included. It describes a low cost, non-destructive and efficient method for mechanically counting fruits on a coffee tree branch. Farmers make wrong decisions in choosing pesticides and fertilizers for pest control. But with the application of precision agriculture, variation within the field can be measured and farmers can change strategies accordingly. It results in better pest management. Not only in pest management, smart farming techniques helpful in monitoring the needs and health of individual animals. Consequently their diet can be adjusted to make it more nutrients which protect them from unwanted diseases and enhance herd health.

The first proposal of using AI techniques in crop management was given by McKinion and Lemmon in their paper "Expert Systems for Agriculture" (J. M. McKinion, 1985) in 1985. In doctoral thesis of Boulanger (A G. Boulanger, 1983) corn crop protection expert system was proposed. Roach et al. suggested an expert system POMME for management of apple plantation (J. Roach, 1987) in 1987. Similarly for cotton crop management Stone and Toman came up with an expert system COTFLEX (N. D. Stone,

1989). In the same lines Lemmon proposed another rule based expert system COMAX for cotton crop management (H. Lemmon, 1990).

2.1 Weed Control: Blue River Technology

This technology is used in manufacturing smart farm machines to handle crops. Computer vision and Artificial intelligence in their smart machines can perform different categories of plant management efficiently. See and Spray robot developed by them can spray herbicides only when and where needed. This smart machine provides farmer with precise way of controlling and preventing herbicide resistant weeds. Sensors and cameras used to detect weeds are using machine learning where the machine has been taught in different weeds.

2.2 Crop Harvesting: Use of Robotics

Harvest CROO is working on agriculture robots. Certain farming areas in many countries are facing lack of labours which leads to significant money loss in these regions. Cost of harvest labours can be reduced by replacing them with robots which can pick and pack crops and fruits. It is only one time investment and use many times. Robots developed by Harvest CROO Robotics are employed for picking and packing fruits.

2.3 Plantix App: For Diagnosis Plant Diseases

Plantix App is developed by an agricultural tech startup PEAT in Berlin. It is used for detecting defects and deficiencies in soil. App makes use of images of plants to identify diseases. Collection of such images is kept in smart phone and is matched with image in server for diagnosis.

2.4 Cloud Technology: Prospera

Prospera, a company for data analytics, is working on changing agricultural produce into predictable and optimized assets. A cloud based solution is developed by them which combines all kind of data farmers are having such as data related to soil and water, images of crops etc. Prospera device makes sense of it all with the help of variety of sensors, computer vision and machine learning and makes predictions. It can be used in both open fields as well as in green houses.

2.5 Autopiloted Tractors

Tractors are now connected with GPS so that it can track the different lines of work in agricultural fields. The trackers have trackers attached to their steering systems, and tractors can also move in curved lines. The controlled mechanism keeps a track of the balance of machines and their working efficiencies.

2.6 Use of Artificial Intelligence in Seed Selection

High strength, good germination and the seedling emergence rate of seeds have always ensured emergence may under varying agricultural conditions and have been the key to optimizing yields and ensuring uniformity in production. Generally, farmers have optimized seed choice based on experience, and any laboratory experiments for seed- choice optimization are laborious and prone to error. The method that individual seed varieties react to different weather conditions and disease resistance, etc., are understood by AI technical devices by analyzing the previous data to a greater amount than could be accessed by a general farmer.

2.6.1 A Cost-Effective Phenotyping Platform: SeedGerm

Efficient seed germination and establishment are important concept for field and glasshouse crops. Large-scale germination experiments are very difficult and laborious and prone to find errors, leading to the necessity for automated.

The SeedGerm system, which combines cost-effective hardware and open-source software for seed germination experiments, automated seed imaging and machine-learning based phenotypic analysis. The software can process multiple image series simultaneously and produce reliable analysis of germination- and establishment related methods, in both comma separated values (CSV form) and processed images (PNG) formats.

2.7 Use of Artificial Intelligence in Crop Management Practices

Sensors and embedded systems have been developed that support the growth conditions in a growth chamber, such as light intensity, humidity, levels. It can control crop conditions per prevailing crop growth data in real-time to match maximized parameters. Trace Genomics is a technological firm that extracts DNA from the soil samples of agricultural lands and quantifies the microbes dwelling within. The data from the soil is analyzed with machine learning technologies. This biological data is combined with the chemical parameters of the soil sample to complete recommend solutions to the farmer, which would be evidence- based on past occurrence data the past. This may help in selecting the best crop to suit the land or vice versa.

Now the main concept for water irrigation, a continuous and accessible water supply is required for crop cultivation. Due to the scarcity of freshwater, it is highly advised not to exploit more water resources than is necessarily needed by the crop. Hence, AI technologies, which record real time data regarding soil moisture content and weather conditions, could manipulate the amount of water needed and automate the supply and ceasing of the water.

2.8 Use of Artificial Intelligence in Yield Prediction

Prediction models are one of the foremost Artificial Intelligence techniques to be widely accepted by farmers, as yield and profit are the main targets of all forms of agriculture. Soil type, soil nutrient content, crop information, and weather conditions are analyzed before predicting the yield.

2.9 Use of Artificial Intelligence in Pest and Weed Management

Artificial Intelligence based method for developing automated machines that could specifically find weeds and spray them with agrochemicals, which reduces the wastage of weedicide and reduces the exposure of the crop to the agrochemicals. Pasqual and Mansfield, SMARTSOY, and CORAC are examples of pest management systems.

2.10 Use of AI in Storing and Marketing Products

The storage of agricultural products in comfortable conditions is focused task for maintaining quality before reaching the customer. Various sensors have been developed in storage chambers for lengthening the post- harvest life of these products. Common farmers only understand the conventional markets of their products, but the latest market trends, decisions about the products' price, and information about the consumption pattern of consumers are precisely analyzed by market data and can suggest the next round of crops to the farmers.

3. POPULAR DEEP LEARNING ALGORITHM

This section describes the popular neural network algorithms used for deep learning, such as Feed-Forward Network with Back Propagation, Convolution Network, Recurrent Network and Generative Adversarial Networks, which when implemented in technology solutions of problems in agriculture are producing better results in context of farming. Applications of these deep learning algorithms are widely apparent in the field of agriculture.

3.1 Feed-Forward Neural Network and Back Propagation

In the field of Artificial Neural Networks Feed-Forward Back Propagation algorithm is a supervised learning way of multilayer networks. Back propagation approach works on the principle of modeling given function by adjusting internal weights of input signals by considering error to produce expected output signal (Farooq, 2016). Figure 2 represents the working in pictorial form. Training of the system is done with the help of supervised learning method where the error between the system's output and predefined expected output is back propagated in the system to modify internal weights.

Figure 2. Simple feed-forward network with back-propagation

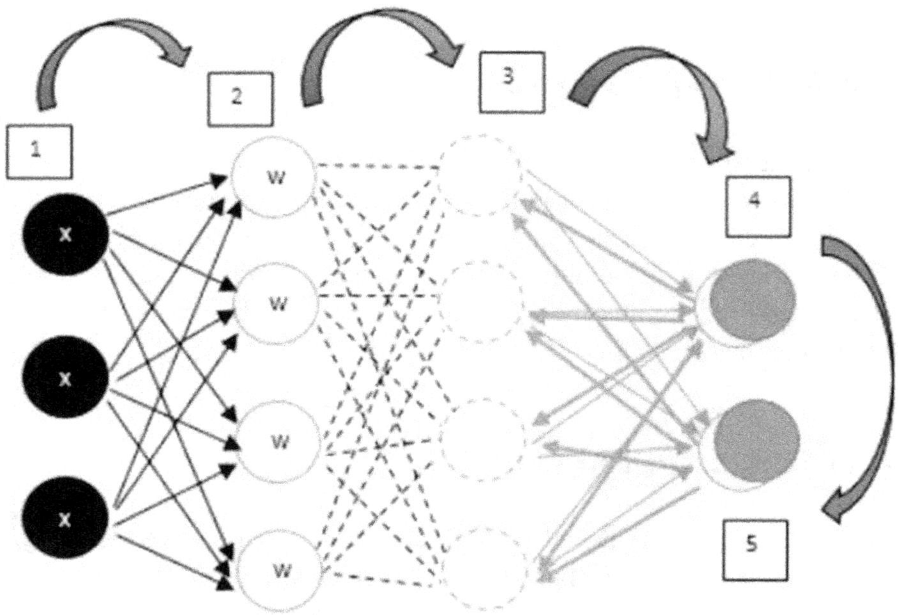

1. Input Layer
2. Weights
3. Hidden Layers
4. Output Layer
5. Back propagation for weight adjustment after calculating error

3.2 Convolution Neural Networks (CNN)

Convolution Neural Network, another deep learning algorithm, works on images as input. To these provided inputs, it gives learnable weights and biases to different identifiable objects in image. The basic architecture of CNN is inspired by the connectivity pattern of the Neurons in human brain. Receptive field is the restricted area of visual field where individual neuron gives response to stimuli. The complete visual area is covered by collection of these fields overlap.

3.3 Recurrent Neural Networks (RNN)

As name suggests in recurrent neural networks output from last executed step is fed to current step (Garcia, 2018). In conventional neural networks all input and output are independent of one another. But many times it is required to remember the previous state. For example to predict the next word of the sentence, words written before are needed in order to give suggestions. This requirement of memory is fulfilled with the help of hidden layer in RNN. It is only this hidden layer used for remembering the state makes RNN different than other algorithms.

3.4 Generative Adversarial Networks (GAN)

Under the category of unsupervised learning another powerful class of neural networks is Generative Adversarial Networks. It makes use of probabilistic models to generate data and thus is Generative. It is Adversarial as training in done under adversarial settings. And for training purpose it makes use of deep neural network algorithms (Habibi, 2021). GAN consists of generator and discriminator. Generator produces mock samples of image or audio data and aims to dodge discriminator. While discriminator is responsible for differentiating real and fake samples. Both, Discriminator and Generator are designed as neural networks and proceed in contest with each other during their training stage. The whole process is iterated numerous times and performance of discriminator and generator keeps on improving after each pass in loop.

4. THE ROLE OF ARTIFICIAL INTELLIGENCE USING INTERNET OF THINGS IN ADVANCED FARMING

As we head towards more cultured and urban farming, the necessity and engagement of fresh scientific developments such as IoT- based technology are becoming increasingly vital in diverse farming systems for numerous applications. They help to improve a variety of farming practices in order to increase yield output while preserving or minimizing the impact on the originality of the product.

4.1 IoT-Based Soil Sampling

Manufacturers currently present a wide range of sensors and toolkits to support farmers in monitoring the quality of soil and provide solutions to prevent degradation. They enable the intensive care of soil qualities such as water- holding capacity, texture, and absorption rate, which aids in decreasing densification, salinization, acidification, pollution, and erosion by avoiding the overconsumption of fertilizers. The Soil Moisture and Ocean Salinity (SMOS) satellite, which gives maps detailing the global soil moisture every one to two days, was launched in 2009 for this purpose (Crapolicchio et al., 2010).

4.2 IoT- Based Disease and Pest Monitoring

Farmers may drastically decrease their usage of pesticides by accurately recognizing crop pests utilizing IoT- based smart devices, including wireless sensors, drones, and robots. Contemporary IoT- based pest management offers real- time monitoring, disease forecasting, and modeling, making it more fruitful than conventional pest control approaches (Kim, 2018). Cutting- edge pest and disease detection techniques depend on image processing, with raw images collected across the farming region using remote sensing satellites or field sensors. Remote sensing imagery typically covers huge areas and provides more effectiveness at a reduced cost. Field sensors, conversely, can support more functions in data collection, such as environmental sampling, plant condition monitoring, and pest threats, in every phase of the crop cycle. IoT- based automatic traps may collect, count, and even describe pest varieties, then upload the data to the cloud for detailed analysis (Ayaz, 2019). This IoT based pest monitoring system is capable of minimizing the total costs while also assisting in the restoration of the natural climate (Oberti, 2016).

4.3 IoT-Based Fertilization

IoT- based fertilization technologies aid in the accurate estimation of spatial patterns of fertilizer requirements while requiring minimal labor. The normalized difference vegetation index (NDVI), for instance, which is based entirely on the reflection of visible and near- infrared light from vegetation, examines the status of crop nutrition utilizing satellite images and measures crop health, vegetation vigor, and density(Benincasa, 2017). It also helps to analyze soil nutrient levels. Such exact execution can considerably boost fertilizer efficiency while also avoiding environmental side effects. Geo- mapping, GPS accuracy, autonomous vehicles, and variable rate technology (VRT) are now contributing to IoT- based smart fertilization. Besides precision fertilization, other IoT benefits include fertigation and chemigation.

4.4 IoT-Based Yield Monitoring

A yield monitor developed using IoT- based technologies can be mounted on any associated harvester and connected to the FarmTRX mobile app, which demonstrates real- time harvest data and instantly uploads it to the manufacturers' web- based platform (Ayaz, 2019). This app can create high- quality yield maps that the farmer may export to other farm management tools for further analysis. Fruit growth measurement can be really beneficial in the precise evaluation of the quality and production of the yield. Satellite photographs can be a useful tool for monitoring the output of large- scale crops. Color (RGB) depth photographs are utilized to track the various fruit stages in mango fields. Similarly, several optical sensors are being used to measure papaya shrinkage, especially during drying conditions.

4.5 IoT-Based Irrigation

Embracing upcoming IoT technology is predicted to change the current status of irrigation practices. The application of IoT- based strategies, such as crop water stress index (CWSI) based irrigation management, is projected to lead to a major enhancement in crop efficiency. CWSI computation necessitates the achievement of crop canopy at various times as well as air temperature (Tekelioğlu, 2017). A wireless sensor- based monitoring system has been created in which all field sensors are linked to assemble the measured data, which is subsequently delivered to a processing centre where the farm data is analyzed using appropriate intelligent software programs. Various other data, such as satellite imaging and meteorological data are also fed into CWSI models to analyze water needs, and an exclusive irrigation index value is created for each site. Variable rate irrigation (VRI) optimization by Crop Metrics, which functions in relation to soil variability or topography and ultimately develops the effectiveness of water usage, is also a good example.

Table 1. Common mobile app and their diverse applications

Mobile Apps	Applications
PocketLAI	Irrigation
LandPKS	Soil assessment
AMACA	Machinery/ tools
Ecofert	Fertilizer management
AgriMaps	Land management
SnapCard	Spraying applications
SWApp	Irrigation
WeedSmart	Weed management
VillageTree	Pest management
EVAPO	Irrigation
BioLeaf	Health monitoring
cFertigUAL	Fertigation

5. USE OF DEEP LEARNING IN SMART FARMING

Applications of Deep Learning have gained momentum in past few years and its applications are increasing day by day. Study of applications of DL algorithm is becoming popular in recent works. Table 1 lists the application of deep learning algorithms in smart farming.

Table 2. List of applications of DL algorithms in agriculture

Deep Learning Algorithm	Applications	Examples
Back Propagation (BP)	Pattern recognition, Classification	Leaf classification, Leaf disease detection, crop type classification etc.
Convolution Neural Network (CNN)	Image Processing	Plant disease detection, Fruit counting, yield prediction, weather forecasting etc.
Recurrent Neural Network (RNN)	Time Series Analysis	Phenotype identification, land cover classification, crop yield estimation, weather forecasting etc.
Generative Adversarial Network (GAN)	Image Generation	Recovery of lost features of images

5.1 Some Applications of CNN in Smart Farming

CNN is most widely used in agricultural research and applications because of its strong capability of image processing. Plant disease detection –Leaf image classification and pattern recognition are used in plant disease identification .Berkley Vision and Learning Centre developed a deep learning framework to identify diseases in plants. The model was capable of identifying 13 categories of diseases in plants. Similar kinds of approaches have been (Tang J L, 2017, Srbinovska M, 2015,Ge Z Y, 2015) used to identify features of plants using image recognition. In all works CNN models have been used for image processing.

Fruit counting- Fruit counting is used in robotic harvesting and is most significant as far as yield prediction is concerned. Conventional methods of counting from mobile camera images or counting fruits manually are very time consuming. A full convolution network has been proposed which uses blob detection method.

Weather Forecasting –Complete process of harvesting is dependent on weather conditions. For weather forecasting also CNN models are being used.

Yield prediction – Estimation of cost is significant for every stakeholder including farmers, consumers and government. Complete strategies for selling, purchasing and market are dependent on this. CNN models are used to predict crop yield in agriculture. Use of CNN in yield prediction is not limited to crops only but can be applied on animals also to study their behaviors.

5.2 RNN Applications in Smart Agriculture

Utility of Recurrent neural networks can be observed in time series data. It is currently being used in farming field for phenotype identification, land cover classification, leaf area index, crop yield estimation, soil moisture approximation, weather prediction and animal research. In addition, recurrent network models are applied to identify land cover classes but also to detect changes in land state like convolution networks, recurrent networks are also used for estimation of yield. It makes use of time series data to reduce biasing. Recurrent networks have also been applied in research on animals.

5.3 GAN Applications in Smart Agriculture

Not much literature is available in depicting the application of GAN in smart farming. But GAN is very useful to solve the problem of feature loss due to poor samples. Mostly on compression features of an image are lost or become inaccurate and need of appropriate recovery is there. Ledig demonstrated the use of GAN to resolve and regain the loss occurred because of poor sampling.

5.4 Libraries of Deep Learning

Deep Learning Frameworks consists of pre-defined and optimized components for designing deep learning models. These libraries and interface provide clear, easy, quick and concise way of defining models without getting onto details of underlying algorithms. Numbers of frameworks are available in market with their comparative analysis. Common deep learning frameworks or libraries are PyTorch on Python, Google's TensorFlow, Caffe, Keras, MATLAB, Amazon Machine Learning, Azure ML Studio and so on.

6. COMPUTER VISION WITH DEEP LEARNING MODELS

Computer vision possesses dual and interrelated goals. In biological science, computer vision aims to represent the human visual system using computational models, and in the engineering perspective, computer vision attempts to create autonomous systems that can do tasks that often human visual systems cannot perform. Computer vision imparts visual capability to machines through cameras, data, models, and algorithms rather than retinas and the visual cortex. Optical character recognition (OCR) technology and intelligent character recognition were some major tasks that employed computer vision to accomplish tasks such as document and invoice processing, vehicle plate detection, etc. In the early stages of computer vision research, the main focus was to build algorithms to detect edges, curves, corners and other basic shapes. Before the era of deep learning, image processing relied on gray level segmentation and this approach wasn't robust enough to represent complex classes. Modern computer vision algorithms rely extensively on artificial neural networks that provide a dramatic improvement in performance and accuracy compared to traditional approaches for image processing. Deep learning-based computation models allow multiple processing layers to learn and infer complex patterns mimicking the human brain. It runs and inspects the data over several iterations until it discerns distinctions and identifies or recognizes the features in the images. The recent surge of interest in deep learning is due to the fact that it can handle massive amounts of heterogeneous data (visual, audio, text, etc.) and is capable of embedding solutions into several hardwares. Deep Learning allows automatic feature extraction and can be utilized in numerous image processing tasks and is well known for its effectiveness in handling vision-based activities like image classification, object detection, semantic segmentation, etc. In fact, these tasks are the backbone for modeling and automating agricultural activities such as disease identification, weed detection, yield estimation, etc.

6.1 Some Application Areas in Agriculture: Deep Learning-Driven Computer Vision

6.1.1 Seed Quality Analysis

The commercial seed industry is focused on the supply of the right quality seeds to the farmers at the right time in the right quantity. Filtering out low-quality of seeds from high-quality ones, is not only laborious, but it requires focused equipments, infrastructure, and time. The testing of seeds for their quality can indeed gain momentum by the use of computer vision technology which can extract the morphological information of different seed lots and grade it according to the internationally prescribed quality standards. The different seed testing modules are likely to address their physical purity, genetic purity, seed health, vigour, patterns of deterioration etc., which in general may indeed cover the physical or visually attributable characters such as the seed length, shape, size, visual impairments, and presence of foreign bodies which can indeed be captured by the advanced computer vision technology. Performance issues of traditional computer vision have greatly been improved by deep learning-based computer vision, resulting in larger adoption for seed variety identification. The seed quality evaluation process using computer vision is shown in Figure 3. Often, spectral imaging techniques are also merged with these approaches to enhance the accuracy.CNN models were found to be effective in identifying the seed varieties. The machine learning models showed an accuracy of more than 80% in classifying the cotton seeds based on the feature extracted by the CNN model. In another investigation, SeedSortNet built from computer vision CNN models, was found to be promising, with accuracies 97.33% and 99.56% in sorting the maize and sunflower seeds. CNN deep learning was also utilized for cognizing the viable and non-viable seeds and was found to be successful with 90% viability prediction accuracy for naturally aged seeds.

Figure 3. Overview of training process in GAN (generative adversarial network)

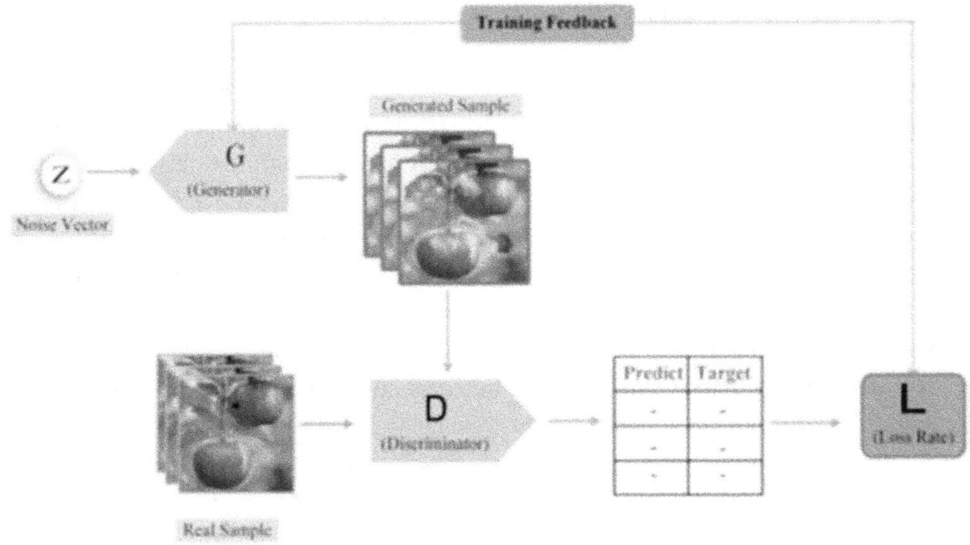

6.2 Soil Analysis

The preservation and improvement of dynamic soil characteristics is the main emphasis of soil management in agriculture for increasing crop productivity. Traditional soil texture analysis entails taking soil samples and bringing them to a laboratory, where they are dried, crushed, and sieved before being used. For coarse textured or sandy soils, sieving is the most typical laboratory analytical method, while for smaller textured particles, a hydrometer or pipette approach based on sedimentation theory is used. With the advancement of image processing power and the development of image acquisition like cameras systems in recent years, computer vision-based image analysis approaches have gotten a lot of interest in a lot of sectors, including soil science. This method collects soil images (dynamic or static) with cameras and then uses simple computer programmes to classify and categories them. For example, after matching textural patterns, the size of the soil particles might be estimated straight from the image.

7. SMART PREDICTION IN AGRICULTURE APPLICATION: DRONES

The work starts with a verifiable assessment of the use of flying vehicles in farming,as precursors of their application in present-day accuracy horticulture strategies,which are currently focused on the use of various applications in the agricultural field. This is the motivation of the chapter to work out the application of drones with sensors in the agricultural field. These sensors can distinguish any risky situations, for example, water system needs, crop sickness and irritation on the board with early location, compost planning with keen application techniques and supplement unevenness conditions in crop plants during their development cycle. In agribusiness, a lot of herbicides and manures are used, which lessens usefulness as well as disturbs the dirt biology. Thus, high hereditary yielding and pesticide and herbicide opposition variations of numerous harvests are in incredible interest and researchers are presently in a situation to create such encouraging assortments to address the momentum circumstance.

The present-day approach for looking over crops on the field and giving otherworldly pictures provides data on crop development status, illness location and climate-based boundary expectation. Drones are generally the unmanned aerial vehicles (UAVs) used in agriculture and other sectors for monitoring, surveying, data image collection, etc. Drones are also used in precision farming, livestock farming, smart greenhouse and horticulture and forestry sectors. These are advanced, low-cost, aerial-camera

equipped with GPS systems and have various sensors for all types of data collection in agriculture. The multispectral sensors can capture various images of both healthy and diseased/unhealthy crops and detect other problems which cannot be seen in the visible spectrum; soil and nutrient mapping is also possible by drones. The progress of digitalization and estimating advancements has empowered computerized gadgets and sensors to create monstrous measures of information. Image-based total information amassing and evaluation has quite a few promises to help with those targets. Visual facts obtained from agricultural fields can be used to automate evaluation operations and provide real-time crop and leaf health information. Drones with sensors are used to monitor the health condition of crops in the agricultural field through image processing which is the interesting part of this chapter.

7.1 Sensors Used in Drones

Accelerometer: This sensor is responsible for the stability of the drones.

Gyroscope: This sensor provides angular motion to the drone.

Magnetometer: This type of sensor is present in the drones with GPS modules and helps in detecting a magnetic field of the earth and is responsible for direction for the fly to the drones.

Barometer: It is also known as a pressure sensor. The pressure variation is seen with increasing height from sea level. A barometer sensor is used to measure accurate height above mean sea level.

7.3 Different Sensors Used in Drone for Agricultural Application

Sensors are small and very simple devices that are used to measure or detect different properties or parameters very precisely with real-time-based observations. Sensors also detect the circumstances such as gesticulation, warmness or grace and transform it into digital form for better understanding and analysis of observed data. Various types of sensors used for different purposes in the agricultural monitoring process are as follows:

7.3.1 Electromagnetic Sensors

Electromagnetic sensors use electric circuits to quantify the conduction or accumulation of electric charges by the soil particles. The whole soil system becomes a part of that circuit and any slight changes in electrical conductivity are measured in the logger.

7.3.2 Optoelectronic Sensors

Optoelectronic sensors integrate the electronic processes with light and optical processes. It is tranquil of a light source that emits light source of diverse frequency and a sensor that can sense these different wavelengths. It can cover the distance of several hundreds of kilometers. It can measure soil dampness and cation trade limit.

7.3.3 Electrochemical Sensors

These sensors measure the electrochemical phenomena of the soil system such as nutrient status and pH. Apart from that, it can detect nitrate and potassium ions.

7.3.4 Ion-Selective Electrode Sensors

This sensor estimates the capability of an explicit particle in an answer and can decide the nitrogen gratified existent in soil. Another reference electrode of the stable constant property was taken into consideration and the result potential was measured against this perspective. The possible contrast between two electrodes relies on the action of an explicit particle in the arrangement.

7.3.5 Optical Sensors

Optical sensors utilize light sources to quantify the diverse soil properties. The light energy interferes with different properties and those changes are analyzed properly.

7.3.6 Location Sensors

Location sensors are the sensors used to determine latitude and longitude along altitude which are needed most.

7.3.7 Mechanical Sensors

Mechanical sensors measure the mechanical antagonism of the soil. These devices go through the soil and measure the strength of the soil system with the help of a strain gauge.

7.3.8 Nitrate Sensors

These sensors measure the nitrate content in both soil and water systems. Nitrate ions are easily leached down into the soil system and stored mostly in groundwater causing blue baby syndrome disease in humans when the nitrate concentration is > 10 ppm. These nitrate sensors are of great use to track the nitrate ion path and also to track the transformations.

7.3.9 Soil pH Sensors

They measure the acidity or alkalinity of the soil system. This sensor reading is also helpful in knowing the causes of poor plant growth, fertility problems of soil, etc.

7.3.10 Ammonium Sensors

They precisely determine the ammonium and nitrogen content in the soil and water system.

7.3.11 Potassium Sensors

This sensor is specially designed to detect the potassium ion concentration in soil and water content.

7.3.12 Soil-Water Sensors

These sensors give the details about the status of the soil-water system; thus they are helpful in irrigation management, nutrient mobility, chemical and water balance status, etc.

7.3.13 Nanobiosensors

Nanobiosensors are very much advanced and important sensors used in agriculture that take the help of bio-organisms in sensing operations. Nanobiosensors are compact and analytic devices that use biologically sensitized element in their sensors for further analysis (Kumar, 2018).

7.3.14 Pneumatic (Magnetic Proximity Sensor)

This is the most common type of sensor used for detecting the magnetic fields of the system.

8. DRONES AND SENSORS IN ADVANCED FARMING

With the fitting sensors ready, the drone can be utilized for a wide assortment of utilizations, for example, valuation of plant inexperience or photosynthetic active biomass, crop stress, weed stress, etc.

8.1 Soil Analysis and Mapping for Field Planning

Drones are used to capture 3D images of the field so that proper analysis of soil can be performed for the planning of crops to be grown on that soil. Different high-resolution images are also analyzed to estimate the moisture percentage of soil, nitrogen content and other nutrient content in the soil. Planting-related aspects along with irrigation requirements can also be observed by using drones in agricultural fields. Sensors are also programmed to determine the various soil physical and chemical properties such as soil pH, cation exchange capacity, bulk density, moisture content and other nutrients present and the sensors used to determine such properties.

8.2 Seed Planting

Proper planting of seeds with maintaining distance and depth can be achieved by using drones. Drones are programmed to throw the seeds in a pod to the previously prepared soil with applied doses of fertilizer in that soil. The drones also save time and labor costs for planting to be done.

8.3 Soil Quality and Plant Disease Assessment

Nanobiosensors are capable to detect the various diseases caused by viruses, bacteria, fungi and other microorganisms by measuring the oxygen depletion status caused by microorganisms. The sensors are capable of detecting this oxygen depletion status, thus giving the amount of infestation of these microorganisms in the plants causing diseases which can be estimated in time so that control measures can be taken.

8.4 Crop Monitoring

Crop monitoring is considered the toughest task in the field of agriculture. Large areas with standing crops are difficult to manage for the farmers on their own. The use of high-resolution drones and the field can monitor the crops on a large scale and multispectral, geospatial images captured by the drones help in analyzing crop development as well as give an idea about microclimate which is very much important for crop growth.

8.5 Spraying of Pesticides, Chemicals, and Fertilizers on Crops

The drones integrated with sensor-based technologies can formulate and calculate the required doses of pesticides, fertilizers and other plant protection chemicals for increasing crop growth along with efficiency enhancement of applied materials. The drone-based spraying can save time and reduce the cost of operation by checking the losses and overdose of chemical application in plants. Required doses of fertilizers are important to check the toxicity of other nutrients in soil and plant systems as fertilizers are considered as plant growth substances. Nutrient losses from fertilizer materials can be checked, thus minimizing the risk of soil and environmental pollutions caused by the excess amount of nutrients.

9. DISCUSSION AND CONCLUSION

The summary of applications of Deep Learning in smart prediction in agriculture, thus making it smart, has been presented. Brief review of concepts and techniques of deep learning applied in the field of yield prediction, fruit counting, crop disease detection, classification, weed detection, weather tracking and forecasting and behaviour classification is also given. Research with the applications of Deep Learning is growing with pace and the field is very diverse and vast. Work presented here has tried to bring out the usage of different deep learning algorithms in different areas and sub fields of agriculture. Finally it can be concluded that smart prediction farming is more profitable, efficient and sustainable now a days.

REFERENCES

Ayaz, M., Ammad-Uddin, M., Sharif, Z., Mansour, A., & Aggoune, E.-H. M. (2019). Internet- ofthings (IoT)- based smart agriculture: Toward making the fields talk. *IEEE Access : Practical Innovations, Open Solutions*, *7*, 129551–129583. doi:10.1109/ACCESS.2019.2932609

Baker, D. N., Lambert, J. R., & McKinion, J. M. (1983). *GOSSYM: A simulator of cotton crop growth and yield, Technical bulletin*. Agricultural Experiment Station.

Benincasa, P., Antognelli, S., Brunetti, L., Fabbri, C., Natale, A., Sartoretti, V., Modeo, G., Guiducci, M., Tei, F., & Vizzari, M. (2017). Reliability of NDVI derived by high resolution satellite and UAV compared to in- field methods for the evaluation of early crop n status and grain yield in wheat. *Experimental Agriculture*, *54*(4), 604–622. doi:10.1017/S0014479717000278

Boulanger, A. G. (1983). *The expert system PLANT/CD: A case study in applying the general purpose inference system ADVISE to predicting black cutworm damage in corn* [Ph.D. Thesis]. University of Illinois at Urbana-Champaign.

Burney, J., & Ramanathan, V. (2014). Recent climate and air pollution impacts on Indian agriculture. *Proceedings of the National Academy of Sciences of the United States of America*, *111*(46), 16319–16324. doi:10.1073/pnas.1317275111 PMID:25368149

Crapolicchio, R., Ferrazzoli, P., Meloni, M., Pinori, S., & Rahmoune, R. (2010). Soil Moisture and Ocean Salinity (SMOS) mission: System overview and contribution to vicarious calibration monitoring. *European Journal of Remote Sensing*, 37– 50. doi:10.5721/ItJRS20104214

Farooq, W., Butt, N., Shukat, S., Baig, N. A., & Ahmed, S. M. (2016). Wirelessly Controlled Mines Detection Robot. *International Conference on Intelligent Systems Engineering (ICISE)*. 10.1109/INTELSE.2016.7475162

Garcia, F. M., Alvarez, L. Y., Heras, F. L., Gonzalez, V. B., Rodriguez, V. Y., Pino, A., & Arboleya, A. A. (2018). GPR System Onboard a UAV for Non-invasive Detection of Buried Objects. *2018 IEEE Antennas and Propagation Society International Symposium and USNC/URSI National Radio Science Meeting, APSURSI 2018 – Proceedings*, 1967–1968. 10.1109/APUSNCURSINRSM.2018.8608907

García-Berná, J. A., Ouhbi, S., Benmouna, B., García-Mateos, G., Fernández-Alemán, J. L., & Molina-Martínez, J. M. (2020). Systematic Mapping Study on Remote Sensing in Agriculture. *Applied Sciences (Basel, Switzerland)*, *10*(10), 3456. doi:10.3390/app10103456

Ge, Z. Y., McCool, C., Sanderson, C., & Corke, P. (2015). *Content specific feature learning for fine-grained plant classification. CLEF*. Working Notes.

Habibi, L., Watanabe, T., Matsui, T., & Tanaka, T. (2021). Machine Learning Techniques to Predict Soybean Plant Density Using UAV and Satellite-Based Remote Sensing. *Remote Sensing (Basel)*, *13*(13), 2548. doi:10.3390/rs13132548

Kim, S., Lee, M., & Shin, C. (2018). IoT- based strawberry disease prediction system for smart farming. *Sensors (Basel)*, *18*(11), 4051. doi:10.339018114051 PMID:30463363

Kumar, S. A., & Ilango, P. (2018). The Impact of Wireless Sensor Network in the Field of Precision Agriculture: A Review. *Wireless Personal Communications*, *98*(1), 685–698. doi:10.100711277-017-4890-z

Lemmon, H. (1990). Comax: An expert system for cotton crop management. *Computer Science in Economics and Management*, *3*(2), 177–185. doi:10.1007/BF00436714

Martiniello, P. (1988). Development of a database computer management system for retrieval on varietal field evaluation and plant breeding information in agriculture. *Computers and Electronics in Agriculture*, *2*(3), 183–192. doi:10.1016/0168-1699(88)90023-3

McKinion, J. M., & Lemmon, H. E. (1985). Expert systems for agriculture. *Computers and Electronics in Agriculture*, *1*(1), 31–40. doi:10.1016/0168-1699(85)90004-3

Oberti, R., Marchi, M., Tirelli, P., Calcante, A., Iriti, M., Tona, E., Hočevar, M., Baur, J., Pfaff, J., Schütz, C., & Ulbrich, H. (2016). Selective spraying of grapevines for disease control using a modular agricultural robot. *Biosystems Engineering*, *146*, 203–215. doi:10.1016/j.biosystemseng.2015.12.004

Ramos, P. J., Prieto, F. A., Montoya, E. C., & Oliveros, C. E. (2017). Automatic fruit count on coffee branches usingcomputer vision. *Computers and Electronics in Agriculture*, *137*, 9–22. doi:10.1016/j.compag.2017.03.010

Roach, J., Virkar, R., Drake, C., & Weaver, M. (1987). An expert system for helping apple growers. *Computers and Electronics in Agriculture*, *2*(2), 97–108. doi:10.1016/0168-1699(87)90020-2

Srbinovska, M., Gavrovski, C., Dimcev, V., Krkoleva, A., & Borozan, V. (2015). Environmental parameters monitoring in precision agriculture using wireless sensor networks. *Journal of Cleaner Production*, *88*, 297–307. doi:10.1016/j.jclepro.2014.04.036

Stone, N. D., & Toman, T. W. (1989). A dynamically linked expert-database system for decision support in Texas cotton production. *Computers and Electronics in Agriculture*, *4*(2), 139–148. doi:10.1016/0168-1699(89)90031-8

Tang, J. L., Wang, D., Zhang, Z. G., He, L. J., Xin, J., & Xu, Y. (2017). Weed identificationbased on K-means feature learning combined with convolutional neural network. *Computers and Electronics in Agriculture*, *135*, 63–70. doi:10.1016/j.compag.2017.01.001

Tekelioğlu, B., Büyüktaş, D., Baştuğ, R., Karaca, C., Aydinşakir, K., & Dinç, N. (2017). Use of crop water stress index for irrigation scheduling of soybean in Mediterranean conditions. *Journal of Experimental Agriculture International*, *18*(6), 1–8. doi:10.9734/JEAI/2017/37058

Thorpe, K. W., Ridgway, R. L., & Webb, R. E. (1992). A computerized data management and decision support system for gypsy moth management in suburban parks. *Computers and Electronics in Agriculture*, *6*(4), 333–345. doi:10.1016/0168-1699(92)90004-7

Chapter 10
Soil Quality Prediction Using Deep Learning

C. V. Suresh Babu
https://orcid.org/0000-0002-8474-2882
Hindustan Institute of Technolgy and Science, India

K. Yadavamuthiah
Hindustan Institute of Technology and Science, India

ABSTRACT

This research introduces a state-of-the-art method for predicting soil quality using deep learning algorithms. It utilizes a comprehensive dataset of physical, chemical, and biological parameters collected from multiple sites. The model combines long short-term memory (LSTM) networks to capture temporal relationships and convolutional neural networks (CNNs) to extract features from soil samples. Extensive experiments demonstrate the model's superiority over conventional machine learning methods, accurately predicting soil quality. The implications extend to sustainable land management, environmental monitoring, and precision agriculture. The CNN model achieves high accuracy in classifying soil quality and identifies influential variables. The study showcases its proficiency in predicting various soil measures and employs cross-validation to ensure consistency. This research contributes to the field by offering a precise and reliable approach to soil quality prediction, aiding decision-making in sustainable land management.

1. INTRODUCTION

Crop productivity, environmental sustainability, and human health are intricately linked to the intrinsic properties of soil, necessitating the comprehensive collection and analysis of a wide range of diverse physical, chemical, and biological soil characteristics. However, this process entails substantial temporal and financial commitments. Consequently, researchers and practitioners in the fields of agriculture, ecology, and environmental science are actively seeking precise and effective methodologies for accurate soil quality prediction. Deep learning, a highly successful paradigm in domains such as speech recognition,

DOI: 10.4018/979-8-3693-1722-8.ch010

image classification, and natural language processing, emerges as a promising avenue in this research endeavor (Suresh Babu et al., 2023).

This study presents a state-of-the-art methodology for soil quality prediction leveraging cutting-edge deep learning techniques. A vast and extensive data-set encompassing a comprehensive array of soil parameters, spanning intricate physical, chemical, and biological attributes, is harnessed. The proposed model synergistically integrates long short-term memory (LSTM) networks to adeptly capture the temporal dynamics and relationships among variables, and convolutional neural networks (CNNs) to extract highly discriminative features from soil samples. Rigorous and meticulous experimentation substantiates the model's undeniable superiority over conventional machine learning models, yielding remarkable accuracy in soil quality prediction. The implications of this research reverberate across the realms of sustainable land management, environmental monitoring, and precision agriculture.

A salient advantage of deploying deep learning in soil quality prediction lies in its inherent capacity to assimilate and integrate a plethora of heterogeneous data sources, encompassing intricate soil chemical and physical parameters, intricate climatic data, and sophisticated remote sensing data. This comprehensive and holistic approach fosters highly precise and comprehensive estimation of soil quality, thereby empowering informed and enlightened decision-making in the domains of soil management, precision farming, and land use planning strategies.

Deep learning models have exhibited exceptional prowess in tackling a myriad of complex soil quality prediction challenges, spanning the accurate prognostication of fundamental soil attributes such as soil organic matter content, soil water retention characteristics, and soil nutrient availability. Diverging from traditional statistical models, deep learning models excel in capturing the intricate nonlinear interactions between various soil qualities and the diverse array of environmental factors influencing them. However, challenges, including the acquisition and cu-ration of extensive, high-quality data-sets, as well as the inherent risks associated with over-fitting, necessitate diligent attention and concerted efforts from researchers in order to foster the development of highly reliable and accurate deep learning models for soil quality prediction. The research community in this domain is actively engaged in surmounting these hurdles, with the overarching goal of enhancing the dependability, robustness, and precision of deep learning models in the context of soil quality prediction.

2. PROBLEM STATEMENT

To effectively comprehend and manage soil health and production for sustainable agriculture and environmental protection, it is crucial to employ deep learning algorithms to predict soil quality. Soil quality encompasses a complex and diverse set of factors influenced by various elements, including management practices, environmental conditions, and the chemical and physical properties of the soil. Traditional methods of soil quality assessment are often time-consuming, expensive, and may not fully capture the intricacies of soil-plant interactions. Hence, there is a growing interest in developing more precise and efficient deep learning-based algorithms for soil quality prediction.

The main challenge in this problem lies in developing deep learning models that can effectively extract relevant features from large and complex soil data-sets while considering the spatial and temporal variability of soil parameters. This requires the creation of unique deep learning architectures capable of handling the high-dimensional and heterogeneous nature of the data. Additionally, the integration of multiple data sources, including soil chemical and physical properties, climate data, and remote sensing data, is essential. Ensuring model interpretability, generalization, and avoiding bias and over-fitting are additional challenges that need to be addressed. Incorporating domain knowledge and expert insights into the modeling process, as well as employing appropriate model selection and evaluation procedures, are vital.

The problem of predicting soil quality using deep learning techniques is both significant and challenging, with wide-ranging implications for environmentally friendly farming and sustainable agriculture. Harnessing the power of deep learning can enhance our understanding of soil-plant interactions and enable more informed and sustainable land management practices. However, it necessitates the development of novel and interdisciplinary techniques to effectively utilize deep learning capabilities and leverage the wealth of available data. By addressing these challenges, we can unlock the potential of deep learning to revolutionize soil quality prediction and contribute to the advancement of sustainable land management and agricultural practices.

3. LITERATURE REVIEW

3.1 Arid Soil Study

This study addresses the challenge of predicting soil nutrient levels in a highly variable arid environment. Accurate soil nutrient prediction is crucial for effective land management, agriculture, and environmental monitoring. However, the complexity and heterogeneity of arid environments present significant obstacles to traditional soil nutrient assessment methods. To overcome these limitations, the study proposes the utilization of machine learning models. By leveraging advanced algorithms, the research analyzes various environmental and soil-related variables to establish their relationships with soil nutrient content. This approach enables the identification of key predictors and the development of predictive models capable of accurately estimating soil nutrient levels in highly variable arid environments. The study explores different machine learning techniques, evaluating their performance in terms of accuracy and reliability. By combining expertise from soil science, environmental monitoring, and machine learning, this research pioneers innovative approaches for soil nutrient prediction. The integration of machine learning technology allows for data-driven analysis and modeling techniques, revolutionizing soil science by enabling accurate and efficient assessment of soil nutrient levels in arid environments. Ultimately, this study contributes to the advancement of soil nutrient prediction methodologies in challenging environmental conditions, while also adding to the growing body of knowledge in the application of machine learning in environmental and agricultural sciences (Liu et al., 2021).

3.2 Arid Soil Exploration

This study focuses on the challenge of predicting soil organic carbon levels in hilly regions, where accurately estimating soil organic carbon can be difficult due to complex terrain and diverse soil properties. Soil organic carbon serves as a critical indicator of soil health and plays a vital role in ecosystem processes and agricultural productivity. To overcome the limitations of traditional prediction methods, this research combines expertise from soil science, machine learning, and geospatial analysis. The study aims to develop reliable and accurate prediction models using random forest and deep learning techniques. By analyzing the relationships between soil properties, terrain attributes, and soil organic carbon content, the researchers enhance our understanding of soil organic carbon dynamics in hilly landscapes. Additionally, the integration of geospatial analysis techniques allows for the incorporation of spatial information into the prediction models. This specialized approach contributes to advancing soil organic carbon prediction methodologies, providing valuable insights for sustainable land management and environmental planning in hilly regions (Wu et al., 2021).

3.3 Semi-Arid Soil

The motive of this study is to predict soil organic carbon and total nitrogen levels in a semi-arid region. Soil organic carbon and total nitrogen are critical indicators of soil fertility and play a crucial role in understanding ecosystem dynamics and agricultural productivity. However, accurately predicting these soil properties in semi-arid regions can be challenging due to the complex interplay of environmental factors. The study aims to address this challenge by utilizing machine learning algorithms to develop robust prediction models that overcome the limitations of traditional methods. By accurately estimating soil organic carbon and total nitrogen levels, this research contributes to a better understanding of soil health and aids in sustainable land management and agricultural practices in semi-arid regions. This study lies at the intersection of soil science and machine learning. By combining expertise from these domains, the research specializes in developing and applying machine learning algorithms to predict soil organic carbon and total nitrogen levels. The study investigates various machine learning techniques and evaluates their performance in predicting soil properties in the specific context of a semi-arid region. This specialized approach enhances our knowledge of soil fertility dynamics in semi-arid environments, providing valuable insights for improved land management and sustainable agricultural practices in similar regions (Gholizadeh et al., 2020).

3.4 Soil Spectral

This study aims to predict soil cation exchange capacity by employing machine learning techniques and utilizing soil spectral data. Cation exchange capacity is a vital soil property that influences nutrient availability, soil fertility, and overall soil health. Accurate estimation of cation exchange capacity is crucial for optimizing agricultural practices and understanding soil functionality. Traditional measurement methods for cation exchange capacity can be time-consuming and costly. To overcome these limitations, this research focuses on the intersection of soil science and machine learning, specializing in the development and application of machine learning algorithms. By leveraging soil spectral data as input, the study aims to develop prediction models that provide a more efficient and cost-effective approach for estimating cation exchange capacity. By integrating soil science knowledge with machine learning expertise, the research contributes to the advancement of soil property prediction methodologies. The investigation of various machine learning techniques enhances our understanding of the relationship between soil spectral characteristics and cation exchange capacity. The findings of this study have implications for improved soil management practices, nutrient management strategies, and the application of precision agriculture in agricultural systems (Behzad et al., 2020).

3.5 Soil Water Study

This study compares and evaluates different machine learning techniques for predicting soil water content, focusing on the domain of hydrology and machine learning. Soil water content is a critical parameter in hydrological studies, agricultural irrigation management, and water resource planning. Accurate prediction of soil water content is essential for understanding water availability, assessing drought conditions, and optimizing water management strategies. Traditional methods for measuring soil water content have limitations in terms of time consumption and spatial coverage (Suresh Babu et al., 2023a). To address these challenges, the study explores the potential of machine learning algorithms to provide efficient and accurate predictions of soil water content.

By specifically investigating the application of machine learning techniques in predicting soil water content, the research aims to enhance our understanding of their capabilities and limitations. Various machine learning algorithms, including regression-based models and artificial neural networks, are compared and evaluated in terms of their performance. The findings of this study contribute to the advancement of predictive modeling in hydrology, supporting improved water resource management and agricultural irrigation practices (Pham et al., 2019).

3.6 Soil Carbon Study

This study explores the effectiveness of machine learning algorithms in predicting soil organic carbon levels by utilizing visible and near-infrared spectra. Soil organic carbon is a critical factor in soil health and ecosystem processes, influencing soil fertility, carbon sequestration potential, and sustainable land management. Traditional methods for measuring soil organic carbon can be time-consuming and labor-intensive. Hence, the study focuses on investigating the potential of machine learning algorithms to rapidly and accurately predict soil organic carbon based on visible and near-infrared spectral data.

The research lies at the intersection of soil science and machine learning, specializing in the application of machine learning algorithms for soil organic carbon prediction using visible and near-infrared spectra. Various machine learning techniques, including support vector machines, random forests, and artificial neural networks, are evaluated to determine their performance in predicting soil organic carbon content. By specifically considering visible and near-infrared spectral data, the study enhances our understanding of the relationship between spectral information and soil organic carbon levels. The findings contribute to the advancement of predictive modeling in soil science, facilitating improved soil management practices and strategies for carbon sequestration (Wang et al., 2019).

3.7 Nutrient Prediction Comparison

This study, conducted in the domain of soil science, aims to compare and evaluate different models and wavelengths for predicting soil nutrient levels using visible and near-infrared spectroscopy. Soil nutrient levels are vital for understanding soil fertility, nutrient management, and optimizing agricultural practices. However, traditional methods of measuring soil nutrient levels can be time-consuming and costly. To address this challenge, the study investigates the potential of visible and near-infrared spectroscopy combined with machine learning models as a rapid and cost-effective approach for soil nutrient prediction. By comparing various models and wavelengths, the research enhances our understanding of the relationship between spectral information and soil nutrient content. The findings contribute to the advancement of soil nutrient prediction methods, supporting improved nutrient management strategies and sustainable agricultural practices (Duan et al., 2018).

3.8 Organic Carbon Nitrogen Prediction

This study aims to leverage soil spectral data and machine learning algorithms to accurately predict soil organic carbon and total nitrogen levels. Soil organic carbon and total nitrogen are crucial indicators of soil fertility and have significant implications for ecosystem dynamics and agricultural productivity. However, traditional methods for measuring these soil properties can be time-consuming and labor-intensive. To overcome these limitations, the study focuses on the application of machine learning techniques within the domain of soil science and machine learning. By specializing in the integration of soil spectral data and machine learning algorithms, the research explores the potential for a more efficient and accurate approach to predicting soil organic carbon and total nitrogen levels. This specialized approach contributes to the advancement of predictive modeling in soil science and provides valuable insights into the relationship between soil spectral information and soil fertility. The findings support improved soil management practices and sustainable agricultural strategies (Gholizadeh & Ayoubi, 2017).

3.9 Geo Soil Carbon Prediction

The motive of this study is to integrate geostatistical techniques and remote sensing indices to predict soil organic carbon stock. Soil organic carbon is a vital component of soil health and plays a crucial role in ecosystem processes. Accurate estimation of soil organic carbon stock is essential for assessing soil fertility, carbon sequestration potential, and informing land management decisions. Traditional methods for estimating soil organic carbon stock can be limited in spatial coverage and resource-intensive. Hence, the study aims to explore the potential of geostatistical techniques and remote sensing indices to provide a more efficient and spatially explicit approach for predicting soil organic carbon stock.

This study lies within the domain of ecology and environmental science. It specializes in the integration of geostatistical techniques and remote sensing indices for predicting soil organic carbon stock. The research evaluates the performance of geostatistical techniques, such as kriging, in combination with remote sensing indices derived from satellite imagery to estimate soil organic carbon stock at a regional scale. By focusing on this specialized application, the study enhances our understanding of the relationship between remote sensing data and soil organic carbon stock. The findings contribute to the advancement of predictive modeling in ecology and support improved carbon management strategies and land use planning (Mishra et al., 2017).

4. DYNAMIC SOIL ASSESSMENT PLATFORM

4.1 The Need for a Real-Time Soil Quality Testing System

The integration of a real-time soil quality testing system holds significant importance in agricultural research and practice. Such a system offers farmers immediate access to precise and up-to-date feedback on soil conditions, enabling them to make data-driven decisions about crop management. The utilization of such a system yields several key benefits.

Firstly, real-time data on soil conditions provided by a soil quality testing system empowers farmers to optimize crop growth and yield through precise management strategies. By closely monitoring essential soil parameters, farmers can fine-tune irrigation schedules, tailor nutrient application rates, and adjust planting techniques, all of which contribute to improved crop productivity and yield.

Secondly, traditional soil testing methods are often associated with high costs and time requirements. In contrast, a real-time soil quality testing system offers prompt feedback on soil conditions, resulting in significant cost and time savings for farmers. By eliminating the need for extensive laboratory testing and reducing delays in decision-making, farmers can allocate their resources more efficiently and enhance operational effectiveness.

Moreover, a real-time soil quality testing system plays a crucial role in promoting sustainable farming practices. By providing farmers with real-time data on soil conditions, the system facilitates informed decision-making regarding crop management. This enables farmers to minimize the unnecessary use of fertilizers and other inputs, reducing environmental impacts and promoting sustainable agricultural practices that prioritize resource conservation and environmental stewardship.

Furthermore, the immediate availability of soil condition data through a real-time soil quality testing system allows farmers to promptly identify and address soil health issues. By detecting factors such as soil compaction, nutrient deficiencies, or imbalances in real-time, farmers can implement targeted corrective actions. These actions may include precision nutrient application, soil amendment incorporation, or other suitable interventions, leading to improved soil health and long-term productivity.

In conclusion, the integration of a real-time soil quality testing system provides farmers with instant feedback on soil conditions, enabling them to make well-informed decisions about crop management and promoting sustainable farming practices. The system's benefits encompass enhanced crop yield, reduced costs, sustainable agricultural approaches, and improved soil health. By harnessing the power of real-time data, farmers can optimize their agricultural practices and contribute to the advancement of sustainable and efficient farming systems (Liakos et al., 2018).

4.2 Unraveling the Thesis: An In-Depth Examination of the Proposition

In recent years, the combination of machine learning algorithms and IoT-based technologies has garnered increasing interest as a means to overcome the limitations of traditional soil testing methods. This integration offers the potential to greatly enhance the accuracy and efficiency of soil testing, empowering farmers and stakeholders with valuable insights for making informed decisions regarding fertilizer usage and other agricultural inputs (Liakos et al., 2018). However, several challenges must be overcome for the successful implementation of these technologies. One significant challenge revolves around the need for reliable and cost-effective IoT devices that can effectively collect and transmit precise data on soil conditions. Another hurdle involves the development of robust machine learning algorithms capable of efficiently processing large datasets and generating accurate predictions of soil quality (Liakos et al., 2018).

To address these challenges, collaborative partnerships among various stakeholders, including farmers, technology companies, and government agencies, are crucial. By pooling their expertise and resources, these stakeholders can identify key issues and devise tailored solutions that account for local conditions and specific requirements. For example, technology companies can focus on designing and manufacturing affordable IoT devices capable of seamlessly gathering soil condition data and transmitting it to a centralized database. Subsequently, farmers and other stakeholders can access this data to make well-informed decisions regarding the optimal use of fertilizers and other agricultural inputs . Furthermore, machine learning algorithms play a critical role in analyzing the collected data and generating accurate predictions of soil quality. By training these algorithms using historical data encompassing soil conditions, crop yields, and relevant factors such as weather patterns, irrigation practices, and crop rotation strategies, it is possible to derive valuable insights to guide agricultural decision-making.

In conclusion, the integration of machine learning algorithms and IoT-based technologies offers substantial potential for revolutionizing soil testing and quality analysis. By effectively addressing challenges related to cost, reliability, and accuracy, these technologies can empower farmers and stakeholders to make more informed decisions about agricultural inputs, ultimately fostering a more sustainable and environmentally friendly approach to farming (Liakos et al., 2018).

4.3 In-Depth Exposition

Soil quality testing and analysis play a vital role in agricultural and environmental management, as they directly impact crop growth and ecosystem health. However, traditional soil testing methods have limitations, such as being time-consuming and expensive. The emergence of machine learning algorithms and IoT-based technologies offers promising solutions to overcome these challenges. By automating the soil testing process, real-time monitoring of soil quality becomes feasible, enabling farmers to make informed decisions promptly. IoT sensors placed in the soil can monitor crucial parameters like moisture content, pH, and nutrient levels, with data transmitted wirelessly for analysis using machine learning algorithms. This automation not only reduces testing time but also cuts costs associated with specialized equipment and personnel. Furthermore, machine learning algorithms aid in analyzing soil data, identifying contaminants, and safeguarding the environment and public health. The spatial variability of soil properties is another challenge addressed by IoT applications, which provide real-time monitoring at multiple locations, allowing targeted management efforts. Accessibility to soil testing facilities is improved through remote access enabled by IoT applications, ensuring farmers in rural areas can benefit from soil testing services without the need for extensive travel. To enhance soil quality prediction, a deep learning (DL)-based method is proposed, utilizing a comprehensive dataset of soil characteristics. The approach involves a two-stage DL model combining LSTM and CNN networks to capture temporal relationships and extract features from soil samples, respectively. The LSTM network captures temporal dependencies between variables, while the CNN network extracts features from soil sample images. By merging the outputs of these networks and utilizing a fully connected layer, the final prediction of soil quality is generated. Extensive experiments and comparisons with conventional machine learning models demonstrate the superiority of the proposed DL method in predicting soil quality accurately. The method's ability to capture temporal dynamics, handle high-dimensional data effectively, and adapt to different soil types and regions highlights its advantages over traditional machine learning approaches (Liakos et al., 2018).

5. OBJECTIVES AND SCOPE OF THE PROJECT

The primary objectives of this research project on soil quality prediction using deep learning are as follows:

Data acquisition: Accumulate extensive datasets of soil samples, environmental data, and pertinent information to facilitate the training of deep learning models.

Data preprocessing: Cleanse and preprocess the datasets through techniques such as data normalization, feature selection, and data augmentation to ensure their suitability for training deep learning models.

Model selection: Determine the most appropriate deep learning models, such as artificial neural networks, convolution neural networks, or recurrent neural networks, based on the specific research objectives and data characteristics.

Model training: Train the selected deep learning models using the pre-processed data-sets, including hyper-parameter tuning, applying regularization techniques, and employing ensemble methods to optimize their performance.

The scope of this research paper encompasses the following aspects:

Model validation: Assess the performance of the trained models by employing evaluation metrics such as mean squared error, root mean squared error, mean absolute error, and coefficient of determination to ascertain their accuracy and reliability.

Model optimization: Fine-tune the trained models to enhance their performance by optimizing hyper-parameters, utilizing advanced optimization techniques such as gradient descent, or incorporating methodologies like transfer learning or domain adaptation.

Model deployment: Implement the optimized models to provide real-time predictions of soil quality based on new data, which may involve developing an intuitive user interface or integrating the models into existing software systems.

Model visualization: Integrate the trained models into an intuitive online or mobile application that enables users to input soil data and receive real-time forecasts of soil quality. Develop suitable visualization and explanation tools to facilitate user comprehension and evaluation of model predictions.

Continual improvement and maintenance: Continuously monitor and update the models and the application to ensure ongoing accuracy and relevance. Establish effective maintenance and update strategies to minimize downtime and ensure user satisfaction.

Model evaluation and optimization: Evaluate the effectiveness and generalizability of the trained models using evaluation metrics such as accuracy, precision, recall, and F1-score. Based on the availability and quality of evaluation data, further optimization of the models can be pursued to enhance their performance (Suresh Babu, 2022).

By achieving these objectives and addressing the defined scope, this research aims to develop a robust and precise soil quality prediction system using deep learning techniques, providing valuable insights for stakeholders involved in agricultural and environmental management (Ananthi et al., 2017).

6. REQUIREMENT ANALYSIS

6.1 Hardware Requirements

- ESP32
- Soil moisture sensor
- Breadboard
- Soil moisture sensor module
- OLED display
- Test setup with soil

- Jumper cables
- Micro USB cable

6.2 Software Requirements

- Arduino IDE
- Processing 3
- CP2102 Driver
- Adafruit IO

Detailed Dataset: A comprehensive dataset comprising the physical, chemical, and biological characteristics of soil is essential. The dataset should encompass a wide range of soil types, land uses, and management practices, ensuring it represents the target area effectively.

Data Pre-Processing: Data pre-processing is crucial to ensure the suitability of the data for deep learning. It involves tasks such as data cleaning, handling missing values, data scaling, and feature engineering.

Model Selection: To achieve accurate predictions of soil quality, selecting the appropriate deep learning model is vital. Convolutional neural networks (CNNs) and long short-term memory (LSTM) networks should be considered for soil quality forecasting.

Training and Validation: To avoid overfitting or underfitting, the model should be trained on one subset of the data and validated on a different subset.

Hyper Parameter Tuning: Optimizing the model's parameters, known as hyperparameter tuning, involves finding the best values for parameters such as learning rate, number of layers, and number of neurons per layer.

Performance Evaluation: Performance evaluation should employ metrics such as accuracy, precision, recall, and F1 score. Comparisons with other conventional machine learning models can provide insights into the model's effectiveness.

Cost-Effectiveness: Deep learning-based soil quality prediction depends on variables such as dataset size, model complexity, computational resources availability, and project objectives. The advantages of deep learning algorithms for soil quality prediction can contribute to cost efficiency.

User-Friendly Interface: The model should be accompanied by an intuitive user interface that is easy to use and understand. The interface should provide clear instructions, visual aids, and interactive elements to facilitate user interaction with the model.

Maintenance and Support: Regular updates to incorporate the latest advancements in deep learning technology and fresh soil quality data are necessary for accurate predictions. The software should undergo regular checks for flaws and defects, and a dedicated technical support staff should be available to assist users. Security checks should be performed to prevent unauthorized access or disclosure of sensitive soil data.

Privacy and Security: The system should prioritize user privacy and security by safeguarding personal data and implementing robust measures to prevent hacking or exploitation of the system.

7. SYSTEM DESIGN AND METHODOLOGY

7.1 Smart Soil Moisture Monitoring System

This research project focuses on developing a soil moisture monitoring system by interfacing a Soil moisture sensor with an ESP8266 micro-controller. The sensor accurately measures the volumetric content of water within the soil and provides the moisture level as an output, which is available in both analog and digital formats. The soil moisture sensor consists of two probes that enable the passage of current through the soil, allowing the measurement of resistance to determine the moisture value. When the soil contains a higher water content, it exhibits enhanced electrical conductivity, resulting in reduced resistance and indicating a higher moisture level. Conversely, in dry soil, the conductivity diminishes, leading to increased resistance and indicating a lower moisture level. By utilizing this system, precise monitoring of soil moisture levels can be achieved, enabling effective irrigation practices, optimizing water usage, and promoting optimal conditions for plant growth (Ananthi et al., 2017).

Figure 1. Soil moisture system

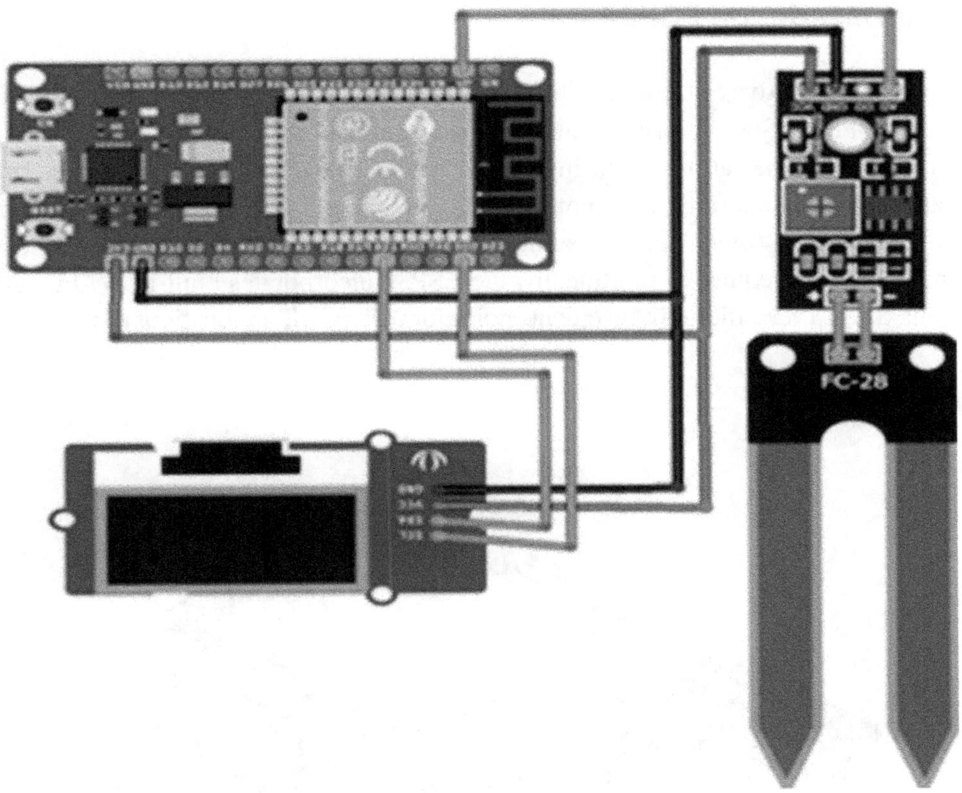

7.2 Soil Moisture Sensor

The soil moisture sensor utilized in this project is a resistive sensor that relies on the correlation between electrical resistance and water content in the soil to determine its moisture levels. These sensors typically consist of two exposed probes that are directly inserted into the soil sample. There are various types of soil moisture sensors commonly used, such as gypsum blocks, tension meters, capacitance sensors, volumetric sensors, and neutron probes. These sensors operate by either measuring soil tension or determining the volumetric water content present in the soil. By leveraging the capabilities of these sensors, accurate and reliable measurements of soil moisture can be obtained, enabling efficient monitoring and management of water resources in agricultural and environmental applications.

7.2.1 Output

The output of the soil moisture monitoring system involves using the Arduino IDE to upload the Moisture Monitoring code to the ESP32 board. To accomplish this, the ESP32 board needs to be connected to a laptop using a Micro USB Cable, and then the upload button is pressed in the Arduino IDE. Once the code is successfully uploaded, the OLED Display and Adafruit IO components will begin displaying the soil moisture value in percentage (%). This real-time display of the soil moisture level provides users with immediate information about the moisture content in the soil, facilitating better decision-making in irrigation and plant management.

7.3 Modules Description ESP32

The ESP32 is a cost-effective System on Chip (SoC) microcontroller developed by Espressif Systems, known for their ESP8266 SoC. It serves as an upgraded version of the ESP8266 and is available in both single-core and dual-core variations, featuring Tensilica's 32-bit Xtensa LX6 microprocessor. What sets the ESP32 apart is its integration of RF components, including a power amplifier, low-noise receive amplifier, antenna switch, filters, and RF balun. This integration simplifies hardware design, as fewer external components are required. Additionally, the ESP32 incorporates built-in Wi-Fi and Bluetooth capabilities, making it a versatile and convenient choice for various IoT applications (Ananthi et al., 2017).

Figure 2. Esp32

The ESP32 is a low-cost Wi-Fi chip with full TCP/IP stack and microcontroller capability produced by Shanghai-based Chinese manufacturer.

7.4 Optimizing Soil Moisture Management for Enhanced Plant Growth

The moisture content of the soil plays a vital role in both agricultural fields and gardens, as it directly affects plant irrigation and growth. Soil nutrients provide essential nourishment for plants, supporting their overall development. Supplying an adequate amount of water is crucial for maintaining optimal soil moisture levels, which not only sustains plant growth but also regulates plant temperature through processes like transpiration. To measure soil moisture, resistive soil moisture sensors are commonly used. These sensors feature two exposed probes that are inserted directly into the soil sample. By analyzing the electrical resistance between the probes, the sensor can accurately determine the moisture content present in the soil. By effectively managing soil moisture levels, it becomes possible to influence plant temperature and create favorable conditions for growth (Liakos et al., 2018).

Figure 3. Soil moisture sensor

7.5 OLED Display

The soil moisture monitoring system incorporates an OLED display module powered by the SSD1306 OLED driver IC. This IC simplifies integration with its compact four-pin configuration, with two pins for power supply and the remaining pins (SCL and SDA) enabling communication through the I2C protocol. The I2C protocol allows for seamless control and interaction with the OLED display, facilitating the presentation of relevant information in the monitoring system.

In addition, the system utilizes the I2C protocol for communication between multiple slave digital integrated circuits and master chips within the same device. This protocol is specifically designed for short-distance communication and requires only two signal wires, enabling efficient data exchange in the system. Furthermore, the system incorporates a GSM module that can transmit alert messages to a central server in critical situations or accidents, ensuring prompt response and appropriate actions (Ananthi et al., 2017).

Figure 4. Flowchart of the soil quality prediction using deep learning

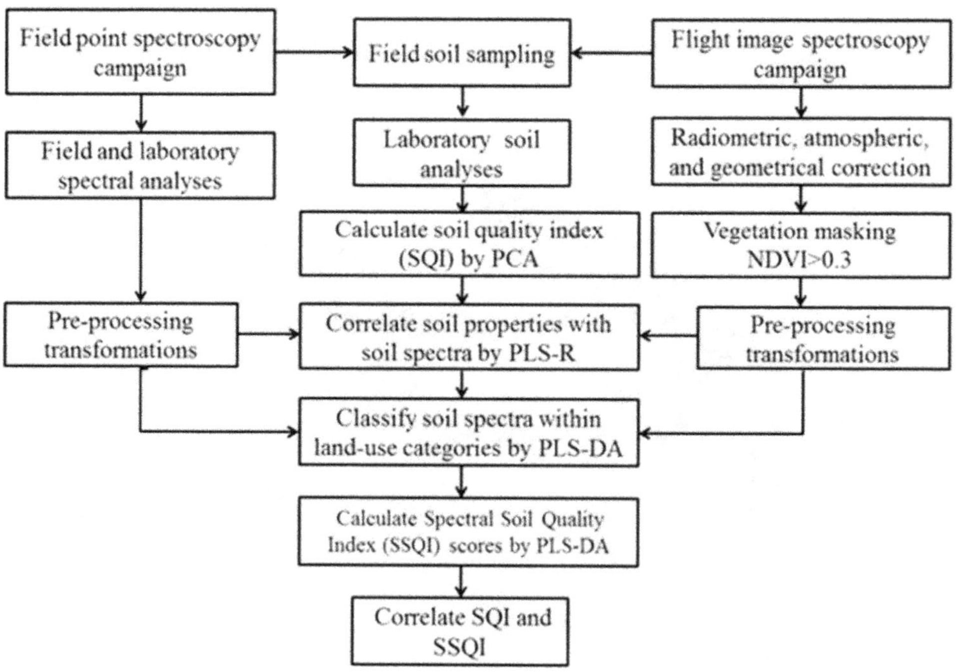

8. SYSTEM IMPLEMENTATION

The Arduino Software (IDE) provides a platform for writing and uploading programs to Arduino boards. There are two options available: the online IDE (Arduino Web Editor) and the desktop IDE. The online IDE is recommended for users with a reliable internet connection, allowing sketches to be saved in the cloud and accessed from any device. It eliminates the need for manual updates or community library installations. Alternatively, the desktop IDE can be used for offline work.

To construct a soil quality prediction system using deep learning, soil information is obtained from various sources such as meteorological data, soil type, and geographic location. The gathered data is cleaned, including filling gaps, eliminating outliers, and structuring it for compatibility with deep learning models. Pertinent features are selected from the pre-processed data for training the deep learning model.

An appropriate deep learning model is chosen, such as Convolutional Neural Networks (CNN), Recurrent Neural Networks (RNN), or Multilayer Perceptrons (MLP), to predict soil quality characteristics like pH levels, nutrient levels, and organic matter content. The chosen model is trained on the pre-processed data using suitable loss functions and optimization techniques to reduce prediction error and improve accuracy.

Evaluation of the trained model's effectiveness is performed using relevant measures like mean absolute error (MAE), mean squared error (MSE), and coefficient of determination (R2). These measures provide insights into the model's performance.

Deployment of the learned deep learning model can be achieved through an on-premises infrastructure or a cloud-based platform. This involves creating an API or web application that allows users to input soil data and receive forecasts. An intuitive interface is designed to enable users to enter soil data, make forecasts, and visualize outcomes effectively. The interface should provide clear visualizations and allow users to adjust settings and parameters.

Continuous maintenance and support of the system are crucial, involving performance monitoring, software updates, and user assistance. Constructing a soil quality prediction system using deep learning requires expertise in data science, machine learning, and software engineering. By following these installation stages, the system can provide precise estimates of soil quality metrics and assist farmers in making informed crop management decisions.

9. RESULT AND PERFORMANCE ANALYSIS

9.1 Result

After lot of errors and problems we have successfully connected the circuit and everything in the circuit works perfectly as we expected.

Figure 5. Sample project

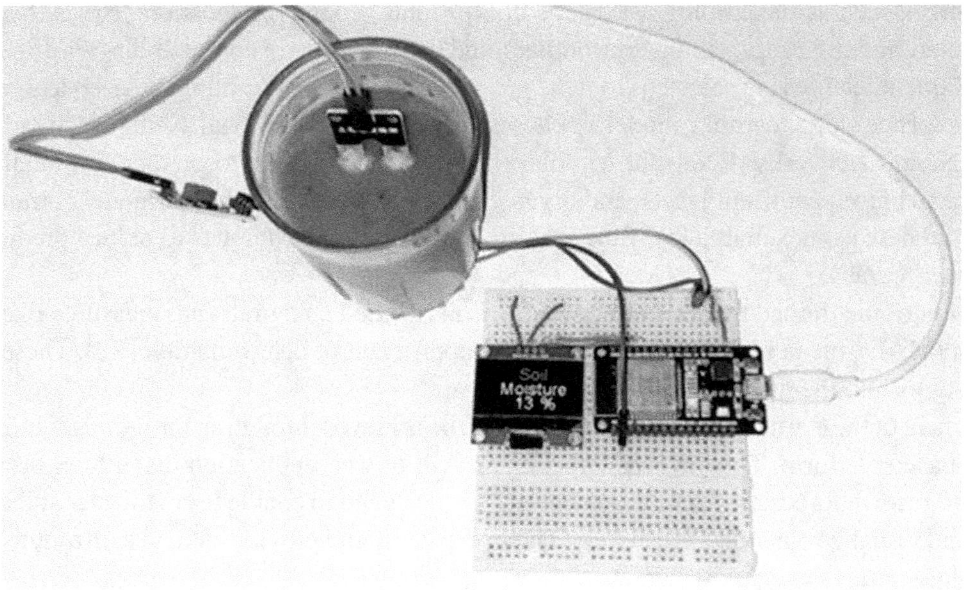

10. PERFORMANCE ANALYSIS

When analyzing the performance of a soil quality prediction system, several factors need to be considered:

Accuracy: The accuracy of the predicted soil quality is crucial to ensure informed decision-making. Performance indicators such as coefficient of determination (R-squared), mean absolute error (MAE), and root mean square error (RMSE) can be used to assess accuracy.

Precision: Precision refers to the consistency and reliability of repeated measurements in soil quality prediction. To establish trust and consistency over time, predictions need to be precise. Performance measures like standard deviation and coefficient of variation can evaluate precision.

Reliability: The reliability of soil quality predictions examines how accurately and consistently a specific approach or model performs over time and across multiple samples. Reliability is essential to ensure the accuracy and consistency of soil quality predictions.

Sensitivity and Specificity: Sensitivity and specificity are important measures of a soil quality prediction method's ability to correctly identify positive and negative soil conditions. High levels of sensitivity and specificity are necessary to ensure accurate and trustworthy soil quality estimates.

Validity: Validity refers to the ability of a soil quality prediction method to accurately represent the health and fertility of the soil. Performance metrics such as face validity, content validity, and criteria validity can be used to assess the validity of soil quality projections.

Cost: The cost of implementing and maintaining the soil quality prediction system is an important aspect of its performance. The system should be cost-effective and provide value for money.

User Experience: The user experience of the system, including ease of use and provision of relevant information, is critical. The system should be user-friendly, intuitive, and provide relevant information to users.

11. FUTURE ENHANCEMENT

Future enhancements in soil quality prediction systems using deep learning can focus on the following technical advancements:

Novel Deep Learning Architectures: Developing innovative deep learning architectures and algorithms that can handle complex and diverse soil data while capturing the non-linear correlations between soil characteristics and environmental factors.

Data Augmentation and Transfer Learning: Addressing challenges related to data scarcity, diversity, and quality by incorporating data augmentation techniques and leveraging transfer learning and domain adaptation methods.

Integration of Additional Data Sources: Expanding the geographical and temporal resolution and coverage of soil quality prediction by integrating deep learning models with additional data sources such as remote sensing, geographic information systems (GIS), and expert knowledge.

Robustness Assessment: Evaluating the effectiveness and robustness of deep learning models under various settings and scenarios, including changing land use, climate variations, and different soil management techniques.

User-Friendly Interfaces and Software: Developing dynamic and user-friendly interfaces and software that can provide accurate soil quality forecasts and suggestions to various stakeholders, including farmers, researchers, and policymakers.

Specific examples of future research in deep learning-based soil quality prediction include:

Deep Learning for Soil Organic Matter Prediction: Proposing a novel method based on deep learning to estimate soil organic matter content from photos captured by unique technology.

Deep Learning Regression Network for Soil Moisture Prediction: Utilizing a deep learning regression network (DNNR) to build a data-driven model for predicting soil moisture levels.

Comparative Study of Machine Learning Algorithms: Conducting a comparative analysis of various machine learning techniques, such as multiple linear regression, support vector regression, and recurrent neural networks, for soil moisture prediction at different time intervals.

12. CONCLUSION

In conclusion, the utilization of deep learning for soil quality prediction has the potential to transform agriculture by providing farmers with precise and timely information about their soils. Deep learning algorithms excel in accurately forecasting soil characteristics, such as pH levels, nutrient content, and organic matter, resulting in increased crop yields, reduced fertilizer usage, and improved soil health. By incorporating diverse data sources and careful model selection, deep learning models can enhance geographical and temporal resolution in soil quality prediction. However, challenges such as interpretability and data availability must be considered. Continued research in this field can further refine sustainable farming practices and enhance soil condition estimates.

REFERENCES

Ananthi, N., Divya, J., Divya, M., & Janani, V. (2017). *IoT based smart soil monitoring system for agricultural production. In 2017 IEEE Technological Innovations in ICT for Agriculture and Rural Development (TIAR)*. IEEE. doi:10.1109/TIAR.2017.8273717

Behzad, M., Kiani-Harchegani, M., Karimi, M., & Mousavi, S. (2020). Machine learning-based prediction of soil cation exchange capacity using soil spectral data. *Catena*, *188*, 104444. doi:10.1016/j.catena.2019.104444

Duan, Y., Zhang, L., Lu, S., Chen, X., & Zhou, X. (2018). Soil nutrient prediction using visible and near-infrared spectroscopy: A comparison of models and wavelengths. *Soil Science Society of America Journal*, *82*(4), 1029–1040. doi:10.2136ssaj2018.01.0038

Gholizadeh, A., & Ayoubi, S. (2017). Predicting soil organic carbon and total nitrogen using soil spectral data and machine learning algorithms. *Catena*, *156*, 35–45. doi:10.1016/j.catena.2017.04.020

Gholizadeh, A., Ayoubi, S., Khormali, F., & Wulfsohn, D. (2020). Predicting soil organic carbon and total nitrogen using machine learning algorithms in a semi-arid region. *Catena*, *193*, 104641. doi:10.1016/j.catena.2020.104641

Liakos, K. G., Busato, P., Moshou, D., Pearson, S., & Bochtis, D. (2018). Machine Learning in Agriculture: A Review. *Sensors (Basel)*, *18*(8), 2674. doi:10.339018082674 PMID:30110960

Liu, X., Zhang, J., Chen, Y., Sun, S., & Wu, L. (2021). Soil nutrient prediction using machine learning models in a highly variable arid environment. *The Science of the Total Environment*, *772*, 144773. doi:10.1016/j.scitotenv.2021.144773

Mishra, A., Sharma, S. K., & Pandey, A. (2017). Predicting soil organic carbon stock using geostatistical techniques and remote sensing indices. *Ecological Indicators*, *78*, 400–412. doi:10.1016/j.ecolind.2017.03.045

Pham, T. V., Jeon, C. H., & Han, D. (2019). A comparative study of machine learning techniques for predicting soil water content. *Journal of Hydrology (Amsterdam)*, *575*, 22–33. doi:10.1016/j.jhydrol.2019.05.059

Suresh Babu, C. V. (2022). *Artificial Intelligence and Expert Systems* (1st ed.). Anniyappa Publications.

Suresh Babu, C. V., Mahalashmi, J., Vidhya, A., Nila Devagi, S., & Bowshith, G. (2023). Save Soil Through Machine Learning. In M. Habib (Ed.), *Global Perspectives on Robotics and Autonomous Systems: Development and Applications* (pp. 345–362). IGI Global., doi:10.4018/978-1-6684-7791-5.ch016

Suresh Babu, C. V., Yadavamuthiah, K., Abirami, S., & Kowsika, S. (2023a). Artificial Intelligence in Wastewater Management. In V. Shikuku (Ed.), *Artificial Intelligence Applications in Water Treatment and Water Resource Management* (pp. 31–45). IGI Global., doi:10.4018/978-1-6684-6791-6.ch002

Wang, Q., Zhou, L., Zhou, Y., & Ma, J. (2019). Machine learning algorithms for soil organic carbon prediction using visible and near-infrared spectra. *Soil & Tillage Research*, *195*, 104384. doi:10.1016/j.still.2019.104384

Wu, Y., Jiang, Z., Zou, H., & Li, F. (2021). Soil organic carbon prediction using random forest and deep learning models in a hilly region. *Catena*, *196*, 105134. doi:10.1016/j.catena.2020.105134

Chapter 11
Succeeding India's Retail Digital Currency

Rajat Deb
https://orcid.org/0000-0002-7009-0051
Tripura University, India

ABSTRACT

The study attempts to critically assess the possibilities of success of the Indian retail digital currency (DC). The Central Bank Digital Currency, popularly known as CBDC, issues in any of the two forms—token and account types—and the Reserve Bank of India (RBI) prefers the former route. A token is a currency or any digital and/or physical asset. Theoretically, tokenization can buy, sell, and transfer digital or real-life assets fully or fractionally. Amending the RBI Act and expanding the scope of the definition of 'bank notes', DC incorporates and enjoys equivalent legal tender like physical currency notes and coins. Albeit the Indians, along with cash, the latter is still preferred and enjoying the status of a 'king' even post-demonetization years. The DC in retail likely could be a game changer in the Indian financial market if the RBI could comprehensively address the teething problems associated with DC.

1. INTRODUCTION

Rapid financial innovation pushes global economies in the era of blockchain and cryptocurrencies. After the first cryptocurrency, Bitcoin (BTC), launched in 2009, it penetrated almost every segment of society, including businesses, consumers, investors, non-profit motive institutions and even public institutions. As proposed by the International Monetary Fund, the Central Bank Digital Currencies (CBDC) is a legal tender in digital form. The emergence and rapid development of digital currencies (DC), such as BTC, Diem, and like, significantly impact the global financial system. Research concedes significant increase in cryptocurrency demands results in substantial market capitalization growth (Kumar & Ajaz, 2019). Apart from BTC and Ethereum, Facebook's DC Diem (erstwhile Libra) also entered the global financial markets, but controversies remain. Considering those, central banks globally engage in developing their unique DCs. CBDC, the blockchain-based version of reserve currencies, is unlikely based on third-party stable coins (Morgan, 2022). Literature reports divergent views regarding the prospects of CBDC, such

DOI: 10.4018/979-8-3693-1722-8.ch011

as the future of money to even short-term investment bubbles, albeit; changes in prioritized investment decisions post-acceptance of CBDC are significantly accelerated globally (Kou *et al.*, 2021). Theoretically, a currency has three primordial functions, a unit of account, a medium of exchange and a store of value. Interestingly, arguments favour cryptocurrency as a medium of exchange and a store of value contested, considering the same merely as a speculative asset rather than money. Furthermore, money referred to as the decoupling of private money from public money in cryptocurrencies contradicted theories of money such as its value derivation from the issuance by governments (Knapp, 1905), the provenance of the state (Wray, 2011), and the credit theory of money (Mitchell-Innes, 1913).

Literature comprehensively reports core differences between cryptocurrency and other financial markets, indicating the ceiling of the number of transactions in the latter. Notably, a lack of control in the supply of digital assets and whopping yielding rates posed severe doubt regarding the security and stability of the former. The research addresses a close association between liquidity and market inefficiency, and the cryptocurrency market's behaviour, such as long memory and multifractality, remains on the research agenda. Studies concede that cryptocurrency markets are opaque, have low liquidity, are exposed to risks and are inefficient (Le *et al.*, 2020). Accordingly, governments intervene by serving notices, bringing them under taxation, or raising tax rates (Renwick & Gleasure, 2021). Although, research argues that asymmetric information has significant spillover effects in the cryptocurrency market. Spillover contributing factors include volatility co-movement, calendar effect, lead/lag effect, and systematic risk. India joins the rally by introducing the e-rupee in the wholesale market through government securities transactions. On 1st December 2022, the Reserve Bank of India (RBI) took the boldest step by flagging off an e-rupee as a pilot project of the retail version (e-Rupee R) of the CBDC with INR 1.71 crores issued to four participating banks based on their indents. For implementing the project, the RBI identifies four banks in the first phase, viz., State Bank of India (SBI), ICICI Bank, YES Bank and IDFC First Bank, for operating in four cities, i.e., Mumbai, New Delhi, Bengaluru, and Bhubaneswar. RBI further notified those four more banks, viz. Bank of Baroda, Union Bank of India, HDFC Bank and Kotak Mahindra Bank, would participate in the pilot project by expanding in nine more cities in December 2022.

The study motivates to critically assess the possibilities of success of the Indian retail digital currency.

The subsequent sections of the qualitative paper include in Section 2 the debate of the DC, Section 3 a description of the Indian DC, Section 4 users' concerns on DC, Section 5 cash preference, Section 6 strategies for addressing cash preference and eventually in Section 7 presents the way forward of the Indian DC.

2. THE DEBATE- BOON OR BANE

Literature paints the pros and cons of CBDC, and the debate is ongoing. One school of thought highlights the benefits associated with CBDC. They primarily report central banks' lower issuance and circulation costs vis-à-vis printed currencies, expanded scope of monetary policy, and avenues for emphasizing other policy issues (Auer *et al.*, 2020). Empirical studies document significant positive impacts, e.g., improved lending, as banks get opportunities for outside deposits by changing interest rates and avoiding bank runs (Fernández Villaverde *et al.*, 2020). Again, CBDC would likely promote financial integration, improve transaction efficiency, enhance security, reduce cross-border payments, and expand financial markets for weaker economies. It will likely address hyperinflation and international sanctions, curb the problems of counterfeit currencies, reduce the cost of issuing and circulating and monitor physical currency. CBDC assists the central banks in aptly accounting for the money supply, its structure, velocity, multiplier, and real-time distribution, i.e., significantly improved operations and attain objectives of the monetary policy. Inclusiveness of the CBDC identifies as the core advantage as anonymous payments without disclosing beneficiary identity, account number, and even without internet connectivity are possible through e-wallets. By accessing existing digital marketing channels, CBDC could provide a new vista of opportunities having a complete ecosystem for economic and financial activities. Moreover, combined with supporting technologies, CBDC would bring the unbanked population under the banking orchestra. Through CBDC, the classification of assets, durables, and livestock, even in small fractions, is possible, and such fractionalization assists in improved liquidity and affordability (Lee *et al.*, 2021). CBDC, in the form of tokens, could track varied household services, transactions pertinent to livestock and numerous unreported and undocumented economic activities having the potential for exploring additional business opportunities.

As every advantage has its tax, multiple challenges and hedges are imminent with the CBDC adoption from technological, economic, legal, ethical, and even social perspectives. Literature acknowledges the negative impacts of CBDC on macro economies. It suggests aspects such as banks' increased liquidity needs coupled with decreased economic outputs, crowding out bank deposits, increased costs of funding and reduced investments, increased costs of deposits and negative impacts on financial stability (Parlour *et al.*, 2020). Admittedly, Nobel laureates (e.g., Paul Krugman and Joseph Stiglitz), investors (e.g., Warren Buffett and Jack Ma), and central bankers (like Alan Greenspan and Vitor Constâncio) indicate most of the cryptocurrencies as speculative bubbles. The literature affirms those observations (see Patterson, 2018). Research cautions that unregulated issuance of CBDCs could lead to a liquidity crunch for banks, a reduction in demand for deposits and bank reserves, and a bank run. Eventually, those may create panic and instability in the financial market. Besides, CBDC opens avenues for launching derivatives and engineered products, which could trigger uncertainties and inherent risks due to the spread of transactions having high volumes. The Flipside of DC includes legal slack in the efficient operation –issuance, circulation, usage, and supervision as banks transited from physical to virtual. In the event of cyber-attacks or system failures, the modalities for indemnifying the victim parties would be completely different from traditional currencies, and relevant amendments in the Acts and Rules are indispensable. Empirical research documents that CBDC would likely catalyse a wide-scale run of bank savings, creating uncertainty in the existing monetary system and adverse impacts on cross-border capital flows and capital regulation policies (Tong & Jiayou, 2021). The literature further demonstrates the ill effects of cryptocurrencies. Cryptocurrencies used in illegal economic activities, such as BTC, are infrequently used, protecting privacy and the possibility of market manipulation (Foley *et al.*, 2019). Apart from contesting schools of thought, another stream of research concludes that CBDCs are neutral to credit provision and bank risk since the impacts of interchangeable public and private money would likely adjust through monetary policy (Brunnermeier & Niepelt, 2019). Authors suggest that post-CBDC banks should increase the interest rates of savings (inclusive wholesale), demand deposits, or both (Chiu *et al.*, 2019).

3. INDIAN DIGITAL CURRENCY

CBDC issuance is taking place in any of the two forms- token and account types. The former is akin to an existing cash or gift voucher combining valuable information with an electronic token allowing the owner to access the value. At the same time, the latter is similar to the demand deposits account of each individual linked with the DC, probably at the central bank. Tokens are the programmability of cryptocurrencies. The design of tokens not only transfers or holds funds but also allows the creation of new cryptocurrencies. A token is a currency or any digital and physical asset. Tokenization can buy, sell, and transfer digital or real-life assets fully or fractionally. The retail DC launched by the RBI is in the form of a token. In the transfer of tokens between addresses, updating the token state (number of tokens involved with each address in the blockchain) and confirmation of token transactions took place simultaneously, avoiding any traditional settlement risk. Tokens with state variables inside the blockchain have been transferrable between various addresses, keeping the total amount of tokens intact. In other words, the result of any such transfer of tokens always remains unchanged on a real-time basis. RBI's preference for token over account type CBDC could be substantiated by the former's different monetary features making those similar to human-made digital gold. Scrutiny of unique features of tokens has shown that those do not possess a liability component having small homogeneous units. For executing token transactions, intermediation of third parties is likely to be dispensed with, and cryptographic technology ensures token holders' anonymity.

Notably, the token-based e-Rupee and the account-based e-Rupee differ in multiple ways. The former represents a digital token on a blockchain, whereas the latter is not representing any blockchain. The former is likely to be treated as a digital asset and transferrable from one person to another through transactions; however, the account-based e-Rupee, unlike the former, is not a standalone digital asset and represents the outstanding balance of any user's account. The token-based e-Rupee has a feature of exchange against other cryptocurrencies or fiat currencies. On the other hand, the account-based e-rupee has a confined use within the system but is not exchangeable against other currencies. Albeit there is a fallacy about the Indian e-Rupee as her unique version of cryptocurrency, the e-Rupee is unlikely to be treated as a cryptocurrency. Like other CBDCs, the e-Rupee is the digital rupee which could have use akin to physical currency notes (Haque & Shoaib, 2023). The provision of e-Rupee would be through the intermediary banks as practices for physical currency notes. The validation process of CBDCs could be through account-based CBDCs and retail-based CBDCs. The former could suit wholesale CBDC applications, while the latter is preferable for retail transactions, and India adopts a hybrid approach.

The wholesale CBDC are created to settle and support interbank payments among banks and financial institutions. On the other hand, the retail CBDC evolves to serve as an alternative to traditional physical money possessed by individuals and public and private business organizations for executing retail transactions. CBDC can introduce in any of the three ways. First, the financial institutions' access (Model FI), whereby individuals are restricted in accessing digital currencies; second, the economy-wide access (Model EW) in which individuals are allowed to use the digital currencies directly and third, the financial institutions plus CBDC backed narrow bank access (Model FI+), a combination of first two models (Kumhof & Noone, 2018). The digital rupee wallet to be used as retail DC would be akin to a physical wallet available or downloaded on smartphones having an Android operating system (OS). Payment is completed by scanning a unique quick response (QR) code accessible at merchant points. The RBI states that the currencies are digitally issued to banks, and on request, the latter will credit the digital rupee to the digital wallets of those customers. After that, the customers could complete transactions by making payments through a digital rupee, a legal tender. Against this back drop, the inherent limitations of the distributed ledger technology (DLT), the RBI concept note, issued in October 2022 prefers a centrally controlled conventional database infrastructure for CBDC. The preference for the latter is likely motivated by the data updating procedure, as data is stored over multiple physical nodes controlled centrally by one authoritative entity, assuring resilience and no restrictions on the volume of transactions.

4. USER'S CONCERNS

Davis (1986) was the pioneer in conceptualising individual technology acceptance by proposing the Technology Acceptance Model (TAM), which extended through developing theories (Venkatesh & Davis, 2000). Literature suggests that socio-demographic characteristics significantly impact information technology (IT) adoption. However, older people show reluctance to accept any specific technology, although the use of IT likely increases their quality of living (Mitzner *et al.*, 2010). Notably, the first cryptocurrency, BTC, although designed as a peer-to-peer (P2P) cash system satisfying one of the characteristics of a currency, high volatility and classified as an investment (Bedi & Nashier, 2020). Although the threat of bank robbery and counterfeiting of physical currency notes no longer persist with DC but likely exposed to cyber-attacks. Research cautions that stolen BTC can easily be convertible into cash could fuel the volatility of BTC. Macroeconomists are unlikely convinced that DC would be a panacea for prompt payment settlement addressing challenges emanating from inconsistent monitoring and governance, grey sections of laws, e.g., anti-money laundering (AML), anti-terrorism, and taxation. The RBI's preference for conventional database infrastructure for retail DC could be transparent. However, cyber-attack vulnerabilities remain, like the existing first payment system (FPS). September 2022 data released by the National Payments Corporation of India (NPC) indicates the Unified Payment Interface (UPI) platform records a whopping 6.8 billion transactions with a volume of INR 11.17 trillion, a 3.05% and 4.06% higher on a month-on-month (m-o-m) basis in terms of volume and value respectively. Again, on a year-on-year (y-o-y) basis, the figure has substantially increased and recorded 85.55% and 70.61%, respectively. Interestingly, consumer spending significantly dropped after the advent of the Covid-19 pandemic, but the cash economy boomed (Mohan, 2022). The RBI data further indicates that the average daily transactions of the e-Rupee W crossed INR 325 crores in November 2022, while in the first two days since launching, the quantum of transactions of e-rupee R crossed INR 3 crores.

Despite of worldwide exponential growth of cryptocurrencies, there are multiple unanswered questions regarding their impacts on global financial, economic, and environmental stability, accounting and taxation aspects, regulations, privacy and anonymity protection, high exposure to cyber-attacks, high protection costs and others (Elsayed & Nasir, 2022). Apprehensions about future significant interoperability problems in the financial system due to increased use of CBDCs are unlikely to be refuted as customers could en masse pull out their bank deposits to invest in risk-free CBDCs which could end with a lack of funds for commercial banks in creating loaned-assets. This phenomenon could destabilise the banking orchestra (Selgin, 2021), especially for economies with a history of unstable banking systems (Yamaoka, 2022). Research on the impact of retail DC further affirms such apprehension (Bindseil, 2019). Authors apprehend central banks could gain monopolistic power over bank deposits which could end with bank run (Sinelnikova-Muryleva, 2020). Interestingly, infamous bank fiascos such as the Yes Bank and exposure of bank frauds in the Indian banking system could also lead to such interoperability problems in future. The possible unregulated issue of private cryptocurrencies could adversely impact global economies, particularly developing economies, as those may significantly reduce the role of intermediaries such as banks. The excessively volatile nature of cryptocurrencies and poor or lack of regulations could adversely affect national and global economies. A cryptocurrency is a DC; the laws of supply and demand determine its value based on blockchain technology, and it operates in its own rules with no regulation by central banks. In contrast, the central banks issue and monitor CBDCs debase the core objective of the cryptocurrencies of state intervention. Research reports that money laundering significantly increased since the evolution of modern cryptocurrency markets (Kaplan, 2021). But proponents of free markets suggest that the market should determine its equilibrium point without central bank interference in a decentralised cryptocurrency-based monetary system (Crandall, 2019). Recent research further concurs that CBDCs could impede price stability (Elsayed & Nasir, 2022) while conditions for a smooth introduction of CBDCs without bank intermediation or credit crisis by the European Central Bank (ECB) also reported (Fegatelli, 2022).

The paucity of a common consensus about the underlying technology of CBDCs concerning privacy and anonymity could jeopardise banks as CBDCs based on distributed ledgers, i.e., blockchains (Bank of England, 2020). Although the designs of blockchains of CBDCs are capable of affording and recording all economic transactions, which could control global financial corruption; however, individual privacy protection concerns remain unaddressed (Goodell & Shen, 2021). As opposed to cryptocurrency, CBDC transactions are unlikely to be anonymous, remain under central banks' surveillance and function like traditional paper currencies in a centralised manner. The pre-purchase complete personal verification of potential buyers of CBDCs differs from modalities practised in investments in cryptocurrencies, but the right to anonymity and privacy protection in cryptocurrency investment is absent in CBDCs. Notably, since central banks issue, ledger and control of CBDCs, aspects of data privacy and transaction monitoring fall under government jurisdiction, implying a lack of corrective mechanisms, reduced competition, and close vigil and transaction recording. Empirical research further suggests that increased acceptance of CBDCs is subject to high levels of security and confidentiality, and disclosure of private information could lead to its abysmal use (Jabbar *et al.*, 2023). Moreover, the pervasive use of digitalised data concerning customer information and behaviour is a high degree of exposure to compromise, jeopardising their protection and privacy (Chen *et al.*, 2021), could lead to discriminating credit decisions (Ichihashi, 2020) and temptation of misuse of those data (Liu *et al.*, 2021).

Regulations, enforcement ability of contractual obligations and property rights, and taxation are other issues of users' concerns about CBDCs' global acceptability, which require explicit clarification (Goodell & Shen, 2021). Despite the substantial growth of DCs lack of specific regulations for transaction verifications and controlling made those vulnerable as CBDC regulations significantly vary across countries (Tran, 2021). The highly volatile speculative investment nature of cryptocurrencies prevents them as a payment unit, while many other countries recognise Bitcoin and other cryptocurrencies as a payment unit (Fomina *et al.*, 2019). Again, the decentralisation and anonymity characteristics of DC catalyse money laundering and other illegal activities, such as terror funding (Dyntu & Dykyi, 2019). Interestingly, a decentralised feature of cryptocurrency blockchains prevents regulators and investigating agencies from tracking the perpetrators. The impacts of DC gains and losses on corporate cash and book taxes are another matter of users' concern. Anonymity or asymmetric information about DC transactions, such as capital gains from cryptocurrencies and multiple global tax laws, could further complicate the taxation issue (Alsalmi *et al.*, 2023). Research indicates CBDCs denominated in national currencies could act as complements instead of substitutes for cash and bank deposits (Goodell & Shen, 2021), and unsettled queries concerning ethics, privacy, and environmental and technological constraints remain (Elsayed & Nasir, 2022).

Literature reports that regulatory technology (RegTech) gained significant momentum among banks for meeting enhanced computational demands of compliance (Currie *et al.*, 2018), and the costs of regulatory compliance motivate the financial sector to RegTech adoption (Butler & O'Brien, 2019). Notably, the post-2008 global financial crisis and persistent geo-political global tensions compelled the banks for enhanced transparency and surveillance in transactions. Again, Basel III norms suggest that banks should comply with anti-money laundering (AML) and counter-financing of terrorism (CFT) regulations. Money laundering (ML) refers to an act of generating a substantial amount of money through illegal activities and giving those a legal status (Kumar, 2012), while terrorism financing (TF) indicates a collection of legal and illegal sources of funds for terrorism (Tofangsaz, 2012). However, instead of their differentiation, banks focus on unearthing sources and the perpetrators; and adopt the same strategies for AML/CFT. To address the challenges of AML/CFT, worldwide banks prefer rule-based systems for detecting and tracking suspicious activities, but those systems are unlikely to be free from flaws. Although the counter-mechanism systems face criticism due to the required expertise for redefining the rules and the significant consumption of time and resources, leading to the under-reporting of crimes (Han *et al.*, 2020). Related literature indicates managing the challenges of rule-based systems, and banks are shifting to artificial intelligence (AI) technologies which are likely to significantly minimise human error and other routine work (Aziz & Dowling, 2019). Admittedly, research also concurs application of AI technologies for countering the problems of ML/TF is more experimental instead systematic (Canhoto, 2020). Those pose a concern about AI applications in combating threats of ML/TF activities as empirical research in this area remains inadequate (Al-Suwaidi & Nobanee, 2020). In the Indian context, it lacks an exhaustive set of rules regulating the AML/CFT concerning CBDC. In compliance with provisions of section 35A of the Banking Regulation Act, 1949, and Rule 9(14) of the Prevention of Money-Laundering (Maintenance of Records) Rules, 2005, (PMLA) RBI requires to verify whether reporting entities following specific client identification procedures for opening accounts and monitoring suspicious transactions for reporting to the competent authorities. The Apex Court intervention setting aside the impugned RBI's Circular debarring virtual currency transactions on the ground of proportionality further indicates RBI has limited power in the context of regulating cryptocurrencies as per the RBI Act, 1949.**1** This decision subsequently compels RBI to issue guidelines for banks and financial institutions trading in cryptocurrencies to adhere to the KYC norms, AML, and CFT, obligations under PMLA and relevant provisions under the Foreign Exchange Management Act (FEMA), 1999, for their overseas remittances. Furthermore, lessons learnt in June 2021 from the controversy involving WazirX, India's largest cryptocurrency exchange platform, suggests the importance of studying the association with AML/CFT and CBDC for enacting new laws or amending the existing one for the success of the e-Rupee.

The success of CBDCs significantly depends on effective counter strategies implementation addressing inherent problems of risk aversion, low user adoption, high cyber security risks, vulnerability testing, and costs of protecting firewalls. Recent literature indicates that symmetric access to news about CBDC uncertainty could channelise future CBDC performance (Lucey *et al.*, 2022). Again, the currency market hedging factor could impact CBDC leading to currency market uncertainty through its moderating effects on risk aversion. Systematic risks to the financial system could also be inevitable through a CBDC due to the redemption of money market mutual funds (MMFs) during a financial crisis, as liquidated funds may be parked in the CBDC, leaving disintermediation risks for MMFs. The exposure of increased cybersecurity risk innates from distributed nature of DLT of CBDCs, albeit DLT could offer cybersecurity benefits in terms of mass rejection by other participants in the network once any data breach is exposed. Notably, irrespective of the nature of the CBDC-centralised or decentralised, counterfeiting and cybersecurity threats are likely to persist, and RBI requires a comprehensive policy to address those risks. The probable solution to the problem of low user adoption includes mass propaganda focusing on the potentiality of CBDC to offer higher resilience, enhanced safety, greater availability, improved liquidity, and lower costs vis-a-vis private cryptocurrencies. Concerning the choice of employed technology of CBDC, it should be scalable with zero tolerance against data breaches and cyberattacks and ensure privacy preservation. Regarding the e-Rupee, RBI could deploy a robust data protection system akin to the present core banking solution (CBS). Furthermore, RBI should chalk out policies for phase-wise substantial investments in building robust digital infrastructure, such as cyber-security, to combat vulnerability and smooth pan India e-Rupee implementation.

Public finance economists doubt the fraud-proof success of the RBI's CBDC and are subject to unveiling a comprehensive rule book containing modalities, roles, responsibilities, governance, instruments, incentives, modes of funds transfer, redemptions and standard operating procedures (SOPs). Financial inclusion can only be treated as a natural and automatic by-product of the CBDC if, eventually, transmitted to cash or credit for the unbanked population. As the recently launched e-Rupee R as a pilot project confines P2P and person-to-merchant (P2M) transactions, the litmus test of its acceptance and success lies in a remote. Replacing the physical cash with e-Rupee R at the point-of-sale (POS), even with immediate delivery unlikely be solved if merchants possess only high-denomination DCs rather than small-denomination DCs.

5. CASH IS STILL KING

Public Finance literature posits framing of monetary policy based on the theoretical underpinning. However, bank data shows persisting cash intensity despite policy efforts for a 'cashless' economy. Digitalisation, demonetisation and formalising businesses through goods and services tax (GST) are prominent in this direction. Inversely related income elasticity of currency demand likely contributes to a surge in e-payments, enactment of GST, demonetisation, and direct benefit transfers. However, such elasticity scored close to unity, contesting a theoretical inverse association. The cash preference of the Indians is also evident from the significantly increasing trend of currency, with the public (CwP) lying above the trends since mid-2000. Interestingly, CwP records an unprecedented surge during the last four financial years ending in 2022, in a timeline having moderated nominal GDP values and exponential growth of e-payments. Again, a higher CwP to demand deposit (DD) ratio for the period FY 2011-22 (1.44) compared to 1991-2000 (1.35) indicate an increasing trend of cash holding by the public (Chandak, 2022). Figure 1 reports currency circulation (CwP + cash held by banks) as a % of GDP showing an increasing trend during the post-demonetisation timeline. This trend poses a tricky question about attaining one of the demonetisation objectives. The significant contributing factors for higher cash intensity include under-invoiced Chinese imports and systematically disrupted trade credit (TC) flows. Research concedes that cash is the preferred mode of payment for financing those illicit and under-invoiced imports. On the other hand, adverse conditions of TC trigger the firms for higher liquidity with a simultaneous reduction in TC flows and average payment timeline. Consequently, lower TC velocity likely accelerates cash intensity (liquidity) holding back and conversely effects velocity of money drops.

Figure 1. Currency in circulation (% of GDP) (Source: RBI, SBI Research)

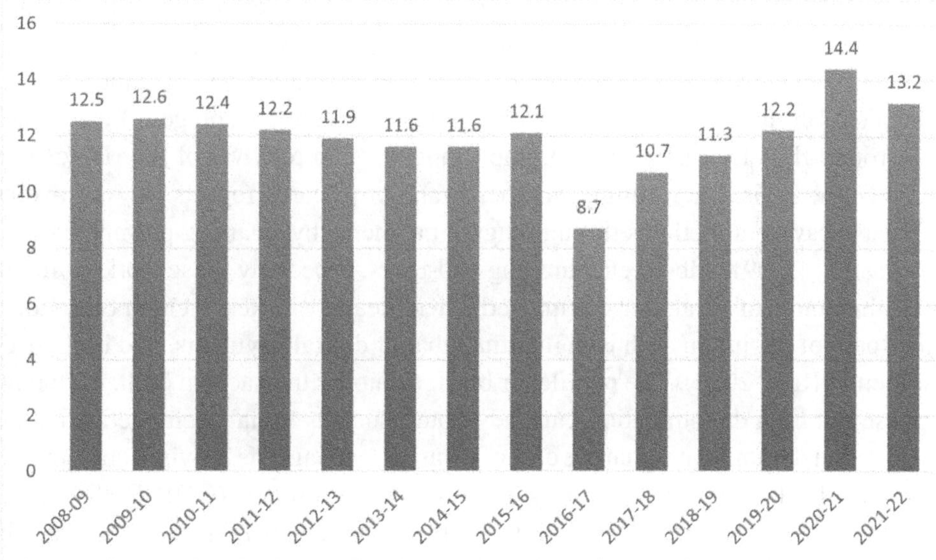

6. ADDRESSING CASH PREFERENCE

Financial literature posits dual reasons for holding cash: transactional and precautionary. For the first motive, people benefit from cash holding as they can reduce transaction costs by utilising it for making payments without raising external funds or liquidating properties (Han & Qiu, 2007). For the second motive, people stockpile cash to meet unprecedented contingencies, hedging against the risk of unforeseen cash shortfalls, which, in turn, is likely to prevent liquidity constraint costs (Faulkender &Wang, 2006). Public finance literature affirms that cash is unlikely to replace entirely. They perform a significant peerless role as a safety cushion during malfunctioning or technical glitches in the e-payment system and higher uncertainty, such as the global financial crisis (Jobst & Stix, 2017). Organisational research reports determinants of marginal cash holding ranging from financial constraints and agency problems to investment opportunities (Lin & Chiu, 2017). The literature shows that self-employed who turned to small merchants have cash preference for twin reasons-tax evasion and higher costs of e-payments (Goodhart & Ashworth 2014). Again, research on behavioural finance documents different causes for customers' cash preference, including privacy concerns, especially for retail transactions and for unorganised sectors, selective users of e-payments, phobia of incurring excessive spending through e-payment modes and cash as a preferred mode for social welfare (Png & Tan, 2020). Literature supporting rCBDCs suggests economies with high cash preference and lack of alternative rCBDCs could motivate the launching of rCBDCs which could further reduce the cash management cost substantially (Khiaonarong & Humphrey, 2019), affirming RBI's decision to e-Rupee introduction.

Interestingly, all merchants are unlikely motivated to use e-payments for their associated fees with e-payment systems and prefer cash, especially for transactions of smaller value. Research on socioeconomic factors explicitly shows a higher propensity to use cash by people at the bottom of the pyramid who devoid of accessing alternative modes of payment and economies with higher income inequalities (Srouji, 2020). Again, infrastructure reliability poses a severe concern to mass acceptance of e-payments, albeit 'go slow' or 'resistance to change' significantly influenced cash preference over e-payments. Admittedly, recent research concludes that during the Covid-19 sanitary crisis, demand for cash for transactional motives declined, but demand for cash for hoarding motives substantially increased (Rogof & Scazzero, 2021).

Literature suggests extensive examination of different e-payment modes, viz., mobile, cards, digital wallets, and cheques (Blumenstock *et al.*, 2015). Studies pointed out advantages of e-payments such as safety, easiness, round-the-clock usage and prompt transfers, and removal of the risk of carrying and handling cash real-time basis. Interestingly, another strand of research reports ways of overcoming the pitfalls of different e-payment methods through digital payments by ensuring prompt and secure transfers (Lehdonvirta *et al.*, 2009). Albeit, encouraging end-users, especially those working in the informal economies and inhabitants of rural areas, remained a herculean task. Research on behavioural finance concurs that the 'pain of paying in cash is higher than that of digital payments, and it likely contributes to deferred payments (Rick, 2018). The parallel or black economy transacts in cash. Different countries attempted to phase out high denomination currency notes, such as India's demonetization saga of November 2016. Research demonstrates that the cost of printing, carriage, destroying, and other operational expenses are estimated to be nearly 1.7% of India's gross domestic product (GDP) (VISA, 2016), 1.5% of the world (Jenkins, 2018), but merely 0.5% in Singapore (Menon, 2016). Furthermore, the perpetration of tax evasion and criminal activities such as terror financing, drug smuggling, prostitution and financial crimes are using cash. Research further cautious against holding cash from a safety perspective since the risk of loss due to theft, robbery, embezzlement, and even pilferage remained significant (Hazra, 2017).

7. THE WAY FORWARD

The protagonists of cryptocurrencies strongly argue for cryptocurrencies. P2P e-cash transfer without an intermediary such as a bank gains momentum after introducing RBI's e-Rupee R. The launching of the e-Rupee R, considering the significant numbers of the unbanked population even after the successful implementation of 'Prime Minister Jan Dhan Yojana (PMJDY), raises a question about the latter's success. E-Rupee R likely opens a new vista for all to participate in financial transactions from any Android smartphone downloaded the app. The use of encryption techniques in DC for controlling the generation of currency units, verifying the transfer of funds and independent operation of a single central unit could suppress the challenges. DCs would facilitate customers to hold and transact risk-freely. Although holding DC would not yield any interest, those can be recoverable in the event of a loss. The policymakers are probably expecting the testing of e-Rupee R in an offline functionality for enhancing financial inclusion for the inclusion of unbanked people in rural areas with lower internet penetration or suffering from problems of low bandwidth rates. The concern about anonymity is likely to be resolved as RBI has proposed the government amend the RBI Act to include the term 'digital currency' by widening the scope of the definition of 'bank note'. Notably, as a currency would include DC, the ceiling on cash withdrawals as per the Income Tax Act will also be applicable, which probably encourages transactions through e-Rupee R in preference to cash. The RBI envisaged that anonymity, a fundamental cash feature, would also be embedded in DC through technological solutions depending on fintech innovation.

It is reverting to the functions of a currency, the form of currency-physical, virtual or digital unlikely to have any significant impact on the unit of account. As far as the second function is concerned, the currency in its current physical and virtual forms comfortably serves the purpose of a medium of exchange. The third function, i.e., store of value is likely to change significantly, having the uniqueness the e-Rupee

R possesses. Traditionally cash holding involved logistical challenges apart from security concerns but no accumulation for such holding; while assuming credit risk, banks compensate the customers with interest. In contrast, the e-Rupee R would provide a logistically superior and risk-free alternative for the digital holding of currency. In conclusion, the RBI's vision of comprehensively addressing teething problems associated with the e-Rupee R, the DC, will likely be a game changer in the Indian financial market.

DECLARATION

The author hereby declares that the study has carried out exclusively for academic purpose, without any financial aid from any funders, the contents are free from plagiarism, there is no conflict of interest (COI) and all other usual disclaimer is applicable.

NOTE

Internet and Mobile Association of India vs Reserve Bank of India, reported in (2020)10SCC274.

REFERENCES

Al-Suwaidi, N. A., & Nobanee, H. (2020). Anti-money laundering and anti-terrorism financing: A survey of the existing literature and a future research agenda. *Journal of Money Laundering Control*, *24*(2), 396–426. doi:10.1108/JMLC-03-2020-0029

Alsalmi, N., Ullah, S., & Rafique, M. (2023). Accounting for digital currencies. *Research in International Business and Finance*, *64*, 101897. doi:10.1016/j.ribaf.2023.101897

Auer, R., Cornelli, G., & Frost, J. (2020). *Covid-19, cash, and the future of payments.* BIS Bulletin No. 3, Bank for International Settlements.

Aziz, S., & Dowling, M. (2019). Machine learning and AI for risk management. In *Disrupting finance* (pp. 33–50). Palgrave Pivot. doi:10.1007/978-3-030-02330-0_3

Bank of England. (2020). *Central Bank Digital Currency Opportunities, challenges and design.* https://www.bankofengland.co.uk/-/media/boe/files/paper/2020/central-bank-digital-currency-opportunities-challenges-and design.pdf?la=en&hash=DFAD18646A77C00772AF1C5B18E63E71F68E4593

Bedi, P., & Nashier, T. (2020). On the investment credentials of Bitcoin: A cross-currency perspective. *Research in International Business and Finance*, *51*, 101087. doi:10.1016/j.ribaf.2019.101087

Bindseil, U. (2019). Central bank digital currency: Financial system implications and control. *International Journal of Political Economy*, *48*(4), 303–335. doi:10.1080/08911916.2019.1693160

Blumenstock, J. E., Callen, M., Ghani, T., & Koepke, L. (2015). Promises and pitfalls of mobile money in Afghanistan: evidence from a randomized control trial. In *ICTD'15. Proceedings of the Seventh International Conference on Information and Communication Technologies and Development, Article no.* 15. New York: ACM. 10.1145/2737856.2738031

Brunnermeier, M. K., & Niepelt, D. (2019). On the equivalence of private and public money. *Journal of Monetary Economics, 106*, 27–41. doi:10.1016/j.jmoneco.2019.07.004

Butler, T., & O'Brien, L. (2019). Understanding RegTech for digital regulatory compliance. In T. Lynn, J. Mooney, P. Rosati, & M. Cummins (Eds.), *Disrupting Finance. Palgrave Studies in Digital Business & Enabling Technologies* (pp. 85–102). Palgrave Pivot.

Canhoto, A. I. (2020). Leveraging machine learning in the global fight against money laundering and terrorism financing: An affordances perspective. *Journal of Business Research, 131*, 441–452. doi:10.1016/j.jbusres.2020.10.012 PMID:33100427

Chandak, B. (2022, November 25). Why cash is still king in India. *The Business Line*, p. 4.

Chen, L., Huang, Y., Ouyang, S., & Xiong, W. (2021). *The Data Privacy Paradox and Digital Demand.* NBER Working Paper No. 28854.

Crandall, J. (2019). Blockchains and the "chains of empire": Contextualizing blockchain, cryptocurrency, and neoliberalism in Puerto Rico. *Design and Culture, 11*(3), 279–300. doi:10.1080/17547075.2019.1673989

Currie, W. L., Gozman, D. P., & Seddon, J. J. (2018). Dialectic tensions in the financial markets: A longitudinal study of pre-and postcrisis regulatory technology. *Journal of Information Technology, 33*(4), 304–325. doi:10.105741265-017-0047-5

Davis, F. D. (1986). *A technology acceptance model for empirically testing new end-user information systems: theory and results* [Doctoral dissertation]. Sloan School of Management, Massachusetts Institute of Technology.

Dyntu, V., & Dykyi, O. (2019). Cryptocurrency in the system of money laundering. *Baltija Journal of Economic Studies, 4*(5), 75–81. doi:10.30525/2256-0742/2018-4-5-75-81

Elsayed, A. H., & Nasir, M. A. (2022). Central Bank digital currencies: An Agenda for future research. *Research in International Business and Finance, 62*, 101736. doi:10.1016/j.ribaf.2022.101736

Faulkender, M., & Wang, R. (2006). Corporate financial policy and the value of cash. *The Journal of Finance, 61*(4), 1957–1990. doi:10.1111/j.1540-6261.2006.00894.x

Fegatelli, P. (2022). A central bank digital currency in a heterogeneous monetary union: Managing the effects on the bank lending channel. *Journal of Macroeconomics, 71*(C), 103392. doi:10.1016/j.jmacro.2021.103392

Fernández-Villaverde, J., Sanches, D., Schilling, L., & Uhlig, H. (2020). *Central bank digital currency: central banking for all?* Working paper, Vol. 26753, National Bureau of Economic Research.

Foley, S., Karlsen, J. R., & Putniš, T. J. (2019). Sex, Drugs, and Bitcoin: How Much Illegal Activity Is Financed through Cryptocurrencies. *Review of Financial Studies, 32*(5), 1798–1853. doi:10.1093/rfs/hhz015

Fomina, O., Moshkovska, O., Avhustova, O., Romashko, O., & Holovina, D. (2019). Current aspects of the cryptocurrency recognition in Ukraine. *Banks and Bank Systems, 14*(2), 203–213. doi:10.21511/bbs.14(2).2019.18

Goodell, J. W., & Shen, D. (2021). The Chinese sovereign digital currency as a catalyst for change: A new trilemma? In C. Shaen (Ed.), *Understanding Cryptocurrency Fraud: The Challenges and Headwinds to Regulate Digital Currencies* (pp. 177–186). De Gruyter. doi:10.1515/9783110718485-014

Goodhart, C., & Ashworth, J. (2014). *Trying to glimpse the 'grey economy'*. Available at: https://voxeu.org/article/trying-glimpse-grey-economy

Han, J., Huang, Y., Liu, S., & Towey, K. (2020). Artificial intelligence for anti-money laundering: A review and extension. *Digital Finance, 2*(3), 211–239. doi:10.100742521-020-00023-1

Han, S., & Qiu, J. (2007). Corporate precautionary cash holdings. *Journal of Corporate Finance, 13*(1), 43–57. doi:10.1016/j.jcorpfin.2006.05.002

Haque, M. A., & Shoaib, M. (2023). E-Rupee-The digital currency in India: Challenges and prospects. *Bench Council Transactions on Benchmarks. Standards and Evaluations, 3*, 100107.

Hazra, D. (2017). Monetary policy and alternative means of payment. *The Quarterly Review of Economics and Finance, 65*(C), 378–387. doi:10.1016/j.qref.2016.11.002

Ichihashi, S. (2020). Online Privacy and Information Disclosure by Consumer. *The American Economic Review, 110*(2), 569–595. doi:10.1257/aer.20181052

Jabbar, A., Geebren, A., Hussain, Z., Dani, S., & Ul-Durar, S. (2023). Investigating individual privacy within CBDC: A privacy calculus perspective. *Research in International Business and Finance, 64*, 101826. doi:10.1016/j.ribaf.2022.101826

Jenkins, P. (2018, May 10). We Don't Take Cash: Is this the Future of Money? *The Financial Times.*

Jobst, C., & Stix, H. (2017). *Doomed to disappear?* CEPR Discussion Paper Series: The surprising return of cash across time and across countries.

Kaplan, A. (2021). Cryptocurrency and corruption: auditing with blockchain. In *Auditing Ecosystem and Strategic Accounting in the Digital Era* (pp. 325–338). Springer. doi:10.1007/978-3-030-72628-7_15

Khiaonarong, T., & Humphrey, D. (2019). *Cash use Across Countries and the Demand for Central Bank Digital Currency.* International Monetary Fund. doi:10.5089/9781484399606.001

Knapp, G. F. (1905). *The State Theory of Money.* https://socialsciences.mcmaster.ca/econ/ugcm/3ll3/knapp/StateTheoryMoney.pdf

Kou, G., Akdeniz, Ö. O., Dinçer, H., & Yüksel, S. (2021). Fintech investments in European banks: A hybrid IT2 fuzzy multidimensional decision-making approach. *Financial Innovation, 7*(1), 1–28. doi:10.118640854-021-00256-y PMID:35024283

Kumar, A. S., & Anandarao, S. (2019). Volatility spillover in crypto-currency markets: Some evidences from GARCH and wavelet analysis. *Physica A*, *524*, 448–458. doi:10.1016/j.physa.2019.04.154

Kumar, V. A. (2012). Money laundering: Concept, significance and its impact. *European Journal of Business and Management*, *4*(2), 113–119.

Kumhof, M., & Noone, C. (2018). *Central bank digital currencies-design principles and balance sheet implications*. Staff Working Paper, Vol. 725, Bank of England.

Le Tran, V., & Leirvik, T. (2020). Efficiency in the markets of crypto-currencies. *Finance Research Letters*, *35*, 101382. doi:10.1016/j.frl.2019.101382

Lee, D., Yan, L., & Wang, Y. (2021). A Global Perspective on Central Bank Digital Currency. *China Economic Journal*, *14*(1), 52–66. doi:10.1080/17538963.2020.1870279

Lehdonvirta, V., Soma, H., Ito, H., Yamabe, T., Kimura, H., & Nakajima, T. (2009). Ubipay: Minimizing transaction costs with smart mobile payments. In *Proceedings of the6th international conference on mobile technology, application & systems*. ACM.

Lin, H. C., & Chiu, S. C. (2017). Trade off on corporate cash holdings: A theoretical and empirical analysis. *Review of Quantitative Finance and Accounting*, *49*(3), 727–763. doi:10.100711156-016-0606-9

Liu, J., Sockin, M., & Xiong, W. (2021). *Data Privacy and Consumer Vulnerability*. Princeton University Working Paper.

Lucey, B. M., Vigne, S. A., Yarovaya, L., & Wang, Y. (2022). The cryptocurrency uncertainty index. *Finance Research Letters*, *45*(C), 102147. doi:10.1016/j.frl.2021.102147

Menon, R. (2016, August 19). *An Electronic Payments Society*. Speech at Sim Kee Boon Institute Conference on FinTech and Financial Inclusion, Singapore.

Mitchell-Innes, A. (1913). What is money. *Bank Law Journal*, (May), 377–408.

Mitzner, T. L., Boron, J. B., Fausset, C. B., Adams, A. E., Charness, N., Czaja, S. J., Dijkstra, K., Fisk, A. D., Rogers, W. A., & Sharit, J. (2010). Older adults talk technology: Technology usage and attitudes. *Computers in Human Behavior*, *26*(6), 1710–1721. doi:10.1016/j.chb.2010.06.020 PMID:20967133

Mohan, R. (2022, December 5). *King Cash's castle*. The Business Standard.

Morgan, J. (2022). Systemic stable coin and the defensive case for Central Bank Digital Currency: A critique of the Bank of England's framing. *Research in International Business and Finance*, *62*, 101716. doi:10.1016/j.ribaf.2022.101716

Parlour, C. A., Rajan, U., & Walden, J. (2020). *Payment system externalities and the role of central bank digital currency*. Working Paper.

Patterson, M. (2018). *Crypto's 80% plunge is now worse than the Dot-Com crash*. Bloomberg.

Png, I., & Tan, C. (2020). Privacy, Trust in Banks and Use of Cash. *Monetary Authority of Singapore. Special Feature*, *C*, 109–116.

Renwick, R., & Gleasure, R. (2021). Those who control the code control the rules: How different perspectives of privacy are being written into the code of blockchain systems. *Journal of Information Technology*, *36*(1), 16–38. doi:10.1177/0268396220944406

Rick, S. I. (2018). Tightwads and spendthrifts: An interdisciplinary review. *Financial Planning Review*, *1*(1–2), e1010. doi:10.1002/cfp2.1010

Rogof, K., & Scazzero, J. (2021). *COVID Cash.* CMFA Working Paper 002.

Selgin, G. (2021). Central bank digital currency as a potential source of financial instability. *The Cato Journal*, 333–341.

Sinelnikova-Muryleva, E. V. (2020). Central Bank Digital Currencies: Potential Risks and Benefits. *Voprosy Ekonomiki*, *4*(4), 147–159. doi:10.32609/0042-8736-2020-4-147-159

Srouji, J. (2020). Digital payments, the cashless economy, and financial inclusion in the United Arab Emirates: Why is everyone still transacting in cash? *Journal of Risk and Financial Management*, *13*(11), 1–10. doi:10.3390/jrfm13110260

Tofangsaz, H. (2012). A new approach to the criminalization of terrorist financing and its compatibility with Sharia law. *Journal of Money Laundering Control*, *15*(4), 396–406. doi:10.1108/13685201211265980

Tong, W., & Jiayou, C. (2021). A study of the economic impact of central bank digital currency under global competition. *China Economic Journal*, *14*(1), 78–101. doi:10.1080/17538963.2020.1870282

Tran, H. (2021). *Regulation: The solution to Bitcoin's risks and unrealized benefits*. Available at: https://www.atlanticcouncil.org/blogs/new-atlanticist/regulation-thesolution-to-bitcoins-risks-and-unrealized-benefits/

Venkatesh, V., & Davis, F. D. (2000). A theoretical extension of the technology acceptance model: Four longitudinal field studies. *Management Science*, *46*(2), 186–204. doi:10.1287/mnsc.46.2.186.11926

VISA. (2016). *Accelerating the growth of digital payments in India: A five-year outlook*. VISA.

Wray, L. R. (2011). *Keynes after 75 years: Rethinking money as a public monopoly*. Levy Economics Institute, Working Paper No. 658.

Yamaoka, H. (2022). Digital Currencies and the Future of Money. In *The Future of Financial Systems in the Digital Age* (pp. 49–73). Springer. doi:10.1007/978-981-16-7830-1_4

Chapter 12
Sustainable Development Using IoT and AI Techniques for Water Utilization in Agriculture

Sampath Boopathi
https://orcid.org/0000-0002-2065-6539
Mechanical Engineering, Muthayammal Engineering College, India

ABSTRACT

Water scarcity and poor quality are major challenges in agriculture, affecting crop growth and food security. IoT and AI techniques are being explored for sustainable development, including water management, precision irrigation, and data analytics. IoT sensors collect real-time data, while AI algorithms predict availability and optimize irrigation schedules. Precision irrigation improves water use efficiency and productivity by utilizing data analytics and clustering algorithms. IoT and AI in agriculture offer economic benefits like increased crop yields, water savings, and sustainable practices. However, initial investment costs, social acceptance, and policy considerations hinder widespread adoption. Future directions should focus on scaling, collaboration, investment, customizable solutions, farmer-to-farmer knowledge transfer, and research funding. Addressing data privacy, security, and connectivity concerns is crucial for trust and confidence among stakeholders.

INTRODUCTION

Water is crucial for agriculture, providing essential nutrients and sustaining food production. However, water scarcity and deteriorating quality are interconnected challenges affecting crop yields, food security, and environmental sustainability. Inefficient water management practices and wasteful utilization exacerbate these issues. To address these issues and promote sustainable agricultural development, the integration of IoT and AI techniques in water treatment and utilization is gaining attention as a transformative approach. Agriculture accounts for a substantial portion of the world's freshwater consumption, representing approximately 70% of global water withdrawals. As the global population is projected to reach 9 billion by 2050, the demand for food and water is expected to increase significantly (Karthik et

DOI: 10.4018/979-8-3693-1722-8.ch012

al., 2023; Koshariya, Kalaiyarasi, et al., 2023; Maguluri et al., 2023; Syamala et al., 2023). Concurrently, climate change-induced uncertainties, such as irregular precipitation patterns and more frequent extreme weather events, are further straining water availability. To safeguard food production and mitigate the impact of water scarcity, innovative and sustainable solutions are urgently needed.

Traditional agricultural practices often rely on conventional irrigation methods, such as flood irrigation or overhead sprinklers, which result in significant water wastage and uneven distribution across fields. Moreover, the indiscriminate use of fertilizers and pesticides contaminates water sources, compromising water quality and posing risks to human health and ecosystems. To address these issues, a paradigm shift is required in water management practices, emphasizing resource efficiency, precision irrigation, and conservation-oriented practices. The integration of IoT and AI technologies offers a promising avenue to revolutionize water management in agriculture (Boopathi, 2023c; Hema et al., 2023). IoT devices, including sensors and connected devices, enable real-time data collection and monitoring of various environmental parameters, such as soil moisture levels, weather conditions, and water quality. These devices create a networked ecosystem that facilitates the continuous exchange of information between agricultural systems and decision-makers. By providing accurate and timely data, IoT devices enhance the understanding of water dynamics and enable informed decision-making (Reddy et al., 2023; Samikannu et al., 2022).

AI, on the other hand, empowers agricultural systems with the ability to analyze vast datasets and extract meaningful insights. Machine learning algorithms can process historical and real-time data to predict water demand, optimize irrigation schedules, and identify anomalies, leading to more efficient water usage (Anitha et al., 2023; Boopathi, Sureshkumar, et al., 2022; Vanitha et al., 2023). AI-driven precision irrigation systems tailor water application to the specific needs of crops and soil conditions, reducing water wastage and increasing crop productivity. Additionally, AI techniques can assist in water quality monitoring, enabling early detection of contamination and timely remediation measures. One of the primary applications of IoT and AI integration in agriculture is smart irrigation. Smart irrigation systems utilize IoT sensors to monitor soil moisture levels, temperature, humidity, and other relevant parameters (Bikash Chandra Saha, 2022; Boopathi, Lewise, Sarojwal, et al., 2022; Jeevanantham et al., 2022). This data is then analyzed using AI algorithms to determine the precise amount of water required by each crop, ensuring that water is delivered in optimal quantities and at the right time. This targeted approach to irrigation minimizes water wastage, reduces energy consumption, and fosters sustainable water use practices.

Moreover, IoT and AI technologies enable remote monitoring and control of irrigation systems, providing farmers with real-time access to data and the ability to adjust irrigation schedules as needed. This level of automation and data-driven decision-making enhances agricultural efficiency and resilience, especially in regions facing water scarcity or erratic rainfall patterns. In addition to smart irrigation, IoT and AI integration supports water treatment and quality monitoring in agriculture. Advanced IoT devices can be deployed to monitor water sources for pollutants and pathogens, ensuring that water used for irrigation is safe and free from contamination (Koshariya, Kalaiyarasi, et al., 2023; Koshariya, Khatoon, et al., 2023; Ramudu et al., 2023). AI algorithms can aid in the detection of water quality anomalies, alerting farmers and authorities to potential issues before they escalate into major crises. The combination of IoT and AI also promotes the adoption of precision agriculture techniques, wherein resources are utilized more judiciously. IoT sensors can continuously monitor crop health and growth patterns, enabling farmers to identify stress factors and implement targeted interventions (Boopathi & Kanike,

2023; Sengeni et al., 2023). By integrating AI algorithms, farmers can analyze historical data and identify trends, making informed decisions on crop selection, planting times, and nutrient application.

In developed economies, where technology adoption is more widespread, several successful case studies demonstrate the effectiveness of IoT and AI integration in agriculture. These examples highlight the positive impact of such technologies on water conservation, increased crop yields, and overall economic viability (Boopathi, Pandey, et al., 2023; Venkateswaran, Vidhya, Ayyannan, et al., 2023). However, in developing economies, challenges related to technology accessibility, infrastructure, and cost can hinder widespread adoption. To overcome these challenges, governments, international organizations, and private sectors need to collaborate to develop tailored solutions that align with the socioeconomic context of each region. Initiatives to promote technology transfer, provide training and capacity building, and offer financial incentives can facilitate the integration of IoT and AI in agriculture across different geographies (Boopathi, 2021; Boopathi, Lewise, Subbiah, et al., 2022; Boopathi & Sivakumar, 2014).

The integration of IoT and AI in water treatment and utilization in agriculture also holds significant promise for sustainable development on a broader scale. By optimizing water usage, reducing wastage, and minimizing environmental impacts, this approach aligns with the United Nations Sustainable Development Goals (SDGs), particularly Goal 2 (Zero Hunger) and Goal 6 (Clean Water and Sanitation). Thus, water scarcity and declining water quality pose formidable challenges to the agricultural sector, threatening food security and environmental sustainability (Boopathi, Thillaivanan, Mohammed, et al., 2022; Vanitha et al., 2023). Embracing the integration of IoT and AI techniques in water treatment and utilization can drive transformative change in agricultural practices. By enabling efficient water management, precision irrigation, and real-time monitoring of water quality, IoT and AI technologies empower farmers to make informed decisions that increase productivity and resource efficiency (Sathish et al., 2023; Syamala et al., 2023; Venkateswaran, Vidhya, Naik, et al., 2023). To fully realize the potential of this approach, global collaboration, targeted investments, and supportive policies are essential to ensure equitable access to these technologies, especially in regions where agricultural economies are vulnerable to water-related challenges. Embracing IoT and AI in water management represents a pivotal step towards achieving a sustainable and resilient future for agriculture and the broader ecosystem.

Background

Agriculture consumes a substantial portion of the world's freshwater resources, accounting for approximately 70% of global water withdrawals. With the population projected to reach 9 billion by 2050, the demand for food and water is expected to escalate significantly. Concurrently, climate change-induced uncertainties further intensify water availability issues, making it imperative to enhance water management practices in agriculture (Gnanaprakasam et al., 2023; Koshariya, Khatoon, et al., 2023; Kumar et al., 2023). Traditional agricultural practices often involve inefficient irrigation methods, leading to substantial water wastage and uneven distribution across fields. Additionally, the excessive use of fertilizers and pesticides can contaminate water sources, further compromising water quality. Addressing these challenges requires innovative and sustainable solutions that not only optimize water usage but also ensure ecological preservation and long-term agricultural viability.

Problem Statement

The primary challenge lies in developing an integrated approach that combines advanced water treatment techniques with cutting-edge IoT and AI technologies to optimize water usage in agriculture. This necessitates the creation of smart systems that can efficiently monitor water quality and quantity, predict crop water requirements, and enable precision irrigation, tailored to the specific needs of crops and soil conditions. Moreover, the adoption of such technologies must be economically viable and socially acceptable, especially in regions where agricultural economies are heavily reliant on conventional practices.

Objectives

This research study aims to explore and analyze the potential of integrating IoT and AI techniques in water treatment and utilization to achieve sustainable agricultural development. The specific objectives of this research are as follows:

- Investigate existing water treatment technologies and their applicability in agricultural settings.
- Examine the role of IoT devices in monitoring and managing water resources in agriculture.
- Evaluate the effectiveness of AI algorithms in optimizing water usage and crop yield in different agricultural contexts.
- Assess the socioeconomic implications and potential barriers to the widespread adoption of IoT and AI technologies in agriculture.
- Provide recommendations and guidelines for policymakers, researchers, and stakeholders to promote the integration of IoT and AI in water management practices for sustainable agriculture.

Scope and Limitations

This research will focus on the integration of IoT and AI techniques specifically in water treatment and utilization within the agricultural sector. While the study will explore diverse water treatment methods and cutting-edge AI algorithms, it will primarily emphasize their practical application in agriculture. Additionally, the research will consider both developed and developing economies to understand the potential challenges and opportunities faced by different regions in adopting these technologies.

LITERATURE REVIEW

Water Management in Agriculture

Water management in agriculture is a critical area of research aimed at addressing water scarcity and optimizing water usage to ensure sustainable agricultural practices. Various studies have explored the challenges posed by water scarcity, particularly in regions with limited water resources, and have proposed innovative approaches to enhance water efficiency in irrigation. Research in this domain emphasizes the adoption of water-saving irrigation techniques, such as drip irrigation and sprinkler irrigation, as well as the implementation of water conservation practices, such as rainwater harvesting and water recycling. Integrated Water Resources Management (IWRM) has been recognized as an effective approach to balance water needs across different sectors and foster sustainable water management in agriculture (Gnanaprakasam et al., 2023; Koshariya, Kalaiyarasi, et al., 2023; Sankar et al., 2023).

Water Treatment Techniques

Water treatment techniques play a vital role in ensuring the availability of clean and safe water for agricultural purposes. The literature review in this area highlights various water treatment methods, including physical, chemical, and biological processes. Common water treatment techniques, such as sedimentation, coagulation, filtration, and disinfection, are discussed in the context of agricultural water usage. Additionally, emerging water treatment technologies, such as advanced oxidation processes and membrane filtration, are explored for their potential application in agriculture. Research in this domain underscores the importance of treating water from various sources, such as surface water, groundwater, and reclaimed water, to safeguard crops and prevent waterborne diseases (Alghazzawi et al., 2021; Al-Tarawneh et al., 2022; Burugari et al., 2021).

IoT Applications in Agriculture

The Internet of Things (IoT) has revolutionized agriculture by enabling real-time data collection and monitoring. Studies have focused on the deployment of IoT devices, such as soil moisture sensors, weather stations, and drones, to monitor various environmental parameters relevant to agriculture. The integration of IoT in agriculture enables precision farming practices, such as precision irrigation and precision fertilization, by providing farmers with actionable insights based on data analytics. Research in this area also highlights the potential of IoT in optimizing water usage through smart water management systems that automatically control irrigation schedules based on real-time data (Boopathi, 2023a; Hema et al., 2023; Sampath et al., 2022).

AI Techniques for Agricultural Optimization

Artificial Intelligence (AI) techniques are increasingly being explored for optimizing agricultural processes and resource management. Machine learning algorithms, in particular, have been applied to predict crop water demand, optimize irrigation scheduling, and identify crop diseases. AI-driven decision support systems aid farmers in making informed choices regarding crop selection, planting times, and pest management. The literature review delves into different AI models, such as neural networks, support vector machines, and random forests, and their applications in agricultural optimization. Research in this domain emphasizes the potential of AI in increasing crop productivity while minimizing resource wastage (Boopathi, Pandey, et al., 2023; Rahamathunnisa et al., 2023; Veeranjaneyulu, Boopathi, Kumari, et al., 2023).

Sustainable Development in Agriculture

Sustainable development in agriculture is a multidimensional concept that encompasses economic, social, and environmental aspects. Studies have explored the role of agriculture in achieving the United Nations Sustainable Development Goals (SDGs) and the importance of adopting sustainable agricultural practices to ensure food security and environmental preservation. Research in this area highlights the significance of sustainable water management practices in agriculture, promoting resource efficiency, reducing water pollution, and fostering climate resilience. The literature review also examines the socio-economic implications of sustainable agriculture, including the well-being of farmers, rural communities, and the overall agricultural sector (Boopathi, 2022; Boopathi, Kumar, et al., 2023; Domakonda et al., 2022; Samikannu et al., 2022).

Hence, the literature review on water management in agriculture, water treatment techniques, IoT applications in agriculture, AI techniques for agricultural optimization, and sustainable development in agriculture reveals the interconnected nature of these topics. Efficient water management and treatment are crucial for sustainable agriculture, and the integration of IoT and AI technologies further enhances resource efficiency and productivity. Sustainable agriculture, aligned with the principles of environmental stewardship and social equity, is essential for meeting global food demands while safeguarding natural resources for future generations (Harikaran et al., 2023; Janardhana et al., 2023; Mohanty et al., 2023; Selvakumar et al., 2023). The combination of innovative technologies and sustainable practices provides a promising pathway towards achieving a more resilient and prosperous agricultural sector.

WATER TREATMENT TECHNOLOGIES IN AGRICULTURE

Water treatment technologies in agriculture are essential to ensure the availability of clean and safe water for irrigation and other agricultural purposes. As water quality directly affects crop health and productivity, employing effective water treatment methods becomes crucial in optimizing agricultural practices. This section explores various water treatment techniques used in agriculture, including traditional methods, advanced water purification technologies, and the emerging role of nanotechnology in water treatment (Figure 1).

Figure 1. Water treatment technologies in agriculture

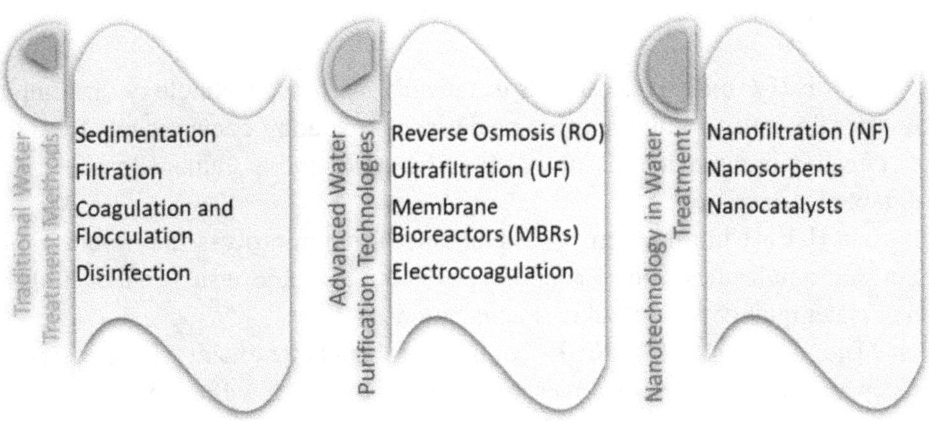

Traditional Water Treatment Methods

Traditional water treatment methods have been employed for centuries to make water suitable for agricultural use. These methods mainly focus on physical and chemical processes to remove impurities and contaminants from water. Common traditional water treatment methods include:

- Sedimentation: Sedimentation involves allowing water to stand undisturbed, allowing heavier particles and sediments to settle at the bottom. This process can remove larger impurities, such as sand and silt, from the water.
- Filtration: Filtration uses porous materials, such as sand, gravel, or fabric, to trap and remove suspended particles and impurities from the water.
- Coagulation and Flocculation: Coagulation involves the addition of chemicals (coagulants) to water, which destabilize and aggregate small particles. Flocculation follows coagulation, encouraging the formation of larger particles (flocs) that can be easily removed by sedimentation or filtration.
- Disinfection: Disinfection methods, such as chlorination or UV treatment, are used to eliminate harmful microorganisms and pathogens from water, reducing the risk of waterborne diseases.

While traditional methods are effective in basic water treatment, they may not fully address emerging water quality challenges, such as emerging contaminants, agricultural runoff, and persistent pollutants.

Advanced Water Purification Technologies

Advanced water purification technologies in agriculture aim to address complex water quality issues and emerging contaminants that may be present in agricultural water sources (Boopathi, Pandey, et al., 2023; Boopathi, Umareddy, et al., 2023; Pramila et al., 2023; Ramudu et al., 2023). These technologies utilize cutting-edge processes to achieve higher levels of water purity. Some key advanced water purification technologies include:

- Reverse Osmosis (RO): Reverse osmosis is a membrane-based technology that employs pressure to force water through a semipermeable membrane, separating contaminants from the water. RO is highly effective in removing dissolved salts, ions, and other pollutants, producing high-quality water suitable for irrigation.
- Ultrafiltration (UF): Ultrafiltration is a membrane filtration process that removes particles, colloids, and macromolecules from water. UF can effectively remove suspended solids and bacteria, improving water quality for agricultural applications.
- Membrane Bioreactors (MBRs): MBRs combine biological treatment with membrane filtration to treat wastewater. The system uses microorganisms to break down organic matter, and the membrane filters out suspended solids and bacteria, resulting in treated water suitable for agricultural use.
- Electrocoagulation: Electrocoagulation involves the use of electrical current to destabilize and aggregate particles and contaminants in water, facilitating their removal. This technology is effective in treating water with high turbidity and organic content.

Nanotechnology in Water Treatment

Nanotechnology is an emerging field that shows promising potential in water treatment applications, including agriculture. Nanotechnology involves manipulating materials at the nanoscale (one billionth of a meter) to create novel structures and properties (Boopathi, Umareddy, et al., 2023; Boopathi & Davim, 2023a, 2023b; Fowziya et al., 2023). In water treatment, nanotechnology can enhance the efficiency and effectiveness of existing treatment processes. Some nanotechnology applications in water treatment include:

- Nanofiltration (NF): Nanofiltration is a membrane-based process that utilizes nanoscale pores to selectively remove ions and organic compounds from water. NF is particularly effective in softening water and removing natural organic matter.
- Nanosorbents: Nanoscale materials, such as nanoscale adsorbents or nanoparticles, can be used to capture and remove contaminants from water. Nanosorbents have high surface area and reactivity, making them efficient in removing pollutants, heavy metals, and organic compounds.
- Nanocatalysts: Nanocatalysts can be employed to facilitate chemical reactions that degrade or neutralize contaminants in water. Nanocatalytic processes can be used for the removal of organic pollutants and the degradation of harmful chemicals.

While nanotechnology shows promise, its widespread adoption in water treatment faces challenges related to cost, scalability, and potential environmental impacts of nanomaterials. Water treatment technologies are crucial for ensuring clean and safe water for irrigation and other agricultural purposes. Traditional methods like sedimentation, filtration, and disinfection are effective, but advanced technologies like reverse osmosis, ultrafiltration, and membrane bioreactors offer sophisticated solutions. Nanotechnology offers new opportunities for improving water quality and resource sustainability in agriculture. To optimize water treatment, a combination of traditional, advanced, and emerging technologies should be tailored to specific contexts and challenges.

IOT INTEGRATION IN WATER MANAGEMENT

The integration of Internet of Things (IoT) technologies in water management has revolutionized how water resources are monitored and managed in various sectors, including agriculture (Boopathi, 2023b, 2023c; Koshariya, Kalaiyarasi, et al., 2023; Koshariya, Khatoon, et al., 2023). IoT sensors for water monitoring play a crucial role in collecting real-time data on water quality, quantity, and usage, enabling data-driven decision-making and optimizing water resource management. This section explores the significance of IoT sensors in water monitoring and their applications in agriculture (Figure 2).

Figure 2. IoT integration in water management

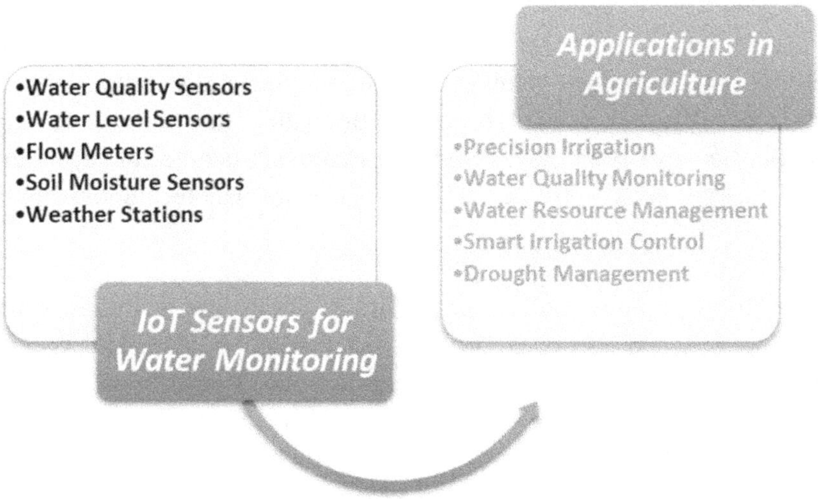

Importance of IoT Sensors in Water Monitoring

Traditional water monitoring methods often involve manual data collection and periodic sampling, which may not capture real-time variations in water parameters. IoT sensors provide a cost-effective and efficient solution by continuously monitoring water quality and quantity. These sensors can be deployed at various points in water systems, such as rivers, lakes, reservoirs, wells, and irrigation networks, to provide a comprehensive understanding of water dynamics (Boopathi, 2023b; Maguluri et al., 2023; Sankar et al., 2023).

Types of IoT Sensors for Water Monitoring

- Water Quality Sensors: These sensors measure various water quality parameters, such as pH, dissolved oxygen (DO), turbidity, temperature, conductivity, and levels of nutrients and pollutants. Water quality sensors help detect changes in water conditions and identify potential contamination events.
- Water Level Sensors: Water level sensors monitor the water levels in reservoirs, rivers, and wells. By tracking water levels in real-time, water managers can better manage water resources and prevent issues such as flooding or water scarcity.
- Flow Meters: Flow meters measure the rate of water flow in pipes or channels. They are crucial for understanding water usage patterns and optimizing irrigation schedules.
- Soil Moisture Sensors: Soil moisture sensors provide information about the moisture content in the soil. By integrating soil moisture data with weather forecasts and crop water requirements, farmers can implement precision irrigation practices, reducing water wastage and enhancing crop productivity.
- Weather Stations: Weather stations equipped with IoT sensors collect data on atmospheric conditions, such as temperature, humidity, wind speed, and precipitation. This information is vital for predicting water demand and optimizing irrigation schedules.

Applications in Agriculture

In agriculture, IoT sensors for water monitoring offer numerous benefits and applications (Boopathi, Khare, et al., 2023; Boopathi, Pandey, et al., 2023; Maheswari et al., 2023; Sampath et al., 2023):

- Precision Irrigation: IoT sensors provide real-time data on soil moisture levels and weather conditions, enabling farmers to implement precision irrigation practices. By delivering water precisely when and where it is needed, precision irrigation optimizes water usage, reduces water wastage, and enhances crop yield.
- Water Quality Monitoring: IoT water quality sensors help monitor irrigation water sources for pollutants, salinity, and other contaminants. This ensures that crops are not exposed to harmful substances, safeguarding both crop health and consumer safety.
- Water Resource Management: By continuously monitoring water levels and flow rates, IoT sensors facilitate efficient water resource management. Water managers can make informed decisions on water allocation and distribution, ensuring equitable access to water resources.
- Smart Irrigation Control: IoT sensors integrated with automated irrigation systems allow for remote control and monitoring. Farmers can adjust irrigation schedules, turn on/off irrigation systems, and receive alerts on water usage or anomalies, even when away from the field.
- Drought Management: During drought conditions, IoT sensors provide crucial data on soil moisture levels and water availability. This information helps farmers and water authorities implement drought management strategies, such as water rationing and crop selection.

Challenges and Future Directions

Despite the numerous benefits, the widespread adoption of IoT sensors in water monitoring faces challenges such as data security and privacy concerns, sensor calibration and maintenance, and the need for standardized communication protocols to ensure interoperability between different sensor systems. Overcoming these challenges requires collaborative efforts from governments, technology providers, and researchers to develop robust, scalable, and user-friendly IoT solutions for water management in agriculture (Ramudu et al., 2023).

In the future, advancements in IoT technology, including the miniaturization of sensors, improved battery life, and enhanced connectivity options, are expected to further enhance the capabilities and accessibility of IoT sensors for water monitoring. Moreover, integrating IoT data with AI-driven analytics will enable more sophisticated water management strategies, improving agricultural productivity while conserving water resources in the face of increasing water scarcity and climate variability.

AI TECHNIQUES FOR WATER MANAGEMENT IN AGRICULTURE

Artificial Intelligence (AI) techniques have emerged as powerful tools in water management in agriculture, offering data-driven insights and optimization capabilities to enhance water efficiency and agricultural productivity (Boopathi & Kanike, 2023; Maheswari et al., 2023; Ramudu et al., 2023; Syamala et al., 2023). This section explores how AI techniques, particularly machine learning algorithms, are applied in water prediction, precision irrigation, and data analytics for water resource optimization in agriculture (Figure 3).

Figure 3. AI techniques for water management in agriculture

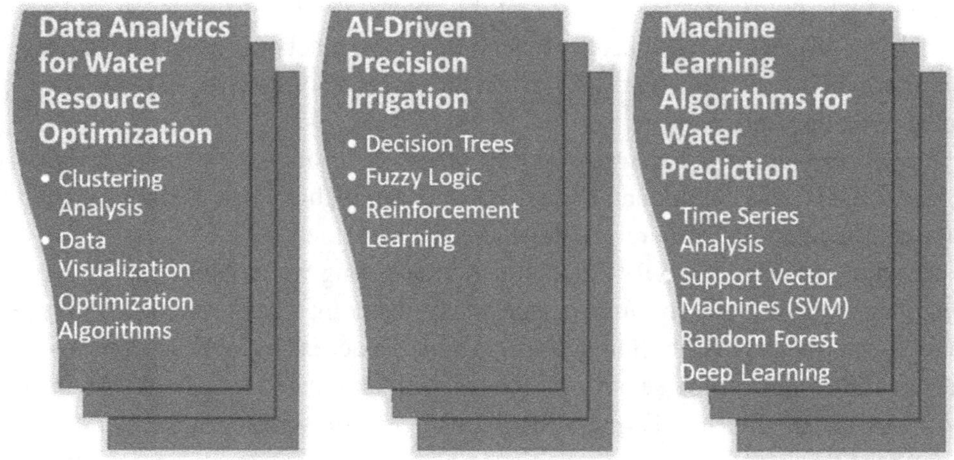

Machine Learning Algorithms for Water Prediction

Machine learning algorithms are extensively used in water prediction models to forecast water availability, demand, and water-related events. These algorithms analyze historical data on weather patterns, hydrological conditions, and water usage to make accurate predictions (Anitha et al., 2023; Boopathi, Arigela, Raman, et al., 2022; Subha et al., 2023; Veeranjaneyulu, Boopathi, Kumari, et al., 2023; Veeranjaneyulu, Boopathi, Narasimharao, et al., 2023). Some commonly used machine learning algorithms for water prediction include:

- Time Series Analysis: Time series analysis models, such as Autoregressive Integrated Moving Average (ARIMA) and Seasonal Autoregressive Integrated Moving-Average (SARIMA), are applied to predict water availability and usage trends based on historical time series data.
- Support Vector Machines (SVM): SVM algorithms are used for water demand prediction, identifying patterns and correlations in various factors influencing water consumption, such as climate, population, and agricultural activities.
- Random Forest: Random Forest algorithms are employed to predict water levels in reservoirs and rivers based on multiple environmental variables, including rainfall, evaporation, and water release.
- Deep Learning: Deep learning techniques, such as recurrent neural networks (RNNs) and long short-term memory networks (LSTMs), are used for more complex water prediction tasks, such as forecasting extreme weather events and floods.

Machine learning-based water prediction models provide valuable information for water resource planning and allocation, enabling better management of water supply and demand.

AI-Driven Precision Irrigation

Precision irrigation is a data-driven approach that tailors water application to the specific needs of crops and soil conditions. AI-driven precision irrigation systems utilize real-time data from IoT sensors and weather stations to optimize irrigation schedules and delivery (Boopathi, Balasubramani, et al., 2023; Boopathi et al., 2021; Domakonda et al., 2022). Key AI techniques applied in precision irrigation include:

- Decision Trees: Decision trees analyze soil moisture data, weather conditions, and crop water requirements to determine the optimal irrigation schedule for different crops and growth stages.
- Fuzzy Logic: Fuzzy logic-based controllers adjust irrigation rates based on soil moisture levels, taking into account crop water stress thresholds and environmental factors.
- Reinforcement Learning: Reinforcement learning algorithms enable irrigation systems to learn and adapt their strategies based on feedback from crop performance and water usage.

Precision irrigation powered by AI reduces water wastage, minimizes nutrient leaching, and maximizes crop productivity, contributing to sustainable water management in agriculture.

Data Analytics for Water Resource Optimization

AI-driven data analytics play a crucial role in optimizing water resource management in agriculture. Data analytics techniques process vast amounts of data to identify patterns, trends, and anomalies, leading to more informed decision-making (Pramila et al., 2023; Ramudu et al., 2023). Key data analytics techniques applied in water resource optimization include:

- Clustering Analysis: Clustering algorithms group water resource data into clusters based on similarity, enabling targeted interventions and tailored water management strategies.
- Optimization Algorithms: Optimization algorithms, such as genetic algorithms and linear programming, help find the best allocation and distribution of water resources to meet agricultural needs.
- Data Visualization: Data visualization tools aid in representing complex water resource data in intuitive visual formats, enabling stakeholders to comprehend and interpret the information effectively.

By leveraging data analytics, water managers and farmers can gain deeper insights into water usage patterns, identify areas for improvement, and implement evidence-based water resource optimization strategies.

AI techniques, especially machine learning algorithms, are revolutionizing water management in agriculture by enabling water prediction, precision irrigation, and data-driven optimization. These approaches improve efficiency, reduce resource wastage, and contribute to sustainable practices amidst water scarcity and climate variability. AI integration holds promise for addressing water challenges and promoting food security globally.

Case Studies: Successful Implementation of IoT AI Techniques in Agriculture

Case Study 1: Smart Water Management in Israel

Water scarcity and limited water resources pose significant challenges to agriculture in arid regions, such as Israel. To address these challenges and ensure sustainable agricultural development, Israel has successfully implemented smart water management systems using IoT and AI techniques (Maheswari et al., 2023; Sankar et al., 2023; Venkateswaran, Vidhya, Ayyannan, et al., 2023). This case study explores the key components of Israel's smart water management approach, the implementation details, and the remarkable results achieved through the integration of innovative technologies.

Smart Water Management Implementation

1. IoT Sensors Deployment: Israel's agricultural fields are equipped with an extensive network of IoT sensors, strategically placed to collect real-time data on various environmental parameters. These sensors include soil moisture sensors, weather stations, water level sensors, and flow meters. The data collected by these sensors provides valuable insights into soil conditions, weather patterns, water availability, and irrigation requirements.
2. AI-Driven Precision Irrigation: Sophisticated AI algorithms are employed to analyze the data collected by IoT sensors and make data-driven decisions regarding irrigation. These algorithms consider multiple factors, such as crop type, growth stage, soil moisture levels, weather forecasts, and historical data, to optimize irrigation schedules and delivery. AI-driven precision irrigation ensures that each crop receives the precise amount of water it needs at the right time, minimizing water wastage and maximizing water use efficiency.
3. Drip Irrigation Adoption: Drip irrigation, a water-efficient technique, is widely adopted in Israel's agricultural practices. This method involves delivering water directly to the plant's root zone through a network of pipes and emitters. By minimizing water contact with the soil surface, drip irrigation reduces evaporation losses and minimizes weed growth. Drip irrigation is particularly effective for high-value crops and water-sensitive plants.

Results and Achievements

1. Enhanced Water Use Efficiency: The integration of IoT and AI technologies has significantly improved water use efficiency in Israel's agriculture. Precision irrigation techniques ensure that water is used judiciously, avoiding over-irrigation and reducing water wastage. As a result, farmers can produce more crops with the same amount of water, maximizing agricultural output while conserving water resources.
2. Increased Crop Yields: The precise control over water application provided by AI-driven precision irrigation has led to increased crop yields. Crops receive the optimal amount of water, nutrients, and care, leading to healthier and more productive plants. This has resulted in improved quality and quantity of agricultural produce, benefiting both farmers and consumers.
3. Water Resource Conservation: Smart water management practices have contributed to water resource conservation in Israel. By using IoT data to manage water distribution efficiently, the country has

reduced water stress on natural water sources, such as rivers and groundwater reserves. This conservation approach helps maintain ecosystem health and supports sustainable water management for future generations.

4. Agricultural Innovation and Export: The success of smart water management in Israel's agriculture has fostered the growth of agro-tech innovation in the country. Israeli companies involved in developing IoT and AI technologies for agriculture have become leaders in the global market. They export their expertise and technologies to other water-scarce regions, helping countries worldwide address water challenges in agriculture and enhance food security.

Israel's smart water management system serves as a compelling example of how IoT and AI technologies can be harnessed to overcome water scarcity challenges and promote sustainable agricultural practices. The integration of IoT sensors and AI algorithms has revolutionized irrigation practices, leading to enhanced water efficiency, increased crop yields, and water resource conservation. This case study demonstrates the crucial role of innovation and technology in ensuring food security and environmental sustainability in regions facing water scarcity. The success of Israel's smart water management approach paves the way for other countries to adopt similar strategies and leverage the power of IoT and AI in addressing pressing water challenges in agriculture.

Case Study 2: Precision Agriculture in the Netherlands

The Netherlands is renowned for its innovative and advanced agricultural practices, particularly in precision agriculture. In this case study, we explore how the Netherlands has successfully implemented precision agriculture using IoT and AI techniques. Precision agriculture has enabled farmers in the Netherlands to optimize resource utilization, enhance crop productivity, and achieve sustainable agricultural practices (Karthik et al., 2023; Koshariya, Kalaiyarasi, et al., 2023; Maguluri et al., 2023; Syamala et al., 2023).

Precision Agriculture Implementation

- IoT-Enabled Greenhouses: The Netherlands is a global leader in greenhouse agriculture. IoT sensors are extensively deployed in greenhouses to monitor key environmental parameters, including temperature, humidity, CO2 levels, soil moisture, and nutrient concentrations. The real-time data collected from these sensors provides a comprehensive understanding of the greenhouse environment.
- AI-Driven Data Analytics: Sophisticated AI algorithms analyze the data collected by IoT sensors to derive valuable insights into crop health, growth patterns, and environmental conditions. These algorithms use machine learning techniques to identify correlations and patterns, helping farmers make data-driven decisions.
- Smart Water Management: In precision agriculture, water management is a critical aspect. The Netherlands uses IoT and AI to optimize water usage in greenhouse environments. Sensors continuously monitor soil moisture levels, and AI algorithms determine precise irrigation schedules based on crop water requirements and weather forecasts.
- Nutrient Management: Precision agriculture in the Netherlands extends to nutrient management. IoT sensors monitor nutrient levels in the soil and plant tissues, allowing farmers to adjust fertil-

ization practices accordingly. AI algorithms help optimize nutrient application, minimizing wastage and maximizing crop uptake.

Results and Achievements

- High Crop Yields: The integration of IoT and AI technologies in precision agriculture has led to higher crop yields in the Netherlands. By precisely controlling environmental conditions and providing crops with optimal water and nutrient levels, farmers can achieve maximum crop productivity throughout the year.
- Resource Efficiency: Precision agriculture practices in the Netherlands have significantly improved resource efficiency. Smart water management and targeted nutrient application minimize water and fertilizer wastage, reducing the environmental impact of agriculture.
- Quality and Consistency: The controlled environment of greenhouses, supported by AI-driven data analytics, ensures consistent crop quality and production. This is particularly valuable for high-value crops, such as vegetables and flowers, where uniformity and quality are essential for market demand.
- Environmental Sustainability: Precision agriculture in the Netherlands promotes environmental sustainability by reducing the use of agrochemicals and conserving water resources. The IoT-enabled greenhouses and AI-driven decision-making help minimize the ecological footprint of agricultural operations.
- Export of Expertise: The success of precision agriculture in the Netherlands has made the country a global hub for agro-tech innovation. Dutch companies involved in developing IoT and AI solutions for agriculture export their expertise and technologies worldwide, contributing to sustainable agricultural practices in different regions.

The precision agriculture practices in the Netherlands exemplify the transformative power of IoT and AI in modern agriculture. By leveraging advanced technologies, Dutch farmers have achieved high crop yields, optimized resource utilization, and promoted environmental sustainability. The integration of IoT sensors, AI-driven data analytics, and smart water and nutrient management has established the Netherlands as a leader in precision agriculture, inspiring other countries to adopt similar approaches for sustainable and productive farming (Pramila et al., 2023; Ramudu et al., 2023; Venkateswaran, Vidhya, Naik, et al., 2023). The success of precision agriculture in the Netherlands showcases the potential of technology to drive agricultural innovation and ensure food security in a rapidly changing world.

SOCIOECONOMIC IMPLICATIONS AND CHALLENGES

The socioeconomic implications and challenges are illustrated in Figure 4.

Figure 4. Socioeconomic implications and challenges

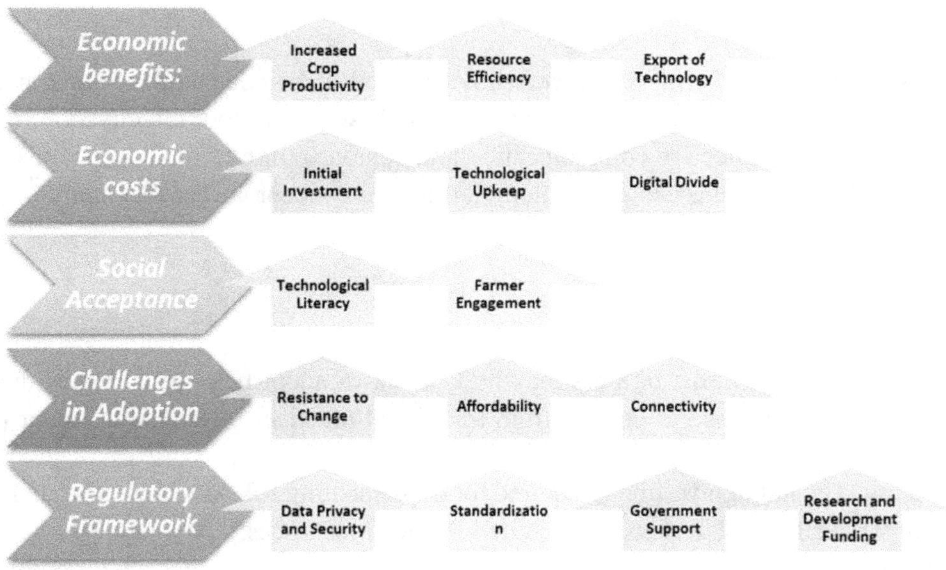

Economic Benefits and Costs

Economic Benefits

- Increased Crop Productivity: IoT and AI-driven precision agriculture can lead to higher crop yields and improved productivity, resulting in higher revenues for farmers and increased food production.
- Resource Efficiency: Optimized water and nutrient management can reduce input costs, making agriculture more cost-effective and sustainable.
- Export of Technology: Countries that develop and implement IoT AI techniques in agriculture can become exporters of agro-tech solutions, generating economic growth and job opportunities.

Economic Costs

- Initial Investment: Implementing IoT AI technologies in agriculture requires significant upfront costs for purchasing sensors, AI systems, and related infrastructure.
- Technological Upkeep: Regular maintenance, updates, and skilled personnel may lead to ongoing operational costs for farmers adopting these technologies.

- Digital Divide: High-tech solutions may not be accessible to small-scale or resource-limited farmers, leading to an economic disparity in agriculture.

Social Acceptance and Adoption

Social Acceptance

- Technological Literacy: Farmers and stakeholders need to be adequately trained and educated about IoT and AI technologies to embrace and adopt these innovations effectively.
- Farmer Engagement: Effective communication and demonstration of the benefits of IoT AI techniques can enhance social acceptance among farmers and encourage broader adoption.

Challenges in Adoption

- Resistance to Change: Some farmers may be hesitant to adopt new technologies due to a fear of the unknown, reluctance to deviate from traditional practices, or concerns about technology complexities.
- Affordability: The initial investment required for implementing IoT AI techniques can be a barrier, especially for small-scale farmers with limited financial resources.
- Connectivity: Reliable internet connectivity is essential for the seamless functioning of IoT systems. In rural areas with poor connectivity, the adoption of IoT technologies can be challenging.

Policy and Regulatory Considerations

Regulatory Framework

- Data Privacy and Security: The collection and use of data in IoT AI systems raise concerns about data privacy and security. Robust regulations and safeguards are needed to protect farmers' data and prevent misuse.
- Standardization: Establishing standards and protocols for IoT devices and AI algorithms can ensure interoperability and compatibility between different systems, promoting seamless integration.

Incentives and Support

- Government Support: Policymakers can offer financial incentives, subsidies, or tax breaks to encourage farmers to adopt IoT AI technologies, promoting sustainable agriculture and resource efficiency.
- Research and Development Funding: Investments in research and development can drive innovation and the development of cost-effective IoT AI solutions.

IoT AI techniques in agriculture offer numerous socioeconomic benefits, including increased crop productivity, resource efficiency, and export potential. However, challenges related to initial costs, social acceptance, and policy considerations need to be addressed to ensure widespread adoption and equitable benefits. Policymakers, agricultural organizations, and technology providers play crucial roles in fostering an enabling environment for the successful integration of IoT AI technologies in agriculture, leading to a more sustainable and productive agricultural sector (Boopathi & Davim, 2023a; Ramudu et al., 2023; Sengeni et al., 2023).

FUTURE DIRECTIONS AND RECOMMENDATIONS

Potential for Scaling IoT AI Integration

Customization and Adaptation: Develop customizable IoT AI solutions that can be tailored to different agricultural contexts and crops, allowing farmers to implement technology that aligns with their specific needs and resources. Modular Approach: Adopt a modular approach to IoT AI integration, allowing farmers to start with basic systems and gradually expand and integrate additional components as they become more familiar with the technology. Open Platforms: Promote the development of open-source platforms and APIs (Application Programming Interfaces) that facilitate interoperability between different IoT AI systems, encouraging seamless integration and scalability (Boopathi & Kanike, 2023; Koshariya, Kalaiyarasi, et al., 2023; Koshariya, Khatoon, et al., 2023; Sengeni et al., 2023).

Promoting Collaboration and Knowledge Exchange

- Public-Private Partnerships: Foster collaborations between governments, private companies, research institutions, and agricultural organizations to pool resources, expertise, and knowledge for the development and adoption of IoT AI technologies.
- Farmer-to-Farmer Knowledge Transfer: Facilitate farmer-to-farmer knowledge exchange programs and workshops to share best practices, success stories, and challenges related to IoT AI integration in agriculture.
- Agricultural Extension Services: Strengthen agricultural extension services that provide farmers with training and information on the benefits and practicalities of using IoT AI technologies.

Encouraging Investment and Innovation

- Research and Development Funding: Governments and private sectors should allocate funds for research and development initiatives focused on advancing IoT AI technologies tailored to agricultural applications.
- Start-up Support: Create incubators and accelerator programs that support agro-tech start-ups working on innovative IoT AI solutions, providing them with mentorship, funding, and market access.

- Demonstration Projects: Establish demonstration farms or pilot projects to showcase the benefits and practicality of IoT AI integration in agriculture, encouraging other farmers and stakeholders to adopt the technology.

Addressing Concerns and Challenges

- Data Privacy and Security: Develop robust data privacy and security measures to address concerns related to the collection, storage, and use of agricultural data in IoT AI systems.
- Training and Capacity Building: Invest in training programs that equip farmers and agricultural professionals with the skills needed to effectively use and manage IoT AI technologies.
- Connectivity and Infrastructure: Improve rural connectivity and infrastructure to ensure that farmers in remote areas have access to reliable internet and technology support for IoT AI integration.

The future of agriculture lies in the successful integration of IoT AI technologies, enabling resource-efficient and sustainable farming practices. By embracing potential scaling opportunities, promoting collaboration, encouraging investment, and addressing concerns, the agricultural sector can harness the full potential of IoT AI integration (Boopathi, 2023c, 2023b; Karthik et al., 2023; Koshariya, Kalaiyarasi, et al., 2023). Policymakers, researchers, technology providers, and farmers must work together to create an enabling environment for the widespread adoption of IoT AI technologies, leading to enhanced agricultural productivity, reduced environmental impact, and improved food security in the years to come.

CONCLUSION

The integration of Internet of Things (IoT) and Artificial Intelligence (AI) techniques in agriculture has the potential to revolutionize the way we produce food, address water challenges, and promote sustainable development. Smart water management systems in developed economies, such as Israel and precision agriculture in the Netherlands, serve as compelling case studies showcasing the successful implementation and transformative impact of IoT AI technologies in agriculture.

From the case studies, it is evident that IoT AI integration offers a range of significant benefits:

- AI-driven precision irrigation and data-driven decision-making lead to improved crop yields, contributing to enhanced food production and economic prosperity.
- Smart water management practices reduce water consumption in agriculture, conserving this valuable resource and mitigating water scarcity concerns.
- IoT and AI techniques support sustainable agricultural practices by optimizing resource utilization, minimizing environmental impacts, and promoting ecological balance.
- The adoption of IoT and AI technologies in agriculture enhances economic viability by reducing input costs, increasing productivity, and creating opportunities for technology export.

Despite the evident advantages, challenges remain to realize the full potential of IoT AI integration in agriculture. These challenges include initial investment costs, social acceptance and adoption barriers, and policy and regulatory considerations. To address these challenges and unlock the benefits of IoT AI technologies, several future directions and recommendations are proposed.

To promote scaling IoT AI integration, customizable solutions, modular approaches, and open platforms can enhance accessibility and adaptability for different agricultural contexts. Collaboration and knowledge exchange among stakeholders, including farmers, researchers, and private sectors, can facilitate learning and foster innovation. Encouraging investment in research and development, supporting start-ups, and implementing demonstration projects can drive technological advancements and adoption.

Addressing concerns related to data privacy, security, connectivity, and training is essential to instill confidence and promote widespread adoption. By collectively addressing these challenges and adopting the recommended strategies, the agricultural sector can harness the transformative potential of IoT AI technologies to ensure sustainable and resilient agricultural development.

In conclusion, IoT AI integration in agriculture holds immense promise for meeting the growing global demand for food, overcoming water scarcity challenges, and fostering sustainable development. By embracing innovation, collaboration, and sound policies, we can create a future where technology-driven agriculture ensures food security, conserves natural resources, and supports the well-being of farmers and communities worldwide.

ABBREVIATIONS

IoT: Internet of Things
AI: Artificial Intelligence
ARIMA: Autoregressive Integrated Moving Average
SARIMA: Seasonal Autoregressive Integrated Moving-Average
SVM: Support Vector Machines
RNNs: Recurrent Neural Networks
LSTMs: Long Short-Term Memory Networks
CO2: Carbon Dioxide
API: Application Programming Interface

REFERENCES

Al-Tarawneh, L., Mehyar, A., Alasasaf, S. E., & Al-Mariat, M. (2022). Environmental Tracking System using IoT Based WSN: Smart Agriculture. *2022 4th IEEE Middle East and North Africa COMMunications Conference, MENACOMM 2022*, 147–152. 10.1109/MENACOMM57252.2022.9998269

Alghazzawi, D., Bamasaq, O., Bhatia, S., Kumar, A., Dadheech, P., & Albeshri, A. (2021). Congestion Control in Cognitive IoT-Based WSN Network for Smart Agriculture. *IEEE Access : Practical Innovations, Open Solutions*, *9*, 151401–151420. doi:10.1109/ACCESS.2021.3124791

Anitha, C., Komala, C., Vivekanand, C. V., Lalitha, S., & Boopathi, S. (2023). Artificial Intelligence driven security model for Internet of Medical Things (IoMT). *IEEE Explore*, 1–7.

Bikash Chandra Saha, M. S., Deepa, R., Akila, A., & Sai Thrinath, B. V. (2022). IOT based smart energy meter for smart grid. Academic Press.

Boopathi, S. (2021). *Pollution monitoring and notification: Water pollution monitoring and notification using intelligent RC boat*. Academic Press.

Boopathi, S. (2022). An extensive review on sustainable developments of dry and near-dry electrical discharge machining processes. *ASME: Journal of Manufacturing Science and Engineering*, *144*(5), 050801–1.

Boopathi, S. (2023a). Deep Learning Techniques Applied for Automatic Sentence Generation. In Promoting Diversity, Equity, and Inclusion in Language Learning Environments (pp. 255–273). IGI Global. doi:10.4018/978-1-6684-3632-5.ch016

Boopathi, S. (2023b). Internet of Things-Integrated Remote Patient Monitoring System: Healthcare Application. In *Dynamics of Swarm Intelligence Health Analysis for the Next Generation* (pp. 137–161). IGI Global. doi:10.4018/978-1-6684-6894-4.ch008

Boopathi, S. (2023c). Securing Healthcare Systems Integrated With IoT: Fundamentals, Applications, and Future Trends. In Dynamics of Swarm Intelligence Health Analysis for the Next Generation (pp. 186–209). IGI Global.

Boopathi, S., Arigela, S. H., Raman, R., Indhumathi, C., Kavitha, V., & Bhatt, B. C. (2022). Prominent Rule Control-based Internet of Things: Poultry Farm Management System. *IEEE Explore*, 1–6.

Boopathi, S., Balasubramani, V., & Kumar, R. S. (2023). Influences of various natural fibers on the mechanical and drilling characteristics of coir-fiber-based hybrid epoxy composites. *IOP: Engineering Research Express*, *5*(1), 015002. doi:10.1088/2631-8695/acb132

Boopathi, S., Balasubramani, V., Kumar, R. S., & Singh, G. R. (2021). The influence of human hair on kenaf and Grewia fiber-based hybrid natural composite material: An experimental study. *Functional Composites and Structures*, *3*(4), 045011. doi:10.1088/2631-6331/ac3afc

Boopathi, S., & Davim, J. P. (2023a). Applications of Nanoparticles in Various Manufacturing Processes. In *Sustainable Utilization of Nanoparticles and Nanofluids in Engineering Applications* (pp. 1–31). IGI Global. doi:10.4018/978-1-6684-9135-5.ch001

Boopathi, S., & Davim, J. P. (2023b). *Sustainable Utilization of Nanoparticles and Nanofluids in Engineering Applications*. IGI Global. doi:10.4018/978-1-6684-9135-5

Boopathi, S., & Kanike, U. K. (2023). Applications of Artificial Intelligent and Machine Learning Techniques in Image Processing. In *Handbook of Research on Thrust Technologies' Effect on Image Processing* (pp. 151–173). IGI Global. doi:10.4018/978-1-6684-8618-4.ch010

Boopathi, S., Khare, R., KG, J. C., Muni, T. V., & Khare, S. (2023). Additive Manufacturing Developments in the Medical Engineering Field. In Development, Properties, and Industrial Applications of 3D Printed Polymer Composites (pp. 86–106). IGI Global.

Boopathi, S., Kumar, P. K. S., Meena, R. S., & Sudhakar, M. (2023). Sustainable Developments of Modern Soil-Less Agro-Cultivation Systems: Aquaponic Culture. In Human Agro-Energy Optimization for Business and Industry (pp. 69–87). IGI Global.

Boopathi, S., Lewise, K. A. S., Sarojwal, A., Arulvendhan, K., Sandeepkumar, S., & Subbiah, R. (2022). *An improved aqueous lithium-ion battery with IoT connectivity*. Academic Press.

Boopathi, S., Lewise, K. A. S., Subbiah, R., & Sivaraman, G. (2022). Near-dry wire-cut electrical discharge machining process using water–air-mist dielectric fluid: An experimental study. *Materials Today: Proceedings*, *50*(5), 1885–1890. doi:10.1016/j.matpr.2021.08.077

Boopathi, S., Pandey, B. K., & Pandey, D. (2023). Advances in Artificial Intelligence for Image Processing: Techniques, Applications, and Optimization. In Handbook of Research on Thrust Technologies' Effect on Image Processing (pp. 73–95). IGI Global.

Boopathi, S., & Sivakumar, K. (2014). Study of water assisted dry wire-cut electrical discharge machining. *Indian Journal of Engineering and Materials Sciences*, *21*, 75–82.

Boopathi, S., Sureshkumar, M., & Sathiskumar, S. (2022). Parametric Optimization of LPG Refrigeration System Using Artificial Bee Colony Algorithm. *International Conference on Recent Advances in Mechanical Engineering Research and Development*, 97–105.

Boopathi, S., Thillaivanan, A., Mohammed, A. A., Shanmugam, P., & VR, P. (2022). Experimental investigation on Abrasive Water Jet Machining of Neem Wood Plastic Composite. *IOP: Functional Composites and Structures, 4*.

Boopathi, S., Umareddy, M., & Elangovan, M. (2023). Applications of Nano-Cutting Fluids in Advanced Machining Processes. In *Sustainable Utilization of Nanoparticles and Nanofluids in Engineering Applications* (pp. 211–234). IGI Global. doi:10.4018/978-1-6684-9135-5.ch009

Burugari, V. K., Selvaraj, P., & Palaniappan, K. (2021). Smart agriculture using WSN and IoT. In *Artificial Intelligence and IoT-Based Technologies for Sustainable Farming and Smart Agriculture* (pp. 192–212). IGI Global. doi:10.4018/978-1-7998-1722-2.ch012

Domakonda, V. K., Farooq, S., Chinthamreddy, S., Puviarasi, R., Sudhakar, M., & Boopathi, S. (2022). Sustainable Developments of Hybrid Floating Solar Power Plants: Photovoltaic System. In Human Agro-Energy Optimization for Business and Industry (pp. 148–167). IGI Global.

Fowziya, S., Sivaranjani, S., Devi, N. L., Boopathi, S., Thakur, S., & Sailaja, J. M. (2023). Influences of nano-green lubricants in the friction-stir process of TiAlN coated alloys. *Materials Today: Proceedings*. Advance online publication. doi:10.1016/j.matpr.2023.06.446

Gnanaprakasam, C., Vankara, J., Sastry, A. S., Prajval, V., Gireesh, N., & Boopathi, S. (2023). Long-Range and Low-Power Automated Soil Irrigation System Using Internet of Things: An Experimental Study. In Contemporary Developments in Agricultural Cyber-Physical Systems (pp. 87–104). IGI Global.

Harikaran, M., Boopathi, S., Gokulakannan, S., & Poonguzhali, M. (2023). Study on the Source of E-Waste Management and Disposal Methods. In *Sustainable Approaches and Strategies for E-Waste Management and Utilization* (pp. 39–60). IGI Global. doi:10.4018/978-1-6684-7573-7.ch003

Hema, N., Krishnamoorthy, N., Chavan, S. M., Kumar, N., Sabarimuthu, M., & Boopathi, S. (2023). A Study on an Internet of Things (IoT)-Enabled Smart Solar Grid System. In *Handbook of Research on Deep Learning Techniques for Cloud-Based Industrial IoT* (pp. 290–308). IGI Global. doi:10.4018/978-1-6684-8098-4.ch017

Janardhana, K., Singh, V., Singh, S. N., Babu, T. R., Bano, S., & Boopathi, S. (2023). Utilization Process for Electronic Waste in Eco-Friendly Concrete: Experimental Study. In Sustainable Approaches and Strategies for E-Waste Management and Utilization (pp. 204–223). IGI Global.

Jeevanantham, Y. A., Saravanan, A., Vanitha, V., Boopathi, S., & Kumar, D. P. (2022). Implementation of Internet-of Things (IoT) in Soil Irrigation System. *IEEE Explore*, 1–5.

Karthik, S., Hemalatha, R., Aruna, R., Deivakani, M., Reddy, R. V. K., & Boopathi, S. (2023). Study on Healthcare Security System-Integrated Internet of Things (IoT). In Perspectives and Considerations on the Evolution of Smart Systems (pp. 342–362). IGI Global.

Koshariya, A. K., Kalaiyarasi, D., Jovith, A. A., Sivakami, T., Hasan, D. S., & Boopathi, S. (2023). AI-Enabled IoT and WSN-Integrated Smart Agriculture System. In *Artificial Intelligence Tools and Technologies for Smart Farming and Agriculture Practices* (pp. 200–218). IGI Global. doi:10.4018/978-1-6684-8516-3.ch011

Koshariya, A. K., Khatoon, S., Marathe, A. M., Suba, G. M., Baral, D., & Boopathi, S. (2023). Agricultural Waste Management Systems Using Artificial Intelligence Techniques. In *AI-Enabled Social Robotics in Human Care Services* (pp. 236–258). IGI Global. doi:10.4018/978-1-6684-8171-4.ch009

Kumar, P., Sampath, B., Kumar, S., Babu, B. H., & Ahalya, N. (2023). Hydroponics, Aeroponics, and Aquaponics Technologies in Modern Agricultural Cultivation. In Trends, Paradigms, and Advances in Mechatronics Engineering (pp. 223–241). IGI Global.

Maguluri, L. P., Ananth, J., Hariram, S., Geetha, C., Bhaskar, A., & Boopathi, S. (2023). Smart Vehicle-Emissions Monitoring System Using Internet of Things (IoT). In Handbook of Research on Safe Disposal Methods of Municipal Solid Wastes for a Sustainable Environment (pp. 191–211). IGI Global.

Maheswari, B. U., Imambi, S. S., Hasan, D., Meenakshi, S., Pratheep, V., & Boopathi, S. (2023). Internet of Things and Machine Learning-Integrated Smart Robotics. In Global Perspectives on Robotics and Autonomous Systems: Development and Applications (pp. 240–258). IGI Global. doi:10.4018/978-1-6684-7791-5.ch010

Mohanty, A., Venkateswaran, N., Ranjit, P., Tripathi, M. A., & Boopathi, S. (2023). Innovative Strategy for Profitable Automobile Industries: Working Capital Management. In Handbook of Research on Designing Sustainable Supply Chains to Achieve a Circular Economy (pp. 412–428). IGI Global.

Pramila, P., Amudha, S., Saravanan, T., Sankar, S. R., Poongothai, E., & Boopathi, S. (2023). Design and Development of Robots for Medical Assistance: An Architectural Approach. In Contemporary Applications of Data Fusion for Advanced Healthcare Informatics (pp. 260–282). IGI Global.

Rahamathunnisa, U., Sudhakar, K., Murugan, T. K., Thivaharan, S., Rajkumar, M., & Boopathi, S. (2023). Cloud Computing Principles for Optimizing Robot Task Offloading Processes. In *AI-Enabled Social Robotics in Human Care Services* (pp. 188–211). IGI Global. doi:10.4018/978-1-6684-8171-4.ch007

Ramudu, K., Mohan, V. M., Jyothirmai, D., Prasad, D., Agrawal, R., & Boopathi, S. (2023). Machine Learning and Artificial Intelligence in Disease Prediction: Applications, Challenges, Limitations, Case Studies, and Future Directions. In Contemporary Applications of Data Fusion for Advanced Healthcare Informatics (pp. 297–318). IGI Global.

Reddy, M. A., Reddy, B. M., Mukund, C., Venneti, K., Preethi, D., & Boopathi, S. (2023). Social Health Protection During the COVID-Pandemic Using IoT. In *The COVID-19 Pandemic and the Digitalization of Diplomacy* (pp. 204–235). IGI Global. doi:10.4018/978-1-7998-8394-4.ch009

Samikannu, R., Koshariya, A. K., Poornima, E., Ramesh, S., Kumar, A., & Boopathi, S. (2022). Sustainable Development in Modern Aquaponics Cultivation Systems Using IoT Technologies. In *Human Agro-Energy Optimization for Business and Industry* (pp. 105–127). IGI Global.

Sampath, B., Pandian, M., Deepa, D., & Subbiah, R. (2022). Operating parameters prediction of liquefied petroleum gas refrigerator using simulated annealing algorithm. *AIP Conference Proceedings*, *2460*(1), 070003. doi:10.1063/5.0095601

Sampath, B., Sasikumar, C., & Myilsamy, S. (2023). Application of TOPSIS Optimization Technique in the Micro-Machining Process. In Trends, Paradigms, and Advances in Mechatronics Engineering (pp. 162–187). IGI Global.

Sankar, K. M., Booba, B., & Boopathi, S. (2023). Smart Agriculture Irrigation Monitoring System Using Internet of Things. In *Contemporary Developments in Agricultural Cyber-Physical Systems* (pp. 105–121). IGI Global. doi:10.4018/978-1-6684-7879-0.ch006

Sathish, T., Sunagar, P., Singh, V., Boopathi, S., Al-Enizi, A. M., Pandit, B., Gupta, M., & Sehgal, S. S. (2023). Characteristics estimation of natural fibre reinforced plastic composites using deep multi-layer perceptron (MLP) technique. *Chemosphere*, *337*, 139346. doi:10.1016/j.chemosphere.2023.139346 PMID:37379988

Selvakumar, S., Adithe, S., Isaac, J. S., Pradhan, R., Venkatesh, V., & Sampath, B. (2023). A Study of the Printed Circuit Board (PCB) E-Waste Recycling Process. In Sustainable Approaches and Strategies for E-Waste Management and Utilization (pp. 159–184). IGI Global.

Sengeni, D., Padmapriya, G., Imambi, S. S., Suganthi, D., Suri, A., & Boopathi, S. (2023). Biomedical Waste Handling Method Using Artificial Intelligence Techniques. In *Handbook of Research on Safe Disposal Methods of Municipal Solid Wastes for a Sustainable Environment* (pp. 306–323). IGI Global. doi:10.4018/978-1-6684-8117-2.ch022

Subha, S., Inbamalar, T., Komala, C., Suresh, L. R., Boopathi, S., & Alaskar, K. (2023). A Remote Health Care Monitoring system using internet of medical things (IoMT). *IEEE Explore*, 1–6.

Syamala, M., Komala, C., Pramila, P., Dash, S., Meenakshi, S., & Boopathi, S. (2023). Machine Learning-Integrated IoT-Based Smart Home Energy Management System. In *Handbook of Research on Deep Learning Techniques for Cloud-Based Industrial IoT* (pp. 219–235). IGI Global. doi:10.4018/978-1-6684-8098-4.ch013

Vanitha, S., Radhika, K., & Boopathi, S. (2023). Artificial Intelligence Techniques in Water Purification and Utilization. In *Human Agro-Energy Optimization for Business and Industry* (pp. 202–218). IGI Global. doi:10.4018/978-1-6684-4118-3.ch010

Veeranjaneyulu, R., Boopathi, S., Kumari, R. K., Vidyarthi, A., Isaac, J. S., & Jaiganesh, V. (2023). Air Quality Improvement and Optimisation Using Machine Learning Technique. *IEEE Explore*, 1–6.

Veeranjaneyulu, R., Boopathi, S., Narasimharao, J., Gupta, K. K., Reddy, R. V. K., & Ambika, R. (2023). Identification of Heart Diseases using Novel Machine Learning Method. *IEEE Explore*, 1–6.

Venkateswaran, N., Vidhya, K., Ayyannan, M., Chavan, S. M., Sekar, K., & Boopathi, S. (2023). A Study on Smart Energy Management Framework Using Cloud Computing. In 5G, Artificial Intelligence, and Next Generation Internet of Things: Digital Innovation for Green and Sustainable Economies (pp. 189–212). IGI Global. doi:10.4018/978-1-6684-8634-4.ch009

Venkateswaran, N., Vidhya, R., Naik, D. A., Raj, T. M., Munjal, N., & Boopathi, S. (2023). Study on Sentence and Question Formation Using Deep Learning Techniques. In *Digital Natives as a Disruptive Force in Asian Businesses and Societies* (pp. 252–273). IGI Global. doi:10.4018/978-1-6684-6782-4.ch015

Compilation of References

Abonazel, M. R. (2018). A practical guide for creating monte carlo simulation studies using r. *International Journal of Mathematics and Computer Science*, *4*, 18–33.

Afik, Z., Arad, O., & Galil, K. (2016). Using merton model for default prediction: An empirical assessment of selected alternatives. *Journal of Empirical Finance*, *35*, 43–67. doi:10.1016/j.jempfin.2015.09.004

Aggarwal, N., & Singh, D. (2021). Technology assisted farming: Implications of IoT and AI. *IOP Conference Series. Materials Science and Engineering*, *1022*(1), 012080. doi:10.1088/1757-899X/1022/1/012080

Ahmad, L., & Nabi, F. (2021). *Agriculture 5.0: Artificial Intelligence, IoT and Machine Learning*. CRC Press.

Akisawa, A., Kang, Y. T., Shimazaki, Y., & Kashiwagi, T. (1999). Environmentally friendly energy system models using material circulation and energy cascade—The optimization work. *Energy*, *24*(7), 561–578. doi:10.1016/S0360-5442(99)00023-7

Alanezi, M. A., Mohammad, A., Sha'aban, Y. A., Bouchekara, H. R., & Shahriar, M. S. (2022). Auto-Encoder Learning-Based UAV Communications for Livestock Management. *Drones (Basel)*, *6*(10), 276. doi:10.3390/drones6100276

Aldaej, A., Ahanger, T. A., Atiquzzaman, M., Ullah, I., & Yousufudin, M. (2022). Smart Cybersecurity Framework for IoT-Empowered Drones: Machine Learning Perspective. *Sensors (Basel)*, *22*(7), 2630. doi:10.339022072630 PMID:35408244

Alex, B., & Mulvenna, M. D. (1998). Discovering Internet Marketing Intelligence through Online Analytical Web Usage Mining. *SIGMOD Record*, *27*(4), 54–61. doi:10.1145/306101.306124

Alghazzawi, D., Bamasaq, O., Bhatia, S., Kumar, A., Dadheech, P., & Albeshri, A. (2021). Congestion Control in Cognitive IoT-Based WSN Network for Smart Agriculture. *IEEE Access : Practical Innovations, Open Solutions*, *9*, 151401–151420. doi:10.1109/ACCESS.2021.3124791

Aljaghtham, M. (n.d.). *Design of cascade thermoelectric generation systems with improved thermal reliability*. Elsevier. Retrieved August 12, 2023, from https://www.sciencedirect.com/science/article/pii/S0360544221032813

Al-khafajiy, M., Kolivand, H., Baker, T., Tully, D., & Waraich, A. (2019). Smart hospital emergency system Via mobile-based requesting services. *Multimedia Tools and Applications*, *78*(14), 20087–20111. doi:10.100711042-019-7274-4

Alsalmi, N., Ullah, S., & Rafique, M. (2023). Accounting for digital currencies. *Research in International Business and Finance*, *64*, 101897. doi:10.1016/j.ribaf.2023.101897

Alsamhi, S. H., Ma, O., Ansari, M. S., & Almalki, F. A. (2019). Survey on collaborative smart drones and internet of things for improving smartness of smart cities. *IEEE Access : Practical Innovations, Open Solutions*, *7*, 128125–128152. doi:10.1109/ACCESS.2019.2934998

Al-Suwaidi, N. A., & Nobanee, H. (2020). Anti-money laundering and anti-terrorism financing: A survey of the existing literature and a future research agenda. *Journal of Money Laundering Control*, *24*(2), 396–426. doi:10.1108/JMLC-03-2020-0029

Al-Tarawneh, L., Mehyar, A., Alasasaf, S. E., & Al-Mariat, M. (2022). Environmental Tracking System using IoT Based WSN: Smart Agriculture. *2022 4th IEEE Middle East and North Africa COMMunications Conference, MENACOMM 2022*, 147–152. 10.1109/MENACOMM57252.2022.9998269

Altman, E. I., & Saunders, A. (1997). Credit risk measurement: Developments over the last 20 years. *Journal of Banking & Finance*, *21*(11-12), 1721–1742. doi:10.1016/S0378-4266(97)00036-8

Alvino, F. C., Aleman, C. C., Filgueiras, R., Althoff, D., & da Cunha, F. F. (2020). Vegetation indices for irrigated corn monitoring. *Engenharia Agrícola*, *40*(3), 322–333. doi:10.1590/1809-4430-eng.agric.v40n3p322-333/2020

Ananthi, N., Divya, J., Divya, M., & Janani, V. (2017). *IoT based smart soil monitoring system for agricultural production. In 2017 IEEE Technological Innovations in ICT for Agriculture and Rural Development (TIAR)*. IEEE. doi:10.1109/TIAR.2017.8273717

Andersen, T. G., & Sørensen, B. E. (1996). Gmm estimation of a stochastic volatility model: A monte carlo study. Journal of Business amp. *Economie & Statistique*, *14*, 328–352.

Anderson, C. R. (2002). *A Machine Learning Approach to Web Personalization* [Ph.D. Thesis]. University of Washington.

Angelini, E. (2012). Credit default swaps (cds) and their role in the credit risk market. *International Journal of Academic Research in Business & Social Sciences*, *2*, 584.

Anitha, C., Komala, C., Vivekanand, C. V., Lalitha, S., & Boopathi, S. (2023). Artificial Intelligence driven security model for Internet of Medical Things (IoMT). *IEEE Explore*, 1–7.

Aronson. (1977). The lancet on the telephone 1876-1975. *Medical History, 21*, 69-87.

Asensio, O. I., Alvarez, K., Dror, A., Wenzel, E., Hollauer, C., & Ha, S. (2020). Real-time data from mobile platforms to evaluate sustainable transportation infrastructure. *Nature Sustainability*, *3*(6), 463–471. doi:10.103841893-020-0533-6

Ashbaugh-Skaife, H., Collins, D. W., & LaFond, R. (2006). The effects of corporate governance on firms' credit ratings. *Journal of Accounting and Economics*, *42*(1-2), 203–243. doi:10.1016/j.jacceco.2006.02.003

Ashton, K. (2009). That 'internet of things' thing. *RFID Journal, 22*(7), 97-114.

ASTM. (2008). *Developing sustainable transportation infrastructure.* Citeseer. https://citeseerx.ist.psu.edu/document?repid=rep1&type=pdf&doi=f2d9506dee70808a8803f8955d58eecd715df05b

Auer, R., Cornelli, G., & Frost, J. (2020). *Covid-19, cash, and the future of payments.* BIS Bulletin No. 3, Bank for International Settlements.

Ayadi, R., & Behr, P. (2009). On the necessity to regulate credit derivatives markets. *Journal of Banking Regulation*, *10*(3), 179–201. doi:10.1057/jbr.2009.3

Ayaz, M., Ammad-Uddin, M., Sharif, Z., Mansour, A., & Aggoune, E.-H. M. (2019). Internet- ofthings (IoT)- based smart agriculture: Toward making the fields talk. *IEEE Access : Practical Innovations, Open Solutions*, *7*, 129551–129583. doi:10.1109/ACCESS.2019.2932609

Aziz, S., & Dowling, M. (2019). Machine learning and AI for risk management. In *Disrupting finance* (pp. 33–50). Palgrave Pivot. doi:10.1007/978-3-030-02330-0_3

Badassa, B. B., Sun, B., & Qiao, L. (2020). Sustainable Transport Infrastructure and Economic Returns: A Bibliometric and Visualization Analysis. *Sustainability (Basel)*, *12*(5), 2033. doi:10.3390u12052033

Baig, Z., Khan, M. A., Mohammad, N., & Brahim, G. B. (2022). Drone forensics and machine learning: Sustaining the investigation process. *Sustainability (Basel)*, *14*(8), 4861. doi:10.3390u14084861

Baker, D. N., Lambert, J. R., & McKinion, J. M. (1983). *GOSSYM: A simulator of cotton crop growth and yield, Technical bulletin*. Agricultural Experiment Station.

Balamash, A., & Krunz, M. (2004). An Overview of Web Caching Replacement Algorithms. *IEEE Communications Surveys and Tutorials*, *6*(2), 44–56. doi:10.1109/COMST.2004.5342239

Bamshad, M. (2007). *Data Mining for Web Personalization*. LCNS, Springer-Verleg Berlin.

Bank of England. (2020). *Central Bank Digital Currency Opportunities, challenges and design*. https://www.bankofengland.co.uk/-/media/boe/files/paper/2020/central-bank-digital-currency-opportunities-challenges-and design.pdf?la=en&hash=DFAD18646A77C00772AF1C5B18E63E71F68E4593

Batty, M., Axhausen, K. W., Giannotti, F., Pozdnoukhov, A., Bazzani, A., Wachowicz, M., Ouzounis, G., & Portugali, Y. (2012). Smart cities of the future. *The European Physical Journal. Special Topics*, *214*(1), 481–518. doi:10.1140/epjst/e2012-01703-3

Bedi, P., & Nashier, T. (2020). On the investment credentials of Bitcoin: A cross-currency perspective. *Research in International Business and Finance*, *51*, 101087. doi:10.1016/j.ribaf.2019.101087

Behzad, M., Kiani-Harchegani, M., Karimi, M., & Mousavi, S. (2020). Machine learning-based prediction of soil cation exchange capacity using soil spectral data. *Catena*, *188*, 104444. doi:10.1016/j.catena.2019.104444

Ben Ayed, R., & Hanana, M. (2021). Artificial intelligence to improve the food and agriculture sector. *Journal of Food Quality*, *2021*, 1–7. doi:10.1155/2021/5584754

Benincasa, P., Antognelli, S., Brunetti, L., Fabbri, C., Natale, A., Sartoretti, V., Modeo, G., Guiducci, M., Tei, F., & Vizzari, M. (2017). Reliability of NDVI derived by high resolution satellite and UAV compared to in- field methods for the evaluation of early crop n status and grain yield in wheat. *Experimental Agriculture*, *54*(4), 604–622. doi:10.1017/S0014479717000278

Benos, A., & Papanastasopoulos, G. (2007). Extending the merton model: A hybrid approach to assessing credit quality. *Mathematical and Computer Modelling*, *46*(1-2), 47–68. doi:10.1016/j.mcm.2006.12.012

Bhatore, S., Mohan, L., & Reddy, Y. R. (2020). Machine learning techniques for credit risk evaluation: A systematic literature review. *Journal of Banking and Financial Technology*, *4*(1), 111–138. doi:10.100742786-020-00020-3

Bhowmik, S., Spee, R., & Enslin, J. H. R. (1999). Performance optimization for doubly fed wind power generation systems. *IEEE Transactions on Industry Applications*, *35*(4), 949–958. doi:10.1109/28.777205

Bidirectional LSTM. (n.d.). Retrieved May 27, 2023, from https://www.baeldung.com/cs/bidirectional-vs-unidirectional-lstm#:~:text=Bidirectional%20LSTM%20(BiLSTM)%20is%20a,utilizing%20information%20from%20both%20sides

Bikash Chandra Saha, M. S., Deepa, R., Akila, A., & Sai Thrinath, B. V. (2022). IOT based smart energy meter for smart grid. Academic Press.

Bindseil, U. (2019). Central bank digital currency: Financial system implications and control. *International Journal of Political Economy*, *48*(4), 303–335. doi:10.1080/08911916.2019.1693160

Blumenstock, J. E., Callen, M., Ghani, T., & Koepke, L. (2015). Promises and pitfalls of mobile money in Afghanistan: evidence from a randomized control trial. In *ICTD'15. Proceedings of the Seventh International Conference on Information and Communication Technologies and Development, Article no.* 15. New York: ACM. 10.1145/2737856.2738031

Boopathi, S. (2021). *Pollution monitoring and notification: Water pollution monitoring and notification using intelligent RC boat*. Academic Press.

Boopathi, S. (2023a). Deep Learning Techniques Applied for Automatic Sentence Generation. In Promoting Diversity, Equity, and Inclusion in Language Learning Environments (pp. 255–273). IGI Global. doi:10.4018/978-1-6684-3632-5.ch016

Boopathi, S. (2023c). Securing Healthcare Systems Integrated With IoT: Fundamentals, Applications, and Future Trends. In Dynamics of Swarm Intelligence Health Analysis for the Next Generation (pp. 186–209). IGI Global.

Boopathi, S., Arigela, S. H., Raman, R., Indhumathi, C., Kavitha, V., & Bhatt, B. C. (2022). Prominent Rule Control-based Internet of Things: Poultry Farm Management System. *IEEE Explore*, 1–6.

Boopathi, S., Khare, R., KG, J. C., Muni, T. V., & Khare, S. (2023). Additive Manufacturing Developments in the Medical Engineering Field. In Development, Properties, and Industrial Applications of 3D Printed Polymer Composites (pp. 86–106). IGI Global.

Boopathi, S., Kumar, P. K. S., Meena, R. S., & Sudhakar, M. (2023). Sustainable Developments of Modern Soil-Less Agro-Cultivation Systems: Aquaponic Culture. In Human Agro-Energy Optimization for Business and Industry (pp. 69–87). IGI Global.

Boopathi, S., Lewise, K. A. S., Sarojwal, A., Arulvendhan, K., Sandeepkumar, S., & Subbiah, R. (2022). *An improved aqueous lithium-ion battery with IoT connectivity*. Academic Press.

Boopathi, S., Pandey, B. K., & Pandey, D. (2023). Advances in Artificial Intelligence for Image Processing: Techniques, Applications, and Optimization. In Handbook of Research on Thrust Technologies' Effect on Image Processing (pp. 73–95). IGI Global.

Boopathi, S., Thillaivanan, A., Mohammed, A. A., Shanmugam, P., & VR, P. (2022). Experimental investigation on Abrasive Water Jet Machining of Neem Wood Plastic Composite. *IOP: Functional Composites and Structures, 4.*

Boopathi, S. (2022). An extensive review on sustainable developments of dry and near-dry electrical discharge machining processes. *ASME: Journal of Manufacturing Science and Engineering*, *144*(5), 050801–1.

Boopathi, S. (2023b). Internet of Things-Integrated Remote Patient Monitoring System: Healthcare Application. In *Dynamics of Swarm Intelligence Health Analysis for the Next Generation* (pp. 137–161). IGI Global. doi:10.4018/978-1-6684-6894-4.ch008

Boopathi, S., Balasubramani, V., & Kumar, R. S. (2023). Influences of various natural fibers on the mechanical and drilling characteristics of coir-fiber-based hybrid epoxy composites. *IOP: Engineering Research Express*, *5*(1), 015002. doi:10.1088/2631-8695/acb132

Boopathi, S., Balasubramani, V., Kumar, R. S., & Singh, G. R. (2021). The influence of human hair on kenaf and Grewia fiber-based hybrid natural composite material: An experimental study. *Functional Composites and Structures*, *3*(4), 045011. doi:10.1088/2631-6331/ac3afc

Boopathi, S., & Davim, J. P. (2023a). Applications of Nanoparticles in Various Manufacturing Processes. In *Sustainable Utilization of Nanoparticles and Nanofluids in Engineering Applications* (pp. 1–31). IGI Global. doi:10.4018/978-1-6684-9135-5.ch001

Boopathi, S., & Davim, J. P. (2023b). *Sustainable Utilization of Nanoparticles and Nanofluids in Engineering Applications*. IGI Global. doi:10.4018/978-1-6684-9135-5

Boopathi, S., & Kanike, U. K. (2023). Applications of Artificial Intelligent and Machine Learning Techniques in Image Processing. In *Handbook of Research on Thrust Technologies' Effect on Image Processing* (pp. 151–173). IGI Global. doi:10.4018/978-1-6684-8618-4.ch010

Boopathi, S., Lewise, K. A. S., Subbiah, R., & Sivaraman, G. (2022). Near-dry wire-cut electrical discharge machining process using water–air-mist dielectric fluid: An experimental study. *Materials Today: Proceedings*, *50*(5), 1885–1890. doi:10.1016/j.matpr.2021.08.077

Boopathi, S., & Sivakumar, K. (2014). Study of water assisted dry wire-cut electrical discharge machining. *Indian Journal of Engineering and Materials Sciences*, *21*, 75–82.

Boopathi, S., Sureshkumar, M., & Sathiskumar, S. (2022). Parametric Optimization of LPG Refrigeration System Using Artificial Bee Colony Algorithm. *International Conference on Recent Advances in Mechanical Engineering Research and Development*, 97–105.

Boopathi, S., Umareddy, M., & Elangovan, M. (2023). Applications of Nano-Cutting Fluids in Advanced Machining Processes. In *Sustainable Utilization of Nanoparticles and Nanofluids in Engineering Applications* (pp. 211–234). IGI Global. doi:10.4018/978-1-6684-9135-5.ch009

Boulanger, A. G. (1983). *The expert system PLANT/CD: A case study in applying the general purpose inference system ADVISE to predicting black cutworm damage in corn* [Ph.D. Thesis]. University of Illinois at Urbana-Champaign.

Brin, S., & Pange, L. (1998). The Anatomy of a Large-scale Hyper Textual Web Search Engine. *Computer Networks and ISDN Systems*, *30*(1-7), 107–117. doi:10.1016/S0169-7552(98)00110-X

Bruggink, A., Schoevaart, R., & Kieboom, T. (2003). Concepts of Nature in Organic Synthesis: Cascade Catalysis and Multistep Conversions in Concert. *Organic Process Research & Development*, *7*(5), 622–640. doi:10.1021/op0340311

Brunnermeier, M. K., & Niepelt, D. (2019). On the equivalence of private and public money. *Journal of Monetary Economics*, *106*, 27–41. doi:10.1016/j.jmoneco.2019.07.004

Burney, J., & Ramanathan, V. (2014). Recent climate and air pollution impacts on Indian agriculture. *Proceedings of the National Academy of Sciences of the United States of America*, *111*(46), 16319–16324. doi:10.1073/pnas.1317275111 PMID:25368149

Burugari, V. K., Selvaraj, P., & Palaniappan, K. (2021). Smart agriculture using WSN and IoT. In *Artificial Intelligence and IoT-Based Technologies for Sustainable Farming and Smart Agriculture* (pp. 192–212). IGI Global. doi:10.4018/978-1-7998-1722-2.ch012

Butler, T., & O'Brien, L. (2019). Understanding RegTech for digital regulatory compliance. In T. Lynn, J. Mooney, P. Rosati, & M. Cummins (Eds.), *Disrupting Finance. Palgrave Studies in Digital Business & Enabling Technologies* (pp. 85–102). Palgrave Pivot.

Canhoto, A. I. (2020). Leveraging machine learning in the global fight against money laundering and terrorism financing: An affordances perspective. *Journal of Business Research*, *131*, 441–452. doi:10.1016/j.jbusres.2020.10.012 PMID:33100427

Chamola, V., Hassija, V., Gupta, V., & Guizani, M. (2020). A comprehensive review of the COVID-19 pandemic and the role of IoT, drones, AI, blockchain, and 5G in managing its impact. *IEEE Access : Practical Innovations, Open Solutions*, *8*, 90225–90265. doi:10.1109/ACCESS.2020.2992341

Chandak, B. (2022, November 25). Why cash is still king in India. *The Business Line*, p. 4.

Chang, C. C., & Lin, C. J. (2011, April). LIBSVM. *ACM Transactions on Intelligent Systems and Technology*, *2*(3), 1–27. doi:10.1145/1961189.1961199

Chang, H. K., & Chien, W. A. (2006). Neural network with multi-trend simulating transfer function for forecasting typhoon wave. *Advances in Engineering Software*, *37*(3), 184–194. doi:10.1016/j.advengsoft.2005.05.001

Chen, L., Huang, Y., Ouyang, S., & Xiong, W. (2021). *The Data Privacy Paradox and Digital Demand.* NBER Working Paper No. 28854.

Chen, X., & Zhang, X. (2002). Popularity-based PPM: An effective Web pre-fetching technique for high accuracy and low storage. *Proceedings of the International Conference on Parallel Processing,* 296-304. 10.1109/ICPP.2002.1040885

Chipade, Mehta, Roham, & Naik. (2020). A review paper on indoor navigation system. *International Journal of Engineering Applied Sciences and Technology, 4*(11).

Choi, U.-M., Blaabjerg, F., & Lee, K.-B. (2015). Study and Handling Methods of Power IGBT Module Failures in Power Electronic Converter Systems. *IEEE Transactions on Power Electronics*, *30*(5), 2517–2533. doi:10.1109/TPEL.2014.2373390

Cohn, S. A. (1995). Radar Measurements of Turbulent Eddy Dissipation Rate in the Troposphere: A Comparison of Techniques. *Journal of Atmospheric and Oceanic Technology*, *12*(1), 85–95. doi:10.1175/1520-0426(1995)012<0085:RMOTED>2.0.CO;2

Crandall, J. (2019). Blockchains and the "chains of empire": Contextualizing blockchain, cryptocurrency, and neoliberalism in Puerto Rico. *Design and Culture*, *11*(3), 279–300. doi:10.1080/17547075.2019.1673989

Crapolicchio, R., Ferrazzoli, P., Meloni, M., Pinori, S., & Rahmoune, R. (2010). Soil Moisture and Ocean Salinity (SMOS) mission: System overview and contribution to vicarious calibration monitoring. *European Journal of Remote Sensing*, 37– 50. doi:10.5721/ItJRS20104214

Currie, W. L., Gozman, D. P., & Seddon, J. J. (2018). Dialectic tensions in the financial markets: A longitudinal study of pre-and postcrisis regulatory technology. *Journal of Information Technology*, *33*(4), 304–325. doi:10.105741265-017-0047-5

Cyrus, S., Zarkessh, A. M., Jafar, A., & Vishal, S. (1997). Knowledge discovery from Users Web Page Navigation. In *Workshop on Research Issues in Data Engineering*, Birmingham, UK.

Darwin, G. H. (1907). *The Harmonic Analysis of Tidal Observations in Scientific Papers, 1, Oceanic Tides and Lunar Disturbances of Gravity*. Cambridge Univ. Press.

Davis, F. D. (1986). *A technology acceptance model for empirically testing new end-user information systems: theory and results* [Doctoral dissertation]. Sloan School of Management, Massachusetts Institute of Technology.

Demuth, H., & Beale, M. (2000). Neural networks toolbox user's guide, version 4. Math Works, Inc.

Deo, M. C., Gondane, D. S., & Kumar, V. S. (2002). Analysis of wave directional spread-ing using neural networks. *Journal of Waterway, Port, Coastal, and Ocean Engineering*, *128*(1), 30–37. doi:10.1061/(ASCE)0733-950X(2002)128:1(30)

Deo, M. C., & Naidu, C. S. (1998). Real time wave forecasting using neural networks. *Ocean Engineering*, *26*(3), 191–203. doi:10.1016/S0029-8018(97)10025-7

De, P. B., Aroyo, L., & Chepegin, V. (2004). The Next Big Thing: Adaptive Web-Based Systems. *Journal of Digital Information*, *5*(1). http://jodi.ecs.soton.ac.uk/Articles/v05/ i01/DeBra/

Derbali, A., & Jamel, L. (2019). Dependence of default probability and recovery rate in structural credit risk models: Case of greek banks. *Journal of the Knowledge Economy*, *10*(2), 711–733. doi:10.100713132-017-0473-1

Desai, S. D. (1996). *Ocean tides from TOPEX/POSEIDON altimetry with some geophysical applications* [Ph.D. dissertation]. Department of Aerospace Engineering Sciences, University of Colorado, Boulder, CO.

Desai, S. D., & Wahr, J. (1995). Empirical ocean tide models estimated from TOPEX/ POSEIDON altimetry. *Journal of Geophysical Research*, *100*(C12, c12), 25205–25228. doi:10.1029/95JC02258

Dharmaraj, V., & Vijayanand, C. (2018). Artificial intelligence (AI) in agriculture. *International Journal of Current Microbiology and Applied Sciences*, *7*(12), 2122–2128. doi:10.20546/ijcmas.2018.712.241

Domakonda, V. K., Farooq, S., Chinthamreddy, S., Puviarasi, R., Sudhakar, M., & Boopathi, S. (2022). Sustainable Developments of Hybrid Floating Solar Power Plants: Photovoltaic System. In Human Agro-Energy Optimization for Business and Industry (pp. 148–167). IGI Global.

Doodson, A. T. (1921). The harmonic development of the tide generating potential. *Proceedings of the Royal Society of London. Series A, Containing Papers of a Mathematical and Physical Character*, *100*(704), 305–329. doi:10.1098/rspa.1921.0088

Duan, Y., Zhang, L., Lu, S., Chen, X., & Zhou, X. (2018). Soil nutrient prediction using visible and near-infrared spectroscopy: A comparison of models and wavelengths. *Soil Science Society of America Journal*, *82*(4), 1029–1040. doi:10.2136ssaj2018.01.0038

Duffie, D., & Singleton, K. J. (2012). *Credit risk: pricing, measurement, and management*. Princeton university press. doi:10.2307/j.ctv30pnvpg

Dunham, M. H. (2006). *Data Mining Introductory and Advanced Topics* (1st ed.). Pearson Education.

Dyntu, V., & Dykyi, O. (2019). Cryptocurrency in the system of money laundering. *Baltija Journal of Economic Studies*, *4*(5), 75–81. doi:10.30525/2256-0742/2018-4-5-75-81

Džaja, J., & Aljinović, Z. (2013). Testing capm model on the emerging markets of the central and southeastern europe. *Croatian Operational Research Review*, *4*, 164–175.

Ekström, J.B., & Sjögren, O. (2014). *Implementation of heston nandi garch model on omxs30*. Academic Press.

Elsayed, A. H., & Nasir, M. A. (2022). Central Bank digital currencies: An Agenda for future research. *Research in International Business and Finance*, *62*, 101736. doi:10.1016/j.ribaf.2022.101736

Eng, L. S., Ismail, R., Hashim, W., & Baharum, A. (2019). The use of VARI, GLI, and VIgreen formulas in detecting vegetation in aerial images. *International Journal of Technology*, *10*(7), 1385–1394. doi:10.14716/ijtech.v10i7.3275

Engle, R. F. (1982). Autoregressive conditional heteroscedasticity with estimates of the variance of united kingdom inflation. *Econometrica*, *50*(4), 987–1007. doi:10.2307/1912773

Enitan, T. (2019). Effectiveness of a Multimodal Digital Psychotherapy Platform for Adult Depression: A Naturalistic Feasibility Study. *JMIR mHealth and uHealth*, *7*(1), e10948. doi:10.2196/10948 PMID:30674448

Facca, F. M., & Lanzi, P. L. (2005). Mining Interesting Knowledge from Web logs: A Survey. *Data & Knowledge Engineering*, *53*(3), 225–241. doi:10.1016/j.datak.2004.08.001

Farooq, W., Butt, N., Shukat, S., Baig, N. A., & Ahmed, S. M. (2016). Wirelessly Controlled Mines Detection Robot. *International Conference on Intelligent Systems Engineering (ICISE)*. 10.1109/INTELSE.2016.7475162

Faulkender, M., & Wang, R. (2006). Corporate financial policy and the value of cash. *The Journal of Finance, 61*(4), 1957–1990. doi:10.1111/j.1540-6261.2006.00894.x

Fegatelli, P. (2022). A central bank digital currency in a heterogeneous monetary union: Managing the effects on the bank lending channel. *Journal of Macroeconomics, 71*(C), 103392. doi:10.1016/j.jmacro.2021.103392

Feng, W., Man, S., & Hu, G. (2009). *Markov Tree Prediction on Web Cache Pre-fetching. In Software Engineering, Artificial Intelligence (SCI)* (Vol. 209). Springer-Verlag.

Fernández-Villaverde, J., Sanches, D., Schilling, L., & Uhlig, H. (2020). *Central bank digital currency: central banking for all?* Working paper, Vol. 26753, National Bureau of Economic Research.

Ferreira, M. A., & Santa-Clara, P. (2011). Forecasting stock market returns: The sum of the parts is more than the whole. *Journal of Financial Economics, 100*(3), 514–537. doi:10.1016/j.jfineco.2011.02.003

Foley, S., Karlsen, J. R., & Putniš, T. J. (2019). Sex, Drugs, and Bitcoin: How Much Illegal Activity Is Financed through Cryptocurrencies. *Review of Financial Studies, 32*(5), 1798–1853. doi:10.1093/rfs/hhz015

Fomina, O., Moshkovska, O., Avhustova, O., Romashko, O., & Holovina, D. (2019). Current aspects of the cryptocurrency recognition in Ukraine. *Banks and Bank Systems, 14*(2), 203–213. doi:10.21511/bbs.14(2).2019.18

Fowziya, S., Sivaranjani, S., Devi, N. L., Boopathi, S., Thakur, S., & Sailaja, J. M. (2023). Influences of nano-green lubricants in the friction-stir process of TiAlN coated alloys. *Materials Today: Proceedings*. Advance online publication. doi:10.1016/j.matpr.2023.06.446

Francq, C., & Zakoian, J. M. (2004). Maximum likelihood estimation of pure garch and arma-garch processes. *Bernoulli, 10*(4), 605–637. doi:10.3150/bj/1093265632

Gabaix, X., Gopikrishnan, P., Plerou, V., & Stanley, E. (2007). A unified econophysics explanation for the power-law exponents of stock market activity. *Physica A, 382*(1), 81–88. doi:10.1016/j.physa.2007.02.030

Garcia, F. M., Alvarez, L. Y., Heras, F. L., Gonzalez, V. B., Rodriguez, V. Y., Pino, A., & Arboleya, A. A. (2018). GPR System Onboard a UAV for Non-invasive Detection of Buried Objects. *2018 IEEE Antennas and Propagation Society International Symposium and USNC/URSI National Radio Science Meeting, APSURSI 2018 – Proceedings*, 1967–1968. 10.1109/APUSNCURSINRSM.2018.8608907

García-Berná, J. A., Ouhbi, S., Benmouna, B., García-Mateos, G., Fernández-Alemán, J. L., & Molina-Martínez, J. M. (2020). Systematic Mapping Study on Remote Sensing in Agriculture. *Applied Sciences (Basel, Switzerland), 10*(10), 3456. doi:10.3390/app10103456

Ge, Z. Y., McCool, C., Sanderson, C., & Corke, P. (2015). *Content specific feature learning for fine-grained plant classification. CLEF.* Working Notes.

Ghazali, M. H. M., Azmin, A., & Rahiman, W. (2022). Drone Implementation in Precision Agriculture—A Survey. *International Journal of Emerging Technology and Advanced Engineering, 12*(4), 67–77. doi:10.46338/ijetae0422_10

Gholizadeh, A., & Ayoubi, S. (2017). Predicting soil organic carbon and total nitrogen using soil spectral data and machine learning algorithms. *Catena, 156*, 35–45. doi:10.1016/j.catena.2017.04.020

Gholizadeh, A., Ayoubi, S., Khormali, F., & Wulfsohn, D. (2020). Predicting soil organic carbon and total nitrogen using machine learning algorithms in a semi-arid region. *Catena, 193*, 104641. doi:10.1016/j.catena.2020.104641

Gnanaprakasam, C., Vankara, J., Sastry, A. S., Prajval, V., Gireesh, N., & Boopathi, S. (2023). Long-Range and Low-Power Automated Soil Irrigation System Using Internet of Things: An Experimental Study. In Contemporary Developments in Agricultural Cyber-Physical Systems (pp. 87–104). IGI Global.

Golechha. (2021). India should ramp up its emergency medicine and critical care infrastructure to combat COVID-19. *Postgraduate Medical Journal, 97.*

Goodell, J. W., & Shen, D. (2021). The Chinese sovereign digital currency as a catalyst for change: A new trilemma? In C. Shaen (Ed.), *Understanding Cryptocurrency Fraud: The Challenges and Headwinds to Regulate Digital Currencies* (pp. 177–186). De Gruyter. doi:10.1515/9783110718485-014

Goodhart, C., & Ashworth, J. (2014). *Trying to glimpse the 'grey economy'.* Available at: https://voxeu. org/article/trying-glimpse-grey-economy

Guo, Z. (2017). Option pricing under the merton model of the short rate in subdiffusive brownian motion regime. *Journal of Statistical Computation and Simulation, 87*(3), 519–529. doi:10.1080/00949655.2016.1218880

Habibi, L., Watanabe, T., Matsui, T., & Tanaka, T. (2021). Machine Learning Techniques to Predict Soybean Plant Density Using UAV and Satellite-Based Remote Sensing. *Remote Sensing (Basel), 13*(13), 2548. doi:10.3390/rs13132548

Hafeez, A., Husain, M. A., Singh, S. P., Chauhan, A., Khan, M. T., Kumar, N., ... Soni, S. K. (2022). Implementation of drone technology for farm monitoring & pesticide spraying: A review. *Information Processing in Agriculture.*

Han, G., Hendry, R., & Ikeda, M. (2000). Assimilating TOPEX/POSEIDON derived tides in a primitive equation model over the Newfoundland Shelf. *Continental Shelf Research, 20*(1), 83–108. doi:10.1016/S0278-4343(99)00058-8

Hanifah, R., Supangkat, S. H., & Purwarianti, A. (2014). Twitter Information Extraction for Smart City. In *2014 International Conference on ICT For Smart Society (ICISS)* (pp. 295-299). 10.1109/ICTSS.2014.7013190

Han, J., Huang, Y., Liu, S., & Towey, K. (2020). Artificial intelligence for anti-money laundering: A review and extension. *Digital Finance, 2*(3), 211–239. doi:10.100742521-020-00023-1

Han, S., & Qiu, J. (2007). Corporate precautionary cash holdings. *Journal of Corporate Finance, 13*(1), 43–57. doi:10.1016/j.jcorpfin.2006.05.002

Hans, A. S. A., & Rao, S. (2021, March 31). A CNN-LSTM based deep neural networks for facial emotion detection in videos. *International Journal of Advances in Signal and Image Sciences, 7*(1), 11–20. doi:10.29284/IJASIS.7.1.2021.11-20

Haque, M. A., & Shoaib, M. (2023). E-Rupee-The digital currency in India: Challenges and prospects. *Bench Council Transactions on Benchmarks. Standards and Evaluations, 3,* 100107.

Harding, D. (2013). *The performance of garch option pricing models – an empirical study on Swedish omxs30 call options.* http: //hj.diva-portal.org/smash/get/diva2:637395/FULLTEXT01.pdf

Hardin, G. (1968, December 13). The Tragedy of the Commons. *Science, 162*(3859), 1243–1248. doi:10.1126cience.162.3859.1243

Harikaran, M., Boopathi, S., Gokulakannan, S., & Poonguzhali, M. (2023). Study on the Source of E-Waste Management and Disposal Methods. In *Sustainable Approaches and Strategies for E-Waste Management and Utilization* (pp. 39–60). IGI Global. doi:10.4018/978-1-6684-7573-7.ch003

Harris, T. (2013). Quantitative credit risk assessment using support vector machines: Broad versus narrow default definitions. *Expert Systems with Applications, 40*(11), 4404–4413. doi:10.1016/j.eswa.2013.01.044

Hassan, S. I., Alam, M. M., Illahi, U., Al Ghamdi, M. A., Almotiri, S. H., & Su'ud, M. M. (2021). A systematic review on monitoring and advanced control strategies in smart agriculture. *IEEE Access : Practical Innovations, Open Solutions*, *9*, 32517–32548. doi:10.1109/ACCESS.2021.3057865

Hazra, D. (2017). Monetary policy and alternative means of payment. *The Quarterly Review of Economics and Finance*, *65*(C), 378–387. doi:10.1016/j.qref.2016.11.002

Hema, N., Krishnamoorthy, N., Chavan, S. M., Kumar, N., Sabarimuthu, M., & Boopathi, S. (2023). A Study on an Internet of Things (IoT)-Enabled Smart Solar Grid System. In *Handbook of Research on Deep Learning Techniques for Cloud-Based Industrial IoT* (pp. 290–308). IGI Global. doi:10.4018/978-1-6684-8098-4.ch017

Henao, A., Piatkowski, D., Luckey, K. S., Nordback, K., Marshall, W. E., & Krizek, K. J. (2015). Sustainable transportation infrastructure investments and mode share changes: A 20-year background of Boulder, Colorado. *Transport Policy*, *37*, 64–71. doi:10.1016/j.tranpol.2014.09.012

Heston, S.L., & Nandi, S. (2000). A closed-form garch option valuation model. *The Review of Financial Studies, 13*(3), 585-625.

Hisakado, M., & Mori, S. (2021). Parameter estimation of default portfolios using the merton model and phase transition. *Physica A*, *563*, 125435. doi:10.1016/j.physa.2020.125435

Hochreiter, S., & Schmidhuber, J. (1997, November 1). Long-Short-Term Memory. *Neural Computation*, *9*(8), 1735–1780. doi:10.1162/neco.1997.9.8.1735 PMID:9377276

Huang, X., Liu, X., & Ren, Y. (2018). Enterprise credit risk evaluation based on neural network algorithm. *Cognitive Systems Research, 52*, 317–324.

Huang, Y., Yi, Q., Wei, G., Kang, J., Li, W., Feng, J., & Xie, K. (2018). Energy use, greenhouse gases emission and cost effectiveness of an integrated high– and low–temperature Fisher–Tropsch synthesis plant from a lifecycle viewpoint. *Applied Energy*, *228*, 1009–1019. doi:10.1016/j.apenergy.2018.07.007

Ibrahim, T. I., & Xu, C. Z. (2000). Neural Nets based Predictive Pre-fetching to Tolerate WWW Latency. *Proceedings of the 20th International Conference on Distributed Computing Systems.*

Ichihashi, S. (2020). Online Privacy and Information Disclosure by Consumer. *The American Economic Review*, *110*(2), 569–595. doi:10.1257/aer.20181052

Israr, A., Abro, G. E. M., Sadiq Ali Khan, M., Farhan, M., & Bin Mohd Zulkifli, S. U. A. (2021). Internet of things (IoT)-Enabled unmanned aerial vehicles for the inspection of construction sites: A vision and future directions. *Mathematical Problems in Engineering*, *2021*, 1–15. doi:10.1155/2021/9931112

Jabbar, A., Geebren, A., Hussain, Z., Dani, S., & Ul-Durar, S. (2023). Investigating individual privacy within CBDC: A privacy calculus perspective. *Research in International Business and Finance*, *64*, 101826. doi:10.1016/j.ribaf.2022.101826

Jabbar, M. A., Tiwari, S., & Ortiz-Rodriguez, F. (Eds.). (2023). *Smart Urban Computing Applications* (1st ed.). River Publishers.

Jackwerth, J. C., & Rubinstein, M. (1996). Recovering probability distributions from option prices. *The Journal of Finance*, *51*(5), 1611–1631. doi:10.1111/j.1540-6261.1996.tb05219.x

Jaczynski, M., & Trousse, B. (1998). WWW Assisted Browsing by Reusing Past Navigations of a Group of Users. *Proceedings of the Advances in Case-Based Reasoning, Forth European Workshop*, *1488*, 160-171.

Janardhana, K., Singh, V., Singh, S. N., Babu, T. R., Bano, S., & Boopathi, S. (2023). Utilization Process for Electronic Waste in Eco-Friendly Concrete: Experimental Study. In Sustainable Approaches and Strategies for E-Waste Management and Utilization (pp. 204–223). IGI Global.

Javaid, N. (2021). *Integration of context awareness in Internet of Agricultural Things*. Academic Press.

Javaid, M., Haleem, A., Khan, I. H., & Suman, R. (2023). Understanding the potential applications of Artificial Intelligence in Agriculture Sector. *Advanced Agrochem*, *2*(1), 15–30. doi:10.1016/j.aac.2022.10.001

Javed, A. R., Ahmed, W., Pandya, S., Maddikunta, P. K. R., Alazab, M., & Gadekallu, T. R. (2023). A Survey of Explainable Artificial Intelligence for Smart Cities. *Electronics (Basel)*, *12*(4), 1020. doi:10.3390/electronics12041020

Jeevanantham, Y. A., Saravanan, A., Vanitha, V., Boopathi, S., & Kumar, D. P. (2022). Implementation of Internet-of Things (IoT) in Soil Irrigation System. *IEEE Explore*, 1–5.

Jenkins, P. (2018, May 10). We Don't Take Cash: Is this the Future of Money? *The Financial Times*.

Jiang, W., & Yin, Z. (2015). Indoor Localization with a Signal Tree. *Proceedings of the 18th International Conference on Information Fusion*, 1724 - 1731.

Jiawei, H., Micheline, K., & Jian, P. (2006). *Data Mining Concepts and Techniques*. Pearson Education.

Jiménez, G., & Saurina, J. (2004). Collateral, type of lender and relationship banking as determinants of credit risk. *Journal of Banking & Finance*, *28*(9), 2191–2212. doi:10.1016/j.jbankfin.2003.09.002

Jobst, C., & Stix, H. (2017). *Doomed to disappear?* CEPR Discussion Paper Series: The surprising return of cash across time and across countries.

Johnson, S. A. (2018, February 26). Discussion of Change Needed Following the Shooting at Marjory Stoneman Douglas High School in Parkland Florida, A Brief Response. *Journal of Forensic Sciences & Criminal Investigation*, *7*(5). Advance online publication. doi:10.19080/JFSCI.2018.07.555725

Kalidindi, E. R., & Ramana Rao, G. V. (2022). The role of 108 GVK EMRI ambulance services in the management of behavioral emergencies in the state of Telangana. *Asian Journal of Psychiatry*, *70*, 103019. doi:10.1016/j.ajp.2022.103019 PMID:35151038

Kang, Y., Kong, N., Ou, M., Wang, Y., Xiao, Q., Mei, L., Liu, B., Chen, L., Zeng, X., & Ji, X. (2023). A novel cascaded energy conversion system inducing efficient and precise cancer therapy. *Bioactive Materials*, *20*, 663–676. doi:10.1016/j.bioactmat.2022.07.007 PMID:35891799

Kaplan, A. (2021). Cryptocurrency and corruption: auditing with blockchain. In *Auditing Ecosystem and Strategic Accounting in the Digital Era* (pp. 325–338). Springer. doi:10.1007/978-3-030-72628-7_15

Kapoor, A., Bhat, S. I., Shidnal, S., & Mehra, A. (2016, October). Implementation of IoT (Internet of Things) and Image processing in smart agriculture. In *2016 International Conference on Computation System and Information Technology for Sustainable Solutions (CSITSS)* (pp. 21-26). 10.1109/CSITSS.2016.7779434

Karoui, N. E., Jeanblanc-Picquè, M., & Shreve, S. E. (1998). Robustness of the black and scholes formula. *Mathematical Finance*, *8*(2), 93–126. doi:10.1111/1467-9965.00047

Karthik, S., Hemalatha, R., Aruna, R., Deivakani, M., Reddy, R. V. K., & Boopathi, S. (2023). Study on Healthcare Security System-Integrated Internet of Things (IoT). In Perspectives and Considerations on the Evolution of Smart Systems (pp. 342–362). IGI Global.

Kazmierkowski, M. (n.d.). *Automatic control of converter-fed drives.* Academia.Edu. Retrieved August 12, 2023, from https://www.academia.edu/download/36319799/PI_controller.PDF

Kenc, T., & Cevik, E. I. (2021). Estimating volatility clustering and variance risk premium effects on bank default indicators. *Review of Quantitative Finance and Accounting, 57*(4), 1373–1392. doi:10.100711156-021-00981-6

Khiaonarong, T., & Humphrey, D. (2019). *Cash use Across Countries and the Demand for Central Bank Digital Currency*. International Monetary Fund. doi:10.5089/9781484399606.001

Kim, S., Lee, M., & Shin, C. (2018). IoT- based strawberry disease prediction system for smart farming. *Sensors (Basel), 18*(11), 4051. doi:10.339018114051 PMID:30463363

Klein, M., & Schmidt, C. J. (2011). CASCADE, neutron detectors for highest count rates in combination with ASIC/FPGA based readout electronics. *Nuclear Instruments & Methods in Physics Research. Section A, Accelerators, Spectrometers, Detectors and Associated Equipment, 628*(1), 9–18. doi:10.1016/j.nima.2010.06.278

Knapp, G. F. (1905). *The State Theory of Money*. https://socialsciences.mcmaster.ca/econ/ugcm/3ll3/knapp/StateTheoryMoney.pdf

Konapala, G., Kao, S. C., Painter, S. L., & Lu, D. (2020, September 21). Machine learning-assisted hybrid models can improve streamflow simulation in diverse catchments across the conterminous US. *Environmental Research Letters, 15*(10), 104022. doi:10.1088/1748-9326/aba927

Kosala, R. & Blockeel, H. (2000). Web Mining Research: A Survey. *SIGKDD Explorations, 2*(1), 1-15.

Koshariya, A. K., Kalaiyarasi, D., Jovith, A. A., Sivakami, T., Hasan, D. S., & Boopathi, S. (2023). AI-Enabled IoT and WSN-Integrated Smart Agriculture System. In *Artificial Intelligence Tools and Technologies for Smart Farming and Agriculture Practices* (pp. 200–218). IGI Global. doi:10.4018/978-1-6684-8516-3.ch011

Koshariya, A. K., Khatoon, S., Marathe, A. M., Suba, G. M., Baral, D., & Boopathi, S. (2023). Agricultural Waste Management Systems Using Artificial Intelligence Techniques. In *AI-Enabled Social Robotics in Human Care Services* (pp. 236–258). IGI Global. doi:10.4018/978-1-6684-8171-4.ch009

Koskela, T.J., Heikkonen, & Kaski, K. (2003). Web cache optimization with nonlinear model using object feature. *Computer Networks Journal, 43*(6), 805-817.

Kou, G., Akdeniz, Ö. O., Dinçer, H., & Yüksel, S. (2021). Fintech investments in European banks: A hybrid IT2 fuzzy multidimensional decision-making approach. *Financial Innovation, 7*(1), 1–28. doi:10.118640854-021-00256-y PMID:35024283

Kroeger, T. M., Long, D. D. E., & Mogul, J. C. (1997). Exploring the Bounds of Web Latency Reduction from Caching and Pre-fetching. *Proceedings of the USENDC Symposium on Internet Technology and Systems*, 13-22.

Kumar, P., Sampath, B., Kumar, S., Babu, B. H., & Ahalya, N. (2023). Hydroponics, Aeroponics, and Aquaponics Technologies in Modern Agricultural Cultivation. In Trends, Paradigms, and Advances in Mechatronics Engineering (pp. 223–241). IGI Global.

Kumar, A. S., & Anandarao, S. (2019). Volatility spillover in crypto-currency markets: Some evidences from GARCH and wavelet analysis. *Physica A, 524*, 448–458. doi:10.1016/j.physa.2019.04.154

Kumar, A., & Minocha, V. K. (2001). A Discussion on Back-propagation Neural Network in Tidal-level Forecasting. Port, Coast., and Oc. Eng.

Kumar, I., Rawat, J., Mohd, N., & Husain, S. (2021). Opportunities of artificial intelligence and machine learning in the food industry. *Journal of Food Quality, 2021*, 1–10. doi:10.1155/2021/4535567

Kumar, R., Kumar, P., Tripathi, R., Gupta, G. P., Gadekallu, T. R., & Srivastava, G. (2021). SP2F: A secured privacy-preserving framework for smart agricultural Unmanned Aerial Vehicles. *Computer Networks, 187*, 107819. doi:10.1016/j.comnet.2021.107819

Kumar, S. A., & Ilango, P. (2018). The Impact of Wireless Sensor Network in the Field of Precision Agriculture: A Review. *Wireless Personal Communications, 98*(1), 685–698. doi:10.100711277-017-4890-z

Kumar, V. A. (2012). Money laundering: Concept, significance and its impact. *European Journal of Business and Management, 4*(2), 113–119.

Kumhof, M., & Noone, C. (2018). *Central bank digital currencies-design principles and balance sheet implications.* Staff Working Paper, Vol. 725, Bank of England.

Lai, J.-S., & Fang, Z. P. (1996). Multilevel converters-a new breed of power converters. *IEEE Transactions on Industry Applications, 32*(3), 509–517. doi:10.1109/28.502161

Lan, B., Bressan, S., Ooi, B. C., & Tan, K. L. (2000). Rule-Assisted Pre-fetching in Web-Server Caching. *Proceedings of the 9th International Conference on Information and Knowledge Management*, 504-511.

Lander, E. S., Linton, L. M., Birren, B., Nusbaum, C., Zody, M. C., Baldwin, J., Devon, K., Dewar, K., Doyle, M., FitzHugh, W., Funke, R., Gage, D., Harris, K., Heaford, A., Howland, J., Kann, L., Lehoczky, J., LeVine, R., McEwan, P., ... Morgan, M. J. (2001, February 15). Initial sequencing and analysis of the human genome. *Nature, 409*(6822), 860–921. doi:10.1038/35057062 PMID:11237011

Landoni, G., Biselli, C., Maj, G., & Zangrillo, A. (2007). Faster rings in the survival chain: Mobile phones could improve the response to the dedicated emergency call system. *Resuscitation, 75*(3), 547. doi:10.1016/j.resuscitation.2007.05.022 PMID:17629388

Le Provost, C., Lyard, F., Molines, J. M., Genco, M. L., & Rabilloud, F. (1998). A hydrodynamic ocean tide model improved by assimilating a satellite altimeter-derived data set. *Journal of Geophysical Research, 103*(C3), 5513–5529. doi:10.1029/97JC01733

Le Tran, V., & Leirvik, T. (2020). Efficiency in the markets of crypto-currencies. *Finance Research Letters, 35*, 101382. doi:10.1016/j.frl.2019.101382

Lee, J., Edil, T., & Benson, C. (2013). *Building environmentally and economically sustainable transportation infrastructure: green highway rating system.* Ascelibrary.Org. https://ascelibrary.org/doi/abs/10.1061/(ASCE)CO.1943-7862.0000742

Lee, D., Yan, L., & Wang, Y. (2021). A Global Perspective on Central Bank Digital Currency. *China Economic Journal, 14*(1), 52–66. doi:10.1080/17538963.2020.1870279

Lee, H. K., An, B. S., & Kim, E. J. (2009). Adaptive Pre-fetching Scheme Using Web Log Mining in Cluster-Based Web Systems. *IEEE International Conference on Web Services (ICWS)*, 903-910.

Lee, S. S. (2012). Jumps and information flow in financial markets. *Review of Financial Studies, 25*(2), 439–479. doi:10.1093/rfs/hhr084

Lee, T. L. (2004). Back-propagation neural network for long-term tidal predictions. *Ocean Engineering, 31*(2), 225–238. doi:10.1016/S0029-8018(03)00115-X

Lee, T. L., & Jeng, D. S. (2002). Application of artificial neural networks in tide-forecasting. *Ocean Engineering*, *29*(9), 1003–1022. doi:10.1016/S0029-8018(01)00068-3

Lee, T. L., Tsai, C. P., Jeng, D. S., & Shieh, R. J. (2002). Neural network for prediction and supplement of tidal record in Taichung harbor. *Advances in Engineering Software*, *33*(6), 329–338. doi:10.1016/S0965-9978(02)00043-1

Lehdonvirta, V., Soma, H., Ito, H., Yamabe, T., Kimura, H., & Nakajima, T. (2009). Ubipay: Minimizing transaction costs with smart mobile payments. In *Proceedings of the6th international conference on mobile technology, application & systems*. ACM.

Lemmon, H. (1990). Comax: An expert system for cotton crop management. *Computer Science in Economics and Management*, *3*(2), 177–185. doi:10.1007/BF00436714

Liakos, K. G., Busato, P., Moshou, D., Pearson, S., & Bochtis, D. (2018). Machine Learning in Agriculture: A Review. *Sensors (Basel)*, *18*(8), 2674. doi:10.339018082674 PMID:30110960

Liao, S. L., & Huang, H. H. (2005). Pricing black–scholes options with correlated interest rate risk and credit risk: An extension. *Quantitative Finance*, *5*(5), 443–457. doi:10.1080/14697680500362718

Li, K. L., & Wong, H. Y. (2008). Structural models of corporate bond pricing with maximum likelihood estimation. *Journal of Empirical Finance*, *15*(4), 751–777. doi:10.1016/j.jempfin.2008.01.001

Lin, H. C., & Chiu, S. C. (2017). Trade off on corporate cash holdings: A theoretical and empirical analysis. *Review of Quantitative Finance and Accounting*, *49*(3), 727–763. doi:10.100711156-016-0606-9

Liu, J., Sockin, M., & Xiong, W. (2021). *Data Privacy and Consumer Vulnerability*. Princeton University Working Paper.

Liu, Q., Li, Q., Zhu, Z., Ye, T., & Ma, X. (2021). *Inspecting the process of bank credit rating via visual analytics. In 2021 IEEE Visualization Conference (VIS)*. IEEE. doi:10.1109/VIS49827.2021.9623312

Liu, X., Zhang, J., Chen, Y., Sun, S., & Wu, L. (2021). Soil nutrient prediction using machine learning models in a highly variable arid environment. *The Science of the Total Environment*, *772*, 144773. doi:10.1016/j.scitotenv.2021.144773

Livak, K. J., & Schmittgen, T. D. (2001, December). *Analysis of Relative Gene Expression Data Using Real-Time Quantitative PCR and the 2CT Method Methods*. doi:10.1006/meth.2001.1262

Loon, T. S., & Bharghavan, V. (1997). Alleviating the Latency and Bandwidth Problems in WWW Browsing. *Proceedings of the USENIX Symposium on Internet Technologies and Systems (USITS)*.

Losi, A., Mancarella, P., & Vicino, A. (2015). *Integration of demand response into the electricity chain: challenges, opportunities, and Smart Grid solutions*. https://books.google.com/books?hl=en&lr=&id=P2ThCgAAQBAJ&oi=fnd&pg=PP1&dq=Smart+Grid+Integration+and+Demand+Response+&ots=8oTsImjU57&sig=CQ151wzFZQkD0cLQc4TRj8AI2hc

Lucey, B. M., Vigne, S. A., Yarovaya, L., & Wang, Y. (2022). The cryptocurrency uncertainty index. *Finance Research Letters*, *45*(C), 102147. doi:10.1016/j.frl.2021.102147

Maguluri, L. P., Ananth, J., Hariram, S., Geetha, C., Bhaskar, A., & Boopathi, S. (2023). Smart Vehicle-Emissions Monitoring System Using Internet of Things (IoT). In Handbook of Research on Safe Disposal Methods of Municipal Solid Wastes for a Sustainable Environment (pp. 191–211). IGI Global.

Maharjan, L., & Inoue, S. (n.d.). *State-of-charge (SOC)-balancing control of a battery energy storage system based on a cascade PWM converter.* Ieeexplore.Ieee.Org. Retrieved August 12, 2023, from https://ieeexplore.ieee.org/abstract/document/5071730/

Maharjan, L., Inoue, S., & Akagi, H. (2008). A Transformerless Energy Storage System Based on a Cascade Multilevel PWM Converter With Star Configuration. *IEEE Transactions on Industry Applications*, *44*(5), 1621–1630. doi:10.1109/TIA.2008.2002180

Maharjan, L., Yamagishi, T., Akagi, H., & Asakura, J. (2010). Fault-Tolerant Operation of a Battery-Energy-Storage System Based on a Multilevel Cascade PWM Converter With Star Configuration. *IEEE Transactions on Power Electronics*, *25*(9), 2386–2396. doi:10.1109/TPEL.2010.2047407

Maheswari, B. U., Imambi, S. S., Hasan, D., Meenakshi, S., Pratheep, V., & Boopathi, S. (2023). Internet of Things and Machine Learning-Integrated Smart Robotics. In Global Perspectives on Robotics and Autonomous Systems: Development and Applications (pp. 240–258). IGI Global. doi:10.4018/978-1-6684-7791-5.ch010

Makarynskyy, O. (2004). Improving wave predictions with artificial neural networks. *Ocean Engineering*, *31*(5-6), 709–724. doi:10.1016/j.oceaneng.2003.05.003

Maraveas, C., Asteris, P. G., Arvanitis, K. G., Bartzanas, T., & Loukatos, D. (2023). Application of bio and nature-inspired algorithms in agricultural engineering. *Archives of Computational Methods in Engineering*, *30*(3), 1979–2012. doi:10.100711831-022-09857-x

Markatos, E. P., & Chronaki, C. E. (1998). A Top-10 Approach to Pre-fetching on the Web. *Proceedings of INET Geneva,* 276-290.

Mark, R., & Anya, G. (2019). Ethics of Using Smart City AI and Big Data: The Case of Four Large European Cities. *The ORBIT Journal*, *2*(2), 1–36. doi:10.29297/orbit.v2i2.110

Martiniello, P. (1988). Development of a database computer management system for retrieval on varietal field evaluation and plant breeding information in agriculture. *Computers and Electronics in Agriculture*, *2*(3), 183–192. doi:10.1016/0168-1699(88)90023-3

Mat, I., Kassim, M. R. M., Harun, A. N., & Yusoff, I. M. (2018, November). Smart agriculture using internet of things. In *2018 IEEE conference on open systems (ICOS)* (pp. 54-59). IEEE.

Matsumoto, K., Takanezawa, T., & Ooe, M. (2000). Ocean tide model developed by assimilating TOPEX/POSEIDON altimetry data into hydrodynamical model: A global and a regional model around Japan. *Journal of Oceanography*, *56*(5), 567–581. doi:10.1023/A:1011157212596

McKinion, J. M., & Lemmon, H. E. (1985). Expert systems for agriculture. *Computers and Electronics in Agriculture*, *1*(1), 31–40. doi:10.1016/0168-1699(85)90004-3

Menon, R. (2016, August 19). *An Electronic Payments Society*. Speech at Sim Kee Boon Institute Conference on FinTech and Financial Inclusion, Singapore.

Miao, B., Lin, J., Li, H., Liu, C., Li, B., Zhu, X., & Yang, J. (2020). Day-Ahead Energy Trading Strategy of Regional Integrated Energy System Considering Energy Cascade Utilization. *IEEE Access : Practical Innovations, Open Solutions*, *8*, 138021–138035. doi:10.1109/ACCESS.2020.3007224

Mihail, B., Ionel-Sorinel, V., Madalina, T., Nadia, C., & Madlena, N. (2021). Analysis of Abusive 112 Emergency Calls in Romania. *Journal of Administrative Sciences and Technology*, *2021*, 471463. Advance online publication. doi:10.5171/2021.471463

Mishra, A., Sharma, S. K., & Pandey, A. (2017). Predicting soil organic carbon stock using geostatistical techniques and remote sensing indices. *Ecological Indicators*, *78*, 400–412. doi:10.1016/j.ecolind.2017.03.045

Misra, N. N., Dixit, Y., Al-Mallahi, A., Bhullar, M. S., Upadhyay, R., & Martynenko, A. (2020). IoT, big data, and artificial intelligence in agriculture and food industry. *IEEE Internet of Things Journal*, *9*(9), 6305–6324. doi:10.1109/JIOT.2020.2998584

Mitchell-Innes, A. (1913). What is money. *Bank Law Journal*, (May), 377–408.

Mitzner, T. L., Boron, J. B., Fausset, C. B., Adams, A. E., Charness, N., Czaja, S. J., Dijkstra, K., Fisk, A. D., Rogers, W. A., & Sharit, J. (2010). Older adults talk technology: Technology usage and attitudes. *Computers in Human Behavior*, *26*(6), 1710–1721. doi:10.1016/j.chb.2010.06.020 PMID:20967133

Mobasher, B., Dai, H., Luo, T., & Nakagawa, M. (2002). Discovery and Evaluation of Aggregate Usage Profiles for Web Personalization. *Data Mining and Knowledge Discovery*, *6*(1), 61–82. doi:10.1023/A:1013232803866

Mohamed, E. S., Belal, A. A., Abd-Elmabod, S. K., El-Shirbeny, M. A., Gad, A., & Zahran, M. B. (2021). Smart farming for improving agricultural management. *The Egyptian Journal of Remote Sensing and Space Sciences*, *24*(3), 971–981. doi:10.1016/j.ejrs.2021.08.007

Mohan, R. (2022, December 5). *King Cash's castle*. The Business Standard.

Mohanty, A., Venkateswaran, N., Ranjit, P., Tripathi, M. A., & Boopathi, S. (2023). Innovative Strategy for Profitable Automobile Industries: Working Capital Management. In Handbook of Research on Designing Sustainable Supply Chains to Achieve a Circular Economy (pp. 412–428). IGI Global.

Morgan, J. (2022). Systemic stable coin and the defensive case for Central Bank Digital Currency: A critique of the Bank of England's framing. *Research in International Business and Finance*, *62*, 101716. doi:10.1016/j.ribaf.2022.101716

Moss. (2017). The Three-Digit Emergency Number and the Transnational Politics of Welfare Activism, 1937–1979. *Journal of Social History*, *52*(2).

Mu, C., Ding, T., Qu, M., Zhou, Q., Li, F., & Shahidehpour, M. (2020). Decentralized optimization operation for the multiple integrated energy systems with energy cascade utilization. *Applied Energy*, *280*, 115989. doi:10.1016/j.apenergy.2020.115989

Munk, W. H., & Cartwright, D. E. (1996). Tidal spectroscopy and prediction. *Philos. Trans. R. Soc. Lond. Ser. A*, *259*, 533–581.

Murthy, S. (2011). Market-implied risk-neutral probabilities, actual probabilities, credit risk and news. *The Journal of Economic Perspectives*, *18*, 3–24.

Nagi, G. K., Minhas, A. K., Gaur, S., Jain, P., & Mandal, S. (2021). Integration of Algal Biofuels With Bioremediation Coupled Industrial Commodities Towards Cost-Effectiveness. *Frontiers in Energy Research*, *9*, 735141. Advance online publication. doi:10.3389/fenrg.2021.735141

Oberti, R., Marchi, M., Tirelli, P., Calcante, A., Iriti, M., Tona, E., Hočevar, M., Baur, J., Pfaff, J., Schütz, C., & Ulbrich, H. (2016). Selective spraying of grapevines for disease control using a modular agricultural robot. *Biosystems Engineering*, *146*, 203–215. doi:10.1016/j.biosystemseng.2015.12.004

Olmos, R., Tabik, S., & Herrera, F. (2018, January). Automatic handgun detection alarm in videos using deep learning. *Neurocomputing*, *275*, 66–72. doi:10.1016/j.neucom.2017.05.012

Ordouei, M., Broumandnia, A., Banirostam, T., & Gilani, A. (2023). Optimization of energy consumption in smart city using reinforcement learning algorithm. *International Journal of Nonlinear Analysis and Applications*.

Ounejjar, Y., Al-Haddad, K., & Grégoire, L.-A. (2011). Packed U cells multilevel converter topology: Theoretical study and experimental validation. *IEEE Transactions on Industrial Electronics, 58*(4), 1294–1306. Advance online publication. doi:10.1109/TIE.2010.2050412

Pacheco-Torgal, F., Granqvist, C.-G., Vanoli, G. P., Bianco, N., & Kurnitski, J. (2017). *Cost-effective energy efficient building retrofitting: materials, technologies, optimization and case studies.* https://books.google.com/books?hl=en&lr=&id=aWeyDAAAQBAJ&oi=fnd&pg=PP1&dq=Energy-Efficient+Building+Retrofitting+&ots=XAoaAY_zL7&sig=lbu4j6svowujgI9GPp_V1AQLV_I

Padmanabhan, V. N., & Mogul, J. C. (1996). Using Predictive Pre-fetching to Improve World Wide Web Latency. *Computer Communication Review, 26*(3), 23–36. doi:10.1145/235160.235164

Pallis, G., Vakali, A., & Pokorny, J. (2008). A Clustering-Based Pre-Fetching Scheme on A Web Cache Environment. ACM Journal Computers and Electrical Engineering, 34(4).

Pandey & Dani. (2014). Android Mobile Application Build on Eclipse. *International Journal of Scientific and Research Publications, 4*(2).

Papastergiou, M. (2009, January). Digital game-based learning in high school Computer science education: Impact on educational effectiveness and student motivation. *Computers & Education, 52*(1), 1–12. doi:10.1016/j.compedu.2008.06.004

Parasuraman, K., Anandan, U., & Anbarasan, A. (2021, February). IoT based smart agriculture automation in artificial intelligence. In *2021 Third International Conference on Intelligent Communication Technologies and Virtual Mobile Networks (ICICV)* (pp. 420-427). 10.1109/ICICV50876.2021.9388578

Parlour, C. A., Rajan, U., & Walden, J. (2020). *Payment system externalities and the role of central bank digital currency.* Working Paper.

Patterson, M. (2018). *Crypto's 80% plunge is now worse than the Dot-Com crash.* Bloomberg.

Pavković, D., Lobrović, M., Hrgetić, M., & Komljenović, A. (2016). A design of cascade control system and adaptive load compensator for battery/ultracapacitor hybrid energy storage-based direct current microgrid. *Energy Conversion and Management, 114*, 154–167. doi:10.1016/j.enconman.2016.02.005

Pei, C., & Irani, S. (1997). Cost-Aware WWW Proxy Caching Algorithms. *Proceedings of the USENIX Symposium on Internet Technologies and Systems*, 193-206.

Personal Characteristics of Military Personnel and Law Enforcement Officers that Determine Psychological Readiness for Duty with Firearm. (2018). LEX RUSSICA (РУССКИЙ ЗАКОН). doi:10.17803/1729-5920.2018.142.9.119-128

Pham, T. V., Jeon, C. H., & Han, D. (2019). A comparative study of machine learning techniques for predicting soil water content. *Journal of Hydrology (Amsterdam), 575*, 22–33. doi:10.1016/j.jhydrol.2019.05.059

Pirolli, P., Pitkow, J., & Ramna, R. (1996). Extracting Usable Structure from the Web. CHI – 96, 118-125.

Place, B. J., & Field, J. A. (2012, June 15). Identification of Novel Fluorochemicals in Aqueous Film-Forming Foams Used by the US Military. *Environmental Science & Technology, 46*(13), 7120–7127. doi:10.1021/es301465n PMID:22681548

Png, I., & Tan, C. (2020). Privacy, Trust in Banks and Use of Cash. *Monetary Authority of Singapore. Special Feature, C*, 109–116.

Podlipnig, S., & Boszormenyi, L. (2003). A Survey of Web Cache Replacement Strategies. *ACM Computing Surveys, 35*(4), 374–398. doi:10.1145/954339.954341

Prabu, A. V., Kumar, G. S., Rajasoundaran, S., Malla, P. P., Routray, S., & Mukherjee, A. (2022). Internet of things-based deeply proficient monitoring and protection system for crop field. *Expert Systems: International Journal of Knowledge Engineering and Neural Networks, 39*(5), e12876. doi:10.1111/exsy.12876

Pramila, P., Amudha, S., Saravanan, T., Sankar, S. R., Poongothai, E., & Boopathi, S. (2023). Design and Development of Robots for Medical Assistance: An Architectural Approach. In Contemporary Applications of Data Fusion for Advanced Healthcare Informatics (pp. 260–282). IGI Global.

Qazi, S., Khawaja, B. A., & Farooq, Q. U. (2022). *IoT-equipped and AI-enabled next generation smart agriculture: A critical review, current challenges and future trends*. Academic Press.

Rahamathunnisa, U., Sudhakar, K., Murugan, T. K., Thivaharan, S., Rajkumar, M., & Boopathi, S. (2023). Cloud Computing Principles for Optimizing Robot Task Offloading Processes. In *AI-Enabled Social Robotics in Human Care Services* (pp. 188–211). IGI Global. doi:10.4018/978-1-6684-8171-4.ch007

Rajini, N. S., Ramamoorthy, S., Rammohan, S. R., Rajakumar, P., & Niveditha, V. (2020). Reliability of cloud services provided to non-banking financial institutions. *International Journal of Control and Automation, 13*, 165–172165.

Raj, M., Gupta, S., Chamola, V., Elhence, A., Garg, T., Atiquzzaman, M., & Niyato, D. (2021). A survey on the role of Internet of Things for adopting and promoting Agriculture 4.0. *Journal of Network and Computer Applications, 187*, 103107. doi:10.1016/j.jnca.2021.103107

Ramesh, M., & Rajeshkumar, L. (2021). Technological advances in analyzing of soil chemistry. *Applied soil chemistry*, 61-78.

Ramos, P. J., Prieto, F. A., Montoya, E. C., & Oliveros, C. E. (2017). Automatic fruit count on coffee branches using-computer vision. *Computers and Electronics in Agriculture, 137*, 9–22. doi:10.1016/j.compag.2017.03.010

Ramudu, K., Mohan, V. M., Jyothirmai, D., Prasad, D., Agrawal, R., & Boopathi, S. (2023). Machine Learning and Artificial Intelligence in Disease Prediction: Applications, Challenges, Limitations, Case Studies, and Future Directions. In Contemporary Applications of Data Fusion for Advanced Healthcare Informatics (pp. 297–318). IGI Global.

Rathore, N. S. (2021). Application of artificial intelligence in agriculture including horticulture. *International Journal of Innovative Horticulture, 10*(2), 138–141. doi:10.5958/2582-2527.2021.00013.0

Ray, R. D. (1998). Spectral analysis of highly aliased sea-level signals. *Journal of Geophysical Research, 103*(C11), 24991–25003. doi:10.1029/98JC02545

Reddy, M. A., Reddy, B. M., Mukund, C., Venneti, K., Preethi, D., & Boopathi, S. (2023). Social Health Protection During the COVID-Pandemic Using IoT. In *The COVID-19 Pandemic and the Digitalization of Diplomacy* (pp. 204–235). IGI Global. doi:10.4018/978-1-7998-8394-4.ch009

Ren, S., He, K., Girshick, R., & Sun, J. (2017, June 1). Faster R CNN. *IEEE Transactions on Pattern Analysis and Machine Intelligence, 39*(6), 1137–1149. doi:10.1109/TPAMI.2016.2577031 PMID:27295650

Renwick, R., & Gleasure, R. (2021). Those who control the code control the rules: How different perspectives of privacy are being written into the code of blockchain systems. *Journal of Information Technology, 36*(1), 16–38. doi:10.1177/0268396220944406

Retrofitting. (n.d.). *Introduction to cost-effective energy-efficient building retrofitting.* Elsevier. Retrieved August 12, 2023, from https://www.sciencedirect.com/science/article/pii/B9780081011287000010

Reviews. (2013). *Demand response and smart grids—A survey.* Elsevier. doi:10.1016/j.rser.2013.10.022

Rick, S. I. (2018). Tightwads and spendthrifts: An interdisciplinary review. *Financial Planning Review*, *1*(1–2), e1010. doi:10.1002/cfp2.1010

Roach, J., Virkar, R., Drake, C., & Weaver, M. (1987). An expert system for helping apple growers. *Computers and Electronics in Agriculture*, *2*(2), 97–108. doi:10.1016/0168-1699(87)90020-2

Rodriguez, J., Bernet, S., Wu, B., Pontt, J. O., & Kouro, S. (2007). Multilevel Voltage-Source-Converter Topologies for Industrial Medium-Voltage Drives. *IEEE Transactions on Industrial Electronics*, *54*(6), 2930–2945. doi:10.1109/TIE.2007.907044

Rogof, K., & Scazzero, J. (2021). *COVID Cash.* CMFA Working Paper 002.

Romero, D., & Salamea, C. (2019, July 24). Convolutional Models for the Detection of Firearms in Surveillance Videos. *Applied Sciences (Basel, Switzerland)*, *9*(15), 2965. doi:10.3390/app9152965

Ronn, E. I., & Verma, A. K. (1986). Pricing risk-adjusted deposit insurance: An option-based model. *The Journal of Finance*, *41*(4), 871–895. doi:10.1111/j.1540-6261.1986.tb04554.x

Roosevelt, T. S. (1995, November 15). Preventing Firearm Violence. *Annals of Internal Medicine*, *123*(10), 813. doi:10.7326/0003-4819-123-10-199511150-00033 PMID:7574217

Saadane, R., Chehri, A., & Jeon, S. (2022). AI-based modeling and data-driven evaluation for smart farming-oriented big data architecture using IoT with energy harvesting capabilities. *Sustainable Energy Technologies and Assessments*, *52*, 102093. doi:10.1016/j.seta.2022.102093

Saha, A. K., Saha, J., Ray, R., Sircar, S., Dutta, S., Chattopadhyay, S. P., & Saha, H. N. (2018, January). IOT-based drone for improvement of crop quality in agricultural field. In *2018 IEEE 8th Annual Computing and Communication Workshop and Conference (CCWC)* (pp. 612-615). IEEE.

Sahoo, B. P. S. & Rath. (2012). Integrating GPS, GSM and Cellular Phone for Location Tracking and Monitoring. *Proceedings of the International Conference on Geospatial Technologies and Applications, Geomatrix'*12.

Samikannu, R., Koshariya, A. K., Poornima, E., Ramesh, S., Kumar, A., & Boopathi, S. (2022). Sustainable Development in Modern Aquaponics Cultivation Systems Using IoT Technologies. In *Human Agro-Energy Optimization for Business and Industry* (pp. 105–127). IGI Global.

Sampath, B., Sasikumar, C., & Myilsamy, S. (2023). Application of TOPSIS Optimization Technique in the Micro-Machining Process. In Trends, Paradigms, and Advances in Mechatronics Engineering (pp. 162–187). IGI Global.

Sampath, B., Pandian, M., Deepa, D., & Subbiah, R. (2022). Operating parameters prediction of liquefied petroleum gas refrigerator using simulated annealing algorithm. *AIP Conference Proceedings*, *2460*(1), 070003. doi:10.1063/5.0095601

Sankar, K. M., Booba, B., & Boopathi, S. (2023). Smart Agriculture Irrigation Monitoring System Using Internet of Things. In *Contemporary Developments in Agricultural Cyber-Physical Systems* (pp. 105–121). IGI Global. doi:10.4018/978-1-6684-7879-0.ch006

Santangeli, A., Chen, Y., Kluen, E., Chirumamilla, R., Tiainen, J., & Loehr, J. (2020). Integrating drone-borne thermal imaging with artificial intelligence to locate bird nests on agricultural land. *Scientific Reports*, *10*(1), 1–8. doi:10.103841598-020-67898-3 PMID:32665596

Sarker, E., Halder, P., Seyedmahmoudian, M., Jamei, E., Horan, B., Mekhilef, S., & Stojcevski, A. (2021). Progress on the demand side management in smart grid and optimization approaches. *International Journal of Energy Research*, *45*(1), 36–64. doi:10.1002/er.5631

Sasikala, D., & Sharma, K. V. (2022). Optimization of ML techniques with Gaussian Quadrature Numerical Analysis for Precision Agricultural Augmentation. *Journal of Soft Computing Paradigm, 4*(2), 113–120. doi:10.36548/jscp.2022.2.006

Sathish, T., Sunagar, P., Singh, V., Boopathi, S., Al-Enizi, A. M., Pandit, B., Gupta, M., & Sehgal, S. S. (2023). Characteristics estimation of natural fibre reinforced plastic composites using deep multi-layer perceptron (MLP) technique. *Chemosphere, 337*, 139346. doi:10.1016/j.chemosphere.2023.139346 PMID:37379988

Sathiyamoorthi, V., & Murali Bhaskaran, V. (2011b). Data Pre-Processing Techniques for Pre-Fetching and Caching of Web Data through Proxy Server. *International Journal of Computer Science and Network Security, 11*(11), 92-98.

Sathiyamoorthi, V. (2016). A Novel Cache Replacement Policy for Web Proxy Caching System Using Web Usage Mining. *International Journal of Information Technology and Web Engineering, 11*(2), 1–12. doi:10.4018/IJITWE.2016040101

Sathiyamoorthi, V., & Murali Bhaskaran, V. (2010a). Data Preparation Techniques for Mining World Wide Web through Web Usage Mining-An Approach. *International Journal of Recent Trends in Engineering, 2*(4), 1–4.

Sathiyamoorthi, V., & Murali Bhaskaran, V. (2010b). Data mining for intelligent enterprise resource planning system. *International Journal of Recent Trends in Engineering, 2*(3), 1–4.

Sathiyamoorthi, V., & Murali Bhaskaran, V. (2011a). Improving the Performance of Web Page Retrieval through Pre-Fetching and Caching. *European Journal of Scientific Research, 66*(2), 207–217.

Sathiyamoorthi, V., & Murali Bhaskaran, V. (2012). Optimizing the Web Cache performance by Clustering Based Pre-Fetching Technique Using Modified ART1. *International Journal of Computer Application, 44*(1), 51–60.

Sathiyamoorthi, V., & Murali Bhaskaran, V. (2013). Novel Approaches for Integrating MART1 Clustering Based Pre-Fetching Technique with Web Caching. *International Journal of Information Technology and Web Engineering, 8*(2), 18–32. doi:10.4018/jitwe.2013040102

Schaefer, S. M., & Strebulaev, I. A. (2008). Structural models of credit risk are useful: Evidence from hedge ratios on corporate bonds. *Journal of Financial Economics, 90*(1), 1–19. doi:10.1016/j.jfineco.2007.10.006

Selgin, G. (2021). Central bank digital currency as a potential source of financial instability. *The Cato Journal*, 333–341.

Selvakumar, S., Adithe, S., Isaac, J. S., Pradhan, R., Venkatesh, V., & Sampath, B. (2023). A Study of the Printed Circuit Board (PCB) E-Waste Recycling Process. In Sustainable Approaches and Strategies for E-Waste Management and Utilization (pp. 159–184). IGI Global.

Sengeni, D., Padmapriya, G., Imambi, S. S., Suganthi, D., Suri, A., & Boopathi, S. (2023). Biomedical Waste Handling Method Using Artificial Intelligence Techniques. In *Handbook of Research on Safe Disposal Methods of Municipal Solid Wastes for a Sustainable Environment* (pp. 306–323). IGI Global. doi:10.4018/978-1-6684-8117-2.ch022

Shaikh, P. H., Shaikh, F., Sahito, A. A., Uqaili, M. A., & Umrani, Z. (2017). An Overview of the Challenges for Cost-Effective and Energy-Efficient Retrofits of the Existing Building Stock. In *Cost-Effective Energy Efficient Building Retrofitting* (pp. 257–278). Elsevier. doi:10.1016/B978-0-08-101128-7.00009-5

Shaikh, T. A., Mir, W. A., Rasool, T., & Sofi, S. (2022). Machine Learning for Smart Agriculture and Precision Farming: Towards Making the Fields Talk. *Archives of Computational Methods in Engineering, 29*(7), 4557–4597. doi:10.100711831-022-09761-4

Shaikh, T. A., Rasool, T., & Lone, F. R. (2022). Towards leveraging the role of machine learning and artificial intelligence in precision agriculture and smart farming. *Computers and Electronics in Agriculture, 198*, 107119. doi:10.1016/j.compag.2022.107119

Shan, S., Tian, J., Chen, B., Zhang, Y., & Zhou, Z. (2023). Theoretical and technical analysis of the photo-thermal energy cascade conversion for fuel with high-temperature combustion. *Energy, 263*, 125990. doi:10.1016/j.energy.2022.125990

Shao, S., Pipattanasomporn, M., & Rahman, S. (2012). Grid integration of electric vehicles and demand response with customer choice. *IEEE Transactions on Smart Grid, 3*(1), 543–550. doi:10.1109/TSG.2011.2164949

Sharma & Brandler. (2014). Emergency Medical Services in India: The Present and Future. *Prehospital and Disaster Medicine, 29*(3), 1-4. doi:10.1017/S1049023X14000296

Sharma, A., Jain, A., Gupta, P., & Chowdary, V. (2020). Machine learning applications for precision agriculture: A comprehensive review. *IEEE Access : Practical Innovations, Open Solutions, 9*, 4843–4873. doi:10.1109/ACCESS.2020.3048415

ShokrollahiF. (2018). *Pricing european option with the short rate under subdiffusive fractional brownian motion regime.* arXiv:1805.00792.

Sinelnikova-Muryleva, E. V. (2020). Central Bank Digital Currencies: Potential Risks and Benefits. *Voprosy Ekonomiki, 4*(4), 147–159. doi:10.32609/0042-8736-2020-4-147-159

Singh, G., Singh, A., & Kaur, G. (2021). Role of artificial intelligence and the internet of things in agriculture. In Artificial Intelligence to Solve Pervasive Internet of Things Issues (pp. 317-330). doi:10.1016/B978-0-12-818576-6.00016-2

Singh, S., & Jain, P. (2022). Applications of artificial intelligence for the development of sustainable agriculture. In Agro-biodiversity and Agri-ecosystem Management (pp. 303-322). doi:10.1007/978-981-19-0928-3_16

Singh, R. K., Berkvens, R., & Weyn, M. (2021). AgriFusion: An architecture for IoT and emerging technologies based on a precision agriculture survey. *IEEE Access : Practical Innovations, Open Solutions, 9*, 136253–136283. doi:10.1109/ACCESS.2021.3116814

Sitaram, K. A., Ankush, K. R., Anant, K. N., & Raghunath, B. R. (2018, December). Iot based smart management of poultry farm and electricity generation. In *2018 IEEE International Conference on Computational Intelligence and Computing Research (ICCIC)* (pp. 1-4). 10.1109/ICCIC.2018.8782308

Srbinovska, M., Gavrovski, C., Dimcev, V., Krkoleva, A., & Borozan, V. (2015). Environmental parameters monitoring in precision agriculture using wireless sensor networks. *Journal of Cleaner Production, 88*, 297–307. doi:10.1016/j.jclepro.2014.04.036

Srivastava, J., Cooley, R., Deshpande, M., & Tan, P. N. (2000). Web Usage Mining: Discovery and Applications of Usage Patterns from Web Data. *SIGKDD Explorations, 1*(2), 12–23. doi:10.1145/846183.846188

Srouji, J. (2020). Digital payments, the cashless economy, and financial inclusion in the United Arab Emirates: Why is everyone still transacting in cash? *Journal of Risk and Financial Management, 13*(11), 1–10. doi:10.3390/jrfm13110260

Steffen, J., Lengsfeld, S., Jung, M., Ponick, B., Gracia, M. H., Spagnolo, A., Klöpzig, M., Schleicher, K., Schäfer, K., Russo, A., Mazza, A., Musumeci, S., & Pons, E. (2021). *Design of a medium voltage generator with dc-cascade for high power wind energy conversion systems.* Mdpi.Com. doi:10.3390/en14113106

Stone, N. D., & Toman, T. W. (1989). A dynamically linked expert-database system for decision support in Texas cotton production. *Computers and Electronics in Agriculture, 4*(2), 139–148. doi:10.1016/0168-1699(89)90031-8

Subeesh, A., & Mehta, C. R. (2021). Automation and digitization of agriculture using artificial intelligence and internet of things. *Artificial Intelligence in Agriculture, 5*, 278–291. doi:10.1016/j.aiia.2021.11.004

Subha, S., Inbamalar, T., Komala, C., Suresh, L. R., Boopathi, S., & Alaskar, K. (2023). A Remote Health Care Monitoring system using internet of medical things (IoMT). *IEEE Explore*, 1–6.

Su, K., Li, J., & Fu, H. (2011). Smart city and the applications. In *2011 International Conference on Electronics, Communications and Control (ICECC)* (pp. 1028-1031). 10.1109/ICECC.2011.6066743

Suresh Babu, C. V. (2022). *Artificial Intelligence and Expert Systems* (1st ed.). Anniyappa Publications.

Suresh Babu, C. V., Mahalashmi, J., Vidhya, A., Nila Devagi, S., & Bowshith, G. (2023). Save Soil Through Machine Learning. In M. Habib (Ed.), *Global Perspectives on Robotics and Autonomous Systems: Development and Applications* (pp. 345–362). IGI Global., doi:10.4018/978-1-6684-7791-5.ch016

Suresh Babu, C. V., Yadavamuthiah, K., Abirami, S., & Kowsika, S. (2023a). Artificial Intelligence in Wastewater Management. In V. Shikuku (Ed.), *Artificial Intelligence Applications in Water Treatment and Water Resource Management* (pp. 31–45). IGI Global., doi:10.4018/978-1-6684-6791-6.ch002

Syamala, M., Komala, C., Pramila, P., Dash, S., Meenakshi, S., & Boopathi, S. (2023). Machine Learning-Integrated IoT-Based Smart Home Energy Management System. In *Handbook of Research on Deep Learning Techniques for Cloud-Based Industrial IoT* (pp. 219–235). IGI Global. doi:10.4018/978-1-6684-8098-4.ch013

Tang, J. L., Wang, D., Zhang, Z. G., He, L. J., Xin, J., & Xu, Y. (2017). Weed identificationbased on K-means feature learning combined with convolutional neural network. *Computers and Electronics in Agriculture*, *135*, 63–70. doi:10.1016/j.compag.2017.01.001

Tastimur, C., Karakose, M., & Akin, E. (2017). *An Information Extraction Approach with Vehicle and Pedestrian Activity Monitoring for Traffic Management in Smart City*. Academic Press.

Tekelioğlu, B., Büyüktaş, D., Baştuğ, R., Karaca, C., Aydinşakir, K., & Dinç, N. (2017). Use of crop water stress index for irrigation scheduling of soybean in Mediterranean conditions. *Journal of Experimental Agriculture International*, *18*(6), 1–8. doi:10.9734/JEAI/2017/37058

Teng, W., Chang, C., & Chen, M. (2005). Integrating Web Caching and Web Pre-fetching in Client-Side Proxies. *IEEE Transactions on Parallel and Distributed Systems*, *16*(5), 444–455. doi:10.1109/TPDS.2005.56

Thorpe, K. W., Ridgway, R. L., & Webb, R. E. (1992). A computerized data management and decision support system for gypsy moth management in suburban parks. *Computers and Electronics in Agriculture*, *6*(4), 333–345. doi:10.1016/0168-1699(92)90004-7

Tofangsaz, H. (2012). A new approach to the criminalization of terrorist financing and its compatibility with Sharia law. *Journal of Money Laundering Control*, *15*(4), 396–406. doi:10.1108/13685201211265980

Toma, C., Popa, M., Iancu, B., Doinea, M., Pascu, A., & Ioan-Dutescu, F. (2022). Edge Machine Learning for the Automated Decision and Visual Computing of the Robots, IoT Embedded Devices or UAV-Drones. *Electronics (Basel)*, *11*(21), 3507. doi:10.3390/electronics11213507

Tomar, P., & Kaur, G. (Eds.). (2021). *Artificial Intelligence and IoT-based Technologies for Sustainable Farming and Smart Agriculture*. doi:10.4018/978-1-7998-1722-2

Tong, W., & Jiayou, C. (2021). A study of the economic impact of central bank digital currency under global competition. *China Economic Journal*, *14*(1), 78–101. doi:10.1080/17538963.2020.1870282

Tran, H. (2021). *Regulation: The solution to Bitcoin's risks and unrealized benefits*. Available at: https://www.atlanticcouncil.org/blogs/new-atlanticist/regulation-thesolution-to-bitcoins-risks-and-unrealized-benefits/

Tsai, C. P., & Lee, T. L. (1999). Back-propagation neural network in tidal-level forecasting. *Journal of Waterway, Port, Coastal, and Ocean Engineering*, *125*(4), 195–202. doi:10.1061/(ASCE)0733-950X(1999)125:4(195)

Ünal, Z. (2020). Smart farming becomes even smarter with deep learning—A bibliographical analysis. *IEEE Access : Practical Innovations, Open Solutions*, *8*, 105587–105609. doi:10.1109/ACCESS.2020.3000175

Uscher-Pines, L., Mulcahy, A., Cowling, D., Hunter, G., Burns, R., & Mehrotra, A. (2016). Access and Quality of Care in Direct-to-Consumer Telemedicine. *Telemedicine Journal and e-Health*, *22*(4), 282–287. doi:10.1089/tmj.2015.0079 PMID:26488151

Uthayakumar, J., Vengattaraman, T., & Dhavachelvan, P. (2020). Swarm intelligence based classification rule induction (cri) framework for qualitative and quantitative approach: An application of bankruptcy prediction and credit risk analysis. *Journal of King Saud University-Computer and Information Sciences*, *32*(6), 647–657. doi:10.1016/j.jksuci.2017.10.007

Van Binsbergen, J. H., Diamond, W. F., & Grotteria, M. (2022). Risk-free interest rates. *Journal of Financial Economics*, *143*(1), 1–29. doi:10.1016/j.jfineco.2021.06.012

Vangala, A., Das, A. K., Kumar, N., & Alazab, M. (2020). Smart secure sensing for IoT-based agriculture: Blockchain perspective. *IEEE Sensors Journal*, *21*(16), 17591–17607. doi:10.1109/JSEN.2020.3012294

Vanitha, S., Radhika, K., & Boopathi, S. (2023). Artificial Intelligence Techniques in Water Purification and Utilization. In *Human Agro-Energy Optimization for Business and Industry* (pp. 202–218). IGI Global. doi:10.4018/978-1-6684-4118-3.ch010

Vaziri, M. (1997). Predicting Caspian Sea surface water level by ANN and ARIMA models. *Journal of Waterway, Port, Coastal, and Ocean Engineering*, *123*(4), 158–162. doi:10.1061/(ASCE)0733-950X(1997)123:4(158)

Veeranjaneyulu, R., Boopathi, S., Kumari, R. K., Vidyarthi, A., Isaac, J. S., & Jaiganesh, V. (2023). Air Quality Improvement and Optimisation Using Machine Learning Technique. *IEEE Explore*, 1–6.

Veeranjaneyulu, R., Boopathi, S., Narasimharao, J., Gupta, K. K., Reddy, R. V. K., & Ambika, R. (2023). Identification of Heart Diseases using Novel Machine Learning Method. *IEEE Explore*, 1–6.

Velasquez, J., Bassi, A., Yasuda, H., & Aoki, T. (2004). Mining Web Data to Create Online Navigation Recommendations. *Proceedings of the Fourth IEEE International Conference on Data Mining*, 551-554.

Venkatesh, V., & Davis, F. D. (2000). A theoretical extension of the technology acceptance model: Four longitudinal field studies. *Management Science*, *46*(2), 186–204. doi:10.1287/mnsc.46.2.186.11926

Venkateswaran, N., Vidhya, K., Ayyannan, M., Chavan, S. M., Sekar, K., & Boopathi, S. (2023). A Study on Smart Energy Management Framework Using Cloud Computing. In 5G, Artificial Intelligence, and Next Generation Internet of Things: Digital Innovation for Green and Sustainable Economies (pp. 189–212). IGI Global. doi:10.4018/978-1-6684-8634-4.ch009

Venkateswaran, N., Vidhya, R., Naik, D. A., Raj, T. M., Munjal, N., & Boopathi, S. (2023). Study on Sentence and Question Formation Using Deep Learning Techniques. In *Digital Natives as a Disruptive Force in Asian Businesses and Societies* (pp. 252–273). IGI Global. doi:10.4018/978-1-6684-6782-4.ch015

Verdugo, C., Kouro, S., Rojas, C., Perez, M., & Energies, T. M. (2019). undefined. (2012). Five-level T-type cascade converter for rooftop grid-connected photovoltaic systems. *Mdpi. Com*, *6*(3), 495–504. doi:10.1049/iet-pel.2012.0494

VISA. (2016). *Accelerating the growth of digital payments in India: A five-year outlook*. VISA.

Vítor, G., Rito, P., Sargento, S., & Pinto, F. (2022). A scalable approach for smart city data platform: Support of real-time processing and data sharing. *Computer Networks*, *213*, 109027. doi:10.1016/j.comnet.2022.109027

Wakode, M. S. (2021). Role of AI and Big Data Analytics in UAV-Enabled IoT Applications for Smart Cities. *Unmanned Aerial Vehicles for Internet of Things (IoT) Concepts, Techniques, and Applications,* 193-205.

Waleed, A., Siti M.S. & Abdul S.I. (2011). A Survey of Web Caching and Prefetching. *Int. J. Advance. Soft Comput. Appl., 3*(1).

Walker, G., & Sernia, P. C. (2004a). Cascaded DC-DC converter connection of photovoltaic modules. *IEEE Transactions on Power Electronics, 19*(4), 1130–1139. Advance online publication. doi:10.1109/TPEL.2004.830090

Wang, W., & Suo, W. (2006). *Assessing default probabilities from structural credit risk models.* S&P Global Market Intelligence Research Paper Series.

Wang, Q., Zhou, L., Zhou, Y., & Ma, J. (2019). Machine learning algorithms for soil organic carbon prediction using visible and near-infrared spectra. *Soil & Tillage Research, 195*, 104384. doi:10.1016/j.still.2019.104384

Weng, Z., Li, W., & Jin, Z. (2021, January 11). Human activity prediction using saliency-aware motion enhancement and weighted LSTM network. *EURASIP Journal on Image and Video Processing, 2021*(1). doi:10.1186/s13640-020-00544-0

Wessels & Duane. (2001). Web Caching. O'Reilly Publication.

Wiwekananda, Hamukti, Yogananda, Calisto, & Utomo. (2020). Understanding factors of ambulance delay and crash to enhance ambulance efficiency: An integrative literature review. *Journal of Community Empowerment for Health, 3*(3).

Wongchai, A., Shukla, S. K., Ahmed, M. A., Sakthi, U., Jagdish, M., & kumar, R. (2022). Artificial intelligence-enabled soft sensor and internet of things for sustainable agriculture using ensemble deep learning architecture. *Computers & Electrical Engineering, 102*, 108128. doi:10.1016/j.compeleceng.2022.108128

Wray, L. R. (2011). *Keynes after 75 years: Rethinking money as a public monopoly.* Levy Economics Institute, Working Paper No. 658.

Wu, Y., Jiang, Z., Zou, H., & Li, F. (2021). Soil organic carbon prediction using random forest and deep learning models in a hilly region. *Catena, 196*, 105134. doi:10.1016/j.catena.2020.105134

Yamaoka, H. (2022). Digital Currencies and the Future of Money. In *The Future of Financial Systems in the Digital Age* (pp. 49–73). Springer. doi:10.1007/978-981-16-7830-1_4

Yang, Q., Li, T., & Wang, K. (2004). Building Association-Rule Based Sequential Classifiers for Web-Document Prediction. *Data Mining and Knowledge Discovery, 8*(3), 253–273. doi:10.1023/B:DAMI.0000023675.04946.f1

Yusof, N. M., Alias, I. Q., Kassim, A. J. M., & Zaidi, F. L. N. M. (2021). Determining the credit score and credit rating of firms using the combination of kmv-merton model and financial ratios. *Science and Technology Indonesia, 6*(3), 105–112. doi:10.26554ti.2021.6.3.105-112

Zahboune, H., Zouggar, S., Krajacic, G., Varbanov, S., Elhafyani, M., & Ziani, E. (2016). *Optimal hybrid renewable energy design in autonomous system using Modified Electric System Cascade Analysis and Homer software.* Elsevier. doi:10.1016/j.enconman.2016.08.061

Zaiane, O. (2000). Web Mining: Concepts, Practices and Research. *Proc. SDBD, Conference Tutorial Notes.*

ZhangT. Y. (2018). *Predicting credit default swap (cds) returns with machine learning.* Available at SSRN 3152143.

Zhou, Z., Zhang, S., Wang, C., Zuo, J., He, Q., & Rameezdeen, R. (2016). Achieving energy efficient buildings via retrofitting of existing buildings: A case study. *Journal of Cleaner Production, 112*, 3605–3615. doi:10.1016/j.jclepro.2015.09.046

Ziosi, M., Hewitt, B., Juneja, P., Taddeo, M., & Floridi, L. (2022). Smart cities: Reviewing the debate about their ethical implications. *AI & Society*. Advance online publication. doi:10.100700146-022-01558-0 PMID:36212227

Related References

To continue our tradition of advancing academic research, we have compiled a list of recommended IGI Global readings. These references will provide additional information and guidance to further enrich your knowledge and assist you with your own research and future publications.

Abbasnejad, B., Moeinzadeh, S., Ahankoob, A., & Wong, P. S. (2021). The Role of Collaboration in the Implementation of BIM-Enabled Projects. In J. Underwood & M. Shelbourn (Eds.), *Handbook of Research on Driving Transformational Change in the Digital Built Environment* (pp. 27–62). IGI Global. https://doi.org/10.4018/978-1-7998-6600-8.ch002

Abdulrahman, K. O., Mahamood, R. M., & Akinlabi, E. T. (2022). Additive Manufacturing (AM): Processing Technique for Lightweight Alloys and Composite Material. In K. Kumar, B. Babu, & J. Davim (Ed.), *Handbook of Research on Advancements in the Processing, Characterization, and Application of Lightweight Materials* (pp. 27-48). IGI Global. https://doi.org/10.4018/978-1-7998-7864-3.ch002

Agrawal, R., Sharma, P., & Saxena, A. (2021). A Diamond Cut Leather Substrate Antenna for BAN (Body Area Network) Application. In V. Singh, V. Dubey, A. Saxena, R. Tiwari, & H. Sharma (Eds.), *Emerging Materials and Advanced Designs for Wearable Antennas* (pp. 54–59). IGI Global. https://doi.org/10.4018/978-1-7998-7611-3.ch004

Ahmad, F., Al-Ammar, E. A., & Alsaidan, I. (2022). Battery Swapping Station: A Potential Solution to Address the Limitations of EV Charging Infrastructure. In M. Alam, R. Pillai, & N. Murugesan (Eds.), *Developing Charging Infrastructure and Technologies for Electric Vehicles* (pp. 195–207). IGI Global. doi:10.4018/978-1-7998-6858-3.ch010

Aikhuele, D. (2018). A Study of Product Development Engineering and Design Reliability Concerns. *International Journal of Applied Industrial Engineering*, *5*(1), 79–89. doi:10.4018/IJAIE.2018010105

Al-Khatri, H., & Al-Atrash, F. (2021). Occupants' Habits and Natural Ventilation in a Hot Arid Climate. In R. González-Lezcano (Ed.), *Advancements in Sustainable Architecture and Energy Efficiency* (pp. 146–168). IGI Global. https://doi.org/10.4018/978-1-7998-7023-4.ch007

Related References

Al-Shebeeb, O. A., Rangaswamy, S., Gopalakrishan, B., & Devaru, D. G. (2017). Evaluation and Indexing of Process Plans Based on Electrical Demand and Energy Consumption. *International Journal of Manufacturing, Materials, and Mechanical Engineering*, *7*(3), 1–19. doi:10.4018/IJMMME.2017070101

Amuda, M. O., Lawal, T. F., & Akinlabi, E. T. (2017). Research Progress on Rheological Behavior of AA7075 Aluminum Alloy During Hot Deformation. *International Journal of Materials Forming and Machining Processes*, *4*(1), 53–96. doi:10.4018/IJMFMP.2017010104

Amuda, M. O., Lawal, T. F., & Mridha, S. (2021). Microstructure and Mechanical Properties of Silicon Carbide-Treated Ferritic Stainless Steel Welds. In L. Burstein (Ed.), *Handbook of Research on Advancements in Manufacturing, Materials, and Mechanical Engineering* (pp. 395–411). IGI Global. https://doi.org/10.4018/978-1-7998-4939-1.ch019

Anikeev, V., Gasem, K. A., & Fan, M. (2021). Application of Supercritical Technologies in Clean Energy Production: A Review. In L. Chen (Ed.), *Handbook of Research on Advancements in Supercritical Fluids Applications for Sustainable Energy Systems* (pp. 792–821). IGI Global. https://doi.org/10.4018/978-1-7998-5796-9.ch022

Arafat, M. Y., Saleem, I., & Devi, T. P. (2022). Drivers of EV Charging Infrastructure Entrepreneurship in India. In M. Alam, R. Pillai, & N. Murugesan (Eds.), *Developing Charging Infrastructure and Technologies for Electric Vehicles* (pp. 208–219). IGI Global. https://doi.org/10.4018/978-1-7998-6858-3.ch011

Araujo, A., & Manninen, H. (2022). Contribution of Project-Based Learning on Social Skills Development: An Industrial Engineer Perspective. In A. Alves & N. van Hattum-Janssen (Eds.), *Training Engineering Students for Modern Technological Advancement* (pp. 119–145). IGI Global. https://doi.org/10.4018/978-1-7998-8816-1.ch006

Armutlu, H. (2018). Intelligent Biomedical Engineering Operations by Cloud Computing Technologies. In U. Kose, G. Guraksin, & O. Deperlioglu (Eds.), *Nature-Inspired Intelligent Techniques for Solving Biomedical Engineering Problems* (pp. 297–317). Hershey, PA: IGI Global. doi:10.4018/978-1-5225-4769-3.ch015

Atik, M., Sadek, M., & Shahrour, I. (2017). Single-Run Adaptive Pushover Procedure for Shear Wall Structures. In V. Plevris, G. Kremmyda, & Y. Fahjan (Eds.), *Performance-Based Seismic Design of Concrete Structures and Infrastructures* (pp. 59–83). Hershey, PA: IGI Global. doi:10.4018/978-1-5225-2089-4.ch003

Attia, H. (2021). Smart Power Microgrid Impact on Sustainable Building. In R. González-Lezcano (Ed.), *Advancements in Sustainable Architecture and Energy Efficiency* (pp. 169–194). IGI Global. https://doi.org/10.4018/978-1-7998-7023-4.ch008

Aydin, A., Akyol, E., Gungor, M., Kaya, A., & Tasdelen, S. (2018). Geophysical Surveys in Engineering Geology Investigations With Field Examples. In N. Ceryan (Ed.), *Handbook of Research on Trends and Digital Advances in Engineering Geology* (pp. 257–280). Hershey, PA: IGI Global. doi:10.4018/978-1-5225-2709-1.ch007

Ayoobkhan, M. U. D., Y., A., J., Easwaran, B., & R., T. (2021). Smart Connected Digital Products and IoT Platform With the Digital Twin. In P. Vasant, G. Weber, & W. Punurai (Ed.), Research Advancements in Smart Technology, Optimization, and Renewable Energy (pp. 330-350). IGI Global. https://doi.org/ doi:10.4018/978-1-7998-3970-5.ch016

Baeza Moyano, D., & González Lezcano, R. A. (2021). The Importance of Light in Our Lives: Towards New Lighting in Schools. In R. González-Lezcano (Ed.), *Advancements in Sustainable Architecture and Energy Efficiency* (pp. 239–256). IGI Global. https://doi.org/10.4018/978-1-7998-7023-4.ch011

Bagdadee, A. H. (2021). A Brief Assessment of the Energy Sector of Bangladesh. *International Journal of Energy Optimization and Engineering, 10*(1), 36–55. doi:10.4018/IJEOE.2021010103

Baklezos, A. T., & Hadjigeorgiou, N. G. (2021). Magnetic Sensors for Space Applications and Magnetic Cleanliness Considerations. In C. Nikolopoulos (Ed.), *Recent Trends on Electromagnetic Environmental Effects for Aeronautics and Space Applications* (pp. 147–185). IGI Global. https://doi.org/10.4018/978-1-7998-4879-0.ch006

Bas, T. G. (2017). Nutraceutical Industry with the Collaboration of Biotechnology and Nutrigenomics Engineering: The Significance of Intellectual Property in the Entrepreneurship and Scientific Research Ecosystems. In T. Bas & J. Zhao (Eds.), *Comparative Approaches to Biotechnology Development and Use in Developed and Emerging Nations* (pp. 1–17). Hershey, PA: IGI Global. doi:10.4018/978-1-5225-1040-6.ch001

Bazeer Ahamed, B., & Periakaruppan, S. (2021). Taxonomy of Influence Maximization Techniques in Unknown Social Networks. In P. Vasant, G. Weber, & W. Punurai (Eds.), *Research Advancements in Smart Technology, Optimization, and Renewable Energy* (pp. 351-363). IGI Global. https://doi.org/10.4018/978-1-7998-3970-5.ch017

Beale, R., & André, J. (2017). *Design Solutions and Innovations in Temporary Structures*. Hershey, PA: IGI Global. doi:10.4018/978-1-5225-2199-0

Behnam, B. (2017). Simulating Post-Earthquake Fire Loading in Conventional RC Structures. In P. Samui, S. Chakraborty, & D. Kim (Eds.), *Modeling and Simulation Techniques in Structural Engineering* (pp. 425–444). Hershey, PA: IGI Global. doi:10.4018/978-1-5225-0588-4.ch015

Ben Hamida, I., Salah, S. B., Msahli, F., & Mimouni, M. F. (2018). Distribution Network Reconfiguration Using SPEA2 for Power Loss Minimization and Reliability Improvement. *International Journal of Energy Optimization and Engineering, 7*(1), 50–65. doi:10.4018/IJEOE.2018010103

Bentarzi, H. (2021). Fault Tree-Based Root Cause Analysis Used to Study Mal-Operation of a Protective Relay in a Smart Grid. In A. Recioui & H. Bentarzi (Eds.), *Optimizing and Measuring Smart Grid Operation and Control* (pp. 289–308). IGI Global. https://doi.org/10.4018/978-1-7998-4027-5.ch012

Beysens, D. A., Garrabos, Y., & Zappoli, B. (2021). Thermal Effects in Near-Critical Fluids: Piston Effect and Related Phenomena. In L. Chen (Ed.), *Handbook of Research on Advancements in Supercritical Fluids Applications for Sustainable Energy Systems* (pp. 1–31). IGI Global. https://doi.org/10.4018/978-1-7998-5796-9.ch001

Bhaskar, S. V., & Kudal, H. N. (2017). Effect of TiCN and AlCrN Coating on Tribological Behaviour of Plasma-nitrided AISI 4140 Steel. *International Journal of Surface Engineering and Interdisciplinary Materials Science*, *5*(2), 1–17. doi:10.4018/IJSEIMS.2017070101

Bhuyan, D. (2018). Designing of a Twin Tube Shock Absorber: A Study in Reverse Engineering. In K. Kumar & J. Davim (Eds.), *Design and Optimization of Mechanical Engineering Products* (pp. 83–104). Hershey, PA: IGI Global. doi:10.4018/978-1-5225-3401-3.ch005

Blumberg, G. (2021). Blockchains for Use in Construction and Engineering Projects. In J. Underwood & M. Shelbourn (Eds.), *Handbook of Research on Driving Transformational Change in the Digital Built Environment* (pp. 179–208). IGI Global. https://doi.org/10.4018/978-1-7998-6600-8.ch008

Bolboaca, A. M. (2021). Considerations Regarding the Use of Fuel Cells in Combined Heat and Power for Stationary Applications. In G. Badea, R. Felseghi, & I. Aşchilean (Eds.), *Hydrogen Fuel Cell Technology for Stationary Applications* (pp. 239–275). IGI Global. https://doi.org/10.4018/978-1-7998-4945-2.ch010

Burstein, L. (2021). Simulation Tool for Cable Design. In L. Burstein (Ed.), *Handbook of Research on Advancements in Manufacturing, Materials, and Mechanical Engineering* (pp. 54–74). IGI Global. https://doi.org/10.4018/978-1-7998-4939-1.ch003

Calderon, F. A., Giolo, E. G., Frau, C. D., Rengel, M. G., Rodriguez, H., Tornello, M., ... Gallucci, R. (2018). Seismic Microzonation and Site Effects Detection Through Microtremors Measures: A Review. In N. Ceryan (Ed.), *Handbook of Research on Trends and Digital Advances in Engineering Geology* (pp. 326–349). Hershey, PA: IGI Global. doi:10.4018/978-1-5225-2709-1.ch009

Ceryan, N., & Can, N. K. (2018). Prediction of The Uniaxial Compressive Strength of Rocks Materials. In N. Ceryan (Ed.), *Handbook of Research on Trends and Digital Advances in Engineering Geology* (pp. 31–96). Hershey, PA: IGI Global. doi:10.4018/978-1-5225-2709-1.ch002

Ceryan, S. (2018). Weathering Indices Used in Evaluation of the Weathering State of Rock Material. In N. Ceryan (Ed.), *Handbook of Research on Trends and Digital Advances in Engineering Geology* (pp. 132–186). Hershey, PA: IGI Global. doi:10.4018/978-1-5225-2709-1.ch004

Chen, H., Padilla, R. V., & Besarati, S. (2017). Supercritical Fluids and Their Applications in Power Generation. In L. Chen & Y. Iwamoto (Eds.), *Advanced Applications of Supercritical Fluids in Energy Systems* (pp. 369–402). Hershey, PA: IGI Global. doi:10.4018/978-1-5225-2047-4.ch012

Chen, H., Padilla, R. V., & Besarati, S. (2021). Supercritical Fluids and Their Applications in Power Generation. In L. Chen (Ed.), *Handbook of Research on Advancements in Supercritical Fluids Applications for Sustainable Energy Systems* (pp. 566–599). IGI Global. https://doi.org/10.4018/978-1-7998-5796-9.ch016

Chen, L. (2017). Principles, Experiments, and Numerical Studies of Supercritical Fluid Natural Circulation System. In L. Chen & Y. Iwamoto (Eds.), *Advanced Applications of Supercritical Fluids in Energy Systems* (pp. 136–187). Hershey, PA: IGI Global. doi:10.4018/978-1-5225-2047-4.ch005

Chen, L. (2021). Principles, Experiments, and Numerical Studies of Supercritical Fluid Natural Circulation System. In L. Chen (Ed.), *Handbook of Research on Advancements in Supercritical Fluids Applications for Sustainable Energy Systems* (pp. 219–269). IGI Global. https://doi.org/10.4018/978-1-7998-5796-9.ch007

Chiba, Y., Marif, Y., Henini, N., & Tlemcani, A. (2021). Modeling of Magnetic Refrigeration Device by Using Artificial Neural Networks Approach. *International Journal of Energy Optimization and Engineering, 10*(4), 68–76. https://doi.org/10.4018/IJEOE.2021100105

Clementi, F., Di Sciascio, G., Di Sciascio, S., & Lenci, S. (2017). Influence of the Shear-Bending Interaction on the Global Capacity of Reinforced Concrete Frames: A Brief Overview of the New Perspectives. In V. Plevris, G. Kremmyda, & Y. Fahjan (Eds.), *Performance-Based Seismic Design of Concrete Structures and Infrastructures* (pp. 84–111). Hershey, PA: IGI Global. doi:10.4018/978-1-5225-2089-4.ch004

Codinhoto, R., Fialho, B. C., Pinti, L., & Fabricio, M. M. (2021). BIM and IoT for Facilities Management: Understanding Key Maintenance Issues. In J. Underwood & M. Shelbourn (Eds.), *Handbook of Research on Driving Transformational Change in the Digital Built Environment* (pp. 209–231). IGI Global. doi:10.4018/978-1-7998-6600-8.ch009

Cortés-Polo, D., Calle-Cancho, J., Carmona-Murillo, J., & González-Sánchez, J. (2017). Future Trends in Mobile-Fixed Integration for Next Generation Networks: Classification and Analysis. *International Journal of Vehicular Telematics and Infotainment Systems, 1*(1), 33–53. doi:10.4018/IJVTIS.2017010103

Costa, H. G., Sheremetieff, F. H., & Araújo, E. A. (2022). Influence of Game-Based Methods in Developing Engineering Competences. In A. Alves & N. van Hattum-Janssen (Eds.), *Training Engineering Students for Modern Technological Advancement* (pp. 69–88). IGI Global. https://doi.org/10.4018/978-1-7998-8816-1.ch004

Cui, X., Zeng, S., Li, Z., Zheng, Q., Yu, X., & Han, B. (2018). Advanced Composites for Civil Engineering Infrastructures. In K. Kumar & J. Davim (Eds.), *Composites and Advanced Materials for Industrial Applications* (pp. 212–248). Hershey, PA: IGI Global. doi:10.4018/978-1-5225-5216-1.ch010

Dalgıç, S., & Kuşku, İ. (2018). Geological and Geotechnical Investigations in Tunneling. In N. Ceryan (Ed.), *Handbook of Research on Trends and Digital Advances in Engineering Geology* (pp. 482–529). Hershey, PA: IGI Global. doi:10.4018/978-1-5225-2709-1.ch014

Dang, C., & Hihara, E. (2021). Study on Cooling Heat Transfer of Supercritical Carbon Dioxide Applied to Transcritical Carbon Dioxide Heat Pump. In L. Chen (Ed.), *Handbook of Research on Advancements in Supercritical Fluids Applications for Sustainable Energy Systems* (pp. 451–493). IGI Global. https://doi.org/10.4018/978-1-7998-5796-9.ch013

Daus, Y., Kharchenko, V., & Yudaev, I. (2021). Research of Solar Energy Potential of Photovoltaic Installations on Enclosing Structures of Buildings. *International Journal of Energy Optimization and Engineering, 10*(4), 18–34. https://doi.org/10.4018/IJEOE.2021100102

Daus, Y., Kharchenko, V., & Yudaev, I. (2021). Optimizing Layout of Distributed Generation Sources of Power Supply System of Agricultural Object. *International Journal of Energy Optimization and Engineering, 10*(3), 70–84. https://doi.org/10.4018/IJEOE.2021070104

de la Varga, D., Soto, M., Arias, C. A., van Oirschot, D., Kilian, R., Pascual, A., & Álvarez, J. A. (2017). Constructed Wetlands for Industrial Wastewater Treatment and Removal of Nutrients. In Á. Val del Río, J. Campos Gómez, & A. Mosquera Corral (Eds.), *Technologies for the Treatment and Recovery of Nutrients from Industrial Wastewater* (pp. 202–230). Hershey, PA: IGI Global. doi:10.4018/978-1-5225-1037-6.ch008

Deb, S., Ammar, E. A., AlRajhi, H., Alsaidan, I., & Shariff, S. M. (2022). V2G Pilot Projects: Review and Lessons Learnt. In M. Alam, R. Pillai, & N. Murugesan (Eds.), *Developing Charging Infrastructure and Technologies for Electric Vehicles* (pp. 252–267). IGI Global. https://doi.org/10.4018/978-1-7998-6858-3.ch014

Dekhandji, F. Z., & Rais, M. C. (2021). A Comparative Study of Power Quality Monitoring Using Various Techniques. In A. Recioui & H. Bentarzi (Eds.), *Optimizing and Measuring Smart Grid Operation and Control* (pp. 259–288). IGI Global. https://doi.org/10.4018/978-1-7998-4027-5.ch011

Deperlioglu, O. (2018). Intelligent Techniques Inspired by Nature and Used in Biomedical Engineering. In U. Kose, G. Guraksin, & O. Deperlioglu (Eds.), *Nature-Inspired Intelligent Techniques for Solving Biomedical Engineering Problems* (pp. 51–77). Hershey, PA: IGI Global. doi:10.4018/978-1-5225-4769-3.ch003

Dhurpate, P. R., & Tang, H. (2021). Quantitative Analysis of the Impact of Inter-Line Conveyor Capacity for Throughput of Manufacturing Systems. *International Journal of Manufacturing, Materials, and Mechanical Engineering, 11*(1), 1–17. https://doi.org/10.4018/IJMMME.2021010101

Dinkar, S., & Deep, K. (2021). A Survey of Recent Variants and Applications of Antlion Optimizer. *International Journal of Energy Optimization and Engineering, 10*(2), 48–73. doi:10.4018/IJEOE.2021040103

Dixit, A. (2018). Application of Silica-Gel-Reinforced Aluminium Composite on the Piston of Internal Combustion Engine: Comparative Study of Silica-Gel-Reinforced Aluminium Composite Piston With Aluminium Alloy Piston. In K. Kumar & J. Davim (Eds.), *Composites and Advanced Materials for Industrial Applications* (pp. 63–98). Hershey, PA: IGI Global. doi:10.4018/978-1-5225-5216-1.ch004

Drabecki, M. P., & Kułak, K. B. (2021). Global Pandemics on European Electrical Energy Markets: Lessons Learned From the COVID-19 Outbreak. *International Journal of Energy Optimization and Engineering, 10*(3), 24–46. https://doi.org/10.4018/IJEOE.2021070102

Dutta, M. M. (2021). Nanomaterials for Food and Agriculture. In M. Bhat, I. Wani, & S. Ashraf (Eds.), *Applications of Nanomaterials in Agriculture, Food Science, and Medicine* (pp. 75–97). IGI Global. doi:10.4018/978-1-7998-5563-7.ch004

Dutta, M. M., & Goswami, M. (2021). Coating Materials: Nano-Materials. In S. Roy & G. Bose (Eds.), *Advanced Surface Coating Techniques for Modern Industrial Applications* (pp. 1–30). IGI Global. doi:10.4018/978-1-7998-4870-7.ch001

Elsayed, A. M., Dakkama, H. J., Mahmoud, S., Al-Dadah, R., & Kaialy, W. (2017). Sustainable Cooling Research Using Activated Carbon Adsorbents and Their Environmental Impact. In T. Kobayashi (Ed.), *Applied Environmental Materials Science for Sustainability* (pp. 186–221). Hershey, PA: IGI Global. doi:10.4018/978-1-5225-1971-3.ch009

Ercanoglu, M., & Sonmez, H. (2018). General Trends and New Perspectives on Landslide Mapping and Assessment Methods. In N. Ceryan (Ed.), *Handbook of Research on Trends and Digital Advances in Engineering Geology* (pp. 350–379). Hershey, PA: IGI Global. doi:10.4018/978-1-5225-2709-1.ch010

Faroz, S. A., Pujari, N. N., Rastogi, R., & Ghosh, S. (2017). Risk Analysis of Structural Engineering Systems Using Bayesian Inference. In P. Samui, S. Chakraborty, & D. Kim (Eds.), *Modeling and Simulation Techniques in Structural Engineering* (pp. 390–424). Hershey, PA: IGI Global. doi:10.4018/978-1-5225-0588-4.ch014

Fekik, A., Hamida, M. L., Denoun, H., Azar, A. T., Kamal, N. A., Vaidyanathan, S., Bousbaine, A., & Benamrouche, N. (2022). Multilevel Inverter for Hybrid Fuel Cell/PV Energy Conversion System. In A. Fekik & N. Benamrouche (Eds.), *Modeling and Control of Static Converters for Hybrid Storage Systems* (pp. 233–270). IGI Global. https://doi.org/10.4018/978-1-7998-7447-8.ch009

Fekik, A., Hamida, M. L., Houassine, H., Azar, A. T., Kamal, N. A., Denoun, H., Vaidyanathan, S., & Sambas, A. (2022). Power Quality Improvement for Grid-Connected Photovoltaic Panels Using Direct Power Control. In A. Fekik & N. Benamrouche (Eds.), *Modeling and Control of Static Converters for Hybrid Storage Systems* (pp. 107–142). IGI Global. https://doi.org/10.4018/978-1-7998-7447-8.ch005

Fernando, P. R., Hamigah, T., Disne, S., Wickramasingha, G. G., & Sutharshan, A. (2018). The Evaluation of Engineering Properties of Low Cost Concrete Blocks by Partial Doping of Sand with Sawdust: Low Cost Sawdust Concrete Block. *International Journal of Strategic Engineering*, *1*(2), 26–42. doi:10.4018/IJoSE.2018070103

Ferro, G., Minciardi, R., Parodi, L., & Robba, M. (2022). Optimal Charging Management of Microgrid-Integrated Electric Vehicles. In M. Alam, R. Pillai, & N. Murugesan (Eds.), *Developing Charging Infrastructure and Technologies for Electric Vehicles* (pp. 133–155). IGI Global. https://doi.org/10.4018/978-1-7998-6858-3.ch007

Flumerfelt, S., & Green, C. (2022). Graduate Lean Leadership Education: A Case Study of a Program. In A. Alves & N. van Hattum-Janssen (Eds.), *Training Engineering Students for Modern Technological Advancement* (pp. 202–224). IGI Global. https://doi.org/10.4018/978-1-7998-8816-1.ch010

Galli, B. J. (2021). Implications of Economic Decision Making to the Project Manager. *International Journal of Strategic Engineering*, *4*(1), 19–32. https://doi.org/10.4018/IJoSE.2021010102

Gento, A. M., Pimentel, C., & Pascual, J. A. (2022). Teaching Circular Economy and Lean Management in a Learning Factory. In A. Alves & N. van Hattum-Janssen (Eds.), *Training Engineering Students for Modern Technological Advancement* (pp. 183–201). IGI Global. https://doi.org/10.4018/978-1-7998-8816-1.ch009

Ghosh, S., Mitra, S., Ghosh, S., & Chakraborty, S. (2017). Seismic Reliability Analysis in the Framework of Metamodelling Based Monte Carlo Simulation. In P. Samui, S. Chakraborty, & D. Kim (Eds.), *Modeling and Simulation Techniques in Structural Engineering* (pp. 192–208). Hershey, PA: IGI Global. doi:10.4018/978-1-5225-0588-4.ch006

Gil, M., & Otero, B. (2017). Learning Engineering Skills through Creativity and Collaboration: A Game-Based Proposal. In R. Alexandre Peixoto de Queirós & M. Pinto (Eds.), *Gamification-Based E-Learning Strategies for Computer Programming Education* (pp. 14–29). Hershey, PA: IGI Global. doi:10.4018/978-1-5225-1034-5.ch002

Gill, J., Ayre, M., & Mills, J. (2017). Revisioning the Engineering Profession: How to Make It Happen! In M. Gray & K. Thomas (Eds.), *Strategies for Increasing Diversity in Engineering Majors and Careers* (pp. 156–175). Hershey, PA: IGI Global. doi:10.4018/978-1-5225-2212-6.ch008

Godzhaev, Z., Senkevich, S., Kuzmin, V., & Melikov, I. (2021). Use of the Neural Network Controller of Sprung Mass to Reduce Vibrations From Road Irregularities. In P. Vasant, G. Weber, & W. Punurai (Ed.), *Research Advancements in Smart Technology, Optimization, and Renewable Energy* (pp. 69-87). IGI Global. https://doi.org/10.4018/978-1-7998-3970-5.ch005

Gomes de Gusmão, C. M. (2022). Digital Competencies and Transformation in Higher Education: Upskilling With Extension Actions. In A. Alves & N. van Hattum-Janssen (Eds.), *Training Engineering Students for Modern Technological Advancement* (pp. 313–328). IGI Global. https://doi.org/10.4018/978-1-7998-8816-1.ch015A

Goyal, N., Ram, M., & Kumar, P. (2017). Welding Process under Fault Coverage Approach for Reliability and MTTF. In M. Ram & J. Davim (Eds.), *Mathematical Concepts and Applications in Mechanical Engineering and Mechatronics* (pp. 222–245). Hershey, PA: IGI Global. doi:10.4018/978-1-5225-1639-2.ch011

Gray, M., & Lundy, C. (2017). Engineering Study Abroad: High Impact Strategy for Increasing Access. In M. Gray & K. Thomas (Eds.), *Strategies for Increasing Diversity in Engineering Majors and Careers* (pp. 42–59). Hershey, PA: IGI Global. doi:10.4018/978-1-5225-2212-6.ch003

Güler, O., & Varol, T. (2021). Fabrication of Functionally Graded Metal and Ceramic Powders Synthesized by Electroless Deposition. In S. Roy & G. Bose (Eds.), *Advanced Surface Coating Techniques for Modern Industrial Applications* (pp. 150–187). IGI Global. https://doi.org/10.4018/978-1-7998-4870-7.ch007

Guraksin, G. E. (2018). Internet of Things and Nature-Inspired Intelligent Techniques for the Future of Biomedical Engineering. In U. Kose, G. Guraksin, & O. Deperlioglu (Eds.), *Nature-Inspired Intelligent Techniques for Solving Biomedical Engineering Problems* (pp. 263–282). Hershey, PA: IGI Global. doi:10.4018/978-1-5225-4769-3.ch013

Hamida, M. L., Fekik, A., Denoun, H., Ardjal, A., & Bokhtache, A. A. (2022). Flying Capacitor Inverter Integration in a Renewable Energy System. In A. Fekik & N. Benamrouche (Eds.), *Modeling and Control of Static Converters for Hybrid Storage Systems* (pp. 287–306). IGI Global. https://doi.org/10.4018/978-1-7998-7447-8.ch011

Hasegawa, N., & Takahashi, Y. (2021). Control of Soap Bubble Ejection Robot Using Facial Expressions. *International Journal of Manufacturing, Materials, and Mechanical Engineering, 11*(2), 1–16. https://doi.org/10.4018/IJMMME.2021040101

Hejazi, T., & Akbari, L. (2017). A Multiresponse Optimization Model for Statistical Design of Processes with Discrete Variables. In M. Ram & J. Davim (Eds.), *Mathematical Concepts and Applications in Mechanical Engineering and Mechatronics* (pp. 17–37). Hershey, PA: IGI Global. doi:10.4018/978-1-5225-1639-2.ch002

Hejazi, T., & Hejazi, A. (2017). Monte Carlo Simulation for Reliability-Based Design of Automotive Complex Subsystems. In M. Ram & J. Davim (Eds.), *Mathematical Concepts and Applications in Mechanical Engineering and Mechatronics* (pp. 177–200). Hershey, PA: IGI Global. doi:10.4018/978-1-5225-1639-2.ch009

Hejazi, T., & Poursabbagh, H. (2017). Reliability Analysis of Engineering Systems: An Accelerated Life Testing for Boiler Tubes. In M. Ram & J. Davim (Eds.), *Mathematical Concepts and Applications in Mechanical Engineering and Mechatronics* (pp. 154–176). Hershey, PA: IGI Global. doi:10.4018/978-1-5225-1639-2.ch008

Henao, J., Poblano-Salas, C. A., Vargas, F., Giraldo-Betancur, A. L., Corona-Castuera, J., & Sotelo-Mazón, O. (2021). Principles and Applications of Thermal Spray Coatings. In S. Roy & G. Bose (Eds.), *Advanced Surface Coating Techniques for Modern Industrial Applications* (pp. 31–70). IGI Global. https://doi.org/10.4018/978-1-7998-4870-7.ch002

Henao, J., & Sotelo, O. (2018). Surface Engineering at High Temperature: Thermal Cycling and Corrosion Resistance. In A. Pakseresht (Ed.), *Production, Properties, and Applications of High Temperature Coatings* (pp. 131–159). Hershey, PA: IGI Global. doi:10.4018/978-1-5225-4194-3.ch006

Hrnčič, M. K., Cör, D., & Knez, Ž. (2021). Supercritical Fluids as a Tool for Green Energy and Chemicals. In L. Chen (Ed.), *Handbook of Research on Advancements in Supercritical Fluids Applications for Sustainable Energy Systems* (pp. 761–791). IGI Global. doi:10.4018/978-1-7998-5796-9.ch021

Ibrahim, O., Erdem, S., & Gurbuz, E. (2021). Studying Physical and Chemical Properties of Graphene Oxide and Reduced Graphene Oxide and Their Applications in Sustainable Building Materials. In R. González-Lezcano (Ed.), *Advancements in Sustainable Architecture and Energy Efficiency* (pp. 221–238). IGI Global. https://doi.org/10.4018/978-1-7998-7023-4.ch010

Ihianle, I. K., Islam, S., Naeem, U., & Ebenuwa, S. H. (2021). Exploiting Patterns of Object Use for Human Activity Recognition. In A. Nwajana & I. Ihianle (Eds.), *Handbook of Research on 5G Networks and Advancements in Computing, Electronics, and Electrical Engineering* (pp. 382–401). IGI Global. https://doi.org/10.4018/978-1-7998-6992-4.ch015

Ijemaru, G. K., Ngharamike, E. T., Oleka, E. U., & Nwajana, A. O. (2021). An Energy-Efficient Model for Opportunistic Data Collection in IoV-Enabled SC Waste Management. In A. Nwajana & I. Ihianle (Eds.), *Handbook of Research on 5G Networks and Advancements in Computing, Electronics, and Electrical Engineering* (pp. 1–19). IGI Global. https://doi.org/10.4018/978-1-7998-6992-4.ch001

Ilori, O. O., Adetan, D. A., & Umoru, L. E. (2017). Effect of Cutting Parameters on the Surface Residual Stress of Face-Milled Pearlitic Ductile Iron. *International Journal of Materials Forming and Machining Processes, 4*(1), 38–52. doi:10.4018/IJMFMP.2017010103

Imam, M. H., Tasadduq, I. A., Ahmad, A., Aldosari, F., & Khan, H. (2017). Automated Generation of Course Improvement Plans Using Expert System. *International Journal of Quality Assurance in Engineering and Technology Education*, *6*(1), 1–12. doi:10.4018/IJQAETE.2017010101

Injeti, S. K., & Kumar, T. V. (2018). A WDO Framework for Optimal Deployment of DGs and DSCs in a Radial Distribution System Under Daily Load Pattern to Improve Techno-Economic Benefits. *International Journal of Energy Optimization and Engineering*, *7*(2), 1–38. doi:10.4018/IJEOE.2018040101

Ishii, N., Anami, K., & Knisely, C. W. (2018). *Dynamic Stability of Hydraulic Gates and Engineering for Flood Prevention*. Hershey, PA: IGI Global. doi:10.4018/978-1-5225-3079-4

Iwamoto, Y., & Yamaguchi, H. (2021). Application of Supercritical Carbon Dioxide for Solar Water Heater. In L. Chen (Ed.), *Handbook of Research on Advancements in Supercritical Fluids Applications for Sustainable Energy Systems* (pp. 370–387). IGI Global. https://doi.org/10.4018/978-1-7998-5796-9.ch010

Jayapalan, S. (2018). A Review of Chemical Treatments on Natural Fibers-Based Hybrid Composites for Engineering Applications. In K. Kumar & J. Davim (Eds.), *Composites and Advanced Materials for Industrial Applications* (pp. 16–37). Hershey, PA: IGI Global. doi:10.4018/978-1-5225-5216-1.ch002

Kapetanakis, T. N., Vardiambasis, I. O., Ioannidou, M. P., & Konstantaras, A. I. (2021). Modeling Antenna Radiation Using Artificial Intelligence Techniques: The Case of a Circular Loop Antenna. In C. Nikolopoulos (Ed.), *Recent Trends on Electromagnetic Environmental Effects for Aeronautics and Space Applications* (pp. 186–225). IGI Global. https://doi.org/10.4018/978-1-7998-4879-0.ch007

Karkalos, N. E., Markopoulos, A. P., & Dossis, M. F. (2017). Optimal Model Parameters of Inverse Kinematics Solution of a 3R Robotic Manipulator Using ANN Models. *International Journal of Manufacturing, Materials, and Mechanical Engineering*, *7*(3), 20–40. doi:10.4018/IJMMME.2017070102

Kelly, M., Costello, M., Nicholson, G., & O'Connor, J. (2021). The Evolving Integration of BIM Into Built Environment Programmes in a Higher Education Institute. In J. Underwood & M. Shelbourn (Eds.), *Handbook of Research on Driving Transformational Change in the Digital Built Environment* (pp. 294–326). IGI Global. https://doi.org/10.4018/978-1-7998-6600-8.ch012

Kesimal, A., Karaman, K., Cihangir, F., & Ercikdi, B. (2018). Excavatability Assessment of Rock Masses for Geotechnical Studies. In N. Ceryan (Ed.), *Handbook of Research on Trends and Digital Advances in Engineering Geology* (pp. 231–256). Hershey, PA: IGI Global. doi:10.4018/978-1-5225-2709-1.ch006

Knoflacher, H. (2017). The Role of Engineers and Their Tools in the Transport Sector after Paradigm Change: From Assumptions and Extrapolations to Science. In H. Knoflacher & E. Ocalir-Akunal (Eds.), *Engineering Tools and Solutions for Sustainable Transportation Planning* (pp. 1–29). Hershey, PA: IGI Global. doi:10.4018/978-1-5225-2116-7.ch001

Kose, U. (2018). Towards an Intelligent Biomedical Engineering With Nature-Inspired Artificial Intelligence Techniques. In U. Kose, G. Guraksin, & O. Deperlioglu (Eds.), *Nature-Inspired Intelligent Techniques for Solving Biomedical Engineering Problems* (pp. 1–26). Hershey, PA: IGI Global. doi:10.4018/978-1-5225-4769-3.ch001

Kostić, S. (2018). A Review on Enhanced Stability Analyses of Soil Slopes Using Statistical Design. In N. Ceryan (Ed.), *Handbook of Research on Trends and Digital Advances in Engineering Geology* (pp. 446–481). Hershey, PA: IGI Global. doi:10.4018/978-1-5225-2709-1.ch013

Kumar, A., Patil, P. P., & Prajapati, Y. K. (2018). *Advanced Numerical Simulations in Mechanical Engineering*. Hershey, PA: IGI Global. doi:10.4018/978-1-5225-3722-9

Kumar, G. R., Rajyalakshmi, G., & Manupati, V. K. (2017). Surface Micro Patterning of Aluminium Reinforced Composite through Laser Peening. *International Journal of Manufacturing, Materials, and Mechanical Engineering*, *7*(4), 15–27. doi:10.4018/IJMMME.2017100102

Kumar, N., Basu, D. N., & Chen, L. (2021). Effect of Flow Acceleration and Buoyancy on Thermalhydraulics of sCO2 in Mini/Micro-Channel. In L. Chen (Ed.), *Handbook of Research on Advancements in Supercritical Fluids Applications for Sustainable Energy Systems* (pp. 161–182). IGI Global. doi:10.4018/978-1-7998-5796-9.ch005

Kumari, N., & Kumar, K. (2018). Fabrication of Orthotic Calipers With Epoxy-Based Green Composite. In K. Kumar & J. Davim (Eds.), *Composites and Advanced Materials for Industrial Applications* (pp. 157–176). Hershey, PA: IGI Global. doi:10.4018/978-1-5225-5216-1.ch008

Kuppusamy, R. R. (2018). Development of Aerospace Composite Structures Through Vacuum-Enhanced Resin Transfer Moulding Technology (VERTMTy): Vacuum-Enhanced Resin Transfer Moulding. In K. Kumar & J. Davim (Eds.), *Composites and Advanced Materials for Industrial Applications* (pp. 99–111). Hershey, PA: IGI Global. doi:10.4018/978-1-5225-5216-1.ch005

Kurganov, V. A., Zeigarnik, Y. A., & Maslakova, I. V. (2021). Normal and Deteriorated Heat Transfer Under Heating Turbulent Supercritical Pressure Coolants Flows in Round Tubes. In L. Chen (Ed.), *Handbook of Research on Advancements in Supercritical Fluids Applications for Sustainable Energy Systems* (pp. 494–532). IGI Global. https://doi.org/10.4018/978-1-7998-5796-9.ch014

Li, H., & Zhang, Y. (2021). Heat Transfer and Fluid Flow Modeling for Supercritical Fluids in Advanced Energy Systems. In L. Chen (Ed.), *Handbook of Research on Advancements in Supercritical Fluids Applications for Sustainable Energy Systems* (pp. 388–422). IGI Global. https://doi.org/10.4018/978-1-7998-5796-9.ch011

Loy, J., Howell, S., & Cooper, R. (2017). Engineering Teams: Supporting Diversity in Engineering Education. In M. Gray & K. Thomas (Eds.), *Strategies for Increasing Diversity in Engineering Majors and Careers* (pp. 106–129). Hershey, PA: IGI Global. doi:10.4018/978-1-5225-2212-6.ch006

Macher, G., Armengaud, E., Kreiner, C., Brenner, E., Schmittner, C., Ma, Z., ... Krammer, M. (2018). Integration of Security in the Development Lifecycle of Dependable Automotive CPS. In N. Druml, A. Genser, A. Krieg, M. Menghin, & A. Hoeller (Eds.), *Solutions for Cyber-Physical Systems Ubiquity* (pp. 383–423). Hershey, PA: IGI Global. doi:10.4018/978-1-5225-2845-6.ch015

Madhu, M. N., Singh, J. G., Mohan, V., & Ongsakul, W. (2021). Transmission Risk Optimization in Interconnected Systems: Risk-Adjusted Available Transfer Capability. In P. Vasant, G. Weber, & W. Punurai (Ed.), *Research Advancements in Smart Technology, Optimization, and Renewable Energy* (pp. 183-199). IGI Global. https://doi.org/10.4018/978-1-7998-3970-5.ch010

Mahendramani, G., & Lakshmana Swamy, N. (2018). Effect of Weld Groove Area on Distortion of Butt Welded Joints in Submerged Arc Welding. *International Journal of Manufacturing, Materials, and Mechanical Engineering*, *8*(2), 33–44. doi:10.4018/IJMMME.2018040103

Makropoulos, G., Koumaras, H., Setaki, F., Filis, K., Lutz, T., Montowtt, P., Tomaszewski, L., Dybiec, P., & Järvet, T. (2021). 5G and Unmanned Aerial Vehicles (UAVs) Use Cases: Analysis of the Ecosystem, Architecture, and Applications. In A. Nwajana & I. Ihianle (Eds.), *Handbook of Research on 5G Networks and Advancements in Computing, Electronics, and Electrical Engineering* (pp. 36–69). IGI Global. https://doi.org/10.4018/978-1-7998-6992-4.ch003

Meric, E. M., Erdem, S., & Gurbuz, E. (2021). Application of Phase Change Materials in Construction Materials for Thermal Energy Storage Systems in Buildings. In R. González-Lezcano (Ed.), *Advancements in Sustainable Architecture and Energy Efficiency* (pp. 1–20). IGI Global. https://doi.org/10.4018/978-1-7998-7023-4.ch001

Mihret, E. T., & Yitayih, K. A. (2021). Operation of VANET Communications: The Convergence of UAV System With LTE/4G and WAVE Technologies. *International Journal of Smart Vehicles and Smart Transportation*, *4*(1), 29–51. https://doi.org/10.4018/IJSVST.2021010103

Mir, M. A., Bhat, B. A., Sheikh, B. A., Rather, G. A., Mehraj, S., & Mir, W. R. (2021). Nanomedicine in Human Health Therapeutics and Drug Delivery: Nanobiotechnology and Nanobiomedicine. In M. Bhat, I. Wani, & S. Ashraf (Eds.), *Applications of Nanomaterials in Agriculture, Food Science, and Medicine* (pp. 229–251). IGI Global. doi:10.4018/978-1-7998-5563-7.ch013

Mohammadzadeh, S., & Kim, Y. (2017). Nonlinear System Identification of Smart Buildings. In P. Samui, S. Chakraborty, & D. Kim (Eds.), *Modeling and Simulation Techniques in Structural Engineering* (pp. 328–347). Hershey, PA: IGI Global. doi:10.4018/978-1-5225-0588-4.ch011

Molina, G. J., Aktaruzzaman, F., Soloiu, V., & Rahman, M. (2017). Design and Testing of a Jet-Impingement Instrument to Study Surface-Modification Effects by Nanofluids. *International Journal of Surface Engineering and Interdisciplinary Materials Science*, *5*(2), 43–61. doi:10.4018/IJSEIMS.2017070104

Moreno-Rangel, A., & Carrillo, G. (2021). Energy-Efficient Homes: A Heaven for Respiratory Illnesses. In R. González-Lezcano (Ed.), *Advancements in Sustainable Architecture and Energy Efficiency* (pp. 49–71). IGI Global. https://doi.org/10.4018/978-1-7998-7023-4.ch003

Msomi, V., & Jantjies, B. T. (2021). Correlative Analysis Between Tensile Properties and Tool Rotational Speeds of Friction Stir Welded Similar Aluminium Alloy Joints. *International Journal of Surface Engineering and Interdisciplinary Materials Science*, *9*(2), 58–78. https://doi.org/10.4018/IJSEIMS.2021070104

Muigai, M. N., Mwema, F. M., Akinlabi, E. T., & Obiko, J. O. (2021). Surface Engineering of Materials Through Weld-Based Technologies: An Overview. In S. Roy & G. Bose (Eds.), *Advanced Surface Coating Techniques for Modern Industrial Applications* (pp. 247–260). IGI Global. doi:10.4018/978-1-7998-4870-7.ch011

Mukherjee, A., Saeed, R. A., Dutta, S., & Naskar, M. K. (2017). Fault Tracking Framework for Software-Defined Networking (SDN). In C. Singhal & S. De (Eds.), *Resource Allocation in Next-Generation Broadband Wireless Access Networks* (pp. 247–272). Hershey, PA: IGI Global. doi:10.4018/978-1-5225-2023-8.ch011

Mukhopadhyay, A., Barman, T. K., & Sahoo, P. (2018). Electroless Nickel Coatings for High Temperature Applications. In K. Kumar & J. Davim (Eds.), *Composites and Advanced Materials for Industrial Applications* (pp. 297–331). Hershey, PA: IGI Global. doi:10.4018/978-1-5225-5216-1.ch013

Mwema, F. M., & Wambua, J. M. (2022). Machining of Poly Methyl Methacrylate (PMMA) and Other Olymeric Materials: A Review. In K. Kumar, B. Babu, & J. Davim (Eds.), *Handbook of Research on Advancements in the Processing, Characterization, and Application of Lightweight Materials* (pp. 363–379). IGI Global. https://doi.org/10.4018/978-1-7998-7864-3.ch016

Mykhailyshyn, R., Savkiv, V., Boyko, I., Prada, E., & Virgala, I. (2021). Substantiation of Parameters of Friction Elements of Bernoulli Grippers With a Cylindrical Nozzle. *International Journal of Manufacturing, Materials, and Mechanical Engineering*, *11*(2), 17–39. https://doi.org/10.4018/IJMMME.2021040102

Náprstek, J., & Fischer, C. (2017). Dynamic Stability and Post-Critical Processes of Slender Auto-Parametric Systems. In V. Plevris, G. Kremmyda, & Y. Fahjan (Eds.), *Performance-Based Seismic Design of Concrete Structures and Infrastructures* (pp. 128–171). Hershey, PA: IGI Global. doi:10.4018/978-1-5225-2089-4.ch006

Nautiyal, L., Shivach, P., & Ram, M. (2018). Optimal Designs by Means of Genetic Algorithms. In M. Ram & J. Davim (Eds.), *Soft Computing Techniques and Applications in Mechanical Engineering* (pp. 151–161). Hershey, PA: IGI Global. doi:10.4018/978-1-5225-3035-0.ch007

Nazir, R. (2017). Advanced Nanomaterials for Water Engineering and Treatment: Nano-Metal Oxides and Their Nanocomposites. In T. Saleh (Ed.), *Advanced Nanomaterials for Water Engineering, Treatment, and Hydraulics* (pp. 84–126). Hershey, PA: IGI Global. doi:10.4018/978-1-5225-2136-5.ch005

Nikolopoulos, C. D. (2021). Recent Advances on Measuring and Modeling ELF-Radiated Emissions for Space Applications. In C. Nikolopoulos (Ed.), *Recent Trends on Electromagnetic Environmental Effects for Aeronautics and Space Applications* (pp. 1–38). IGI Global. https://doi.org/10.4018/978-1-7998-4879-0.ch001

Nogueira, A. F., Ribeiro, J. C., Fernández de Vega, F., & Zenha-Rela, M. A. (2018). Evolutionary Approaches to Test Data Generation for Object-Oriented Software: Overview of Techniques and Tools. In M. Khosrow-Pour, D.B.A. (Ed.), Incorporating Nature-Inspired Paradigms in Computational Applications (pp. 162-194). Hershey, PA: IGI Global. https://doi.org/ doi:10.4018/978-1-5225-5020-4.ch006

Nwajana, A. O., Obi, E. R., Ijemaru, G. K., Oleka, E. U., & Anthony, D. C. (2021). Fundamentals of RF/Microwave Bandpass Filter Design. In A. Nwajana & I. Ihianle (Eds.), *Handbook of Research on 5G Networks and Advancements in Computing, Electronics, and Electrical Engineering* (pp. 149–164). IGI Global. https://doi.org/10.4018/978-1-7998-6992-4.ch005

Ogbodo, E. A. (2021). Comparative Study of Transmission Line Junction vs. Asynchronously Coupled Junction Diplexers. In A. Nwajana & I. Ihianle (Eds.), *Handbook of Research on 5G Networks and Advancements in Computing, Electronics, and Electrical Engineering* (pp. 326–336). IGI Global. https://doi.org/10.4018/978-1-7998-6992-4.ch013

Orosa, J. A., Vergara, D., Fraguela, F., & Masdías-Bonome, A. (2021). Statistical Understanding and Optimization of Building Energy Consumption and Climate Change Consequences. In R. González-Lezcano (Ed.), *Advancements in Sustainable Architecture and Energy Efficiency* (pp. 195–220). IGI Global. https://doi.org/10.4018/978-1-7998-7023-4.ch009

Osho, M. B. (2018). Industrial Enzyme Technology: Potential Applications. In S. Bharati & P. Chaurasia (Eds.), *Research Advancements in Pharmaceutical, Nutritional, and Industrial Enzymology* (pp. 375–394). Hershey, PA: IGI Global. doi:10.4018/978-1-5225-5237-6.ch017

Ouadi, A., & Zitouni, A. (2021). Phasor Measurement Improvement Using Digital Filter in a Smart Grid. In A. Recioui & H. Bentarzi (Eds.), *Optimizing and Measuring Smart Grid Operation and Control* (pp. 100–117). IGI Global. https://doi.org/10.4018/978-1-7998-4027-5.ch005

Padmaja, P., & Marutheswar, G. (2017). Certain Investigation on Secured Data Transmission in Wireless Sensor Networks. *International Journal of Mobile Computing and Multimedia Communications*, *8*(1), 48–61. doi:10.4018/IJMCMC.2017010104

Palmer, S., & Hall, W. (2017). An Evaluation of Group Work in First-Year Engineering Design Education. In R. Tucker (Ed.), *Collaboration and Student Engagement in Design Education* (pp. 145–168). Hershey, PA: IGI Global. doi:10.4018/978-1-5225-0726-0.ch007

Panchenko, V. (2021). Prospects for Energy Supply of the Arctic Zone Objects of Russia Using Frost-Resistant Solar Modules. In P. Vasant, G. Weber, & W. Punurai (Eds.), *Research Advancements in Smart Technology, Optimization, and Renewable Energy* (pp. 149-169). IGI Global. https://doi.org/10.4018/978-1-7998-3970-5.ch008

Panchenko, V. (2021). Photovoltaic Thermal Module With Paraboloid Type Solar Concentrators. *International Journal of Energy Optimization and Engineering*, *10*(2), 1–23. https://doi.org/10.4018/IJEOE.2021040101

Pandey, K., & Datta, S. (2021). Dry Machining of Inconel 825 Superalloys: Performance of Tool Inserts (Carbide, Cermet, and SiAlON). *International Journal of Manufacturing, Materials, and Mechanical Engineering*, *11*(4), 26–39. doi:10.4018/IJMMME.2021100102

Panneer, R. (2017). Effect of Composition of Fibers on Properties of Hybrid Composites. *International Journal of Manufacturing, Materials, and Mechanical Engineering*, *7*(4), 28–43. doi:10.4018/IJMMME.2017100103

Pany, C. (2021). Estimation of Correct Long-Seam Mismatch Using FEA to Compare the Measured Strain in a Non-Destructive Testing of a Pressurant Tank: A Reverse Problem. *International Journal of Smart Vehicles and Smart Transportation*, *4*(1), 16–28. doi:10.4018/IJSVST.2021010102

Paul, S., & Roy, P. (2018). Optimal Design of Power System Stabilizer Using a Novel Evolutionary Algorithm. *International Journal of Energy Optimization and Engineering*, *7*(3), 24–46. doi:10.4018/IJEOE.2018070102

Paul, S., & Roy, P. K. (2021). Oppositional Differential Search Algorithm for the Optimal Tuning of Both Single Input and Dual Input Power System Stabilizer. In P. Vasant, G. Weber, & W. Punurai (Eds.), *Research Advancements in Smart Technology, Optimization, and Renewable Energy* (pp. 256-282). IGI Global. https://doi.org/10.4018/978-1-7998-3970-5.ch013

Pavaloiu, A. (2018). Artificial Intelligence Ethics in Biomedical-Engineering-Oriented Problems. In U. Kose, G. Guraksin, & O. Deperlioglu (Eds.), *Nature-Inspired Intelligent Techniques for Solving Biomedical Engineering Problems* (pp. 219–231). Hershey, PA: IGI Global. doi:10.4018/978-1-5225-4769-3.ch010

Pioro, I., Mahdi, M., & Popov, R. (2017). Application of Supercritical Pressures in Power Engineering. In L. Chen & Y. Iwamoto (Eds.), *Advanced Applications of Supercritical Fluids in Energy Systems* (pp. 404–457). Hershey, PA: IGI Global. doi:10.4018/978-1-5225-2047-4.ch013

Plaksina, T., & Gildin, E. (2017). Rigorous Integrated Evolutionary Workflow for Optimal Exploitation of Unconventional Gas Assets. *International Journal of Energy Optimization and Engineering*, *6*(1), 101–122. doi:10.4018/IJEOE.2017010106

Popat, J., Kakadiya, H., Tak, L., Singh, N. K., Majeed, M. A., & Mahajan, V. (2021). Reliability of Smart Grid Including Cyber Impact: A Case Study. In R. Singh, A. Singh, A. Dwivedi, & P. Nagabhushan (Eds.), *Computational Methodologies for Electrical and Electronics Engineers* (pp. 163–174). IGI Global. https://doi.org/10.4018/978-1-7998-3327-7.ch013

Quiza, R., La Fé-Perdomo, I., Rivas, M., & Ramtahalsing, V. (2021). Triple Bottom Line-Focused Optimization of Oblique Turning Processes Based on Hybrid Modeling: A Study Case on AISI 1045 Steel Turning. In L. Burstein (Ed.), *Handbook of Research on Advancements in Manufacturing, Materials, and Mechanical Engineering* (pp. 215–241). IGI Global. https://doi.org/10.4018/978-1-7998-4939-1.ch010

Rahmani, M. K. (2022). Blockchain Technology: Principles and Algorithms. In S. Khan, M. Syed, R. Hammad, & A. Bushager (Eds.), *Blockchain Technology and Computational Excellence for Society 5.0* (pp. 16–27). IGI Global. https://doi.org/10.4018/978-1-7998-8382-1.ch002

Ramdani, N., & Azibi, M. (2018). Polymer Composite Materials for Microelectronics Packaging Applications: Composites for Microelectronics Packaging. In K. Kumar & J. Davim (Eds.), *Composites and Advanced Materials for Industrial Applications* (pp. 177–211). Hershey, PA: IGI Global. doi:10.4018/978-1-5225-5216-1.ch009

Ramesh, M., Garg, R., & Subrahmanyam, G. V. (2017). Investigation of Influence of Quenching and Annealing on the Plane Fracture Toughness and Brittle to Ductile Transition Temperature of the Zinc Coated Structural Steel Materials. *International Journal of Surface Engineering and Interdisciplinary Materials Science*, *5*(2), 33–42. doi:10.4018/IJSEIMS.2017070103

Robinson, J., & Beneroso, D. (2022). Project-Based Learning in Chemical Engineering: Curriculum and Assessment, Culture and Learning Spaces. In A. Alves & N. van Hattum-Janssen (Eds.), *Training Engineering Students for Modern Technological Advancement* (pp. 1–19). IGI Global. https://doi.org/10.4018/978-1-7998-8816-1.ch001

Rondon, B. (2021). Experimental Characterization of Admittance Meter With Crude Oil Emulsions. *International Journal of Electronics, Communications, and Measurement Engineering*, *10*(2), 51–59. https://doi.org/10.4018/IJECME.2021070104

Rudolf, S., Biryuk, V. V., & Volov, V. (2018). Vortex Effect, Vortex Power: Technology of Vortex Power Engineering. In V. Kharchenko & P. Vasant (Eds.), *Handbook of Research on Renewable Energy and Electric Resources for Sustainable Rural Development* (pp. 500–533). Hershey, PA: IGI Global. doi:10.4018/978-1-5225-3867-7.ch021

Sah, A., Bhadula, S. J., Dumka, A., & Rawat, S. (2018). A Software Engineering Perspective for Development of Enterprise Applications. In A. Elçi (Ed.), *Handbook of Research on Contemporary Perspectives on Web-Based Systems* (pp. 1–23). Hershey, PA: IGI Global. doi:10.4018/978-1-5225-5384-7.ch001

Sahli, Y., Zitouni, B., & Hocine, B. M. (2021). Three-Dimensional Numerical Study of Overheating of Two Intermediate Temperature P-AS-SOFC Geometrical Configurations. In G. Badea, R. Felseghi, & I. Aşchilean (Eds.), *Hydrogen Fuel Cell Technology for Stationary Applications* (pp. 186–222). IGI Global. https://doi.org/10.4018/978-1-7998-4945-2.ch008

Sahoo, P., & Roy, S. (2017). Tribological Behavior of Electroless Ni-P, Ni-P-W and Ni-P-Cu Coatings: A Comparison. *International Journal of Surface Engineering and Interdisciplinary Materials Science*, *5*(1), 1–15. doi:10.4018/IJSEIMS.2017010101

Sahoo, S. (2018). Laminated Composite Hypar Shells as Roofing Units: Static and Dynamic Behavior. In K. Kumar & J. Davim (Eds.), *Composites and Advanced Materials for Industrial Applications* (pp. 249–269). Hershey, PA: IGI Global. doi:10.4018/978-1-5225-5216-1.ch011

Sahu, H., & Hungyo, M. (2018). Introduction to SDN and NFV. In A. Dumka (Ed.), *Innovations in Software-Defined Networking and Network Functions Virtualization* (pp. 1–25). Hershey, PA: IGI Global. doi:10.4018/978-1-5225-3640-6.ch001

Salem, A. M., & Shmelova, T. (2018). Intelligent Expert Decision Support Systems: Methodologies, Applications, and Challenges. In T. Shmelova, Y. Sikirda, N. Rizun, A. Salem, & Y. Kovalyov (Eds.), *Socio-Technical Decision Support in Air Navigation Systems: Emerging Research and Opportunities* (pp. 215–242). Hershey, PA: IGI Global. doi:10.4018/978-1-5225-3108-1.ch007

Samal, M. (2017). FE Analysis and Experimental Investigation of Cracked and Un-Cracked Thin-Walled Tubular Components to Evaluate Mechanical and Fracture Properties. In P. Samui, S. Chakraborty, & D. Kim (Eds.), *Modeling and Simulation Techniques in Structural Engineering* (pp. 266–293). Hershey, PA: IGI Global. doi:10.4018/978-1-5225-0588-4.ch009

Samal, M., & Balakrishnan, K. (2017). Experiments on a Ring Tension Setup and FE Analysis to Evaluate Transverse Mechanical Properties of Tubular Components. In P. Samui, S. Chakraborty, & D. Kim (Eds.), *Modeling and Simulation Techniques in Structural Engineering* (pp. 91–115). Hershey, PA: IGI Global. doi:10.4018/978-1-5225-0588-4.ch004

Samarasinghe, D. A., & Wood, E. (2021). Innovative Digital Technologies. In J. Underwood & M. Shelbourn (Eds.), *Handbook of Research on Driving Transformational Change in the Digital Built Environment* (pp. 142–163). IGI Global. https://doi.org/10.4018/978-1-7998-6600-8.ch006

Sawant, S. (2018). Deep Learning and Biomedical Engineering. In U. Kose, G. Guraksin, & O. Deperlioglu (Eds.), *Nature-Inspired Intelligent Techniques for Solving Biomedical Engineering Problems* (pp. 283–296). Hershey, PA: IGI Global. doi:10.4018/978-1-5225-4769-3.ch014

Schulenberg, T. (2021). Energy Conversion Using the Supercritical Steam Cycle. In L. Chen (Ed.), *Handbook of Research on Advancements in Supercritical Fluids Applications for Sustainable Energy Systems* (pp. 659–681). IGI Global. doi:10.4018/978-1-7998-5796-9.ch018

Sezgin, H., & Berkalp, O. B. (2018). Textile-Reinforced Composites for the Automotive Industry. In K. Kumar & J. Davim (Eds.), *Composites and Advanced Materials for Industrial Applications* (pp. 129–156). Hershey, PA: IGI Global. doi:10.4018/978-1-5225-5216-1.ch007

Shaaban, A. A., & Shehata, O. M. (2021). Combining Response Surface Method and Metaheuristic Algorithms for Optimizing SPIF Process. *International Journal of Manufacturing, Materials, and Mechanical Engineering, 11*(4), 1–25. https://doi.org/10.4018/IJMMME.2021100101

Shafaati Shemami, M., & Sefid, M. (2022). Implementation and Demonstration of Electric Vehicle-to-Home (V2H) Application: A Case Study. In M. Alam, R. Pillai, & N. Murugesan (Eds.), *Developing Charging Infrastructure and Technologies for Electric Vehicles* (pp. 268–293). IGI Global. https://doi.org/10.4018/978-1-7998-6858-3.ch015

Shah, M. Z., Gazder, U., Bhatti, M. S., & Hussain, M. (2018). Comparative Performance Evaluation of Effects of Modifier in Asphaltic Concrete Mix. *International Journal of Strategic Engineering, 1*(2), 13–25. doi:10.4018/IJoSE.2018070102

Sharma, N., & Kumar, K. (2018). Fabrication of Porous NiTi Alloy Using Organic Binders. In K. Kumar & J. Davim (Eds.), *Composites and Advanced Materials for Industrial Applications* (pp. 38–62). Hershey, PA: IGI Global. doi:10.4018/978-1-5225-5216-1.ch003

Shivach, P., Nautiyal, L., & Ram, M. (2018). Applying Multi-Objective Optimization Algorithms to Mechanical Engineering. In M. Ram & J. Davim (Eds.), *Soft Computing Techniques and Applications in Mechanical Engineering* (pp. 287–301). Hershey, PA: IGI Global. doi:10.4018/978-1-5225-3035-0.ch014

Shmelova, T. (2018). Stochastic Methods for Estimation and Problem Solving in Engineering: Stochastic Methods of Decision Making in Aviation. In S. Kadry (Ed.), *Stochastic Methods for Estimation and Problem Solving in Engineering* (pp. 139–160). Hershey, PA: IGI Global. doi:10.4018/978-1-5225-5045-7.ch006

Siero González, L. R., & Romo Vázquez, A. (2017). Didactic Sequences Teaching Mathematics for Engineers With Focus on Differential Equations. In M. Ramírez-Montoya (Ed.), *Handbook of Research on Driving STEM Learning With Educational Technologies* (pp. 129–151). Hershey, PA: IGI Global. doi:10.4018/978-1-5225-2026-9.ch007

Sim, M. S., You, K. Y., Esa, F., & Chan, Y. L. (2021). Nanostructured Electromagnetic Metamaterials for Sensing Applications. In M. Bhat, I. Wani, & S. Ashraf (Eds.), *Applications of Nanomaterials in Agriculture, Food Science, and Medicine* (pp. 141–164). IGI Global. https://doi.org/10.4018/978-1-7998-5563-7.ch009

Singh, R., & Dutta, S. (2018). Visible Light Active Nanocomposites for Photocatalytic Applications. In K. Kumar & J. Davim (Eds.), *Composites and Advanced Materials for Industrial Applications* (pp. 270–296). Hershey, PA: IGI Global. doi:10.4018/978-1-5225-5216-1.ch012

Skripov, P. V., Yampol'skiy, A. D., & Rutin, S. B. (2021). High-Power Heat Transfer in Supercritical Fluids: Microscale Times and Sizes. In L. Chen (Ed.), *Handbook of Research on Advancements in Supercritical Fluids Applications for Sustainable Energy Systems* (pp. 424–450). IGI Global. https://doi.org/10.4018/978-1-7998-5796-9.ch012

Sözbilir, H., Özkaymak, Ç., Uzel, B., & Sümer, Ö. (2018). Criteria for Surface Rupture Microzonation of Active Faults for Earthquake Hazards in Urban Areas. In N. Ceryan (Ed.), *Handbook of Research on Trends and Digital Advances in Engineering Geology* (pp. 187–230). Hershey, PA: IGI Global. doi:10.4018/978-1-5225-2709-1.ch005

Stanciu, I. (2018). Stochastic Methods in Microsystems Engineering. In S. Kadry (Ed.), *Stochastic Methods for Estimation and Problem Solving in Engineering* (pp. 161–176). Hershey, PA: IGI Global. doi:10.4018/978-1-5225-5045-7.ch007

Strebkov, D., Nekrasov, A., Trubnikov, V., & Nekrasov, A. (2018). Single-Wire Resonant Electric Power Systems for Renewable-Based Electric Grid. In V. Kharchenko & P. Vasant (Eds.), *Handbook of Research on Renewable Energy and Electric Resources for Sustainable Rural Development* (pp. 449–474). Hershey, PA: IGI Global. doi:10.4018/978-1-5225-3867-7.ch019

Sukhyy, K., Belyanovskaya, E., & Sukhyy, M. (2021). *Basic Principles for Substantiation of Working Pair Choice*. IGI Global. doi:10.4018/978-1-7998-4432-7.ch002

Suri, M. S., & Kaliyaperumal, D. (2022). Extension of Aspiration Level Model for Optimal Planning of Fast Charging Stations. In A. Fekik & N. Benamrouche (Eds.), *Modeling and Control of Static Converters for Hybrid Storage Systems* (pp. 91–106). IGI Global. https://doi.org/10.4018/978-1-7998-7447-8.ch004

Tallet, E., Gledson, B., Rogage, K., Thompson, A., & Wiggett, D. (2021). Digitally-Enabled Design Management. In J. Underwood & M. Shelbourn (Eds.), *Handbook of Research on Driving Transformational Change in the Digital Built Environment* (pp. 63–89). IGI Global. https://doi.org/10.4018/978-1-7998-6600-8.ch003

Terki, A., & Boubertakh, H. (2021). A New Hybrid Binary-Real Coded Cuckoo Search and Tabu Search Algorithm for Solving the Unit-Commitment Problem. *International Journal of Energy Optimization and Engineering, 10*(2), 104–119. https://doi.org/10.4018/IJEOE.2021040105

Tüdeş, Ş., Kumlu, K. B., & Ceryan, S. (2018). Integration Between Urban Planning and Natural Hazards For Resilient City. In N. Ceryan (Ed.), *Handbook of Research on Trends and Digital Advances in Engineering Geology* (pp. 591–630). Hershey, PA: IGI Global. doi:10.4018/978-1-5225-2709-1.ch017

Ulamis, K. (2018). Soil Liquefaction Assessment by Anisotropic Cyclic Triaxial Test. In N. Ceryan (Ed.), *Handbook of Research on Trends and Digital Advances in Engineering Geology* (pp. 631–664). Hershey, PA: IGI Global. doi:10.4018/978-1-5225-2709-1.ch018

Valente, M., & Milani, G. (2017). Seismic Assessment and Retrofitting of an Under-Designed RC Frame Through a Displacement-Based Approach. In V. Plevris, G. Kremmyda, & Y. Fahjan (Eds.), *Performance-Based Seismic Design of Concrete Structures and Infrastructures* (pp. 36–58). Hershey, PA: IGI Global. doi:10.4018/978-1-5225-2089-4.ch002

Vargas-Bernal, R. (2021). Advances in Electromagnetic Environmental Shielding for Aeronautics and Space Applications. In C. Nikolopoulos (Ed.), *Recent Trends on Electromagnetic Environmental Effects for Aeronautics and Space Applications* (pp. 80–96). IGI Global. https://doi.org/10.4018/978-1-7998-4879-0.ch003

Vasant, P. (2018). A General Medical Diagnosis System Formed by Artificial Neural Networks and Swarm Intelligence Techniques. In U. Kose, G. Guraksin, & O. Deperlioglu (Eds.), *Nature-Inspired Intelligent Techniques for Solving Biomedical Engineering Problems* (pp. 130–145). Hershey, PA: IGI Global. doi:10.4018/978-1-5225-4769-3.ch006

Verner, C. M., & Sarwar, D. (2021). Avoiding Project Failure and Achieving Project Success in NHS IT System Projects in the United Kingdom. *International Journal of Strategic Engineering*, *4*(1), 33–54. https://doi.org/10.4018/IJoSE.2021010103

Verrollot, J., Tolonen, A., Harkonen, J., & Haapasalo, H. J. (2018). Challenges and Enablers for Rapid Product Development. *International Journal of Applied Industrial Engineering*, *5*(1), 25–49. doi:10.4018/IJAIE.2018010102

Wan, A. C., Zulu, S. L., & Khosrow-Shahi, F. (2021). Industry Views on BIM for Site Safety in Hong Kong. In J. Underwood & M. Shelbourn (Eds.), *Handbook of Research on Driving Transformational Change in the Digital Built Environment* (pp. 120–140). IGI Global. https://doi.org/10.4018/978-1-7998-6600-8.ch005

Yardimci, A. G., & Karpuz, C. (2018). Fuzzy Rock Mass Rating: Soft-Computing-Aided Preliminary Stability Analysis of Weak Rock Slopes. In N. Ceryan (Ed.), *Handbook of Research on Trends and Digital Advances in Engineering Geology* (pp. 97–131). Hershey, PA: IGI Global. doi:10.4018/978-1-5225-2709-1.ch003

You, K. Y. (2021). Development Electronic Design Automation for RF/Microwave Antenna Using MATLAB GUI. In A. Nwajana & I. Ihianle (Eds.), *Handbook of Research on 5G Networks and Advancements in Computing, Electronics, and Electrical Engineering* (pp. 70–148). IGI Global. https://doi.org/10.4018/978-1-7998-6992-4.ch004

Yousefi, Y., Gratton, P., & Sarwar, D. (2021). Investigating the Opportunities to Improve the Thermal Performance of a Case Study Building in London. *International Journal of Strategic Engineering*, *4*(1), 1–18. https://doi.org/10.4018/IJoSE.2021010101

Zindani, D., & Kumar, K. (2018). Industrial Applications of Polymer Composite Materials. In K. Kumar & J. Davim (Eds.), *Composites and Advanced Materials for Industrial Applications* (pp. 1–15). Hershey, PA: IGI Global. doi:10.4018/978-1-5225-5216-1.ch001

Related References

Zindani, D., Maity, S. R., & Bhowmik, S. (2018). A Decision-Making Approach for Material Selection of Polymeric Composite Bumper Beam. In K. Kumar & J. Davim (Eds.), *Composites and Advanced Materials for Industrial Applications* (pp. 112–128). Hershey, PA: IGI Global. doi:10.4018/978-1-5225-5216-1.ch006

About the Contributors

Rajeev Kumar, Serving as Professor at Computer Science and Engineering Department, Moradabad Institute of Technology, Moradabad. He is having more than 14 Years of experience in academic as well in research, his research area is Cloud Computing, e-Governance, AI. Dr. Kumar received his Ph.D in Computer Science, D.Sc. (CS), Postdoctoral Fellowship (Malaysia) and he is Visited international countries London, United Kingdom and Mauritius as professional activities. Under his supervision awarded 9 scholar their Ph.D. and 5 Scholar is Ongoing their research work. He is awarded 3 times Best supervisor award; He is delivered a guest lecture, keynote speaker, chaired a session in many National and International conferences, Faculty Development program and workshop; He is completed one Research Project from DST in Bhimtal; He is organized many IEEE international conferences and workshop. He is authored and co-authored more than 105 papers in refereed international journal (SCI and Non- SCI) and conferences like IEEE, Springer, American Institute of Physics, New York Science international Journal New York City (USA), American Science Journal, BioInfo science Journal, Academic science of international journal (USA), International Journal of researcher, American Journal of Physics (USA) and many international Conferences and National Conferences, like IIT Roorkee (International Conference) etc.

Abu Bakar A. Hamid chose academia as his profession in 1992, beginning as a lecturer and later rising to a Professor of Marketing and Supply Chain Management. He holds a BBA and an MBA from Northrop University (USA) and a PhD from the University of Derby, UK. He has demonstrated an excellent record of teaching and supervision for more than 25 years in the academic field, at both undergraduate and postgraduate levels. Above all, his achievement in graduating more than 35 PhD candidates proves his ability, capability, and passion in postgraduate supervisions. He has also produced impactful research and publications which directly strengthen his expertise in his area of interest. In particular, he has published more than 300 articles in competitive international journals, proceedings, books, and book chapters. He also managed to secure several competitive national grants and consultancies for various projects. Such commitment is truly a landmark of an academician. His accolades, academic recognition, and leadership demonstrate his level of professorship. His notable contributions are recognised locally and internationally, as proven by the multiple invitations he has received to be an invited speaker, reviewer, editor in journals, external assessor, and internal or external examiner. With such calibre, he has much to contribute to any academic institution in the world.

Dato' Dr Noor Inayah Yaakub serves as Professor at Faculty of Economics and Management, Faculty of Law and Institute of West Asian Studies, University Kebangsaan Malaysia since 1998 until

2014. She serves as a Director of the Centre for Corporate Planning & Leadership, Deputy Dean for Research Graduate School of Business, and the -rst Head of Quality, Faculty of Law UKM. She serves at Global Wisdom Centre, University Islam Malaysia. She was admitted to the Malaysian Bar as an Advocate & Solicitor of the High Court of Malaya in 1996 became a quali-ed Shariah lawyer. She practiced law with Messrs. Abraham & Ooi and Co from 1996 to 1998S. She is also a quali-es Syarie lawyer of Negeri Sembilan. She has more than 20 years of experience in teaching Islamic Law, Syariah and Conventional Banking Law, Takaful and Insurance Law, Equity & Trust Law and Business Law and Ethics. She serves as Member of the Board Shariah Committee at CIMB Bank Berhad and Sun Life Malaysia Takaful Berhad. She served as Member of Board Shariah Committee at CIMB Islamic Bank Berhad until March 24, 2017.

Hari Om Sharan serving as Dean – Academics at Amity University Kolkata (India), he is having more than 17 Years of experience in academic as well in research, his research area is Networking, AI, Security and High Performance Computing. . Dr. Sharan received his Ph.D in DNA Computing: A Novel Approach towards the solution of NP-Complete Problems, and his UG (B.Tech) & PG (M.Tech) in Computer Science and Engineering, He has done International certification in Data Science and Artificial Intelligence Machine Learning Deep Learning and its Application. Dr. Sharan guides the college towards academic excellence; promotes a culture of research, innovation and leads new curricula and program development efforts. He is expert in designing & deployment academic curriculum, and Program inception. As the chairman of IPR cell, he organizes the seminar, workshops for the students and faculty to promote the research. Dr. Sharan also published two books on Mobile Network Technology and Database. Dr. Sharan developed short term course on Artificial Intelligence Machine Learning Deep Learning and its Application, and published 43 patents (National/International) & copyrights mostly in Computer Science and Engineering to serve the nation in the field of research. Dr. Sharan authored and coauthored more than 80 papers in refereed international journal and conferences like IEEE, Springer, International Journal of researcher, American Journal of Physics (USA) and many international Conferences and National Conferences, like IIT (International Conference) etc. and serve as editor of different international journal and Reviewer in SCI and Non-SCI journal, serve as a committee member in many IEEE Society, Springer International Conferences. He delivered a many guest lectures and expert talk on the recent technologies of Computer Science & Engineering and on Curriculum Design and Development, keynote speaker, chaired a session in many National and International conferences, webinars, Faculty Development program and workshops. Dr. Sharan associated in many highly impact Society Membership like IEEE, ACM, CSI, IAENG, ISC.

Sandeep Kumar is CEO of RightZone Technologies Private Limited Company. He has around 13 years of experience in IT industries with different MNC's and winners of Hackathons in MNC's companies. providing their Consulting and trainings in Multiple IT companies. He has expertise in different domains Like, CMS, Image processing, Python etc. He was Visited international countries Denmark, United Kingdom and Mauritius as professional activities. He has delivered Lectures and speaks in different FDP's, seminars and universities. He is authored and coauthored more then to 8 papers in refereed international journal (SCI and Non- SCI) and conferences like IEEE, Springer etc.

***

C.V. Suresh Babu is a pioneer in content development. A true entrepreneur, he founded Anniyappa Publications, a company that is highly active in publishing books related to Computer Science and Management. Dr. C.V. Suresh Babu has also ventured into SB Institute, a center for knowledge transfer. He holds a Ph.D. in Engineering Education from the National Institute of Technical Teachers Training & Research in Chennai, along with seven master's degrees in various disciplines such as Engineering, Computer Applications, Management, Commerce, Economics, Psychology, Law, and Education. Additionally, he has UGC-NET/SET qualifications in the fields of Computer Science, Management, Commerce, and Education. Currently, Dr. C.V. Suresh Babu is a Professor in the Department of Information Technology at the School of Computing Science, Hindustan Institute of Technology and Science (Hindustan University) in Padur, Chennai, Tamil Nadu, India.

A. Bhuvaneswari, working as Assistant Professor (Senior Grade) in School of Computer Science Engineering, VIT University, Chennai, India. She is an active Researcher and Mentoring students/research scholars in specific research domains including Social Network Analysis, Big Data Analytics, Machine Learning, Network Graphs, Web Mining, Recommendation Engines. She has published several International Journals, Book Chapters and presented her research findings in Reputed International Conferences apart from several papers at national level. She has 10+ years of teaching & research experience. She is been a reviewer for reputed journals indexed in SCOPUS, Web of Science and SCI/SCI-E.

Sampath Boopathi is an accomplished individual with a strong academic background and extensive research experience. He completed his undergraduate studies in Mechanical Engineering and pursued his postgraduate studies in the field of Computer-Aided Design. Dr. Boopathi obtained his Ph.D. from Anna University, focusing his research on Manufacturing and optimization. Throughout his career, Dr. Boopathi has made significant contributions to the field of engineering. He has authored and published over 130 research articles in internationally peer-reviewed journals, highlighting his expertise and dedication to advancing knowledge in his area of specialization. His research output demonstrates his commitment to conducting rigorous and impactful research. In addition to his research publications, Dr. Boopathi has also been granted one patent and has three published patents to his name. This indicates his innovative thinking and ability to develop practical solutions to real-world engineering challenges. With 17 years of academic and research experience, Dr. Boopathi has enriched the engineering community through his teaching and mentorship roles. He has served in various engineering colleges in Tamilnadu, India, where he has imparted knowledge, guided students, and contributed to the overall academic development of the institutions. Dr. Sampath Boopathi's diverse background, ranging from mechanical engineering to computer-aided design, along with his specialization in manufacturing and optimization, positions him as a valuable asset in the field of engineering. His research contributions, patents, and extensive teaching experience exemplify his expertise and dedication to advancing engineering knowledge and fostering innovation.

Rajat Deb, Assistant Professor, Department of Commerce, Tripura University, Tripura, India; did M. Com., MBA and Ph. D. from the same institution. A UGC-NET qualifier and recipient of three Gold Medals for top ranks in UG & PG examinations; has around 16 years teaching experience in PG courses, 2 years experience in Government Audit & Accounting; Assistant Co-coordinator, IGNOU Tripura University study Centre, Ph. D. supervisor, life member of six academic associations and has 61 publications in his credit; presented papers in seminars and conferences.

Jagadamba G. is working as an Assistant Professor in the Department of Information Science and Engineering, Siddaganga Institute of Technology, Tumakuru, Karnataka after aquiring her BE, M.Tech, and Ph.D. degree from VTU, Belagavi. She has 20 years of teaching and research experience. Her research interests include security issues in the ubiquitous computing environment, adaptive and biometric authentication systems, trust and context-based security systems, and applications for e-commerce, e-learning, m-banking, and healthcare. She has published many book chapters in CRC press and IGI publications. She has also authored many research articles in reputed international journals and conferences. Aparrt from teaching, she has completed many industry projects from Continental, CISCO, Cyphertek, and Information systems, Bangalore. She has also conducted many certification courses such as "Introduction to computer networks", Introduction to Routing and Switching", "Internet of Things", "Advanced Python Programming", etc. She also delivered many seminars, webinars, and faculty development workshops. She has secured the "Best Project Award" in national level competition, "Best Paper Award" in conferences, "Best teacher Award 2021" from the Institute of Scholars, "Best Scholar Award 2021" from the International Research Awards on Science, Health and Engineering, 2021, and "Instructor of the Year 2021" from CISCO, Bangalore. Apart from academic activities, she has been very keen on serving society and the environment. With a group of like-minded friends, she has planted more than 5000 seedlings in dry lands around Tumakuru by keeping a motto of going green.

I. Daniel Lawrence is an researcher from Garuda Aerospace Pvt Ltd, Chennai. The author has published 41 Research articles and contributed to research in topic(s): Materials, Design and Optimization. The author has an h index of 6, receiving 116 citation(s).

Yadavamuthiah K. student of Hindustan Institute of Technology and Science exploring the role of technology in agriculture, with a focus on AI, ML, IOT, and Robotics. Yadavamuthiah has developed software applications to help farmers make informed decisions and optimize crop yields. He aims to create sustainable and equitable solutions for the challenges facing the agricultural sector.

Dipali Kasat possesses 18+ years of experience including teaching, administration and management of College and Departmental activities in various positions. Currently working as an Associate Professor and Head, Dept. of Computer Engg, Sarvajanik College of Engineering and Technology, Surat. IPR contributions include 2 patents, 2 copyrights and 20 research publications in Computer Vision area at various International/National journals and conferences and a book titled "Management Information System", Tech Max Publication. Associated as Editor of open access International Journal of Advancements in Engg and Technology (IJAET). On Board of IFERP - Professional Ambassador. My research interest is in domains of Computer Vision, Information Retrieval, NLP, Information security, Data Analytics and Statistical modelling.

A.V. Senthil Kumar is working as a Director & Professor in the Department of Research and PG in Computer Applications, Hindusthan College of Arts and Science, Coimbatore since 05/03/2010. He has to his credit 11 Book Chapters, 265 papers in International and National Journals, 25 papers in International Conferences, 5 papers in National Conferences, and edited Nine books (IGI Global, USA). He is an Editor-in-Chief for various journals. Key Member for India, Machine Intelligence Research Lab (MIR Labs). He is an Editorial Board Member and Reviewer for various International Journals. He is also a Committee member for various International Conferences. He is a Life member of International

Association of Engineers (IAENG), Systems Society of India (SSI), member of The Indian Science Congress Association, member of Internet Society (ISOC), International Association of Computer Science and Information Technology (IACSIT), Indian Association for Research in Computing Science (IARCS), and committee member for various International Conferences

Rajendra Kumar is working as a Professor in Rama University, Kanpur U.P. India in Department of Physics; He received B.Sc. and M.Sc. from Kanpur University with gold medal and Ph. D from CCS University Meerut U.P. with collaboration of NPL India in 2009, qualified CSIR-UGC-NET in 2002. He is teaching last 20 years in UG, PG and research students. So Many Students are doing doctorial research work under the supervision of him. His research work is in the field of Plasma Polymer thin films, Sensor Technology, solar cell, IOT health care system, Material Physics and Luminescence, OLED etc, He is author of more than 50 research papers in national as well as international Journals, and 50 national and international conferences research papers, copyright, and Patents. He is author of international book and book chapter for research which is also in the field of plasma polymerization thin films and other fields. He is the member of different Academic and Professional Societies. He is also editors and reviver of various national and international Journals. He has awarded Young Academician Award for his contribution in the field of Engineering & Technology from the Executive Council of Hindustan Agricultural Research Welfare Society, Agra.

Rohaya Latip is an Associate Professor at Faculty of Computer Science and Information Technology, University Putra Malaysia. She holds a Ph.D in Distributed Database in year 2009 and Msc. in Distributed System in 2001 both from University Putra Malaysia, Malaysia. She graduated her Bachelor of Computer Science from University Technology Malaysia, Malaysia in 1999. She was the Head of Department of Communication Technology and Network in 2017-2022. She served as an Associate Professor at Najran University, Kingdom of Arab Saudi (2012-2013). She is the Head of HPC section in Institute for Mathematic Research (INSPEM)., University Putra Malaysia (2011-2012) and consulted the Campus Grid project and also the Wireless for hostel in Campus UPM project. She is also a Co-researcher at INSPEM. She is the editorial board of International Journal of Computer Networks and Communications Security (IJCNCS), editorial board of International Journal of Digital Contents and Applications (IJDCA) and editorial board for International Journal of Computer Networks and Applications (IJCNA). Her research interests include Big Data, Cloud and Grid Computing, Network management, and Distributed database. For her research work, she won Gold medal at ICANS 2019, Canada, and two medals at The World Inventor Award Festival (WIAF) 2014 organized by Korea Invention News. She was awarded Gold medal at IMIT-SIC Innovation Expo in 2018, Riau Indonesia, I-RIA 2018 (Best of the best award), Malaysia Technology Expo (MTE2014) and Malaysian Innovation Expo (MiExpo2013). She also won Silver medal at National Design, Research and Innovation Expo (PRPI) 2010 and Bronze medal at National Design, Research and Innovation Expo (PRPI) 2007 and 2006 respectively. She has published more than 80 papers in international and national journals, proceedings and posters.

Ashutosh Lembhe is an enthusiastic researcher, committed to advancing knowledge and making a positive impact on our world through my work. With a strong educational background and a deep-rooted curiosity, Lembhe strives to explore the frontiers of research.

C. S. Raghuvanshi is a Professor, Department of Computer Science and Engineering (CSE) in Faculty of Engineering & Technology, Rama University Uttar Pradesh, Kanpur. He is having 19+ years of teaching and research experience in various institutions. He has awarded his Ph.D. degree in Computer Science and Engineering from Jiwaji University (Established in 1964), Gwalior, Madhya Pradesh in year 2014 on the topic "Design and Analysis of Innovative Algorithm for Mining Frequent Pattern from Large Database". He has done his M.Tech. in Information Technology in year 2006. His research interests are in Data Mining, Database, Machine Learning, Information Retrieval etc. So far, he has published 15 patents and 46 research papers in reputed international/national journals and conferences. In addition, he has also participated in many reputed national conferences/ FDP/ Workshop etc.

C. S. Raghuvanshi is a Professor, Department of Computer Science and Engineering (CSE) in Faculty of Engineering & Technology, Rama University Uttar Pradesh, Kanpur. He is having 19+ years of teaching and research experience in various institutions. He has awarded his Ph.D. degree in Computer Science and Engineering from Jiwaji University (Established in 1964), Gwalior, Madhya Pradesh in year 2014 on the topic "Design and Analysis of Innovative Algorithm for Mining Frequent Pattern from Large Database". He has done his M.Tech. in Information Technology in year 2006. His research interests are in Data Mining, Database, Machine Learning, Information Retrieval etc. So far, he has published 15 patents and 46 research papers in reputed international/national journals and conferences. In addition, he has also participated in many reputed national conferences/ FDP/ Workshop etc.

Radhika Selvamani, working as Assistant Professor (Senior Grade II) in School of Computer Science Engineering, VIT University, Chennai, India. She is an active Researcher and Mentoring students/ research scholars in specific research domains including Artificial Intelligence, Machine Learning. She has published several International Journals, Book Chapters and presented her research findings in Reputed International Conferences.

Priyanka Sharma is born in Jaipur, Rajasthan, India, in 1991. She Received her B.Tech. degree from Rajasthan Technical University, Kota, Rajasthan India, in 2012 in Information Technology and M.Tech. degree from Rajasthan Technical University, Kota, Rajasthan India, in 2016 in Computer Science. She is working as an Assistant Professor in the department of Computer Science & Engineering, Swami Keshvanand Institute of Technology, Management & Gramothan, Jaipur, Rajasthan, India. She has guided various M.Tech. and UG scholars. She is member of IEEE, ACM and various professional societies. She has published more than 15 research papers in national and international journals/conferences, book chapters. Also, she has taken part in forums hosted by Infosys, TCS, Oracle, and IBM. Her area of interest is investigating the advancements in machine learning and deep learning applications. She has received accolades on a number of times in a variety of fields, including Designation as an Active Reviewer by some well-known journals. She was also given recognition by Infosys, India, for her remarkable performance in the Campus Link Program.

Rashi Shukla is an Assistant Professor, Department of Computer Science and Engineering (CSE) in Faculty of Engineering & Technology, Rama University Uttar Pradesh, Kanpur. He is having 5 years of teaching and industrial experience in various institutions/ organization. He has Completed his Ph.D. degree in Computer Science and Engineering from Rama University, Kanpur, Uttar Pradesh on the topic "Human Pose Estimation using Region based Convolution Neural Network (R-CNN)". He has done his

M.Tech. Computer Science and Engineering from Rama University, Kanpur, Uttar Pradesh. He has done his B.tech (Computer Science and Engineering) from AKTU (Dr. Abdul Kalam Technical University), Lucknow in 2015. His research work are in Data Science Data Mining, Database, Machine Learning, Information Retrieval etc. So far, he has 20 research papers in reputed international/national journals (Scopus/ SCIE) and conferences and having more than 8 Patents . In addition, he has also participated in many reputed national conferences/ FDP/ Workshop etc.

V. Sathiyamoorthi is currently working as Lecturer in Computer Engineering Department at Government Polytechnic College, Dharmapuri,Tamil Nadu, India. He was born on June 21, 1983, at Omalur in Salem District, Tamil Nadu, India. He received his Bachelor of Engineering degree in Information Technology from Periyar University, Salem with First Class. He obtained his Master of Engineering degree in Computer Science and Engineering from Anna University, Chennai with Distinction and secured 30th University Rank.He received his Ph.D degree from Anna University, Chennai in Web Mining. His areas of specialization include Web Usage Mining, Data Structures, Design and Analysis of Algorithm and Operating System. He has published many papers in International Journals and conferences. He has published many books and book chapters in various renowned international publishers. He has also participated in various National level Workshops and Seminars conducted by various reputed institutions.

Index

www.ingramcontent.com/pod-product-compliance
Lightning Source LLC
LaVergne TN
LVHW062154300926
849161LV00010B/2662